V. BASHKIROVA
A. SOLOVIEV
V. DOROFEYEV

HEROES OF THE 90s

THE CHARACTERS, THE MONEY
A NEW HISTORY OF CAPITALISM IN RUSSIA

GLAGOSLAV PUBLICATIONS

HEROES OF THE '90S
THE CHARACTERS, THE MONEY
A NEW HISTORY OF CAPITALISM IN RUSSIA

BY VALERIA BASHKIROVA, ALEXANDER SOLOVIEV,
AND VLADISLAV DOROFEYEV

TRANSLATED BY HUW DAVIES

© 2014, GLAGOSLAV PUBLICATIONS, UNITED KINGDOM

GLAGOSLAV PUBLICATIONS LTD
88-90 HATTON GARDEN
EC1N 8PN LONDON
UNITED KINGDOM
WWW.GLAGOSLAV.COM

CATALOGUE RECORD OF THIS BOOK IS AVAILABLE FROM THE BRITISH LIBRARY

ISBN 978-1-78267-041-4

CONTENTS

This book was made possible thanks to the efforts of journalists from the financial weekly Kommersant Money, among others.

FOREWORD FROM THE PUBLISHER

This book tells the story of the 1990s, when the USSR was consigned to the dustbin of history in a process which seemed to happen as quickly as the unravelling of Byzantium some five hundred years earlier. The successor to the great Soviet state which had disappeared was the Russian Federation, a nation which could go one of two ways — either establish itself as a state or become a grubby stain on the map of the world. The making of Russia, of all its executive, social, economic and civil institutes, took place in the last decade of the 20th century. In other words, this book is about the new country's first decade. Written in the style of a documentary narrative, it contains a combination of facts, opinions and appraisals from those who lived through the events described.

For your enjoyment, we have 'run the rule over' of all the characters, events, actions, decisions and phenomena which determined Russia's fate in the past and are still determining its fate today. In effect we travelled back in time to look at the seeds from which we are continuing to grow, along with the rest of the country, today. And the end result turned out to be of greater import, more substantial and more entertaining – and a book should always entertain, you will agree! – than we thought it would be when we began working on the project roughly a year ago.

The book begins with a list of the concepts and terms which emerged in that decade and which to this day account for a considerably large portion of our socio–political jargon. The main narrative is contained in two sections – *The Economics of*

Change and *A Policy of Interference*, which are divided into 10 chapters: *A wild, wild market: the first entrepreneurs; Shock: the advocates and enemies of 'shock therapy'; The great redistribution. Privatization: vouchers and shares–for–loans auctions; The scum: embezzlers, criminals and bandits; The masters of life: oligarchs and ordinary rich people; The end of an era: the crisis of 1998; The biggest geopolitical catastrophe in history. How the USSR became Russia; The masters of thought: from Solzhenitsyn to the entertainment industry; With a few kind words and a gun: security agents, terrorists and peacekeepers;* and *Politics as a business: reformers, conservatives, deputies and civil servants.*

The third part of the book, *Events and characters*, provides a detailed chronology of the key events which took place during the first decade of the new Russia, and the main cast of characters from that era. The book's structure is fairly straightforward and clear. You can dip into it at any page and find out something that will add to your understanding of Russia's recent past. I can't guarantee it will be an easy read, however, and it certainly won't be a laugh a minute. There's a good reason why the period became known colloquially as the 'wild '90s'. A considerable amount of courage was displayed in those days, too.

And I would like to note in passing that work has already begun on a book about what Russia was like in the first decade of the 21st century. To be continued.

Vladislav Dorofeyev

INTRODUCTION

GLOSSARY

A box for photocopying paper

On the evening of 19th June 1996, staff from the Presidential Security Service (PSS) arrested Sergei Lisovsky and Arkady Yevstafiev, activists in Boris Yeltsin's campaign team, at the exit to the House of government. The activists had on them a box for A4 photocopying paper, containing $500,000. The former head of the PSS, Alexander Korzhakov, said: "I suspected that money which was supposed to be used in the presidential election campaign was being siphoned off at the campaign HQ, in the most banal way imaginable." The directors of Boris Yeltsin's campaign team energetically set about trying to secure the release of their employees. After midnight a special edition of the programme *Sevodnya* was broadcast, in which Yevgeny Kiselov used the phrase 'a box of photocopies' for the first time. The next day Alexander Korzhakov, the director of the FSB Mikhail Barsukov and the first deputy prime minister Oleg Soskovets were fired. At the same time, the General prosecutor opened a criminal investigation into the unlawful currency operations. The version of events which eventually obtained official status was that the box of photocopies had been intended to cover the costs of the 'Vote or lose' campaign. On 7th April 1997 the criminal investigation was closed.

A man bearing a striking resemblance to the procurator general

This phrase was first heard on 17th March 1999 in an edition
of the news programme *Vesti*, in which a video clip was shown of
a man who looked like the procurator general meeting two girls
who looked like prostitutes. As the former editor of *Vesti* Aleksei
Abakumov told Kommersant at the time, the film containing the
scandalous video clip had been delivered to the All–Russia State
Television and Radio Broadcasting Company anonymously on
15th March. According to the newspaper, the order to show
parts of the recording on air was given to the chairman of
the All–Russia State Television and Radio Broadcasting
Company, Mikhail Shvydkom, following a meeting at the
offices of the President's Administration. This was how Boris
Yeltsin's entourage planned to force the disgraced procurator
general to step down. Aleksei Abakumov explained why the
compromising material was shown in his own inimitable way
in an interview with *Kommersant*: "This film became a part of
public life. The main reason for this was that Skuratov himself
referred to the material as being compromising and said that
he was being blackmailed with it. Until the film was made
public, any individual or legal entity could use it against him.
And after it was made public, there would no longer be any
reason to blackmail him. So in this particular instance we were
genuinely defending the interests of the state." The chairman
of the All–Russia State Television and Broadcasting Company
personally ordered that the newsreaders use the circumspect,
non–committal phrase "a man bearing a striking resemblance to
the procurator general". The phrase was subsequently used about
any compromising material of this nature.

"According to observers"

This expression appeared on 29th January 1990 in the
weekly newspaper *Kommersant*. "Generally speaking, according

to observers, the conference can be considered quite a success. Without question, the most important outcome of it is that tenants, who were once isolated, have at last created a structure which represents their interests and protects their rights." This was what the paper had to say about the results of the first founding congress of the Association of Agricultural administrations and co–ops in Russia, held in Moscow. Subsequently all journalists starting talking like that.

Administrative resource

On 9th August 1995, Dmitry Olshansky, the director of the Centre for Strategic Analysis and Forecasting, gave journalists a list of the parties, blocs and movements which were due to take part in the upcoming elections for the State Duma, complete with ratings. When they compiled the ratings, the centre's experts looked at 100 parameters, which, in addition to the level of development of organizational structures, the extent of their intellectual potential (whether or not they had analytical centres, etc.), the extent to which the provisions in their manifestos satisfied the public's expectations, how much money they had and how attractive their leaders were, there was also a parameter called 'extent of administrative resource'. This term would subsequently be used by journalists in their coverage of elections at various levels.

Authoritative entrepreneur

This term was a combination of the phrase 'criminal authority', which was popular among staff at the Ministry of Internal Affairs, and the word 'entrepreneur'. 'Authoritative entrepreneurs' was a term that began to be used to describe businessmen who had close ties to criminal circles. The first recorded use of the phrase was on 27th October 1994 in the newspaper *KommersantDaily,* in an article by Viktor Smirnov with the headline: 'An authoritative entrepreneur dies before his case goes to court': 'Yesterday the well–known local businessman Viktor Kasintsev, whom the police considered to be a criminal authority, was killed. Kasintsev, two of his bodyguards and a driver who was with them in the car at the time, were shot dead by three gunmen.'

Black Tuesday

The phrase 'black Tuesday' achieved fame following the collapse in the exchange rate for the rouble (in the space of a single day the dollar went up by 35.5 roubles to 241 roubles). The Russian TV channels broadcast a message from ITARTASS in their news bulletins: "There is panic once again on Russia's currency market. The situation that arose on 'black Tuesday' is reminiscent of the currency crisis at the end of August... According to data from the Moscow Inter–bank Currency Exchange's information service, in spite of the value of the dollar shooting up, sales achieved a record level in stock exchange trades for the year of $68.8 million. But the most infamous 'black Tuesday' of all was 11th October 1994. On this day the American currency shot up in value by 845 roubles to 3926 roubles to the dollar. As a result, the chairman of the Central Bank, Viktor Geraschenko and the Minister of Finance Sergei Dubinin were fired.

Black salary

This term is a combination of a phrase popular in criminal circles, 'black income', and the world 'salary'. The first recorded use of it came on 2nd October 1996, in an article in *KommersantDaily* under the headline *The Government has mobilized cocktail lovers*: "The maximum rate of income tax must be increased to 50%, according to experts from the State Tax Service of Russia...The amount of money coming into the budget will probably turn out to be far smaller than the STS is expecting, because many of those who are currently paying 35 percent out of respect for the law will simply refuse to pay and instead go back to their 'black salary'. The term 'white salary' first appeared in 1998: "Employers have become a little bit more fearful lately...They have been putting bigger and bigger sums into 'white salaries', the ones we have to pay tax on. After all, the relatively high costs set against the high salaries of staff at commercial enterprises, which have high profits, arouse the suspicion of the tax agencies (*Ogoniok*. 1998. 23rd February).

Capital flight

This financial term was first used on 29th November 1991 in the newspaper *Rossiskaya Gazeta*, in an article by Nikita Yermakov entitled *External debt: always try before you buy*. That particular article, to be fair, was about the possibility of capital flight from the New World to the Old World. Journalists began discussing capital flight from Russia after an article by Mikhail Leontiev appeared on 15th January 1992 in *Nezavisimaya Gazeta*, entitled *The Pavlovization of liberal reforms*, which contained the following paragraph: "The government is still refusing to bow down to those complaining about the unprecedented levels of taxation, which has led to a massive reduction in manufacturing, the coagulation of commercial activity and capital flight across the border. By showing such sacrificial stubbornness in its fiscal projects, the government is being inexplicably indecisive in putting into effect the projects which are constantly being devised deep in the bowels of its economic team (such as the promised free currency market, which was due to be brought in on 2nd January)'.

Capital of crime

This term was first used on 6th November 1992 in Rossiskaya gazeta in an article entitled 'Moscow – the crime capital': "Moscow has turned into one of the most dangerous cities in Russia from a criminogenic point of view, further evidence of which is provided by the 145 violations of the law recorded on 4th November by staff from the Main Directorate of Internal Affairs (MDIA). For the purposes of comparison, around a hundred similar crimes were recorded in Moscow exactly one year ago." In 1996 this term was used with respect to St Petersburg for the first time by the city's governor, Vladimir Yakovlev: "Last week the article in *Izvestiya*, 'In Russia they take everything', elicited two responses. In one pile there are all sorts of criminal cases, rapid breakthroughs, speculation and rumours. It is my firm conviction that preventing unlawful acts is something that the relevant agencies ought to be dealing with. As for the attempts to make St Petersburg the 'crime capital' of the country, I don't like them, as you might expect." (*Izvestiya*. 1996. 21st December). Novosibirsk, Yekaterinburg and Tolyatti have all been described as the 'crime capital of Russia'.

Chechen insurgents

This term was first used on 14th November 1991 in *Rossiskaya Gazeta* in an article by Lyudmila Leontieva under the headline 'A hijacking: "On 9th November a Tu154 aeroplane flying on the route 63–17 from Minvoda to Yekaterinburg was hijacking by Chechen insurgents with a political objective: as an act of protest against the president of Russia's directive introducing a state of emergency and sending troops from the Ministry of Internal Affairs in Checheno–Ingushetia. On 9th January 1993 the Italian newspaper L'Unita published an interview with the director of the Federal Information Centre Mikhail Poltoranin entitled 'How I broke up a plot against Yeltsin': "You accused him [Khasbulatov. – Kommersant Power] of trying to carry out a coup d'etat. "How else would you characterize what happened? If the Chairman of the Supreme Council, who is creating an armed group for himself of up to 5000 people with a special training school, which has already trained a special forces division, issues an order to the effect that forty thousand more rifles should be obtained. At the same time groups of Chechen insurgents arrived in Moscow, armed to the teeth and occupying the whole of the hotel complex next to VDNKh." (*Rossiskaya Gazeta*. 1993. 14th January). This phrase reached the height of its popularity in 1994, when military operations commenced in Chechnya.

Contract killing

This term was used by staff at the Ministry of Internal Affairs. It was first used in the Russian media in *Ogoniok* magazine on 7th May 1988: "One of the leading experts in the study of organized crime, a member of the Academic Investigative Institute of the Ministry of Internal Affairs of the USSR, Alexander Ivanovich Gurov, told me about the consequences of the spread of this racket throughout our country with an undisguised sense of alarm. "It has already been proved," said Gurov, "that, firstly, the racket is enabling large sums of money to be concentrated among particular groups of people, which in turn leads them to get involved with an increasing number of new criminal groups. Secondly, the racket is enabling a general flourishing of criminality, because when there are so many recidivists, practically any crime can be financed – from the unlawful distribution of drugs to contract killings; thirdly, the racket is actively enabling the corruption of practically every layer of society and, as a result, an erosion of financial clout – after all, the racketeers' money generally tends to be put towards buying up people in authority, amongst other things." The term went into common parlance in the early '90s.

Conventional units, c.u.

On 6th March 1993 a directive was issued by the government of the Russian Federation 'On the tightening of control over currency and exports and the development of the currency market', which recommended, among other things, that the Central Bank impose a ban on "transactions in a foreign currency made between citizens residing in Russia." The citizens found out about this decree when they caught sight of labels in the shops expressed in the form of conventional units – the equivalent of one US dollar. This term first appeared in the press in an article by Georgy Putnikov entitled 'Head to Antikvar if it's medals you're after': "The range of medals currently on offer at Antikvar on Frunzenskaya Embankment is making quite a favourable impression...the shop has introduced a new approach to evaluating medals, orders and stamps. The shop's owners present the prices in conventional units which coincide with the current exchange rate for the US dollar. For example, the highest government award that can be won in Mongolia, the order of SukheBator, is on offer for 500 conventional units, and a Finnish medal that was awarded to snipers who served between 1939 and 1940 was available for 50 conventional units." (*KommersantDaily*. 1993. 10 April) It was in shops' interests to price their goods using conventional units, because the shops could set an exchange rate for the dollar of their own choosing. The conventional unit was therefore a common sight all over Russia in the mid–'90s.

Creative

This term was first used on 3rd October 1995 in the newspaper *Sevodnya*, in a piece by Natalia Krotova headed 'The Menatep group: Buy anything that's Russian!' "In the past the packaging for 'Koloss' was manufactured by a Finnish company...Now the works operates with Russian packaging manufacturers, where creative is of a pretty low standard." A month later, the word 'creative' was deployed by journalists from *Kommersant*: "It must also be admitted that Russian advertisers managed to arrange things in such a way that the only route available for foreigners to the Russian media was via the local agencies. This means that international clients have an unnecessary middle–man thrown into the mix, in the shape of a foreign agency. Moreover, the Western agencies' royalties were significantly higher (and for 'creative' – incomparably higher) than those of the Russian agencies." (*KommersantDaily*. 23rd November. 1995.).

Currency corridor

This financial term was first used in the Russian media on 18th November 1991 in the newspaper *KommersantDaily* by the director of the Baltic Stock Exchange, Vadim Pchelkin: "In the latest transactions, shares were acquired in exchange for both currency and roubles – taking into account the exchange rate of the so–called 'currency corridor'. The essence of the 'corridor' is that the stock exchange kept $800,000 reserved for the brokers, and shares could be purchased up to this maximum value for roubles, at the exchange rate set by the BSE. On 13th November roubles were exchanged for dollars at the BSE at a rate of 140:1." But the term 'currency corridor' in the sense with which it is used today (i.e. a departure from the medium–term trend in the exchange rate) was used for the first time in *KommersantDaily* on 2nd November 1992 in the article 'A forecast for the exchange rate for the rouble': 'In this edition, Kommersant's experts attempted to provide a prediction for the 'currency corridor' until the end of 1992, based on an extrapolation of the trend in the medium–term."

Default

This financial term was first used in the Russian press on 21st November 1995 in *KommersantDaily*, in a piece by Tatiana Burchilina headed '*The Oil Refinery reconstruction project in Kazakhstan*': "The situation is also being severely exacerbated by the Republic's defaults (failures to fulfil obligations) on several international debt repayments." This term was first used with regard to Russia in 1996, by the director of Vneshekonombank, Andrei Kostin: "As I see it, Vneshekonombank faces three key tasks in the immediate future. Firstly, there is the overarching restructuring of the debts of the former USSR. The most important area, in which VEB will play a key role, is the debts owed to the London club. This is significant for VEB, because it is only by regulating this debt that VEB will be able to formalize its way out of default" (*Sevodnya*, 29th November 1996). The word went into common parlance in Russian after the government and the Central Bank of the Russian Federation froze State Short–term Obligation / Federal Loan Obligation payments and brought in a 90–day moratorium on the banks' fulfilment of their obligations to their foreign partners. The government described this as a "set of measures aimed at ensuring financial stabilization", but independent observers suggested a somewhat shorter description – a 'default'.

Dictatorship of the law

On 1st July 1991, General–Colonel Albert Makashov said in an interview with the weekly newspaper *Volzhskiye novosti*: "I'm a conservative. When it comes to such concepts as patriotism, internationalism and Leninism, I haven't changed my colours, and I have no intention of changing them. There are so many of us nowadays who are striving to get involved in something new, in order to derive some benefit for themselves. People like that see themselves as reformers, when in actual fact they are merely enablers. But I remain a conservative. As if that wasn't enough, I'm also in favour of a dictatorship. I'm in favour of the dicatorship of the law, the dictatorship of the Constitution. Alas, neither the law nor the Constitution are being adhered to at the moment. The phrase 'dictatorship of the law' became popular following a speech by the acting Russian president Vladimir Putin on 31st January 2000 at an extended Collegium of the Ministry of Justice. In a statement containing implied criticism of those journalists who were predicting a dictatorship of the security agencies in Russia, Putin declared: "The dictatorship of the law is the only form of dictatorship to which it is our duty to submit."

Dirty elections, dirty electoral (campaign) technologies

This term first appeared in the new Russia on 16th March 1995, in the newspaper *Izvestiya Tatarstana*, in a piece about the parliamentary elections in Tataria: "A press conference has taken place in Kazan which was attended by prospective parliamentary candidates who did not make it through to the second round of voting. Those present unanimously expressed the view that the elections currently taking place in Tatarstan represent a major violation of the Republic's legislation. According to the honorary president of the All–Tatar Public Centre, Marat Mulyukov, the recent disbandment of the parliament of Kazakhstan goes to show that it is never too late to declare the results of such 'dirty' elections null and void." This term became particularly popular in 1998, when the media dubbed as 'dirty' the elections held in the Sverdlovsk Region and the Krasnoyarsk Region, and the elections held in St Petersburg – the latter are now cited as the archetypal 'dirty' elections.

Equidistant from power

This term was first heard on 28th February 2000 during a meeting between Vladimir Putin and his representatives in the reception room for the public at his campaign HQ: "We must preclude the possibility of anyone clinging to power and using it in their own interests. Not a single clan, not a single oligarch must be allowed too close to the regional and federal executive – they must be equidistant from power." The phrase "equidistant from power" did not quite catch on among the general public. It is often used in the press, however.

Federals

On 21st December 1993 Mikhail Poltoranin, the director of the Federal Information Centre of Russia, characterized federal power in Russia in the following way, in an interview with *Rossiskaya gazeta*: "Where exactly does the balance lie between the interests of the federal autonomous areas and the local ones? Why did the law enforcement bodies prove so ineffective, and are they capable, in their current state, of ensuring that the Constitution, in the form adopted, operates properly?" This word went into common parlance in 1994–1995, when it began to be used in connection with representatives of the Russian armed forces in Chechnya: "Around 250 of Dudaev's insurgents stormed the police station in the city of Argun on Sunday evening, to the east of Grozny, along with four hostages who were local policemen. From the very outset it was clear that Chernomyrdin would not be entering into any negotiations with Khamzatov. Maskhadov, on the other hand, demonstrated just how influential a figure he is. He spent ten minutes talking to the insurgents, after which they supposedly agreed to leave the building and move out of Argun. There was of course no question of the insurgents giving themselves up to the federal authorities." (*KommersantDaily*. 1995. 22nd August).

Financial pyramid

This financial term became widely used following the collapse of the Joint–Stock Company MMM. Its first recorded use in the press came on 28th July 1994 in *KommersantDaily*, in an article by Igor Nikitina entitled 'Shares in JSC MMM have fallen in value': "MMM, by all accounts, has no money left. How else can we explain the fact that only one of the outlets where shares can be purchased was operating as normal yesterday and the day before yesterday? And although the company may well get out of the mess it is in by taking out a bank loan, given that interest rates for such loans are currently fairly low, one gets the feeling that something is broken in the mechanism that has been put in place at JSC MMM, and that the financial pyramid might collapse."

Genocide of the Russian people

The first recorded use of this term came in 1989, in the magazine *Our contemporary*: "Stalin was the fruit of his age, a figure who found himself at the very top as a result of objective and subjective circumstances. It was the old guard that put him forward...Only later did the internecine warfare begin. Effectively they were all part of the same mob. Trotsky, Bukharin, Kamenev, Zinoviev, Kaganovich, Yem. Yaroslavsky (Gubelman), Uritsky, Volodarsky, Epshtein – they were all devotees of mass murder... Yet now people are trying to paint those who orchestrated the genocide of the Russian people, and of other peoples as well, as victims – to put them on a par with saints, and put up a statue to them" (Valentin Pikul, Our contemporary. 1989. No. 2). This phrase became famous in 1995, when Gennady Zyuganov dded it to his arsenal.

Guarantor of the Constitution

This term was first used with regard to the Constitutional Court at the 5th congress of people's deputies of the RSFSR. The deputy Vladimir Kadyshev declared: "The Constitutional Court must be the guarantor of the Constitution and, figuratively speaking, must, whenever the slightest violation of the Constitution occurs, give a "red signal" to the president and the congress, if an unconstitutional law or directive is being adopted, and remind him that the Constitution exists and must be adhere to" (*Rossiskaya gazeta.* 1991. 1st November). On 16th July 1992 the president declared himself to be the 'guarantor of the Constitution': "As reported by the president's press service, Boris Yeltsin has declared that as the guarantor of the Constitution and of law and order in the country he will not allow any changes to be made to the legislative guarantees of freedom of speech and freedom to publish, or a return to the sad times of censorship" (ITARTASS). The president's roles as 'the guarantor of the Constitution' were set out in the Russian Constitution on 12th December 1993 (part 4, clause 80, point 2): "In the procedure established by the Constitution of the Russian Federation the president shall take measures to safeguard the sovereignty of the Russian Federation, its independence and integrity as a state, and ensure that the agencies of executive power in the state operate in the approved way."

"His handshake is firm"

Following his inauguration on 9th August 1996, Boris Yeltsin disappeared from journalists' field of view for a long period. *Time* magazine reported that the Russian president urgently needed an operation on his heart. On 19th August, Yeltsin's newly–appointed press secretary, Sergei Yastrzhembsky, issued an official denial of these reports and told journalists: "The president is undergoing a medical examination, but he is working, and his handshake is firm." On 5th September 1996 Boris Yeltsin said in an interview with RTR that he had agreed to have coronary bypass surgery.

'Hit them when they're on the shitter'

On 24th September 1999, during a press conference, the Russian prime minister Vladimir Putin was asked how the Russian authorities intended to respond to the explosions at apartment blocks in Moscow. Among other things, the prime minister commented: "...we'll get them in the toilets too [the terrorists – Ed.] – we'll hit them when they're on the shitter!"

Imagemaker

On 11th September 1992 Nurali Latypov said in an interview with *Ogoniok* magazine: "During my brief political career I was a political observer for Mironenko, a deputy minister in Silaev's government, an adviser to Dolgolaptev, an imagemaker for Zatulin...I definitely ended up disappointed by some of them, such as Zatulin; I am still on friendly terms with others, such as Mironenko; and I am still enjoying fruitful relations with others, such as Dolgolaptev – he is currently deputy chairman of the Federation Council."

Impeachment

This term was first used in the new Russia in an interview with the Strugatsky brothers, which was published in *Ogoniok* magazine in 1989: "A person who does a good job for society gets ample reward from society. A person who does a bad job for society gets nothing from society. This fundamental principle was breached at the end of the twenties. And our manufacturing capabilities immediately slowed down. At present we seem to be emerging onto this path, with a screech. And we'll emerge from it, we're not going anywhere. But anything could happen. A military coup – 'impeachment, Soviet style'. Or they might say to us: *perestroika* is over – hello and welcome, you're now decades behind where you ought to be. The calmness to which we are accustomed will be reinstated for a few years..." In March 1991 the head of the expert group of the Constitutional Commission of the RSFSR, Valery Zorkin, advocating the establishment of the post of president in the RSFSR, used the word 'impeachment' with regard to the head of state, for the first time: "The congress of people's deputies and the Supreme Soviet of the RSFSR are going to have effective levers of control over the president and the government...At last, in exceptional cases (when the Constitution and laws of the RSFSR are violated), the president may be replaced as the law–maker as a result of a special procedure (impeachment)" (*Rossiskaya gazeta*, 15th March 1991). The term went into common parlance following attempts by the opposition to impeach president Boris Yeltsin in 1999.

Inauguration

The first recorded use of this term in modern Russia was recorded on 6th July 1991 in *Nezavisimaya gazeta*, in an article by Edward Tolchinsky under the headline 'The inauguration of the president of Tatarstan': "An emergency session of the Supreme Soviet of Tatarstan has opened in Kazan. The highlight of the first day was the inauguration of the republic's president, Mintimer Shaimiev, who prior to that had been in charge of the presidium of the republican Supreme Soviet. Mintimer Shaimiev read the text of the oath in both Tatar and Russian." On 10th July 1991 the Russian president Boris Yeltsin was inaugurated: "This week the word 'inauguratsiya' (inauguration) passed from Russian–speaking citizens' passive vocabulary into their active vocabulary. The most apt translation of this transliterated word into ordinary Russian is "a betrothal to the kingdom". The triumphant swearing of the oath by Boris Nikolaevich

Yeltsin was performed amid truly Byzantine levels of splendour, although, as so often happens, there were a fair few fleas in the gold–embroidered cloth. The tickets for the inauguration ceremony, which were allocated to just a 'happy few', looked like ordinary theatre tickets and were dated 18th June 1989, included the fateful statement: "The management reserves the right to replace one member of the cast with another" (*Kommersant* weekly newspaper. 1991. 15th July).

Individual of Caucasian appearance

This term made the leap from journalists' lexicon to the language of the Ministry of Internal Affairs' operations files. The first recorded use of it came on 7th May 1988 in *Ogoniok* magazine, in an article by Dmitry Likhanov entitled 'Long live the King...': "Although this shell game confidence trick is nothing more than well–organized fraud, in which the person on the outside is destined always to lose, very few of those involved end up in the dock. National teams of 'Caucasians' have brought their business into five areas of the city on the Neva without much effort, and succeeded in turning a profit. It was with them that Sergei Vasiliev's career as a racketeer began. According to a cleaner at the Nevsky restaurant, Yevgeny Kargapolov, "at first Vasiliev took control of the swindling that was going on at Ulyanka, by going into business with some faces of Caucasian appearance." In 1991 the expression became quite common colloquially.

Information leak

On 23rd April 1995, Alexander Zhilin commented on the latest scandal surrounding the division of spheres of influence at the company *Rosvooruzheniye*: "Material of this kind is indeed going to emerge in print on the pages of this newspaper fairly frequently, because what we are witnessing is the process of the leaking of information from a variety of political forces to the press, in order to discredit opponents and rivals. We must therefore be selective in the way we approach this information and ask ourselves: who stands to benefit from this? In particular, if we were to touch on Rosbooruzheniye for a moment, we can pick out several political groups who are interested in some shape or form in strengthening their influence on this state structure, which in particular circumstances could provide funding for an election campaign."

"It's all Chubais's fault!

On 16th January 1996 Boris Yeltsin fired the first deputy prime minister, Anatoly Chubais, "for failing to make sufficiently stringent requirements of the subsidiary federal institutions and failing to perform a host of directives from the president of Russia." His decision was accompanied with the comment: "It's all Chubais's fault!" For some time this short statement was even more popular than the sarcastic saying "Who's going to do that then – Pushkin?"

"It sank"

On 9th September 2000, Vladimir Putin was interviewed live on CNN by the TV presenter Larry King. One of the questions King put to him was: "Let's examine the aspects of your activity which, perhaps, do not cause you pleasure. What could have...What happened? Tell us. What happened to the Russian submarine?" Vladimir Putin: "It sank." The president had an ironic smile on his face as he said these words. The Russian media felt that this smile was a serious political mistake on the part of the president. People in the West, however, who were the intended audience of the interview with Vladimir Putin, did not take it too seriously.

Kickback

This term was widely used in criminal circles. The first use of it in the press was recorded on 28th October 1992 in *KommersantDaily*, in an article by Arkin Tuzmukhamedov entitled 'Alan Grubman: on 23rd September 1992 the New York Supreme Court registered a $90 million lawsuit filed by the artist (Billy Joel. – *Vlast*) against his former lawyer – Allen Grubman – and his partners. Among the allegations were fraud: Grubman had invested $1 million in companies controlled by Frank Weber in order to retain Joel as a client; the use of a 'kickback' and "the payment of a thousand dollars to Weber himself and to companies which he controlled."

Killer

This term was borrowed by journalists from criminal slang. In 1992 the word 'killer' had yet to go into common parlance, and a translation was therefore provided whenever it was used in the press: "A contract killer (murderer) nicknamed 'The cannibal', who was notorious in criminal circles and who was responsible for 8 murders, including the killing of two police officers, was recently taken into custody by Moscow's law enforcement agencies. 'The Cannibal' was spotted in the centre of Moscow by people who recognized his face, and the police were called. On seeing uniformed police, the killer realized what was happening in a flash and immediately reached for his gun. But he did not have time to grab hold of it. In front of startled passers–by, 'the Cannibal' was seized and forced into a car." (*Moskovsky komsomolets*. 1992. 21st October). The phrase 'contract killer' did not stick – journalists preferred to use either the term 'hired assassin' or simply 'killer'. The word 'killer' was first applied to politicians by journalists from *Nezavisimaya gazeta*: "The first deputy prime minister, Gennady Burbulis... has earned himself the epithet of 'killer' – so flattering for a politician – from *Nezavisimaya gazeta*, in place of the title of 'grey cardinal'" (*Nezavisimaya gazeta*. 1992. 18th April).

Maski–show (mask show)

On 2nd December 1994, staff from the Main Security Directorate wearing black masks blocked the entrance to the mayor's office on Novy Arbat, where the office of the Most group was located. According to Most's CEO Vladimir Gusinsky, some of his staff were arrested and beaten up. The media dubbed this operation 'Face down in the snow'. The next day Dmitry Gorbachuk, the head of the security service for the Most group, used the term *maski–show* in public for the first time, in connection with the security services' operations: "It all began not even on Friday but a few days before the sad events took place; in our circle we now refer to them as a 'mascarade', because it genuinely was some sort of show. With regard to both the men in masks and their actions, the effect on the public was probably a higher priority than the outcome itself," (the weekly newspaper *Kommersant*, 13th December 1994). It was not uncommon for representatives of the security agencies to wear black masks when conducting searches of the offices of commercial firms and charities, and when carrying out special ops, and this enabled the term 'mask show' to become more popular. The expression was given a second wind in 1999 thanks to new scandals erupting in connection with the Most group.

Media magnate

The first recorded use of this term came on 5th July 1996 in the newpaper Sevodnya, in an article headed 'TV rights 'handed over' for 2 billion': "The German media magnate Leo Kirch, from Bavaria, and the Swiss marketing agency ISL won the 'battle' for the TV rights to broadcast football's World Cup finals in 2002 and 2006, by paying a record $2.24 billion." The term was later used with reference to a Russian company: "Since the middle of 1994 Severstal – one of Russia's three biggest ferrous metallurgy companies – has been performing the unaccustomed role of a media magnate. Through its affiliates Metkombank and the company Meta (the company's main trader), the combine controls the Transmit radio station (Cherepovets and Vologda), the TV channels TV7 (Vologda), 12 (Cherepovets) and 'Provintsiya' (Vologda), the cable TV studio Skat (Cherepovets), the daily newspaper 'Rech' and the weekly newspaper 'Kurier' (*KommersantDaily*. 1996. 3rd October). The word 'media magnate' went into common parlance in 1998 with respect to Boris Berezovsky and Vladimir Gusinsky.

Money–laundering

This term was taken from criminal slang and used by journalists in the early '90s. It made its first appearance on 2nd February 1991 in Nezavisimaya gazeta, in Dmitry Pinsker's article 'The co–op chest against the state 'little commission'': "There was an influx of cheap goods from the 'black market' to the shop floor. All over Moscow the cost of cigarettes, lighters, tapes and all kinds of other paraphernalia went up so much that they were not even affected by the process of the mass buying up of goods in recent days. And everything that has been said lately to the effect that 'dirty' money has been laundered through the commissions was categorically denied by A. Botin: 'That's not possible here, because we don't deal in cash at all. The revenue we make from sales is paid to the person who delivers the goods by cashless transfer.'"

Negotiator

This term was one that journalists appropriated from the language used by members of the security agencies: "The Academy of the Ministry of Internal Affairs is planning to begin training specialist negotiators who will be able to negotiate with criminals who have taken people hostage." In late 1993 the term acquired a broader definition: "The history of Russia's debts and payments, as set out by Alexander Shokhin, enables us to draw at least three conclusions. Firstly, the deputy prime minister cemented his reputation as a 'tough negotiator'. Shokhin's skill was demonstrated in the fact that there was an easing of the terms and conditions for the payment of loans, in spite of the substantial ($21 billion at the end of the year, according to official reports) Russia's balance sheet for the current payments being in the black" (*KommersantDaily*. 1993. 23rd November).

New Russians

This phrase first appeared in *Ogoniok* magazine on 4th March 1992, in an article about businessmen's eating habits entitled '*New Russians* enraged about fat'. But a full deciphering of the term was given in the weekly newspaper Kommersant on 7th September 1992 in an article marking the launch of the daily newspaper *KommersantDaily*. The weekly reported that Russia had seen the formation of a 'narrow social class, whose members are characterized by being at once extremely wealthy and highly educated, and who have a new mentality and consequently a new lifestyle. This is the newly–emergent elite of Russian society...There is a term in sociology which is particularly apt in this instance: 'anticipatory socialization'. *KommersantDaily* was consciously devised and 100% oriented towards serving the interests and informational needs of the New Russians – the 'anticipatory socialization' in Russian society..."

The expression New Russians was borrowed from the Western media – specifically, it was used by the American magazine Newsweek. Staff at the publication's offices were unable to establish, however, when the phrase was first used by looking through the digital archives. Incidentally, Newsweek cannot lay claim to have invented the term, either. The phrase 'new Russians' could justifiably be attributed to Alexander Pushkin:

> *Yet in the villages and towns*
> *Mazurkas are still danced with grace and*
> *Their distinctive hues and colours:*
> *Moustaches, skipping feet, high heels*
> *Are still there: they were not replaced by*
> *Fashion, that tyrant with reckless will,*
> *Of newest Russians the greatest ill.*
> (Eugene Onegin, chapter 5, stanza XLII, 1828)

Newsmaker

This term first appeared on 24th August 1992 in *KommersantDaily*, in a newspaper announcement which promised to track the life and times of 'newsmakers' avidly: "*Newsmakers* (who, at a stretch, could be described in Russian as *deyateli novostey* – makers of news) are the corporations, organizations, companies or individuals who set the agenda in their particular field and thus affect the lives of all the other structures, organizations, companies or individuals around them. Lists of newsmakers have been compiled by experts from all the departments at *Kommersant* based on their interaction with people from the world of politics, business, culture and other fields."

No tie session

The first recorded use of this diplomatic term was on 19th September 1996 in the newspaper Financial Russia, in an article by A. Soloviev headed *Planning and conducting negotiations*, about the rules and etiquette governing diplomatic meetings: "Etiquette dictates that jackets shall not be taken off whilst negotiations are under way, nor shall ties be loosened, except when your partners' heads of delegation propose that this be done, as an indication that the time of informal discussions has now arrived." This phrase became widely used towards the end of 1997 after a series of informal meetings between Boris Yeltsin and the Japanese Prime Minister Ryutaro Hashimoto.

Oil general

This term was first used on 19th June 1991 in Rossiskaya gazeta, in an article by Vladimir Yefimov entitled 'The Volcano of Tyumen': "'Tyumen is a volcano, which could become unpredictable. And that's what people are afraid of in Moscow – at all levels. For whilst Tyumen will survive without the country, the country is very unlikely to survive without Tyumen...' This is the view of the former oil 'general' and current chairman of the regional Council of people's deputies, Yuri Shafranik. Of course, 'generals' always have their extravagant moments – former generals even more so. And it would be entirely possible simply to ignore all these apparently haughty speeches altogether, were it not for the fact that 3/4 of the national reserves of oil and gas, sales of which on the global market account for more than half of the money coming into the country, are concentrated in this region."

Oligarch

The term first appeared on 2nd June 1995 in the newspaper *Century*, in a sketch entitled 'A portrait of the oligarch as a young man. Oleg Boiko at the tip of the political iceberg.' The word 'oligarch' began to be widely used in 1997. On 20th September 1997 an interview was published in the newspaper *Sevodnya* with the president of the bank SBSAgro, Alexander Smolensk, in which the journalist put the following question to him: "Could you be accused of being an oligarch, just like Potanin?" On 10th February 1998, in an article entitled 'Russians in Davos: we aren't from around here...', published in *Moskovsky komsomolets*, Yulia

Kalinina wrote: "'Look,' Minister Yasin said to the journalists, 'don't you know each other yet? Allow me to introduce you. This is Potanin. He's an oligarch.' "That's right, I'm an oligarch," Potanin confirmed, smiling shyly, and assumed a dignified air. It seemed as though he wasn't overly keen on being called an oligarch, but he was too shy to admit as much. Oligarch...It doesn't sound like a particularly nice name. It sounds as though it might be something a bit like a diplodocus or a tyrannosaurus. It probably has a tiny little head, a brain the size of a walnut, plates of bone along its back, a tail with three spikes on it and tufts of hair under its arms. According to some reports, Berezovsky doesn't like it either when people call him an oligarch. But why is that, exactly? The only possible explanation is that it doesn't sound very nice. And that's probably the reason..." This word became part of the Russian language once and for all with the help of the conference 'Russia's Future: democracy or oligarchy', held in March 1988. The man who organized the conference, Boris Nemtsov, called on society to wage a "month–long struggle against the oligarchs", and this garnered a lot of interest in the media.

Parade of sovereignties

The parade of sovereignties was the name given to the declarations of independence which were made immediately by ten republics in the union between August and October 1990. On 10th October 1990, during a speech at an emergency congress of people's deputies of the RSFSR, deputy Pyotr Zerin declared: "At present, due to the intensifying of inter–ethnic relations in our country, and to the processes taking place as the Union of SSRs is broken up, alarm is being expressed not only by all the healthy forces in our country but also by the European Community. The parade of sovereignties is proving to be a war which is causing suffering for everyone, including those who initiated it. The collapse of economic ties, the rise of separatism, discrepancies between the laws of the union and those of the republics…And, as a result, a daily paralysis of power and a universal sense of disorder," (Rossiskaya gazeta. 1990. 11th December).

Party of power

This term was first used on 29th October 1991 in *Nezavisimaya gazeta*, in Mikhail Karpov's article 'There will be a single political bloc in Russia', about the formation of a pro–presidential political coalition: "As might have been expected, the Russian president, when setting about bringing in radical reform in the 'breakthrough regime' which they had declared, simply did not have the right to spend time worrying about who he could rely on in this tense and, without question, extremely difficult time for him and for the country. In his speech yesterday before the Russian parliament, the president declared that there was a need to create a unified block of political parties which supported the reforms he was proposing. The first thing that may come to mind in connection with all this is: we are once again witnessing an attempt to create a party of power." The 'party of power' was a label given at various times to: 'Russia's Choice (1993–1994), 'Our home is Russia' (1996–1998) and 'Unity' ('United Russia') (2001–2003).

Political correctness

This term first appeared in the Russian press on 8th September 1993 in *KommersantDaily* in an article by Andrei Plakhov entitled The results of the Montreal film festival: "Roger Spottiswoode's film 'And the Band Played On…' really tugged at the heart–strings of the Montreal public. This pseudo–documentary drama tells the story of the emergence of the immuno–deficiency virus, the development of the problem of AIDs, and its transformation from a problem that was strictly medical to one with political, moral and social aspects. The film is notable for its political correctness on two issues: race and sexuality. Andrei Plakhov later shortened the term: "Stanley Kramer is a Hollywood dissident who nowadays is a classic exponent of polit–correctness," (*KommersantDaily*. 1993. 15th October). This version of the term was subsequently used far more often than the original version.

Political heavyweight

On 24th November 1992 the Russian president Boris Yeltsin fired the chairman of the TV and radio company Ostankino, Yegor Yakovlev. Igor Malashenko became the acting chairman. In January 1993, when the issue of who was going to be the company's new chairman was being decided, Malashenko declared in an interview in *KommersantDaily* that the role "ought to be given to a political heavyweight, a centrist." This phrase went into common parlance following a TV address by Boris Yeltsin to the Russian people on 24th August 1998: "Yesterday I made a difficult decision. I suggested to Viktor Stepanovich Chernomyrdin that he take charge of the government. Five months ago no–one anticipated that the financial crisis would hit Russia so hard, or that the economic situation in the country would be made so much more complicated. In light of these circumstances, our top priority is not to allow ourselves to take a backward step, and to guarantee stability. The people we need today are those who tend to be described as heavyweights. I believe that Chernomyrdin's experience and weight are essential." Yevgeny Primakov, Yuri Maslyukov and Boris Yeltsin himself were all described as 'political heavyweights' at one time or another.

Political strategists

When he set up the Strategy centre in 1992, Gennady Burbulis anounced that his aim was to encourage the development and deepening of reforms in Russia, by "developing and implementing programmes devised by political strategists." On 27th October 1994 the term was used by Prime Minister Viktor Chernomyrdin in an address to deputies in the State Duma, prior to a vote of no confidence in the government: "The government of the Russian Federation is essentially proposing a new economic policy, in which a concept starts to become a programme of action. This was announced by Viktor Chernomyrdin. According to Chernomyrdin, the government is only just beginning to master the civilized methods of the political strategy of introducing reforms." (*Rossiskiye vesti*. 1994. 28th October). The term 'political strategist' as the name of a particular profession was first used in *Nezavisimaya gazeta* on 16th July 1996, in an article by Titus Sovetologov (aka Vitaly Tretyakov) entitled 'Rocky96': "But surely one of these public figures – Igor Malashenko, perhaps – could sort of accidentally broadcast one of the Rocky films on his TV channel? In one of the films – Rocky 4, if I'm not mistaken – the great Rocky has to fight a Russian of frightening dimensions...So I got to thinking: how could we spin this final bit of fighting in the light of the disputes between the American and the Russian political strategists?"

Popularly elected

This phrase was first used in relation to Boris Yeltsin, even before he became president of the RSFSR. On 12th March 1991, *Rossiskaya gazeta* contained the following report: 'Sverdlovsk. A rally for democracy has become the first in the city's history to take place with the support of the citizens and official authorities of Sverdlovsk, rather than against their will. Various estimates suggest that as many as 100,000 people attended the rally, shouting slogans such as: "Yes to Yeltsin, no to Gorbachev!", "A popularly elected President of Russia is a counterweight to a dictatorship", "Gorbachev out! "Long may the Union of the Federation reign!", "Mikhail Sergeevich, let us live our lives". From 1993 onwards the term 'popularly elected' began to be used as a synonym for the word 'president'.

Positioning

This term, which was used primarily by marketing experts, was first recorded on 12th November 1992 in *KommersantDaily* in an article by Aristarkh Vladimirov entitled 'Alisa to bring in a product for new Russians': "Yesterday the directors of the 'Alisa' system announced that they were going to introduce their Friend Holder cigarette holders in the CIS market, featuring anti–nicotine and anti–tar filters which will be positioned on the market as a product for "self–respecting smokers". In 1998–1999, when more publications began to appear on the market covering a variety of business fields, the verb 'to position' began to be used by the wider public.

Post–Soviet region

The first recorded use of this term came on 7th February 1992 in *Nezavisimaya gazeta*, in Algis Prazauskas's article 'The CIS as a post–colonial area': "The African and Asian countries which have been liberated – the ones which avoided the temptation of the so–called Socialist orientation, at any rate – were able to use the metropolis's political system and, to some extent, its economic system, as a model for growth. The post–Soviet area does not have this sort of reference point, and the possibility of applying the Eastern European model or searching for a 'third way', which the states of central Asia are clearly inclined to do, are dubious to say the least. It will be a historical miracle if any of the former Soviet republics manages to find solutions for three incredibly difficult tasks at the same time: replacing the political and economic systems and overcoming the financial crisis, whilst avoiding any serious socio–political shocks or instability." The term went into common parlance overnight.

PR

This term was first encountered (without a translation) on 19th August 1991 in the weekly newspaper *Kommersant* in an article by Dmitry Bogdanovich, 'RBN decides to work for the public. The Soviet public': "For the first time, a foreign firm specializing in the field of public relations (PR) has been officially accredited in the USSR. The firm in question is the American company RBN Company. It opened a representative office in Moscow on 13th August. Four years later the term 'black PR' crops up in the Russian press: "The chairman of the Guild of press services and 'public relations' services staff, Alexander Popov, maintains that "our country has for many years seen an abomination of PR, a form of charlatanism." Non–professionals make up for the inadequacy of their technologies by being active on the market, explaining that "PR is flowers, champagne, a $150 tie and that so–called black PR is about articles that have been bought." (*KommersantDaily*. 1995. 9th November). In 1995–1996, as the advertising market began to grow and a huge number of companies appeared which specialized in relations with the community, the term became widely used.

Prime time

The term prime time, written in Latin letters, first appears on 8th July 1991 in the weekly newspaper *Kommersant*, in Georgy Plaksin's article 'TVIN will advertise your services on Brighton Beach at low cost': "On 11th July, airtime on the New York–based TV channel RTN (Russian Television Network), which targets a Russian–speaking audience, is going to be set aside for the International Stock Exchange for the Television Industry (IET) TVIN...The average cost of one minute of prime–time advertising on the nation's biggest TV networks (ABC, NBS, CBS) is $100,000, and can sometimes be as much as half a million dollars." The term was first used in its Cyrillic form in an article by Andrei Naumov entitled 'A minute of stupidity. TV advertising to remain Soviet for the time being': 'Many have come unstuck on voices and intonation already. Items featuring heavy breathing and the use of bass registers may be memorable, but when they accompany information aimed at professionals they evoke a negative reaction among the general public. Does it make sense to pay vast sums of money, albeit 'wooden' money, for prime–time (the best time to be on air) just to have people despising you?' (*Nezavisimaya gazeta*. 1992. 18th January).

'Proslushka' (eavesdropping)

This term was one that journalists borrowed from the jargon of the security services: "Experts feel that control of audio monitoring and surveillance conducted by the Ministry of Security should be transferred to the prosecutor's office, so that voluntary access to operational technical resources can be covered in a reliable way and the surveillance services stop watching and listening to ordinary citizens and politicians, because the Chekists think fit to do so, and start using them – after the sanctions have first been imposed by the prosecutor or by a court – in the fight against criminals, regardless of which post these criminals hold. In the United States, incidentally, there is a whole range of grounds for requesting permission to eavesdrop on telephone calls. The suspicion that John Doe broke the law is not enough on its own; definitive proof is required." (*Izvestiya*. 1993. 7th December). The word *proslushka* ('listening in') became popular in 1996. On 8th July an article was published in *Moskovsky komsomolets* entitled 'The favourites' – it was a transcription of a confidential telephone conversation between Boris Berezovsky, Valentin Yumashev, Tatiana Diachenko and the director of the National Sports Foundation, Boris Fyodorov. The subject of the conversation was the "improper" behaviour of Alexander Korzhakov, Mikhail Barsukov and Shamil Tarpischev. Thereafter the results of various instances of "listening in" appeared on numerous occasions in the newspapers and on websites for "compromising material" on the Internet, and the term went into common parlance.

Purge

This term made the jump from police jargon to the media in 1993: "An unaccustomed hush descended at Kazan station, as well. Local detectives, backed by several soldiers from the special forces, undertook a prophylactic 'purge' of waiting rooms, gathering up local 'residents' – homeless teenagers, tramps, etc. Ultimately, the police released several dozen of the people they had checked for the rest of the night, after failing to discover anything incriminating on them." Since 1995 the term has mostly been used in the sense of 'an operation aimed at uncovering the participants in unlawful armed formations in Chechnya" (*Nezavisimaya gazeta.* 1993. 18th February).

Redistribution of property

In 1991 this term was put to use by members of the opposition movement who were critical of the way things stood in the country. The programme for emerging from the crisis, which was adopted by members of the Communists of Russia bloc, contained the following passage: "Russia's fate, and the lives and well–being of its people, are at stake. The enforced redistribution of property and of distribution relationships will only serve to add an extra burden on the shoulders of the overwhelming majority of workers." Points from the Communists of Russia's programme were published in *Rossiskaya gazeta* on 5th April 1991. This phrase went into common parlance during the period of cheque privatization which was brought in in 1992–1993.

Red belt

The first recorded use of this term came on 11th September 1992 in the magazine *Ogoniok*, in Alexander Prasolov's article 'Are the elections already a *fait accompli*?' "Evidence has emerged which suggests that at least some of the heads of administrations have already been given 'targets' which must be 'reached' by particular blocs in the elections. It is also reported that in a range of areas there are lists of 'undesirable' candidates, who must not be allowed to be given a seat in the Duma. Specifically, there have been reports to this effect from Bashkiria, Tataria, Smolensk and a host of other places. And who's to say that the fact that the Communists are voted in so often in the regions in the "red belt" in the south of Russia – the very regions that they control – is only down to whole-hearted and passionate striving for the happiness of the people? The results of the second round of the presidential elections in 1996 provided clear evidence of the existence of this 'red belt'.

Security agents

The phrase "the security structures of the executive" was first used on 23rd July 1990 in the weekly newspaper *Kommersant*, in an article by Maksim Sokolov entitled *Will there be a military coup d'etat in the Soviet Union?* "People have a tendency to talk in terms of a conflict between the current leaders, who are set on reform, and the party machine (the CPSU. – *Vlast*)...It's quite natural that everyone involved in the conflict has their gaze set on the security structures of the executive: the army and the KGB, without whose involvement any attempt to carry out a coup d'etat (article 64 of the Criminal Code of the RSFSR

'Conspiracy with the objective of seizing power') has no chance of succeeding." In 1993 this phrase was shortened to *siloviki*, 'security agents': "The dubious actions of the Ministry of Internal Affairs, the incomprehensible role played by the Ministry of Security and the wavering of the Ministry of Defence led to a situation in which they weren't considered to be the heroes of the hour at all, and consequently, instead of being able to hold the president hostage, the security agents (first and foremost, the militiamen) found that their main concern was how to avoid nasty questions, rather than how to impose their will on the government." (*Kommersant* weekly. 1993. 11 November).

Sequester

This is a financial term which dates back to the 19th century. It made its way into the Russian press thanks to *Rossiskaya gazeta*, which on 14th November 1991 published the law 'On the principles of the budgetary device and the budgetary process in the RSFSR'. The law set out the mechanisms which could be used to reduce the size of the budget: "If, during the process of distributing the budget, the maximum level of the deficit is exceeded or there is a significant reduction in the amount of money coming into the budget from profitable sources, the mechanism of sequestering expenses shall be introduced. Sequestering involves a proportionate reduction in state expenses (by 5, 10, 15% etc.) each month in every category of the budget throughout the remaining period in the current financial year." This word became generally known in May 1997, when the issue of an overall reduction in the size of the budget was up for discussion in the government.

Seven Bankers' Cabal

On 1st November 1996 an interview with Boris Berezovsky was published in the *Financial Times*, in which he identified the seven people who controlled over 50% of the Russian economy and who, together, influenced the taking of all the most important internal political decisions in Russia: Vladimir Potanin, Vladimir Gusinsky, Mikhail Khodorkovsky, Pyotr Aven, Mikhail Fridman, Alexander Smolensk and Boris Berezovsky himself. Two weeks later the journalist Andrei Fadin published an article in *Obschaya gazeta* under the headline: 'The Seven Bankers' Cabal as the new Russia's answer to the Seven Boyars': "They control access to the funds in the budget and practically all the opportunities for investment in the country. They hold in their hands a huge informational resource from the biggest TV channels. They formulate the will of the president. Those who chose not to join up with them have either been throttled or have left that circle...In Russia, however, no victory is ever decisive unless it seems to be just in some way in the eyes of the majority." On 17th February 2003 the head of the Ministry of Economic Development, German Gref, said live on air on NTV: "You know, we used to have the seven bankers' cabal – now we have the seven oil men's cabal." The phrase 'seven bankers' cabal' can therefore be considered a little outdated.

"Take as much sovereignty as you can swallow"

This statement was made by Boris Yeltsin during a speech in Kazan on 8th August 1990. On 26 April 1990 the Supreme Soviet of the USSR adopted the law 'On the delineation of powers between the USSR and the Federation's subjects', which 'evened out' the powers of the autonomous republics and the unions. The Supreme Soviet of the RSFSR saw this law as an attack on Russia's territorial integrity – 16 autonomous territories were to all intents and purposes withdrawn from the Federation, and their leaders were granted the right to take part in decision-making with regard to the fate of the USSR. The leaders of the Union calculated that in any confrontation with the authorities in the RSFSR the Union would be able to secure the backing of regional politicians. Russia's leaders attempted to keep the autonomous regions in the RSFSR, by providing them with as much freedom as possible. Yeltsin's words about sovereignty were later recalled by supporters of the opposition on numerous occasions, when they sought to criticize the way the central powers interacted with the regions.

Talking head

This term was first used in an interview (*Nezavisimaya gazeta*. 1991. 19 March) with the chairman of the All–Russia State Television and Radio Broadcasting Company, Oleg Poptsov: "NG: We have not ended up with a fundamentally new form of TV. Most of RTV's programmes are made using the same archaic, provincial formula: live on air, "talking heads", endless cantillations. Poptsov: Why do they have all these 'talking heads' and live shows? Because they haven't got enough money! There's a terrible shortage of mounting systems, and if you're live on air you don't need these systems. We started completely from scratch, don't forget. We had nothing: no chairs, no nails, no wheels. And that was one of the principles we stuck to, as well: don't go dividing things up, or pinching things – but create another broadcasting centre from scratch." In 1998 the term 'the talking head of the Kremlin' was used for the first time. On 28th November 1998 the information agency Interfax AIF announced: "Zyuganov's latest anti–presidential escapade with regard to "the drunken and degraded Yeltsin" almost became a pretext for an attempt by the Kremlin to haul Gennady Andreevich before the courts. It soon transpired, however, that the threat of legal proceedings was simply the deeply personal view of Oleg Sysuev, who has recently become the Kremlin's main 'talking head'."

"The right place for a thief is behind bars"

On 20th October 1994, Vadim Poegli claimed in the newspaper Moskovsky komsomolets, in an article entitled *Pashamercedes*, that foreign cars being used by the Minister of Defence Pavel Grachev in the course of his work were being bought with money that had been set aside for the construction of homes for army veterans. The article's sub–heading was: "The right place for a thief is behind bars, not in the Ministry of Defence" – a paraphrased version of a line spoken by Gleb Zheglov in the film *The Meeting Place Cannot Be Changed*: "If it weren't for the lies I told, that kleptomaniac thief Saprykin would be in hiding right now, and not in prison! It's true I put the wallet in his pocket, but who did I do that for? For myself, for my father–in–law, for my brother? If Brick's a thief, he belongs behind bars. And no–one cares how I go about putting him there. The right place for a thief is behind bars! That's what people care about."

Tricolore

This first use of this term came on 15th January 1991 in *Nezavisimaya gazeta*, in Vladimir Todres's article 'Demrossiya' calls for strikes': "Demrossii's plans have been disrupted by the events that took place at the end of last week. The traditional Russian tricolore hanging over the table of the presidium was joined by the yellow, green and red flag of Lithuania. The speech can be summarized using the words of Galina Starovoitova: "The process of *perestroika* has come to an end. The result of the year is a shift to the right. The reforms floundered on the attempts to preserve the empire."

Vertical power structure, vertical system of power

The 'vertical system of power' first appeared on 23rd May 1991 in Rossiskaya Gazeta, in an article by Olga Burkaleva, Vyacheslav Doganov, Andrei Zhdanin and Sergei Nagaev entitled 'Do we need to tighten up on time?'. "The deputy A.I. Stelikov proposed that the law on the president be approved, after making a few businesslike statements to go along with his articles. But in all of this he managed to capture the subtleties of the way the future 'vertical system' of executive power is going to be built, and for that reason the deputy's proposals with regard to perfecting the local autonomy did not cause much of a response among his colleagues." A few months later, in Valery Surikov's article 'The Union, Gorbachev, Russia', published on 17th October 1991 in *Nezavisimaya gazeta*, the phrase 'the vertical power structure' was used: "If the president feels it is essential to have a consultative political body headed by the state secretary, then this body, in order not to weaken or deform the vertical power structure, ought to transform itself from the first and decisive chain in the vertical power structure into the leftovers of it, a body acting exclusively through the president." Both expressions went into common parlance after 28th February 2000, when the acting president of Russia Vladimir Putin fired 17 envoys in the regions, declared that it was essential for the vertical structure of power in the country to be strengthened and promised to bring the regional legislation into line with the federal legislation.

Voice

This term was first used on 6th February 1992 in Rossiskaya gazeta in an article by Vladimir Sluzhakov, 'We are not an alternative government body': "The chairman of parliament's Supreme Economic Board, Vladimir Ispravnikov, voiced the board's forecast: unless the measures set out in the emergency plan are taken in the near future, one possible scenario awaiting us will be the collapse of the Russian economy and the break–up of Russia into several economic zones." It must be said that initially this term was put in quotation marks: "Observers point out that the recent hearings were the first open hearings in the history of the Soviet aerospace industry. A host of valuable proposals were 'voiced' for the first time, many of which had been mentioned in a speech by the chief expert of the parliamentary commission on transport, communications, IT and aerospace, Vladimir Postyshev' (*KommersantDaily*). 1992. 11 November). By 1995 the term was firmly established as part of journalists' lexicon.

Vote of no confidence

This was a term borrowed by journalists from legal jargon. It had been used in Soviet newspapers as well, in articles about politicians from the West. The first use of it in the press of the new Russia was in a letter from a Candidate of Jurisprudence named T. Bogolyubovskaya, published in Ogoniok magazine on 6th May 1989: "In every civilized country the government is often on the receiving end of extremely ferocious criticism, and may have to face a vote of no confidence; all this is seen as an integral feature of democracy." At the start of the '90s the phrase 'vote of no confidence' was popular among politicians and journalists. On 10th September 1990 Maksim Sokolov wrote in the weekly newspaper *Kommersant*: "The presidium of the Supreme Soviet of the USSR proposed an agenda for the assembly which bore little relation to the programme put forward by Shatalin, which the president had previously described as the main programme. On behalf of the Inter–regional Deputy Group, Anatoly Sobchak proposed an alternative agenda: one of the most important points in it was a vote of no confidence in the Union's cabinet." The term 'vote of no confidence' is not referred to in the Russian constitution. This procedure is described in the Constitution of the RF as a 'resolution of the State Duma declaring its lack of confidence in the Government of the RF' (article 117).

Vote or lose

The political campaign 'Vote or lose' was dreamed up by Sergei Lisovsky and Boris Zosimov in January 1996 and put into action in April – July of that year. The aim of the campaign was to mobilize the electorate for the presidential candidate Boris Yeltsin, who were more passive than the people who intended to vote for Gennady Zyuganov. They decided to model their campaign on the 'Choose or lose' pre–election campaign conducted by Bill Clinton's team on the American TV channel MTV in 1992. Sociologists estimate that 17.1% of the total number of people who voted did so because of the 'Vote or lose' campaign, and this figure was as high as 30% among voters aged under 27. Sergei Lisovsky was given an honorary diploma for organizing and conducting the campaign.

War of information

This term was first used on 4th February 1991 in the weekly newspaper *Kommersant*, in an article by Sergei Mitrofanov headed 'The wars of information from the era of the twilight of *glasnost*': "A 'war of information' is a concept that is almost unavoidable in a polarized society. In the political and economic confrontation between the political centre and Russia, it has recently taken on clearly defined forms. Thus 'Democratic Russia' and the Russian leadership are trying to conquer a sphere of influence on radio and TV airtime using whichever legitimate methods they can think of. Those in charge of the Union are attempting to slow down this process in various ways." The term went on to be used with regard to any public confrontation between two conflicting parties which was reflected in the media.

"We were hoping for the best, but ended up with the usual."

On 24th July 1993 the Central Bank of Russia announced that banknotes issued between 1961 and 1992 would cease to be accepted from the Russian population as of Monday 26th July 1993, in connection with which Russian citizens would be entitled, up until 27th July, to exchange up to 35,000 roubles in old money for new banknotes printed in 1993. The announcement caused panic among the people, and queues soon formed in the shops as people attempted to convert the savings they held in roubles into whatever product they could think of. Two days later Boris Yeltsin signed an order 'On the provision of normal functioning of the monetary system in the Russian Federation', which increased the maximum amount of money which could be exchanged from 35,000 to 100,000 roubles per person, permitted the free exchange of banknotes printed in 1992 with a face value of 10,000 and extended the deadline up until which money could be exchanged until the end of August 1993. The head of the Russian government, Viktor Chernomyrdin, told a press conference on 6th August how the monetary reforms were progressing, and concluded his remarks by saying: "We had hoped for the best, but ended up with the usual." The phrase instantly caught on among the general public. In 1994, marking the anniversary of the birth of this aphorism, the *Kommersant* columnist Maksim Sokolov wrote: "What Herzen said about Chaadaev: "The only people who can write like that are those who have spent a lot of time thinking, thought about a lot of things and experienced a lot of things; people reach that sort of view not by theorizing but by living," are surprisingly apt with regard to Chernomyrdin; in future, historians are going to relish quoting and commenting on Chernomyrdin's philosophical aphorisms.

"With a single parachute regiment"

On 26th November 1994 an armed association comprised by the Federal Counter–Espionage Service and the Ministry of Defence of the Russian Federation attempted to storm the city of Grozny. The attempt was aborted and 70 servicemen were taken prisoner; 23 tanks were destroyed. At a press conference on 28th November, the Minister of Defence Pavel Grachev denied reports that Russian soldiers had taken part in the storm, and declared: "If the army had been involved, it would have been possible to resolve all of this with a single parachute regiment."

"You're wrong, Boris"

At the 19th conference of the CPSU on 1st July 1988, the first deputy prime minister of the USSR, Boris Yeltsin, gave a speech in which he strongly criticized the party's central administration for failing to keep pace with the *perestroika* processes taking place in the country, and spoke in favour of *glasnost* being extended to cover the internal life of the party; he proposed that universal, direct, secret elections for the leaders of party organizations be introduced. Yegor Ligachev, a member of the Politburo who was present in the assembly hall, interrupted Yeltsin's speech by saying into the microphone: "You're wrong Boris. It's not just the tactics that we disagree on. You've got huge reserves of energy, Boris, but your energy's destructive rather constructive! You've put your region on ration stamps..." Ignoring Ligachev's remark, Yeltsin carried on talking. The Russian public took a liking to the phrase, and it was subsequently recalled on numerous occasions.

"You've got the seating plan wrong"

On 27th April 1999 Boris Yeltsin, against the will of Prime Minister Yevgeny Primakov, appointed Sergei Stepashin first deputy prime minister of the Russian government. On 5th May, at an assembly of the government's organizing committee for greeting the third millennium, Stepashin was seated at some distance from Primakov. Yeltsin saw in this an insurrection by his staff and issued the famous directive: "You've got the seating plan wrong. Stepashin is the first deputy. Rectify this at once!"

Zagogulina ('jiggery–pokery')

This is one of the favourite expressions cherished by Boris Yeltsin. It was used for the first time on 8th October 1998 at an awards ceremony for senior officers in the Armed Forces. The president announced that the security forces "have traditionally been directly subordinate to the president and will always be directly subordinate to the president." "Everything that the state has borrowed from you will be repaid," the chief commanding officer promised. "Supporting you is a top priority for me, but the demands I make of you should be top priorities, too. That's the kind of jiggery–pokery we end up with." Russia's first president characterized many of his political decisions as 'bits of jiggery–pokery'. For example, Yeltsin wrote about the intrigue surrounding the appointment of the prime minister in May 1999 as follows: "It has been decided, then. I am putting Stepashin forward as a candidate. But I am pleased with the way I kept the intrigue regarding Aksenenko going. That was a nice bit of jiggery–pokery. The men in the Duma are all geared up to see him appointed – they're at battle stations. And then I come along and give them a different candidate. Stepashin's candidacy made it through at the first time of asking. And it did so easily, without the slightest tension." (*The presidential marathon*, 2000).

38 snipers

On 9th January 1996 a group of Chechen insurgents under the command of Salman Raduev carried out a terrorist raid on the Dagestani of Kizlyar. The insurgents took hostages and on 10th January strengthened their position in the village of Pervomaiskoye. On 13th January the Russian president Boris Yeltsin announced in a TV interview: "The operation was prepared down to the last detail – let's say, if there were 38 snipers, then each sniper had a particular target, the target would move and the sniper would follow the target constantly with his eyes. And everything else was carefully planned too – how to fill the streets up with smoke, how to create an opportunity for the hostages to escape. When hostages start running in all directions, it's hard to kill them." Military experts still wonder to this day why Boris Yeltsin chose the number 38 when talking about the snipers.

I

THE ECONOMICS OF CHANGE

1. A WILD, WILD MARKET: THE FIRST ENTREPRENEURS

Agents of the free market

Who was the first entrepreneur in post–Soviet Russia? It is unlikely anyone can give a precise answer to that question. In 1987 the Moscow Registration Chamber did not yet exist. Companies submitted their charters to executive committees to be registered. The staff of these committees looked at the documents with horror on their faces. But a little later, after consulting with the party's district committee, they agreed to register the companies. Many of the archives kept by the various executive committees are now lost, and today there are dozens of people who can lay claim to have got the ball rolling.

Staff at the Moscow Small Business Support Foundation suggest several worthy candidates. These include Alexander Staroselsky (whose Teatralny Co–op was registered in February 1987 and specialized in 'recycling raw materials' and 'making ballet shoes'). Or Andrei Fedorov, whose Kropotkinskaya 36 Co–op provided catering services and who owned the country's first ever private café.

To tell the truth, there had been a market in the USSR as well, and not just in collective farming. And there had been millionaires, too. The market at that time was not a free one, however, and the millionaires all went underground. The only entity which could manufacture and sell products was the state; only collective farms or factories could become millionaires; and entrepreneurial activity on the part of individuals was punishable by law. Even in these circumstances, however, people known as 'market players' managed to operate and even thrive – workshop owners, money changers, spivs, speculators and so–called 'necessary people'.

There had been co–ops in Russia, too, ever since the days of collectivization. After all, the collective farms were supposed to be co–operatives, on paper at any rate – i.e. a group of labourers who had voluntarily formed an association for the common good. There had also been consumer co–operatives: little huts in agricultural areas where, in exchange for a basket of hand–picked mushrooms, you could get your hands on a pair of felt boots, of which there was a scarcity.

So it is no coincidence that the start of the reforms to the market was accompanied by a legalization of co–operatives, as a form of 'market growth'. It makes no odds that there was not so much as a whiff of the Rochdale Principles, which governed the operation of co–operatives, in the air: the main thing was that people were given the opportunity to manufacture and sell goods, without having to worry about either the tax man or the police. The market, the key players in which were shamefacedly referred to as co–operators, was now free.

The entrepreneurs, overjoyed by this new–found freedom, threw themselves into the business of making money with gusto. But what could the co–operators achieve whilst all the assets remained in the hands of the state and the people assigned to look after them? The assets in question were enormous, and the individuals assigned to look after them were no idiots. And whereas everyone could see how many co–operative shops and eateries were springing up, oil and gas were being pilfered on the quiet.

The market was now free but it was also very, very wild.

But everything that happened to the Russian economy in the 1990s and thereafter had its origins in the 1980s – with the five directives made by the USSR's Council of Ministers. Two of them – regarding joint enterprise – were released on 13th January 1987, with an interval of just six hours between them (Nos. 48 and 49). And on 5th February directives Nos. 160, 161 and 162 from the Council of Ministers were published: 'On the creation of co–operatives in the field of public catering', 'On the creation of co–operatives in the field of domestic services' and 'On the creation of co–operatives for the manufacture of products consumed by the people'. The law 'On Co–operative Activity in the USSR', which legalized market relations once and for all and irrevocably, was adopted in 1988.

As it turned out, joint ventures did not go on to be the drivers of Soviet Russia's economy, but the names of these first co–ops and their founders still trip off the tongue today. The Microdin co–operative, for example, provided the country with the men who would go on to be the directors of Norilsk Nickel – Dmitry Zelenin and Oleg Deripaska. And the Pchelka co–op (whose director was Vladimir Bryntsalov) gave the nation not only a presidential candidate and a vodka named in his honour, but also a huge assortment of medicines. The former co–operative MMM (owned by the Mavrodi brothers) taught large swathes of the population the ins and outs of 'securities' long before the Federal Securities Commission of Russia had the chance to do so.

The shelves in Moscow's shops were now heaving with saveloys and other delicacies, though they were so expensive that only millionaires would have thought the prices reasonable. Eateries had at long last appeared where one could quite happily have lunch without being at risk of getting a smack in the face from the waiter or the doorman. Andrei Fedorov's restaurant, Kropotkinskaya 36, was established in 1987, whilst in 1990

McDonald's opened its first ever outlet in Russia. People queued for hours to see what it was like.

Everything was happening for the first time, everything was novel. Society's attitude towards the co–operators was ambivalent. On the one hand, everyone was convinced that they would soon be put in jail. On the other hand, though, good old Soviet bureaucracy held firm in its conviction that its decisions were irrevocable: government ministries were already issuing edicts such as "set up seven joint ventures in the sector by the end of the year". Officials were called before the party committees "for failing to meet the plan for the setting up of co–operatives". Before our very eyes, junior researchers, engineers and warehouse managers were transformed almost overnight into millionaires (albeit rouble millionaires), got their hands on new Zhiguli cars and wives who were models, designer denim suits and Rolexes. This irritated the 'conservative forces in society'. The chairman of the Moscow City Trades Union Council, V.P. Scherbakov, declared in a speech to the Congress of People's Deputies in 1989: "The co–operators' activities are exacerbating the scarcity of goods, emptying the shelves in the shops, fuelling corruption, bribery, speculation, and an increase in organized crime." According to the first restaurateur, Andrei Fedorov, the former procurator general, Rekunkov, said of the co–operators: "If we were to bring them out in handcuffs you'd soon see what sort of genie we've let out of the bottle!"

Meanwhile, according to data from the Moscow Union of Co–operators, the amount of goods sold by all the co–operatives in the country in the first seven months of 1989 was no more than 1% of the total amount of goods manufactured in the country, and was therefore incapable of 'exacerbating' anything in the country at all, for all some people's desire that it might. And yet...the co–op owners in Moscow alone earned 2,522,100 roubles in that period. This was the combined profit of 300,000 companies – the number of companies which had set themselves up in the capital in the two years since 'legalization'.

What sort of companies were they, and where had they come from in the chaste Soviet society? The 'first wave' of entrepreneurs met with various fates, but they were similar in nature. They all strove to make "more money than they made yesterday".

One of the founders of the IVS co-op, Sergei Kabaev, had worked as a programmer at a defence industry research centre during the Soviet era, and used to moonlight on his days off. He is now at the helm of Russia's flagship electronics company – the Kvant factory.

Pyotr Zrelov, the president of the joint venture Dialogue, used to drive to different projects with construction units, and juggled four jobs after his children were born: he worked as a lab technician at a university, posed as a life model at the Stroganov art university, assembled TVs and repaired air-conditioning units. And he continued in the same vein until he was appointed deputy CEO of KamAZ.

Herman Sterligov used to moonlight as a private taxi driver.

The first private restaurant owner, Andrei Fedorov, had worked in catering – he used to "fry cutlets and do a bit of pilfering," as he put it.

"I haven't let money spoil me," Sergei Kabaev maintains. "There was a time when my monthly salary was 300 roubles, and my wife's was 120. We're still together today. When it comes to money, it's all relative. All my money is invested in the plant – you can't put that in a suitcase or hide it away in the Canary Islands. We conduct our business in a civilized manner, with hardly any score-settling. But loads of our friends have been killed. Almost all of them have been killed. Every other one, I'd say…"

Pyotr Zrelov's story has all the best features of the traditional Russian fairytale: a millionaire prince who came from overseas bringing a gift of money. And Zrelov multiplied that sum many times over, which is fairly atypical, shall we say. "Many of the first joint ventures from back in 1987 no longer exist," the trendsetter recalls. "We were the only ones who didn't implode;

on the contrary, we expanded. My wife and I spent our whole lives borrowing money before payday," he adds. "At KamAZ alone I was given 600 roubles. How can money spoil people? Some people start making risky investments and lose everything. Others decide that they haven't yet squeezed all they can out of life, and start a second family. Others still left the country. Some died – they were the ones who "refused to share".

There is a general consensus that in the early days of capitalism, setting up a business was the easiest thing in the world – as long as you had the desire. People look back on the tax system that was in force in those days with such affection that it brings tears to their eyes: in a company's first year it was 3%, in the second year it was 5% and in the third year it was 10%! Within a couple of years the tax collectors came to their senses, and put tax rates up to 20, 40 and 60%. And quotes for cash transactions were twice as high as those for bank transfers. Prior to 1990, state companies didn't pay any tax at all. Companies with foreign partners paid 30% income tax, and that was after two years of tax holidays.

People could become dollar millionaires through a single transaction. No–one batted an eyelid when operations had profit margins of 1000% – this seemed entirely normal. Everything was up for sale! Everything could potentially be exported! "There was money in bucket–loads," veterans of the era recall with a sigh. And in those early years, the racketeers were no more than petty thugs. Sometimes you could get close enough to them to give them a punch in the face. Soon, though, the word 'licence' became just as topical as the term *krysha* (a word which translates literally as 'roof' but meant 'protection' or 'protector'). "We were approached at some point during our second year," said one former co–operative owner who is now a successful businessman. "We only just managed to get out of it. They turned out to be reasonable types. And we were reasonable, too. We managed to establish normal business relations with them: they even invested a heap of cash in us. Some of their people worked for us, and they were very professional. That's the sort of joint enterprise we set up. Even now we still work together in some areas. We have other 'investors' in that mould, too."

The entire economy, not just entrepreneurial individuals, was now running on market lines. Companies issued shares and the shares were divided up among the company's staff. Since the workforce didn't usually know what to do with the bits of paper they were given, sooner or later the shares fell into the hands of enterprising people. Or else the companies went bust...

The collapse of a little candle factory was one thing; the fall of the giants which had been propping up the country's economy – firms in the oil and gas industry or the energy sector – was quite another. Moreover, these companies could give their owners profits that the co–operative owners could only dream about...

Given that the gas companies, oil companies and other pillars of the economy were run by people who were pretty clever, the most far–sighted of them managed to rescue their precious offspring – not without lining their own pockets, of course. That was how Gazprom, for instance – now part of the 'national heritage' – was created. The company was set up by Viktor Chernomyrdin.

Viktor Chernomyrdin was appointed deputy minister of the gas industry in the USSR whilst Leonid Brezhnev was in office, in 1982. The following year, under Yuri Andropov, he also took charge of the All–Union Industrial Association Tyumengazprom – the precursor to Gazprom. It was in this post that he was able, for the first time, to combine the roles of a government functionary and a 'red director'. In 1985, under Mikhail Gorbachev, he was appointed minister of the gas industry in the USSR, and in 1989 he set up the state gas concern Gazprom and took up a post as chairman of the board of directors. In the spring of 1992 he was appointed deputy prime minister and minister of fuel and energy in Russia.

In November 1992 Boris Yeltsin signed an edict to the effect that the state consortium Gazprom was to be transformed into RAO (Russian Joint–Stock Company) Gazprom, and in February 1993, by order of the Council of Ministers of the Russian Government, RAO Gazprom was founded.

The inn on Kropotkin Street

Andrei Fedorov's name had first begun to appear in the media back in 1987. He was the man who opened the country's first ever co–op in the field of catering: a café called Kropotkinskaya 36. The café later became a restaurant, expanding into the basement of what had once been an apartment building leased to the Trubetskoy family. The Trubetskoys, incidentally, used to make an annual pilgrimage to Fedorov's restaurant for a big family dinner. Before long Andrei Fedorov had opened several other restaurants in addition to this first one, in Russia and elsewhere.

When asked whether he was indeed the first restaurateur or not, Andrei Fedorov said: "The newspapers certainly seemed to think so. I think they were right, because we first started building the café in the autumn of 1986. No–one was even talking about co–ops back then. But a certain senior civil servant gave me a tip–off just at the right time. I had always wanted to have my own business, and it was at that moment that he said "go on then, get ready...And when those edicts were issued, I headed straight to the executive committee with my charter documents at the ready." When asked by *Kommersant* journalist V. Gendlin who had given him the tip–off, he made no bones about revealing that it had been the head of the Main Directorate of Public Catering in the city of Moscow. "We were on good terms – I had worked in catering for twenty–four years. Back then I was the director of a restaurant at the Solnechny motel on Varshavskoye highway. I knew this type of cuisine inside out." Then, as now, relations with civil servants were the decisive factor in achieving success in business, but things were a little different back then. "No–one would be able to get their hands on the sort of premises we were given these days. That same civil servant gave me a list of seven apartments whose occupants had been kicked out. I opted for this building: two apartments on the ground floor had been vacated." When he opened his restaurant in 1987, Fedorov invested 17,000 roubles in the business, along with two business partners. A further 30,000 roubles were invested by Viktor Geraschenko, who at the time was the chairman of the USSR's State Bank. By way of a loan, of course. "There's an interesting anecdote about that," says Fedorov. "We walk into Sberbank's head office, and say 'Listen, we need a loan to get something off the ground. Equipment, food supplies, that sort of thing.' Their jaws drop so far they almost hit the floor: "What is the meaning of this? Who on Earth do you think you are?" "We're a co–operative," we reply. They look at us as if we're a few sandwiches short of a picnic. It was unheard of for a bank to issue loans to private individuals! At last the first deputy chairman of the Central Bank, Valery Pekshev, deigned to see me. I later spoke to two of his deputies. Then Geraschenko looked into the matter personally and ordered that the funds should be made available. The outcome was that we invested 47,000 roubles in the project, which was enough for us to have 50 covers in the restaurant."

As far as bribes were concerned, Fedorov says: "We kept track of everything, after all. Budding co–operators came to see us from all over the country to learn from what we had been doing. And we kept records of all our expenses – on this, that and the other, and on bribes too. They came to a total of 5000 roubles. That was a lot of money in 1987. The interest rates had not yet levelled off back then. There was a remarkable story that illustrated the extent of corruption, incidentally. I sent an open letter to *Ogoniok* in 1989. In it I set out all my expenses, demonstrating that over the course of a year, the co–op owners in the capital had paid 31 million roubles to civil servants. And then one morning in October I'm watching the morning debates in the Supreme Soviet, on the box. Gennady Yanaev takes to his feet and, shaking my article in his hand, says to Gorbachev: 'Do you have any idea, Mikhail Sergeevich, what this Fedorov has written?' And Gorbachev says to Bakatin: 'Look, there is a need for this issue to be cleared up." And the next morning some men from the Ministry of Internal Affairs and the procurator's office came to see me, and tried to get it out of me: who had given bribes, and who had taken them? I said to them: "No, I'm not saying a word, I value my life."

And as for racketeering: it's always existed! Even during Soviet times people used to arrange to have a *krysha*. After all, there had been underground capitalists in the Caucasus, in Moscow and in other major cities. There had been tradesmen, barmen and waiters.

Then Fedorov opened a restaurant in Milan: a year later he sold it, then opened a place called *Fyodoroff* in New York but lost a lot of money out there...The location turned out to be badly chosen. After that he took charge of a different restaurant in New York – *L'Ermitage*. But Fedorov, in his own words, is "a Russian citizen first and foremost – but one that has businesses both over there and over here."

But what about the money...? Money, says Fedorov, can ruin those who have never had it before. He is referring to the so–called 'new Russians'. "I spent my whole life frying cutlets... What does that signify? In 1968 I was working as the head waiter at the *Arbat*. And each morning, when I heard a knock coming from the stairwell, my heart would skip a beat: they're coming for me! Because I spent 24 years in catering. I spent four years as a chef and ten years as a waiter, then worked as a barman and a head waiter. And we were all light–fingered! Head waiters used to earn 140 roubles a month. I made up the rest by stealing it from the waiters – and it amounted to 1000 roubles in total. I didn't do it because I wanted to steal: I ought to have been making a grand! Because I had to give away 30–40% of it. I took what was left over – about 700 roubles – for myself. That was how come tradesmen like us always had money. I was walking a tightrope, but I always knew how far I could push things. I knew how much I ought to be getting. That was why I always dreamed of owning something.

But it's too late for money to ruin me now – I spent my entire life frying cutlets, don't forget."

The above–board millionaire

The first co–operative owner to become a household name was Artyom Tarasov (of the Technika co–operative). It was an appearance on the TV show *Vzglyad* that made him famous: he announced that he had a salary of 3 million roubles and had paid a million roubles in contributions to the party. The first legitimate Soviet millionaire declared that the co–operative owners were a pillar of capitalism in Russia, but after his legendary appearance on *Vzglyad*, and the mass cull of co–operatives that followed it, capitalism came to an end before it had even got going.   As for Tarasov, he was forced to leave the country... "I appeared on *Vzglyad* on my own, to keep my workforce safe," Tarasov said when interviewed by a reporter from the Kommersant Publishing House, E. Drankina. "We were already in danger by then, and the safest option at the time was to go public with the story. As I have said many times before, we found out that month about the directive that was being prepared, which would see the limit on the amount of cash that co–operatives could hold reduced to 100 roubles a day. That practically killed off our business. And at that moment in time we had 78 million roubles in our account. We had paid this money to ourselves as a salary, so that we would have enough cash for the whole year. We paid our taxes: I paid 180,000 roubles in small–family tax and my deputy, a party member, paid 3% in party dues, i.e. 90,000 roubles. If you were to index it today, the amounts would probably be the same, only in dollars.   And this infuriated the party bosses. They started queuing up to give us a scare: the KGB, the prosecutor's office...They wanted to put me behind bars, and tried to get me using the law on the theft of state property. You could be put in front of the firing squad under that law in the Soviet Union, incidentally. And although we never saw any budgetary funds with our own eyes – of the Technika co–operative's two dozen areas of activity, not one of them had anything to do with the federal budget – they would definitely have done for us, such was their rage. It took them several years to get over it: even after I emigrated the GRU still came after me.

It was at that moment that the co–operative phase came to an end. In us they saw a dangerous new phenomenon, and they began to close 300–400 cooperatives a day. And Gorbachev turned on the co–operative owners: before long he was speaking at a plant in Kirovsk, and his exact words were: 'A Soviet person's pay will never exceed 10,000 roubles a month.'"

What did his fellow co–operators say to Tarasov after his TV appearance? "Some said I was wrong to speak out, that I shouldn't have exposed everyone like that. But others said it was the right thing to do: they felt that society needed to be shaken up a bit, and shown how much money there was to be made, told to be fearless. Do you know who else thanked me? The 'Red Directors'. They too had seen that there were millions to be made if only the forms of ownership could be changed. And the people supported me too, because ultimately I was elected a deputy and later I was able to return from London and take up a seat in the State Duma."

Tarasov did not keep his seat in parliament for long. He later tried to stand for president in the election in 1996, before once again emigrating. "I might have been able to become an oligarch if I hadn't left, but I might equally have ended up being killed or thrown in jail. I don't get people who decide to play things that way. I for one think that Khodorkovsky could have done far more good for himself and the country if he was living in London right now, rather than behind bars. I realise that emigrating isn't all plain sailing, but it's a damn sight better than prison or death."

Tarasov told one interviewer that in the nineties we had had a primitive, communal system of capitalism, that it had been replaced by a slave–owning version, and that eventually, if we kept going at the same rate, we would reach a stage where we had a normal capitalist system. "The key players in our system are rich civil servants who don't create anything at all. Wealthy civil servants are a nonsense for the whole world, and if I had to try and come up with a name for this class in society – it's beyond me. It seems to me we need a new Karl Marx, who could describe our new model of social class and predict where it's taking us."

So when exactly was it that we got side–tracked? "In the late '80s, when privatization began among the *nomenklatura*. The people who carved up the state property and finances lack the desire and the ability to produce anything – in other words, they are incapable of providing growth for the country. They created a corrupt social class full of speculators, and a ruling class of civil servants. And the co–operative owners had something completely different in mind.

I had a spat recently with Sergei Kurginyan. He said that the first co–ops had been created by criminals, shadow businesses and bandits. It wasn't like that. The late '80s – the period I identified as the time when all this capitalism began – was a happy time in Russia, when we had engineers and research scientists becoming co–operative owners. Everyone else used to look at what we were doing and gesture as if to say: you're crazy, doing all this above board and registering your companies. But back then there were some very powerful ideas floating around which could have found their embodiment in a new qualitative form of development for the country. Had the co–operative movement not been killed off in its infancy, we would now be living in a time of well–developed capitalism, with a human face.

And there were quite a lot of co–operatives. In 1989 I was elected first deputy chairman of the USSR's Union of Co–operatives. In effect we were planting the seeds of capitalism, and we knew full well what was going on. There were 6 million of us in the association, and these people were responsible for creating roughly 5% of GDP. All the republics in the Soviet Union were represented in the organization, and we were independent – we had our own independent newspaper, *Kommersant* (Artyom Tarasov was a co–founder the newspaper – Ed.). And I don't mind saying that we had responsibilities of our own, as well. We realized that our activities were going to cause a certain amount of damage. We were killing off the economic system of the USSR. Because as soon as a co–op owner joined a company, he took over the juiciest morsel of the production unit: the best engineers went off to join him, he made sure the best types of raw material and the most advanced technologies started coming his way, and as a result his little chunk of the production unit flourished, whilst the rest of the factory stagnated. We could see what was going on, but we were ordinary people, and weren't trying to ruin the country in which we lived. We came up with the idea of free economic zones. And there is considerable doubt as to who was first to do this – us or China. We sent letters to Gorbachev, Pavlov and Ryzhkov proposing that areas should be set up in which capitalism would be allowed. And, to our surprise, we received backing from the Komi Republic. There had been strikes there in 1989 – miners had taken to the streets with placards that read: 'The co–op owner ate all the soap and matches'. We travelled to this region, spoke to some people there and made friends with them. Then the miners rewrote their placards: they crossed out 'co–op owner' and replaced it with 'civil servant'. Meanwhile we began asking the government to give us this region, so that it could be used as a special zone.

And we promised that we would raise the quality of life in Komi to the same level as that enjoyed by the people of Austria. They refused to give it to us. If they had supported the co–

operative owners back then, rather than killing off both the movement itself and the powerful industrial economy it could have created, things might have been radically different, and that economy would have become efficient once again."

Tarasov acknowledges that entrepreneurialism is nothing less than a way of life: "In the course of their lives, entrepreneurs lose everything and then work their way back up the ladder on countless occasions. If you go through life without ever losing everything and having to lift yourself off the floor, you can't call yourself an entrepreneur: you must be an oligarch or something like that, who's made a load of money and is resting on his laurels. Everyone loses money at some point – perhaps millions, perhaps billions – and then picks themselves up again. And this general rule tells you all about the nature of what I do. Each new project brings with it the risk of losing everything, and the knowledge that I might end up behind bars as well. …I cannot renounce anything…"

Alice's boss in wonderland

As new market relations came into being, the former, administrative–command relations were destroyed, and economics links were broken down. Meanwhile, newly–emergent business was operating as its nature dictated that it would. If the old links had been severed, this meant it was time for some new ones. And the new links were the commodity exchange market.

At the start of the '90s, German Sterligov became a household name: after setting up the first commodity exchange market in Russia, 'Alice' (named after Sterligov's pet dog, a St Bernard), he promptly became one of the country's wealthiest and most famous people. Sterligov later took part in a host of other projects, stood for president of Russia and mayor of Moscow, went bankrupt and moved from the Rublyovka to the middle of nowhere.

The story of Sterligov the millionaire began in the late '80s, however, when he came up with the idea for his first commercial company: he managed to persuade the men in charge of the capital's railway stations that their waiting rooms could serve as outstanding concert venues. Buskers from the Arbat were asked to perform in the concerts. "We made quite a bit of money that way," he recalls. "The musicians would play for about fifteen minutes, then a group of girls would go round collecting money, and the whole group would move on to the next station. And at the next place we'd have different musicians performing. That was the cycle we had in place. We stashed the money in suitcases, and within a couple of months we had made so much that each of us could afford a new car. The biggest difficulty we came up against was exchanging loose change for banknotes. There wasn't even such a thing as rental or hire at the time – even the cops didn't get a cut, which made them pretty angry. This was in 1988. But the Supreme Soviet brought in a ban on what we had been doing with the concerts that year, so we set up one of the first co–operatives and began providing legal services for members of the public. My studies at the faculty of law came in handy. Artyom Tarasov was one of my first customers. Some of Tarasov's documents had recently gone missing from a bank, and we managed to return them to him. And then came the exchange market, 'Alice'. All sorts of other commodities exchange markets in Russia followed our example."

How did the idea for the exchange market come about? By pure chance. When asked about it in an interview with *Kommersant*, Sterligov says: "I was watching an American film and they showed what was going on in Wall Street. And I thought to myself: why can't we do something similar – after all, people need somewhere to buy and sell products and raw materials. I hired a hall, we hung up some screens and put in some computers. We advertised our services; essentially it was the first ever bit of commercial advertising in the country. To fund the opening of the exchange market, I took out a loan of

1 million roubles from Smolensky (the chairman of the board of directors at Stolichny bank – Ed.) and after two months announced that we were selling seats at 300,000 roubles each (back then a new *Zhiguli* cost 8000 roubles, and you could get by on a dollar a day). And on the very first day we earned 6 million roubles! We sold seats throughout the course of the year, and the price of a seat ended up at 3.5 million roubles."

Are there any operations that stick in his memory? "We got lucky with the putsch," Sterligov says. "I was in New York at the time, at our branch there, and the price of debts in Russia fell to almost zero in the blink of an eye. On the very same day we bought up a huge quantity of debt, mostly using funds from a single Egyptian businessman. We sold them three days later. I had predicted that it would all settle down in three days. And sure enough, that's what happened. The profit we made was in the thousands of per cent."

Generally speaking, "they were fun times, there was an edginess to everything, we were in a permanent state of danger. But the opportunities were colossal: I spent time with the presidents (Gorbachev and Yeltsin) on their birthdays and other festive occasions. Before one of these celebrations, on New Year's Eve, my brother and I were offered the chance to have our photo taken with Yeltsin for $50,000 – it was an official offer, on headed paper. I was astonished by such a degree of cynicism. We replied: "We are very grateful for the offer and we will certainly be at the New Year's Eve party, but we would like to propose that Boris Nikolaevich have his photo taken with us, in exchange for a payment of $50,000 to each of us." The powers that be saw no harm in it – they probably thought to themselves: "stupid is as stupid does". Actually, now that I come to think about it, there was one time when we were summoned to the Lubyanka and they demanded, in earnest, that I sign something to the effect that I had joked about Alice's declaration of independence from the state: we had set up our own ministry of internal affairs and security committee, and our own awards (the order of the Cross of Nikolai Georgievsky – that was the name of Alice's CEO); we issued our own banknotes – 'Alisky' – and paid each other using them."

Sterligov never spoke about how much money he had made: "Not because I had anything to hide, but for the simple reason that I didn't know. When they say that Abramovich has made such and such an amount of money, they analyse his property, his shares and his other assets. When it comes to how much money he has in cash, I doubt whether even he knows. Back then, when I was in business, there were no instruments for measuring that sort of thing at all. And by the time those kinds of instruments came into being, I had nothing left. So I can't even say myself how rich I was."

And then there was another soul–destroying story, something straight out of 'Tales from the Crypt': the Sterligov brothers' coffin agency. "When the Iraq campaign began, we offered to supply the Americans with 50,000 coffins. We hung a sign up on the door that said: 'The Sterligov brothers' coffin agency'. But the Americans turned us down, so then we offered to sell the coffins to Saddam Hussein, and he replied that he was willing to buy the coffins as a gesture of goodwill towards the USA. So that the soldiers could come home in nice wooden coffins (costing $1500 each) rather than zinc ones. The effect was astonishing. I was preparing to run for president at the time, and I needed people to remember who this guy Sterligov was."

But Sterligov failed to sell a single coffin. "If we'd been asked to make them, though, we'd have done it – how hard can it be to knock a few planks of wood together? The Americans just don't have a sense of humour. And this was nothing more than a PR stunt, a joke." When it came to PR, there was nobody else in the country in those days to rival Sterligov. "But it was more than just sensationalism: it saved us huge amounts of money that we would have had to spend on advertising. For example, we set up the notorious Millionaires' Club: all we had to do was hold a press conference, then we cobbled it together in a couple of days, the whole thing cost about $1000. And then I spent about three months doing interviews from morning to night! I was just 24 at the time, and we didn't use the type of language you hear now, like "shaping public opinion". We just laughed ourselves silly every day, it was so funny. Things turned out well with the coffins, too. Many people still remember the slogan made up by our classic author Pyotr Sinyavsky: 'No need to diet or keep fit – our coffins are the perfect fit'. The whole ad campaign cost just $7500: we hired a screen in the Sokol district and a handful of advertising banners in the city centre."

When asked what effect big sums of money have on people, Sterligov's response is: "Tell me about it! What delusions of grandeur I had! My attitude was that I had made all this money, and everyone else was poor. Who were they to question me or get in my way?" So what became of his assets? "I gave them away to my partners. I made a statement in which I said that I was giving up all my shares and stakes to the people who were going to stay on as co–owners of these companies...some of them hit the jackpot, but many partners wrote declarations similar to my own. They had simply come to the conclusion that some sort of catastrophe must be on the cards and that it was time to jump ship, if German himself was jumping ship. That was in 1995; there was no exchange market any more, but the holding company 'Centre for advanced financing' was still around. Then we began to provide housing for people who had served in the military: we bought up apartments and sold them to soldiers, and in return we were given plots of land that could be developed in Moscow and the regions. We sold these plots and bought up apartments again – and so the cycle continued. It was the best of times, we had dozens of companies all over the country and overseas, but I was sitting there getting bored. I very nearly drank myself to death. That's of little interest, it's something that can happen when you don't have enough to do...I used to own a Malevich; I sold it to a gallery in Hamburg for more than $1.5 million, but compared to a DT75 tractor it's a worthless piece of shit! To tell the truth I had only paid twopence for it myself, in the early '90s. I had a whole pile of paintings by Kandinsky. A couple of famous art historians came up to me at one point with a proposal: "We'll help you put together a collection: you'll buy up paintings based on our recommendations, and then further down the line you'll be able to recoup all your money with a single sale." It all went off as planned. I bought up countless paintings – and then I sold one of them and made all my money back. There were three paintings by Malevich alone, and big ones at that – and I'm not even counting the small stuff, various watercolours. When I took a Malevich to auction, at Sotheby's, no less, I realised something: everything gets bought and sold over there in exactly the same way, right down to experts' opinions. And the prices are agreed on a long time in advance. They would say: it's 100,000 for this work, and we'll give you a certificate straight away.

I did have a certain amount of money, of course. And it was quite a sizeable sum, it must be said; and I had a house in Rublyovka to go with it...I even had enough for my presidential campaign, to say nothing of my mayoral campaign. I borrowed a good deal more, it must be said – tens of millions of dollars, which went towards setting up a network throughout the country and collecting signatures. The only thing that wrankles is that the money was spent in vain."

What followed was a move to the Russian countryside and life in the sticks. "I had long had what was a pretty fantastical dream in those days: to move to a deep forest somewhere when it all got too much for me. But I realised this dream could never come true because in those days it was impossible to contemplate: how could one simply up sticks and move to the forest when one's wife and children needed to be fed, and when we had damn all to our name? Were it not for that financial disaster, I'd be living in Red Square right now. So I'm extremely indebted to the electoral commission. In all seriousness, though, I would love to become president, so that I could bring about change, and introduce moral reforms, first and foremost. The economy would soon pull itself together after that. The cornerstones of my manifesto were: a ban on abortions and a ban on the sexual abuse of children. It would all be done through the introduction of bans. Since I have five kids myself, I began to think seriously about what their lives are going to be like in the future. At first I used to try and support someone in the elections, then I would see that they weren't doing anything. It made me think: "Why don't you all go off to the bath–house, I'll have a go at running the country myself." This was a naive way to look at it, of course, but I simply saw no other option open to me at the time. This life is so much more interesting, multifaceted and vibrant than what I had on the Rublyovka…"

Komsomol volunteers

More Russian businessmen seem to have come from the Komsomol than anywhere else: all sorts of YSTCs (Young People's Scientific and Technical Centres) flourished deep in its bowels, and it was here that money was concentrated and the skills required for market economics were developed. One of the YSTC activists, incidentally, was a certain Mikhail Khodorkovsky.

Prior to 1990, advanced technologies were considered the star attraction of these centres. Shuttle traders imported computers and flogged them to state bodies, including the security structures. Later it proved more profitable to import computer components, and 'red assembly' – domestic computer manufacturing in Russia – came into being. Pyotr Zrelov tells us that he knows of quite a few firms which made their money selling on computers from the Dialog joint venture: after buying a kit at Dialog for 80,000 to 85,000 roubles, it could then be sold on for 180,000 roubles. It was almost as profitable a business as commodities trading.

"No, we didn't get involved in commodities trading at all prior to 1990," the former co–operative owner says. "The KGB had its hands on it back then." But just a couple of years later the sharpest operators were trading in commodities. Even the computer firm IVS rode the wave of this boom: in 1990 they hired a mine in the Kuzbass, laid down a railway and, according to Sergei Kabaev, "cornered 20% of the country's coal exports," while the rest of the Kuzbass went on strike. The fun came to an end when transport tariffs began to go through the roof.

Smart people put their money in apartments and cars. The streets were filled with a motley patchwork of Russian cars and old foreign models (back then a middle–ranking gang leader would have felt no shame in turning up at a restaurant in a rusty Mercedes). And people began trying to work out the names of all the foreign–made cars by transliterating them, syllable by syllable – there were *skhruslery* (Chryslers), *renaulty*, *peugeoty* and, God forgive us (this word was still written with a small letter back then), *khuyundai* (Hyundais). The private importing of cars from Germany (including stolen ones) was almost a fully–fledged industry, and it was where many of today's wealthiest businessmen began their careers.

As for the ones who didn't manage to leech off the Motherland, they didn't sit around moping either. A popular option was to get a job at a commercial organisation. Some people worked as security guards inside shops. But this was small fry compared to working at the markets or in the underpasses. Back then this was known as 'standing around'. Do you remember those guys in tracksuits who used to stand near kiosks and flea markets? Their 'standing around' would sometimes end in fisticuffs, or even shoot–outs. These guys, who were keen to show off their wads of cash, nunchucks and pistols, used to encourage people to join them, promising a rapid rise up the career ladder: "the only thing is, you'll be banged up in a month, but when you come out you'll be a gang leader." There may have been some who made a success of it, but many of them later featured in the newspapers – in the crime section – in cold–blooded, detailed descriptions of murders.

Konstantin Borovoi, who found the time to be both a co–operative owner and an exchange broker, recalls: "I managed to set up almost 50 co–operatives before 1991. And it was clear that there was no sign of a big leap forward in quality or the development of market entrepreneurship: the state had taken steps to ensure that these companies did not grow stronger. Trading exchanges and banks had already begun to emerge, though. And after the putsch there was a shift in quality. The level of interaction between these private companies became so strong that they were able to work with one another. Up until 1991, each co–operative had to have state companies alongside it, in the form of subcontractors, partners and clients. After 1991 trading exchanges emerged, and state companies reached out to these structures themselves, in which private companies and co–operatives dominated. The first law on joint stock companies was adopted in September 1991. All this taken together gave a huge boost to the economy.

I personally managed to establish a trading exchange out of several hundred state companies and private enterprises. Almost 2000 branches of the exchange were set up throughout the country. Each of them contained several hundred broker companies, each of which had dozens of partners. And during the course of the year the work of these exchanges led to the setting up of several million new commercial companies. Then came a handful of banks, a handful of investment companies, a handful of insurance companies and a handful of retail centres..." But Borovoi considers the exchange his greatest success: "It enabled us to make a breakthrough in the economy that was unlike anything else."

Says Borovoi, "it was a romantic breakthrough at the time, and a lot of the things I did then were to my own detriment. For example, I never paid myself more than $100 a month as a salary throughout my entire tenure as president of the exchange. I felt it was beneath my dignity to make money from my position, from my brainchild."

Alexander Smolensky, one of the first bankers, recalls that Stolichny bank began operating in 1989. Smolensky had also been a co–operative owner for two years prior to this. "By 1991 my family was already living overseas," he says. "Because there was a lot of racketeering at that time, a complete mess, and I could not see any good coming of it." And yet Smolensky believes that he succeeded at that time in building a retail bank that was utterly independent.

Igor Safaryan (of BrokInvestServis), one of the people who created the securities market, refers to the 1990s as a period of economic romanticism: "Back then my comrades and I thought that the model for economic growth was going to be different, and hoped that what ultimately happened would not come to pass. I think the situation at which we have arrived is 'comprador' capitalism in its purest form. At the time I was starting to get involved in the fund market – I didn't just get involved in it, I helped create it. Its story gives us an understanding of what took place. In the first place we do not have a market in securities, as such. Secondly, what we have is nothing more than a market in controlling stakes. And the reasons why are obvious: it is only when you have a controlling stake in a company that you can not only manage it, but also make money out of it. Those hopes never led to anything, of course. But we continued to work in these conditions, in spite of the fact that we had lost a major market which, apart from anything else, I simply enjoyed working in. My pet project, the fund market, simply disappeared. Given that we were the ones who created it, this meant that our plans didn't come to fruition, either. As for what actually did come of it, that's far more straightforward...We wanted to make some money – and we did."

A 'Fact' is a stubborn old thing

The trailblazers in the Russian market included a new kind of organization, as well as individuals. Realizing that they were operating in a hostile environment, the co–operative owners tried to join forces in order to protect their own interests. The Union of Russian Co–operative Owners was set up; it included a co–operative that few had heard of at the time, called 'Fact'. In 1990 the Union of Co–operative Owners began to release a weekly newsletter, revealing to the country a new type of journalism, a new way of doing business and a new way of looking at power. Far from going out of print, the newsletter went on to become the forerunner to today's *Kommersant*.

The paper began life in...a library. It was in a library that members of the Fact co–operative came up with the name of the new publication. There, they came across a respectable, pre–revolutionary business newspaper which had ceased to be published when the Bolsheviks seized power. The new paper for a new country was supposed to continue the traditions of the entrepreneurial class in pre–revolutionary Russia. They decided to choose between two weekly publications: *Kommersant* (The Merchant) and *Ponedelnik* (Monday). Few people are aware today that what we now know as *Kommersant* could quite easily have been called *Ponedelnik* – this was the option that the editorial team favoured at first. Given that the new newspaper came out on Mondays (when no other newspapers were on sale), the title seemed apt. Credit is due to the newspaper's owner, Vladimir Yakovlev, who followed his gut instinct and opted for the name *Kommersant*. It is funny to think that the Kommersant publishing house's current titles could quite easily have been called *MondayMoney* or *MondayPower*...

Right from the outset the new weekly paper not only amazed its readers with its business news and the fact that it reported on the exchange rate for US dollars, but was also striking in that its journalists wrote about the powers that be – the presidents of the

USSR and of Russia, the government and the Supreme Soviet of the USSR – in a way that seemed utterly fearless. This had never happened before in Russia.   For example, *Kommersant* covered the elections for the first president of Russia in 1990 with the headline: *Little Boris for Tsar!* The new paper presented the country's political heroes as ordinary people who had a poor grasp of economics and who were afraid to take tough decisions as they clung desperately to power. Understandably, the paper's attitude caused mixed emotions among government officials – from hysteria to outright hatred. There were occasions when the authorities and *Kommersant* had some real spats, because the newspaper was protecting the interests of a new class of businessmen who, with the paper's help, would soon become known to the world as 'new Russians'. At the same time, though, genuine fans and allies of *Kommersant* began to appear inside the 'enemy camp' – those same 'confidential sources' who put their jobs at risk by telling the newspaper's readers precisely how Russia's ruling classes lived their lives.

When *KommersantDaily* appeared in 1992, the weekly version of the paper began to focus more on the world of big business which by then had emerged in the country. And given that business – even big business – can't exist without forming some sort of union with the executive, politicians and state officials became the main protagonists of the new publications' stories. The famous phrase 'in the opinion of *Kommersant*'s experts' used to strike fear into the hearts of many a civil servant. And it's little wonder given that the paper's experts often proved far more competent than the officials themselves. It reached the point that Alfred Kokh, who was then deputy prime minister of the State Property Committee, in response to the director of a big company who had complained that privatization was taking place in an unlawful manner, advised him to call in at the editorial offices of *Kommersant*, where "they have a much better understanding of these things than I do."

As time passed, the paper's narrow 'business' focus began to seem too stifling for its constantly growing readership. The weekly therefore started to expand the range of subjects it covered, "in response to requests from the workers", as they used to say in the good old days. It was the first to introduce its readers to each of the country's oligarchs, and was the first to describe how huge fortunes were made in Russia.

Many other media representatives began accusing the daily of making friends with one or other of the oligarchs. One story in particular comes to mind. One of the men who, according to public opinion, had made friends with *Kommersant*, arrived at the paper's editorial offices, with numerous bodyguards in tow, to take personal charge of clearing up an item that had featured in the paper. The offended oligarch had some powerful arguments to put forward: "I'm a Jew," he declared. "Jews are almost Italians. The concept of the vendetta is sacrosanct to Italians. I therefore demand, by way of a vendetta, that the person who wrote this article be sacked." They found some way of bringing the conflict to an end. But the author of the offending article later received a number of phone calls in which he was informed that he (the journalist) had lost a large sum of money on the metro. The person who had found it proposed a meeting. But for some reason the author stubbornly declined the invitation. The outcome of all this was that he had his tyres slashed. In the paper's editorial offices, this story became known as *The Oligarch's Revenge*.

Today, government officials, politicians and oligarchs no longer let their eyes glaze over whenever they hear experts from *Kommersant Power* holding forth: they do not shy away from having their own comments and opinions published in the daily. And that tells us that since those days, not only have we changed – the executive itself has changed...

2. SHOCK. THE ADVOCATES AND ENEMIES OF 'SHOCK THERAPY'

From Pavlov to Gaidar

At the start of the nineties, most people were rapidly growing poor and expecting the worst. They refused to believe the assurances they were given to the effect that nobody was going to lose anything. And the state continued to play Thimblerig with the people. First up was the Pavlov reforms.

They were named after Valentin Pavlov, who served as Minister of Finance and then, from January 1991 onwards, as Prime Minister of the USSR. The reforms were designed to take the huge surplus of cash away from the people and bring some stability to the circulation of cash in the country. In other words, to solve the problem of the deficit by taking people's much–loved cash away from them.

The first stage of the Pavlov reforms featured a decree which withdrew 50 and 100–rouble notes from circulation and exchanged them for smaller denominations. It was signed by Gorbachev on 22nd January 1991. The general public found out about the decree late in the evening, when the banks were all closed. The most enterprising among them managed to rescue their savings by using the outlets inside the metro system and at branches of the post office inside stations, by sending postal transfers to themselves. Everyone else was forced to get crushed in a queue or else wave their savings goodbye: they were given just three days in which to exchange their banknotes, and no more than 1000 roubles could be exchanged 'per person per time'. At the banks, people were not allowed to take out more than 500 roubles.

As a result, some 14 billion roubles in cash was removed from circulation. Opinions vary as to whether this was a substantial sum or not. But in the course of those three days, people's trust in the government, which was weak enough as it was, was lost forever. There followed the April reforms (increases) to prices: on 2nd April 1991 all retail prices simultaneously went up between twofold and fourfold. This marked the start of the second phase of the Pavlov reforms.

Viktor Geraschenko, the former director of the State Bank of the USSR and Bank of Russia, recalls of Valentin Pavlov: "He used to work as first deputy in the budget department of the Ministry of Finance, and gave cause for optimism. A group was set up within the Council of Ministers of the USSR which worked on reforms to the economy. Pavlov happened to be one of the main protagonists in this group, along with Abalkin. Pavlov used to work in the State Pricing Committee, where the pricing reforms were prepared, because there can be no such thing as a market economy if all the prices are wrong and there is no taxation system. In the USSR companies did not pay taxes – all their profits went into the state coffers, and then the money was divided up as the state saw fit. There were three main themes in this group: pricing reforms, the taxation system and different forms of ownership. As a result a plan was drawn up containing 400 measures which had to be taken, in order. You can't introduce a taxation system if there has been no pricing reform. And this might then be followed by monetary reform. And so on and so forth."

The Pavlov reforms, though they were in part a reaction against the tectonic shifts in the country's economy, were nonetheless part of the arsenal available to the administrative command. This was by no means the first set of reforms in the USSR which had involved confiscation of funds...

Later, after the putsch, in 1991–1992, there came the Gaidar reforms: a liberalizing of prices, i.e. a rejection of state regulation of pricing policy and privatization. And these were certainly market reforms – they could even be described as market–shock reforms. In a way, it could be said that this was a form of 'shock therapy'.

Shock therapy is used in medicine to treat psychological and neurological diseases, and in economics to find a way out of crisis situations. In both fields, the effectiveness of this method is open to question: it usually has too many dangerous side–effects.

What did Russia get out of the shock therapy at the start of the nineties? Did it provide a cure for a serious illness or merely exacerbate the overall health of the 'patient' – the Russian economy? Ought we to be thanking the people behind the shock therapy – Yegor Gaidar first and foremost – or cursing them? Could we have effected the transition to market economics in a different way, and thus avoided the harmful consequences that it had for the vast majority of the population? No–one really knows the answer. Shock therapy began and ended almost twenty years ago. But the debate still rages to this day.

We need only recall the headlines in the newspaper articles literally on the eve of the monetary reforms: for example, 'Valentin Pavlov said there would be no monetary reform. Well, well!' (*Kommersant*. 1991. January 7).

History does not deal in the subjunctive mood. And whether we like it or not, we currently live in a country which was forcibly subjected to a brutal course of treatment.

For and against

Yegor Gaidar, who passed away in 2009, is referred to variously as the most important architect of the new Russian state and as the man who destroyed the country. The economic reforms that were named after him are considered by some to have saved the country from hunger and national disaster, and by others as an inhuman experiment which prevented millions of people from being able to lead a normal life.

Timur Gaidar, Yegor's father, once said to the writer Alexander Borin: "As early as in his first year studying economics, in 1975, Yegor and a group of his classmates used to print out and stick up leaflets calling on the working classes to rise up in the name of freedom; Yegor and I had our first, and probably last, disagreement about politics. I said to him: 'They'll lock you up like a bunch of puppies, and that will be the end of it. A day will come when we'll need genuine experts. Get ready for that day.'"

In 1991 Gaidar joined the government of the RSFSR – he was appointed deputy prime minister. Between February and April 1992 he served as first deputy prime minister and finance minister of the Russian Federation, then from June to December 1992 he was the acting head of the Russian Federation's Council of Ministers. On 22nd September he was appointed Minister of Economics of the Russian Federation. He found fame as director of the 'government of reformers' and the man behind the 'shock therapy' policy.

Gaidar's relationship with Boris Yeltsin was, in his own words, fairly complicated. "My family is originally from the Urals, as you know," he once said. "That's where my grandparents came from. I remember relatives of ours coming to visit and saying to us: at last our luck's changed, there's a decent bloke as first secretary, he talks like one of us, he's trying to get things done. I remember how he moved to Moscow and began working here. And generally speaking people responded favourably towards him. He used the same old Communist methods, of course, but they tended to be permissive rather than prohibitive. His campaign against the bazaars was a campaign like any other, of course, but he didn't want to prohibit them: on the contrary, he wanted to secure permission for them, and help them. I vividly recall the time he was excluded from the October plenum, and my sense was that for the first time we had among us a politician who was not dependent on power. But at the same time there was also a tremendous amount of caution. The things he said sounded wonderful, but when you did the maths they simply didn't add up. I couldn't work out how he intended to do all this...for me, Yeltsin was at once a source of hope and a threat. But set against the backdrop of Gorbachev's policies, which by that time seemed to lack all backbone, Yeltsin at least seemed to bring something dependable to the table. Some liked him, others didn't, but the future of Russia and of Russian democracy depended in many ways on the issue of whether we could bring him over to our side and make use of his popularity. The thing which allied me to him once and for all – though he was not aware of it at the time, of course – was the putsch of 19th August 1991."

Many words could be used to describe the early days of Yegor Gaidar's political career, but 'promising' was not one of them. Viktor Geraschenko recalls: "Yeltsin found himself in a vacuum. Where had Gaidar suddenly sprung from? There were various types of people in Yeltsin's entourage, but when he came to power, they all ran off to find a cosy place to hide away. Yeltsin had a team of political hangers–on who were incapable of managing real affairs – he didn't have a government. He didn't know who to appoint as prime minister. It was a good thing Burbulis, who was no idiot, brought in Gaidar. Gaidar was appointed acting prime minister. Yeltsin picked a team of youngsters, who got together somewhere and discussed things, and who had their own ideas about how a Western–style economy should work. But in my opinion their understanding of this was based entirely on theory. Chubais, Gaidar and all the others – they had never studied abroad, lived abroad or worked abroad, and they hadn't worked within our economy either. They had read those little books of theirs and seen what was wrong with our economy. It's quite possible their views were based on the example of Chile, where, once Allende's government had 'left the scene', Pinochet took over the country and invited some Americans from the Chicago

Economic School over for a visit. And by bringing an end to the socialization of the economy, they managed to resurrect it."

After becoming deputy prime minister in Boris Yeltsin's government of reform in the autumn of 1991, Yegor Gaidar, along with a group of like–minded friends, assumed responsibility for the new cabinet's economic policy. In order to gain a better understanding of the circumstances in which these people had come to power, it is worth recalling that one of the most popular bits of economic jargon at the time was the phrase 'humanitarian aid', whilst the most important indicators of economic performance was the timetable showing when this aid was going to be supplied to the country. And when the deputy prime minister was asked by one interviewer how he would like to retire, Yegor Gaidar replied: "After the results of the debates about the budget in 1993." It sounded like a joke. But the deputy prime minister was serious.

On 16th January 1992, Yegor Gaidar took questions from members of parliament in the Supreme Soviet of the RSFSR. It was far from being a brutal conflict between the president and the deputies, but the government had already been battered about by both Boris Yeltsin's enemies and his closest allies. The speaker Ruslan Khasbulatov called for a change of government and had even sterner words for vice–president Alexander Rutskoi, on the subject of his pink trousers. Nobody stood on ceremony for lowly deputy prime ministers in those days. What stuck in the mind most about that day, however, was not the harsh words of the parliamentarians but the self–control demonstrated by the deputy prime minister, who began all his answers with the line: "I have the honour of reporting to the respected member of parliament as follows." The ability to keep his composure and presence of mind in any circumstances was one of Gaidar's most distinctive traits as a politician.

His self–control was founded on a firm confidence in himself and on his conviction that he was doing the right thing. Yegor Gaidar had no doubt as to the need for certain measures to be taken between the autumn of 1991 and the winter of 1992, after becoming one of the leaders of the so–called 'Kamikaze cabinet'. His conviction that he was in the right enabled him to take decisions that were unpopular.

Yet Gaidar was also able to make compromises at times when he felt this was essential for the common good. For that reason he decided not to retire in the spring of 1992, when Boris Yeltsin publically fired one of the key players in Gaidar's team – the minister for fuel and energy, Vladimir Lopukhin (his place was taken by Viktor Chernomyrdin). The decision was taken without Yegor Gaidar's involvement, and he gave serious thought to resigning. But "all the things we had achieved were still extremely fragile...the reforms could still quite easily be reversed. I could have made a nice gesture, of course, and left – but that would only have served to strike out all that we had worked so hard to achieve," Yegor Gaidar later recalled about the episode.

And this unwillingness to strike out everything that he had worked so hard to achieve would be a recurring theme in Yegor Gaidar's political career. In December 1994, as leader of the Democratic Choice of Russia party, which was among the parties in the bloc that formed the government, he effectively defected to the opposition to president Boris Yeltsin because of the outbreak of war in Chechnya. The decision cost the Democratic Choice of Russia half its support and its seats in the next Duma, but Gaidar was convinced that the war that was starting represented a greater threat to democracy in Russia. He considered the prospect of Boris Yeltsin losing in the presidential elections in 1996 a threat of similar proportions, and supported his candidacy.

Although Gaidar had had no formal relations towards executive power since January 1994, and had effectively withdrawn from political life at the start of the 2000s, he thought of himself as a statesman. In 1995, when he was formally in the opposition, he proposed a political coalition which ruined a vote of no confidence in Viktor Chernomyrdin's government. And in his later years he threw himself into research and advisory work, because he saw it as more useful than a role in politics. Being able to avoid doing something you don't consider necessary is a luxury few can afford. Yegor Gaidar felt that he could allow himself that luxury.

He was not considered a very good orator, but there were few people who could hold their own in discussions with Gaidar. Indeed, it was one thing to be a good speaker, but quite another to be able to find the strength to say the right thing at the right time. To do that you need to be sure that you are in the right.

To some, Yegor Gaidar was a hero; to others, he was an enemy. It's like the dispute between Westerners and Slavophiles, in which there are two different truths, two world–views and two mind–sets.

When asked about Gaidar's reforms, some young people today reply, without hesitation, that the people in power in Russia at the time destroyed a great country and robbed the people. They have perhaps not been brought up to speed with the fact that by that time, the great country in question was hungry and in ruins, and the people in power had been rendered so feeble that they couldn't even convince people to go to the party meeting. Others will tell you, no less assuredly, that it was a time of liberation from the yoke of communism and liberalization of the economy. They would be extremely surprised to learn that the achievements of the most liberal of all liberals are not only decrees on free trade and the repeal of the state monopoly on foreign trade, but also a rise in income tax from 35% to 40% and a rise in VAT from 18% to 28%.

The feedback from his colleagues – both politicians and academics – is equally contradictory. Sergei Stankevich, who was an advisor to Boris Yeltsin in 1992–1993, said: "Gaidar upset most of his contemporaries and delighted most of his successors." Ruslan Grinberg, director of the Instute of Economics at the Russian Academy of Science, said: "Yegor Gaidar is a metaphor for the impatience of the Russian intelligentsia, the embodiment of its guiding principle, 'we want everything and we want it right now'. He...discredited the very ideas of a market economy and democracy, and this engendered passivity among the public. Gaidar introduced the reforms, without any regard for timing, the state the country was in or the interests of ordinary people." Alexander Nekipelov, vice–president of the Russian Academy of Sciences: "Gaidar was a man who took on a huge amount of political responsibility for decisions that were of fundamental importance to the country. He was not afraid to go against the opinion of the majority and take on his opponents, who were legion."

Gaidar's eternal opponent, the man behind the famous '500 days' programme, Grigory Yavlinsky, said: "In principle I would defend the strategy of reform, because I believe that the objectives which Yegor Timurovich [Gaidar] is currently promoting as being of top priority, and which he promoted in the past – such as, for example, overcoming inflation, stabilizing the budget and creating an effective monetary system – it is my feeling that these objectives cannot be achieved in the manner in which he wishes to achieve them. We are wasting time, our strength is being drained, the level of confrontation in society is society is only growing stronger, and the reforms are progressing in an extremely haphazard manner. Sergei Glaziev observed: "The policy of shock therapy was a complete failure, and as a consequence of this the state lost control over what was happening."

Vitaly Yefimov, president of the Russian Transport Union and a former minister of transport, gave us a balanced assessment: "On the one hand, I was very well disposed towards Gaidar: whilst he was prime minister he paid close attention to problems in the transport industry. On the other hand, though, his 'shock therapy' brought the country to its knees. I used to send him notes but nobody paid attention. When they freed up prices, and took the value off savings and working capital, industry rose up. It was a mistake of epic proportions."

Andrei Nechaev, the president of the bank Russian Financial Corporation and a former minister of the economy, believes that "Gaidar's most important achievement is the fact that he saved his country from chaos, collapse and civil war – all that was genuinely on the cards. And I would probably say that that is even more important than laying the foundations for a market economy in the country, which was undoubtedly another of his achievements."

Vladimir Lopukhin, president of Vangvard and a former minister of fuel and energy, claims that Gaidar "genuinely gave his life in order to change the lives of others for the better. He was an honest man. And how can people criticize him over 'shock therapy'? The first assembly of the commission on currency policy examined the question: how much money is there in the country? The chairman of Vnesheconombank said: "there are the debts, and there are about $60 million in real money. That was the sort of country they gave us. What more can one say?"

Vladimir Bulgak, an advisor to the company Sovintel and a former minister of communications, feels that "Gaidar had two paths open to him: either the collapse of Russia and a civil war, or the path of reform. Gaidar opted for reform – and the reforms he introduced were hard–hitting and painful. But they helped change the course on which the country was headed. Gaidar modernized the country and let entrepreneurship out of its cage. There aren't many politicians like that in the world."

Viktor Mikhailov, the director of the Institute for Strategic Stability and a former atomic energy minister, insists that "Gaidar led us into a market economy, and did so openly and in a way that showed courage. Regrettably, he failed to appreciate that in addition to a market economy, a form of thieves' capitalism was also being set up inside the country..."

Pavel Grachev, director of the board of advisers to the CEO of the A.S. Popov radio manufacturing plant, and a former minister of defence, said: "Gaidar set off on the road to bringing democracy to the country, and set us on course. He was a wonderful young man, competent and honest. His route to high office was via the economic institutes, rather than through working within the economy, but he soon found his feet and put together a government of young democrats. The fact that Russia is treading a democratic path ranks as a huge achievement on the part of Gaidar."

Vladimir Kashin, deputy chairman of the central committee praesidium of the Communist Party of the Russian Federation, said after Gaidar's death: "Of course, the death of any individual is a time of great grief. Dancing on his grave is the last thing we would want to do, but he was certainly an ideological adversary of ours. We are still fighting against the course he set us on even today. His reforms lay at the heart of the collapse of a great country. Practically all the peoples of the former USSR are currently living in abject poverty. The model which he developed, along with the rest of Yeltsin's circle and some American advisors, led to a tragic situation in the economy. A black hole was created. The idea that the farmer could make enough food for everyone was one that the democrats who came next developed. As a result, we saw the destruction of the Russian countryside and the decimation of beef cattle and small livestock. We saw industry collapse in exactly the same way, and there was no room left even for production research centres. They gave out awards to the people who privatized and siphoned off money, whilst anyone who tried to preserve things was stigmatized. Not a single one of the economic treatises he wrote, as an academic, has passed the test of time, or even come close to doing so. His schemes to decrease the role of the state are now described as deluded not only by us but by economic theorists the world over, as well as prominent statesmen. I think the great writer Arkady Gaidar must have turned in his grave a few times as a result of his grandson's actions."

However, one of Gaidar's peers in the government of reform, Anatoly Chubais, is convinced that the economist succeeded in saving Russia "from hunger, civil war and collapse" in the early nineties. "Few men in the history of Russia and the history of the world can match him in terms of the force of his intellect, the clarity of his understanding of the past, present and future, and his willingness to take tough but essential decisions. Throughout his later years he was an intellectual and moral leader for us all. For me he was and will always remain an extremely important example of honour, courage and dependability. I shall feel this loss for the rest of my life," Anatoly Chubais wrote in his blog following Gaidar's death.

Chubais, incidentally, dismissed as "filthy lies" an article written by two of Moscow's mayors, Yury Luzhkov and Gavriil Popov, under the headline 'Another word on Gaidar', which was published in the newspaper *Moskovsky Komsomolets*. The authors of the article described Gaidar's reforms as "the worst method imaginable" of bringing the country out of socialism and maintained that Yeltsin, who "didn't know Gaidar at all", had appointed him prime minister because "the USA had forcibly thrust him on Yeltsin, whilst promising Russia tens of billions in aid." According to the capital's incumbent mayor (at the time) and his predecessor, "all Gaidar's reforms did was exacerbate the raw materials–based model for the development of the Russian economy, destroy Russian manufacturing, and led to an existence based on the sale of oil in exchange for the import of everything else," and they also led to the seizure of "the vast majority of state–owned property by the *nomenklatura* and the oligarchs."

One of Yury Luzhkov's peers, the speaker of the Moscow City Duma, Vladimir Platonov, admitted to *Kommersant* that he had read Yury Luzhkov and Gavriil Popov's article "with interest". "I interpreted this as an article written by two men who wanted to have their say and express their opinion about a famous person. It is a debatable one, but I'm sure there are a lot of people who would agree with it," he said. He did not shares his views on the facts set out in the article, incidentally, explaining that "he had spent a lot of time thinking about Gaidar's role and personality" (in July 1994 Vladimir Platonov was a member of the political council of the Moscow city branch of the party Russia's Democratic Choice, which was led by Yegor Gaidar).

When the deputy Vera Lekareva (of the Just Russia bloc) proposed a minute's silence as a mark of respect to the memory of Gaidar at a plenary session of the State Duma in December 2009, the first deputy speaker Oleg Morozov, who was chairing the session at the time, said only that the speaker Boris Gryzlov had already "sent his condolences to Yegor Timurovich's family" on behalf of the leaders of the State Duma. Morozov added that Yegor Gaidar was "indeed someone who would take his place in our recent political history." Vera Lekareva's proposal was not put to a vote, however, in breach of the Duma's procedural rules, and the minute's silence did not take place. Oleg Morozov explained the thinking behind his decision later, in a blog post. He said that on the day before these events, "representatives of the two blocs had warned him categorically that they would kick up a big public row if any attempt was made to ask the members of parliament to rise." He added that "the people who proposed the minute's silence were aware that plans had been made for a big row to erupt. They were aware of this, and yet they deliberately tried to provoke it!" Mr Morozov stresses. "They were only worried about themselves – not the memory of the deceased!" The deputy speaker said that if he had asked the chamber to rise, "there would have been a mock trial, rather than memories and grief."

Pyotr Mostovoy, the former deputy chairman of the State Property Committee and one of the men who organized privatization in Russia, when interviewed by a reporter from the Kommersant publishing house, E. Drankina, gave the following assessment of what Gaidar had done: "All the transformations to the tax system and budget relations, all the steps that were taken with regard to establishing institutes and financial markets – all of that was based on the ideas put forward by Yegor Timurovich and the people who carried out this colossal amount of work with him, and which is now being done by the people whom Gaidar educated...the main task which he set himself, and, it has to be said, successfully achieved, was to create the most important foundation for any market economy: money."

What was Yegor Gaidar's own opinion on what he had achieved, and on the price of reform? In 1995 he said: "When I accepted the offer to work in the Russian government, I realised that the most frightening accusations I would have to cope with would be the price that would unavoidably have to be paid for the brutal but essential measures we took in order to save the country...Politics tests a person to the limit, particularly during a time of transition. Some people can handle the pressure, some can't..."

Neither the apologists for Gaidar nor his fiercest critics can deny the magnitude of the role he played in the history of Russia in the 1990s and the 2000s. Yegor Gaidar's place in the history books is already assured, and the differing assessments of him are of no more than secondary importance.

The income deficit

What was the government's reaction to the negative consequences of the shock? Alexander Shokhin, the deputy prime minister and minister for labour and employment of the Russian Federation, said: "It's not fair to say that absolutely everyone needs protecting. Many are capable of getting through it on their own. The government's task is to create favourable conditions for this...The budget isn't elastic, you know. What we are trying to do is make sure there is no budget deficit."

As early as October–November 1991, foodstuffs began disappearing one after another from shops in the big cities, and food prices in the state trading market went up 300–400%. Local authorities tried to bring in a practice of using so–called contract prices and subsidizing essential foodstuffs, unable to wait until the government declared that it was introducing free prices. But to no avail. Foodstuffs which were subsidized, and were therefore cheap, were snapped up immediately, and the overall level of food prices in the shops slowly but surely caught up with the prices in the collective farm markets. As a result, there was the threat of an all–encompassing scarcity of food products.

At the Presidium of the Supreme Soviet of the Russian Federation, Ruslan Khasbulatov declared: "The issue here is not the liberalization of prices; the issue is simply the increase in prices, an increase which has been uncontrolled, anarchic and unregulated." Georgy Khizha, the deputy prime minister of the Russian Federation, echoed his words: "The country has seen an increase in prices for which no allowance was made. There has been a 15–fold increase in the amount of goods sold at the new prices, and just a two–fold increase in the money supply, which is simply not enough. If we are to balance the money supply and the supply of goods, we must add significantly to the amount of money in circulation, and increase companies' working capital." Grigorgy Yavlinsky warned: "The complete and irreversible disintegration of Russia is a real prospect within the next year, or two years at most." The leader of the Working Russia movement, Viktor Anpilov, said reassuringly: "We are attempting to establish contact with committees of agricultural workers and backing their demands, and we want to reinstate the union of workers and peasants."

People who had begun some form of entrepreneurial activity certainly had money, but there was a problem with this money too: it was rapidly falling in value. At the start of the year a dollar was worth 30 roubles, in the summer it rose to 35–37 roubles and within the space of a single week in November the exchange rate collapsed from 40 to 80 roubles. Thereafter the collapse of the rouble became a regular monthly event.

By 1992 there was an abundance of goods in the shops, but most of them were too expensive for 99% of the population. A lucky few who had had the good fortune to get a job with a foreign company or joint venture, where they enjoyed salaries of two hundred dollars a month, were able to feel confident about the future (few people trusted Russian private companies). Meanwhile ordinary skilled experts, who had been well off under the Soviet Union, began to be paid a salary equivalent to just a few dollars a month. A pair of boots cost around $50 (back then, the bulk of 'essentials' – beer, chewing gum, tights and ladies' lingerie, boots, jewellery, cameras, musical centres, non–lethal pistols and gas pistols, pump–action arms, souvenir globes and Samurai swords were sold at kiosks in underpasses).

In time–honoured fashion, the people drowned their sorrows in alcohol. Two alcoholic brands in particular dominated the scene in 1992: Amaretto, a liqueur, and Royal, a spirit. These were the season's biggest hits. In 1992 it was quite common to see drunks swigging Amaretto on the pavement – someone had managed to set up a supply chain (rumour has it this was a counterfeit version of the liqueur, made in Poland). Soon another novelty arrived: one–litre bottles of a spirit called Royal. Sales went through the roof, but stories soon began to come out about bad things happening to those who loved drinking Royal. It may have been that they didn't know how to drink it – perhaps they were diluting it with poor quality water…or it may have been that someone had started producing a counterfeit version of this 'noble' Dutch drink.

Meanwhile, changes had begun to take place in the economy which were barely noticeable and yet, as it later emerged, of considerable importance. In 1992 a law was brought in allowing street trading – and at once the whole country took to the streets to start trading, as if they had been ordered to do so. They sold whatever they happened to have at the time: bleached jeans (people used to bleach them at home), domestic bric–a–brac (socks, mittens, old irons, meat grinders and little lanterns), pickled gherkins and pies. And they made a tidy profit. A nation of engineers, academics and cosmonauts had been transformed into a huge array of stall owners.

A handful of stall owners sold serious goods. One of the most serious products of all was Snickers chocolate bars. It was a boom period for Snickers. The most resourceful types made a small fortune importing Mars bars. Trucks would set off each day to pick them up from a factory in Holland. People took out loans at ridiculous rates of interest (tens or even hundreds of percent a month – the banks handed them out gleefully) in order to buy them up, and then sell the whole consignment within a week, making enough of a profit to be able to pay off the balance and the interest comfortably.

Major trading brands emerged, too – the Erlan trading house, which had been founded in 1991, loudly announced itself to the company in 1992 with a mass ad campaign for Gusser beer. At the same time the Partiya firm, which sold computers, came into being (the 'White wind' retail brand had been set up a year earlier). Another big name in retail was a shop called Le Monti, which was opened by the emigré Leon Gandelman and sold cheap American cast–offs. Two major international brands dominated the scene: Uncle Ben's (made by Mars) and Bledina (made by Danone).

Whilst the former, a range of easy–cook foods, caught on in a way that was extremely irritating (the slogan, 'Outstanding results every time', took off and began to be used in all sorts of different contexts), the latter, a range of children's foods, was irritating because of its sheer cynicism. Mums in Russia couldn't quite bring themselves to feed their children something called Bledina, s it looked too much like an offensive Russian word, and after a while it disappeared from the shelves altogether.

Soon trading houses and retail networks were to put an end to the boom in exchange markets (whilst the administrative networks between companies were being destroyed and a huge proportion of wholesale supplies were being handled by the trading exchanges, which had representatives in almost every major city).

But problems arose with the metals trade, in which the country had traditionally been strong. This is illustrated by the fact that the world's leading trader of nickel in 1992, and for a few years thereafter, was Estonia. Our industry flagship, Norilsk Nickel, was lying stricken, as were all the other flagships, whilst some groups of quick–thinking guys (the Tambov gang from St Petersburg are said to have played a particularly active role) stocked up on goods and sent them to fictitious customers in Kaliningrad. As they went through the Baltic region, shipments got into the hands of local middlemen and were diverted into Europe. The profit margins were several hundred percent (this was quite normal for Russian businesses at the time).

Another significant event in Russia's metals industry in 1992 which went largely unnoticed was a new appointment to the offshore company TransCIS Commodities LTD, which was owned by the Chorny brothers. The company appointed Vladimir Lisin as its new vice–president. Lisin had graduated from the Economics Academy and would go on to manage the company's Russian business until 1997 (the company's other manager was a young man named Oleg Deripaska).

And another significant event among private companies was that Pyotr Aven, minister of foreign economic communications, became president of Alfa bank. The ties between the executive and big business were growing stronger and closer. The founder of Gazprom, Viktor Chernomyrdin, was appointed prime minister of the Russian Federation.

3. THE GREAT REDISTRIBUTION. PRIVATIZATION: VOUCHERS AND SHARES-FOR-LOANS AUCTIONS

Comrade cheque, a.k.a. Mr Voucher

Anatoly Chubais, the man who to all intents and purposes got the whole 'voucher game' going, used to admit that he had invested his own voucher in the First Voucher Fund (FVF). This fund, which had once been one of the biggest, is known for having attracted a large number of voucher deposits, which giants such as Morgan Stanley and CSFB later turned into investments in shares in Russian companies. It was the First Voucher Fund that helped the part–Swedish, part–Norwegian company Baltic Beverages Holdings to buy a controlling stake in the joint–stock company Baltika, the biggest player in Russia's beer industry. It's impossible to say how many deals of this kind went under the radar.

It's a moot point as to whether this 'voucher privatization thievery' brought any benefit to the average man in the street. What matters is that it became an instrument by means of which the institution of private property was established in Russia. And the first major fortunes were of course made.

From 1st October 1992 onwards, all citizens of the Russian Federation were entitled to collect a security with a face value of 10,000 roubles from a branch of Sberbank RF – this was a state privatization cheque, which was christened a voucher following the Polish example. This security was considered confirmation of the right of each Russian citizen to a share of the nation's wealth, and every citizen was to be given an equally–sized 'piece of the pie'.

Later – in line with the principle that money begets money – these fortunes helped their owners take possession of the country's biggest companies during the second stage of privatization, the "shares–for–loans" auctions.

Not without benefit to the state, of course.

Privatization, i.e. the transfer of state companies to private ownership, had begun in Russia back in 1988, after the adoption of the USSR law 'On state companies (associations)'. The necessary regulatory framework was not in place during this phase. The legislation required only began to be developed in 1991. It was in 1991 that the law 'On the privatization of state and municipal companies in the Russian Federation', to which amendments had been made in 1992, was brought in.

After Boris Yeltsin signed the relevant directive on 5th July 1992, voucher privatization descended on the country. The rules of the game were determined once and for all on 14th August: that was the day on which the presidential directive 'On the introduction of a system of privatization cheques in the Russian Federation' was signed. Just in case anyone has forgotten what they were, here's a brief reminder: the government of the Russian Federation valued the country's national wealth – the assets of all the state companies – at 4 trillion roubles. Of this, 1.5 trillion roubles (35% of the national wealth) was to be distributed free of charge to the Russian Federation's 150 million–strong population, with 10,000 roubles per person on a single security, the design of which was created on a commission by Deloitte Touche Tohmatsu. People could either sell it, exchange it for shares in the cheque investment fund (CIF) and receive an annual dividend on it, or exchange it for shares in a company at a cheque auction. The auctions were the highlight of privatization. Each company that was put up for auction was supposed to put up for sale at least 29% of its shares for vouchers. The people were free to exchange vouchers for shares in any company whatsoever. If a single voucher bid was put forward by the Cheque Investment Fund, or by an individual, for 29% of the shares in Gazprom, for example, then its owner had to be given 29% of the shares. If there were ten bids, each would receive 2.9% of the shares – and so on and so forth.

It was all a bit more complicated than that in practice. Companies tried in all sorts of ways to complicate the holding of the cheque auctions and drag out their own privatization procedures, so that by 31st December 1993 – the day when vouchers were taken out of circulation (this deadline was later shifted to 1st July 1994) – they could declare that they weren't ready for the cheque auctions, and they also limited the number of voucher owners who were allowed to buy shares.

In 1992 it was quite common to see miserable bums on the pavement holding up cardboard signs saying 'I'll buy vouchers'. You would catch sight of them standing on the pavement, at stations and in all the passages between stations in the metro. But only experts, for whom the shimmer of a pink and green banknote with a picture of the White House on it and a face value of 10,000 roubles (the amount you could actually sell a voucher for was at first $40, then $10, then $5, and it was only in the spring of 1994 that the price stabilized at $20) was the shimmer of big money, were able to make sense of the system. There were three categories of experts. The first (the 'speculators') got in on the voucher game: they bought them up on the cheap and sold them for profit, but didn't get involved in the privatization game. The second ('managers') organized the CIFs, changed vouchers into their own 'securities', invested the vouchers in shares and then sold these shares to whoever was willing to pay for them. This money rarely reached the shareholders – the experts usually stole it for themselves. Lastly, a third category of experts ('investors') bought up vouchers by the sackful using their own money and other people's, and then exchanged them for shares at the cheque auctions, this time for themselves.

The practice of vouchers being bought up from people in the street and subsequently appearing at cheque auctions in the regions created a whole class of entrepreneurs in Russia, who later featured in lists of the country's biggest magnates in finance and industry. "To look at those people! They had snouts like animals..." the vice–president Alexander Rutskoi said of the representatives of this category from Chelyabinsk in February 1993.

Little is known about the first category of 'voucher experts' – the 'speculators' – among the current business elite. And that's hardly surprising: as early as 1994, when the voucher was removed from circulation, they had begun turning their attention to other speculative instruments. Among their number were the founders of the investment company Rinako Plus, which had previously been extremely famous in the business world, as well as bank owners and industrialists.

The representatives of the second class – the 'managers' – were not particularly successful either. In the summer of 1992, Boris Yeltsin said that the CIFs were "designed to reduce the entrepreneurial risk of investing privatization cheques in securities, by means of professional and controlled management of investments."

The most professional of these, in terms of its own wealth, proved to be the cheque investment fund Alfa–Kapital, which became the privatization base for Alfa Group, owned by Mikhail Fridman, German Khan and Pyotr Aven. Alfa–Kapital, which has now been transformed into an investment fund, is still part of Alfa group today. Admittedly it now has far fewer shareholders than the two million that it managed to accumulate among voucher owners in 1993–1994.

This is probably the only occasion on which 'managers' managed to break into the circle of oligarchs. The other 'managers' from the country's 650 CIFs had a less successful fate in store for them. Anatoly Milashevich, the manager of the Partnership CIF, held no fewer than 2.5 million vouchers at one stage – or

1.5% of the securities of all the people in the Russian Federation who owned vouchers. Milashevich's career was hit by a public scandal: it was discovered that some of the vouchers which had been accepted at cheque auctions had not been properly franked, and were being submitted for privatization for a second time by their new owners. It took the State Property Committee seven months to do anything about it.

As secretary of the Theatre Union, Sergei Yursky answered the Union's call to invest his voucher in an international organization called Theatre. Says Alexander Shokhin, who currently chairs the advisory board of the Renaissance Capital group: "My wife was looking after my voucher. She took all our vouchers to some sort of organization that was popular at the time, like the OLBI group – without consulting me, incidentally, but prompted purely by the huge queues which had formed on the streets of Moscow at the time. And our vouchers simply disappeared, of course." TV presenter Tatiana Mitkova can only shrug her shoulders: "I remember having one, but I've no idea what became of it. It's probably lying about at home somewhere. It definitely didn't get invested in anything, I know that much for sure." As for Sergei Yegorov, the chairman of the board of directors at BIN bank, his voucher is "on the table. What could 10,000 roubles buy you back then? All the more so given that when the cheques came out in Russia there wasn't a developed fund market, or a serious mechanism for issuing company shares. Generally speaking, though, it was the right measure to take, but it wasn't quite done in the right way."

Aleksei Venediktov, a presenter on the radio station Echo of Moscow, maintains that he never even got his hands on his voucher. "Through sheer laziness. I just didn't go and get it – and I didn't think anything of it. Chubais and I talked about this on several occasions, and each time I used to say to him: "I don't owe you anything, Anatoly Borisovich. I never went to pick up that voucher of yours." But he used to reply: 'Well you ought to have picked it up.' Perhaps he was right." Says Grigory Yavlinsky:

"My voucher's at home. I'm keeping it so that I can show it to my grandchildren. It's a good example of how to carry out privatization in a way that is completely inefficient, economically, and is also politically inept."

The leader of the Liberal Democratic Party of Russia, Vladimir Zhirinovsky, also keeps his voucher at home: "I keep it as a reminder of something that was fraud on a grand scale, which proved to be merely the latest stage in the robbery of the people that occurred after Gaidar's reforms." Yegor Gaidar "invested in shares in Gazprom". The leader of the Communist Party of the Russian Federation, Gennady Zyuganov, gave his voucher to his wife. She, in turn, "invested the vouchers in shares in the factory where she worked. Unfortunately the factory went bust." Mikhail Chelnokov, a member of parliament, gave a frank assessment of the situation: "Whatever you did with your cheques, you ended up robbed of your money. I'm in favour of privatization – it's an absolutely essential element of civilization. But I am categorically against the form of privatization which the government, in brazen contravention of the law, chose to introduce. Alexander Rutskoi did not mince his words: "Here we are asset stripping when we ought to be setting up a mixed economy which can include state, communal, collective and private property."

25 million Russian citizens entrusted their vouchers to CIFs. Approximately 40 million people decided to invest their securities in shares – and the odd few, such as employees of Rostelekom, can count on getting the two Volgas which Anatoly Chubais promised they would be able to get in exchange for their voucher. People from the 'investors' category got into the voucher privatization game with a clearly defined goal in mind: to obtain big parcels of shares in major companies. Many of them managed to do so.

At one of the first major investment auctions, for example, in early 1993, a firm called Aluminprodukt obtained a parcel of shares (just 4.88% of the total) in Joint–stock company Sayansk

Aluminium Plant, which was directed by a man no–one had heard of at the time named Oleg Deripaska. Legend has it that Deripaska, whilst studying at Moscow State University, personally bought up vouchers and then shares in the Sayansk plant, stamping his feet in the freezing cold by the main gates of the Khakassian plant. This happened two years before Deripaska took control of the plant. And subsequently – a share in Joint–stock Company Russian aluminium and the post of CEO of the second biggest aluminium company in the world. And it all began with that little bag of vouchers.

Another of the oligarchs – Kakha Bendukidze, the director of 'Amalgamated Engineering Plants' (AEP) – was also an 'investor'. Bendukidze's company, Bioprocess, decided to put up for sale, at a cheque auction of shares in JSC Uralmash – now the chief company in AEP – 130,000 vouchers, ten minutes before the auction was due to end. "This was the Chubais method of privatization in action, in its purest form," Bendukidze said a day after this decision, which resulted in him owning 18% of shares in Uralmash, was taken.

That was a genuine success story: in 1993 it was impossible to say for sure which 'sacks of vouchers' might end up at any given auction, and in what numbers. Igor Smolkin, who at the time was the financial director of Alfa capital, complained that there were "no easy ways of selecting such companies: there isn't a single expert, or even organization, that has all the necessary data." The necessary data was replaced by a presentiment, a gut feeling, or a plan drawn up in two minutes flat on the back of an envelope.

Voucher privatization gave the country at least five oligarchs: Mikhail Fridman, Oleg Deripaska, Vladimir Bogdanov, the director of Surgutneftegaz (after a row with the State Property Committee that lasted six months, he managed to make sure that the voucher privatization of his company worked in his favour), Kakha Bendukidze and, to an extent, Vladimir Potanin (the holding company Mikrodin, which had been actively involved in the privatization market, became part of his empire in 1995). If we were to take a broader look at the situation, then of the 126 million citizens who were given vouchers, 25 million gave their privatization cheques away to the Cheque Investment Funds (the vast majority of which didn't bring any dividends at all), and 40 million chose to invest their vouchers as they saw fit. The remaining 61 million cheques were sold, and it was the people who bought them and invested in shares that would go on to own 35% of the nation's wealth, according to estimates made in 1992.

Given that the average, weighted exchange rate for each voucher over the course of this eighteen-month period was around $20, a third of the country's infrastructure was put in the hands of the entrepreneurs who had got the hang of this voucher game, for $1.2 billion. "I don't think anything like this has ever happened before in the history of mankind" – so said Anatoly Chubais, the man who created this big voucher game, when asked to comment on his brainchild in 1995. A few years later, incidentally, he would add: "During the privatization process, we did not manage to create a broad layer of private owners. This was down to the serious mistakes that we made. It didn't work out due to the specific financial institutions, the cheque investment funds, which were working with hundreds of thousands of investors."

Chubais in black and white

Anatoly Chubais, the architect of voucher privatization, is usually associated with Leningrad, although he was in fact born in Belarus. He was taken to Leningrad at the age of 10: the figure who played such a large part in the destruction of the Soviet empire came from a military family. After graduating from the Institute of Engineering and Economics and defending his postgraduate dissertation, he stayed on at the Institute as part of the teaching staff.

According to his official biography, Chubais's area of study was the economics of research and development, as well as issues related to radical economic reform. The latter, naturally, were introduced on a semi–legitimate basis: legend has it that there was an underground circle of economists concealed behind a larger group of young experts. There is more than a passing resemblance here to the epic Korean tale about the young Kim Il–Sung, who, when he was barely old enough to walk, was already said to have been organizing the partisan struggle against the Japanese occupiers. In fact, if any of the Chubais family were to be described as 'dissidents', it would be more likely to be his brother Igor, the deputy prime minister, who, during the second half of the 1980s and the early nineties, was a fairly prominent (though by no means influential) figure in the democratic movement.

People who knew the future deputy prime minister in those days describe him as a social activist who demonstrated as much ambition as he could reasonably combine with his strong self–control. It must have been this that helped him achieve something that was almost impossible for a young academic: he was put forward for membership of the CPSU. His socially oriented activity could be seen in the way he organized the Perestroika club and subsequently got involved in elections as a consultant to parliamentary candidates. Anatoly Chubais gradually went through the same metamorphosis as many Komsomol activists in the late 1980s: they switched from collaborating with the democratic movement to working within it. Thanks to this he was noticed at the right time, and in 1990 he was given the chance to get directly involved in the reforms. At the municipal level, of course. His doctoral thesis remained unfinished. Chubais took up a role as deputy to the last chairman of the Leningrad City Executive Committee, Alexander Shchelkanov. He didn't do anything of great import while in the role. After

Sobchak swapped his seat in parliament for the mayor's office, Chubais followed him, taking charge of the mayoral committee for economic reform.

He brought an original idea with him to the mayor's office. It seemed original at the time, at any rate: to turn Leningrad into a free economic zone. And the concept of a 'zone' hung over the city for six months. No genuine, serious steps were taken, and Chubais gradually fell out of favour. At least that was what the Leningrad establishment thought of his retirement from the post of chairman of the committee for economic reform. It was all dressed up in a very diplomatic way: Sobchak appointed Chubais his chief economic advisor and president of the international centre for socio–economic research, setting up the so–called Leontiev Centre at city hall as a matter of urgency. This first defeat for Anatoly Chubais can be seen as symbolic in many ways: in later years he constantly found himself drawn into conflicts with regional leaders.

Who knows where the St Petersburg economist's downward trajectory, after he fell out of favour with Sobchak, would have taken him, had the president not signed a directive appointing Yegor Gaidar to the post of prime minister.

Chubais had known Gaidar since 1985, when they had met at a guesthouse outside Leningrad, during a seminar on the reforms in Yugoslavia and the problems facing the Hungarian economy. Yegor Gaidar was taking part in the seminar. When interviewed by the local media, Chubais himself referred to this as a historic event. It was clearly one that lived long in the memory: before long Chubais had been invited to join the government.

When he moved to Moscow, Chubais spent quite a long time living in a hotel. It was clear that he did not feel entirely at home in the role of a minister. But those magic words 'voucher' and 'privatization' came along and pushed that unpleasant word 'zone' out of the frame. Thenceforth even the friends who had stayed behind in St Petersburg stopped calling Chubais a 'redhead' –

after all, as Mark Twain once wrote, those in power are never redheads, by definition.

Some journalists from the Kommersant publishing house carried out a survey among the people who had worked for Chubais. It transpired that all of them – both his dedicated supporters and his enemies – were quick to point out Chubais's positive managerial qualities. Most of them listed qualities which are characteristic of any boss: professionalism, self–assurance (his enemies, admittedly, described these same traits as insolence or impudence), and the ability to grasp things quickly. They talked about Chubais's capacity for work – his working day would begin at 8 or 9 o'clock in the morning and end at 11 or 12 at night (the kind of schedule that was not uncommon among bureaucrats of the Soviet school). They were far more reluctant to list his weaknesses: some said that Chubais didn't think in terms of shades of grey, that everything was either 'black' or 'white'; others said that he was too timid in his attitude to his bosses and was reluctant to admit to his mistakes. The latter, let it be said in passing, is a common trait among our politicians.

It should be noted that the country's first deputy prime minister managed to win the trust of all those who stood above him in the pecking order. In the Russian political system, though, this was not the be all and end all: the key thing was that Anatoly Chubais was able to prove his loyalty to Boris Yeltsin. And yet the love of the monarch is just one of the prerequisites (albeit a significant one) for ensuring a good career. The other one, which is perhaps equally as important, is the ability to organize the work of a large number of people, overcoming resistance from opponents within the workplace and ideological enemies.

The first step that any manager with designs on staying in power for a long period must take is to form his own team.

For someone from the provinces, the simplest and most obvious way to do this is to create a team of people who hail from your home town. Alfred Kokh, Sergei Belyaev, Pyotr

Mostovoi, Sergei Vasiliev, Andrei Illarionov, Pyotr Filippov
and many ordinary employees at the State Property Committee
formed the backbone, at various times and in various places (and
without necessarily working at the State Property Committee)
of the Petersburg team in Moscow. People from the same town
as you could be called on to form a loyal (not to say devoted)
entourage. But as for subordinates, they had to be gathered
together in Moscow. For a state body this was quite a thankless
task, given that employers from the world of private enterprise
are in a much stronger position in the struggle to attract the
top talent. There is only one way to assemble, in a government
department, the type of people about whom there would be
grounds for talking of a new class of civil servant, namely young
professionals with no fear of the pressure that comes from the
machine of party and state. And that is by paying them high
salaries. Chubais managed to do just that: on 6th October 1992 a
modest directive was issued by the director of the State Property
Commission entitled 'On the involvement of consultancy firms
and individual consultants in work related to the privatization
of state and municipal companies'. It was this directive that
opened up the door to the SPC to consultants on privatization
from the West.

None of this would have been possible, however, were it not
for Western financial assistance, which was used to pay for the
services of both foreign consultants and Russian specialists. At
the start of 1993 a directive was issued by the deputy chairman of
the SPC, Alexander Ivanenko, 'On the organization of training
for managers and experts for investment funds', under which part
of a $90 million loan given to Russia by the World Bank was put
towards the training of staff at the State Property Commission.

As privatization gradually became almost the symbol of
economic reforms in Russia, the idea of establishing a monetary
fund of $4 billion to support privatization, with the help of the
G7 countries, began to seem an increasingly likely possibility.
The president of the United States was a fierce advocate of such

a fund. With this in prospect, there was a need for appropriate ways of receiving the funds. The key structure was the state and societal fund Russian Privatization Centre, whose CEO was Maxim Boiko, a young advisor to the SPC's chairman. The State Property Committee was the founder of the fund. As a result, it effectively became its controller, and also one of the beneficiaries of the $3 billion targeted loan from the World Bank.

The 31st June 1994 – the day when voucher privatization came to an end – is generally considered the day of the economic triumph of the then chairman of the State Property Committee. This is true to an extent – free privatization, which had been extended for six months, was successfully concluded, and at a celebratory banquet for staff at the 'ministry of privatization' much was said about the next stage of de–nationalization: the monetary stage.

The author of privatization

The first person to have the idea of introducing privatization cheques in Russia was the economist Vitaly Nayshul. It occurred to him back in 1981, and he first discussed it with senior civil servants long before perestroika. By 1992, however, the people behind the idea felt that voucher privatization would be damaging to the country.

Vitaly Naitshul said that the idea of vouchers had come about somewhat earlier than is commonly accepted. In the late 1970s, when he was a senior academic at Gosplan, it was clear that the crisis in the Soviet economy was terminal. A small group of academics – Yuri Rodny, Viktor Konstantinov and Naitshul himself – began to think about what was going to happen next. It was abundantly clear that strong economic decentralization was required, and that a market must therefore be set up. In order to create a market economy, there must be private property. And since all property belonged to the people, a procedure for dividing it up was needed. Property would be divided into equal shares with the help of vouchers – a basic mathematical task. This was the route taken by every country which had tried to divide property up in this way.

In 1981 Naitshul began actively promoting the idea of vouchers, and in 1985 finished his self–published book 'A different life' about the transition to the market economy, which can now be found on the Internet. One of the first public seminars on this subject was held in 1987. It was attended by many of those who would go on to play prominent roles in the economic reforms in Russia, but back then they were merely researchers. Anatoly Chubais talked about this seminar, too…

Naitshul's idea provoked an extremely negative response. When he said that privatization had to happen and vouchers had to be used, everyone was shocked. "One of the delegates at the seminar began to suspect I was an agent provocateur and that I had been sent in so as to chase away all the progressive economists at a later time. After all, when it comes down to it, it's a very simple and logical idea. My chain of logical reasoning had to be extended throughout the whole country: if you want a cup of tea you have to boil some water."

By the start of the nineties, however, Naitshul was already speaking out against the voucher system. It calls for a powerful state, capable of redistributing property in accordance with the privatization scheme adopted. In 1981, when he offered the vouchers for sale, such a state might still have existed, but it certainly didn't exist any more in the nineties. "Imagine you propose some sort of system for dividing up property," Naitshul explained. "But this property is being used by someone, someone has some form of claim on it. The state says: this bit was owned by subject A, but from now on it is going to be owned by subject B. And subject A must agree to this, because that's what the executive has decided. This sort of activity requires quite a lot of force and, accordingly, strength on the side of the state. At the start of the nineties it was abundantly clear that the state simply did not have such strength and that there was no–one who could ensure that the process of voucher privatization would be completed. I'll tell you a funny story to illustrate this. In the autumn of 1992 the same company, including Chubais, held another seminar outside St Petersburg. The economist Simon Kordonsky and I said that the government's executive powers were insufficient to be able to implement voucher privatization. In response Anatoly Chubais, who was at that time the former head of the SPC, said: I have a nominal right to dispose of all this property as I see fit and to make all the transformations required, and I am going to make them. After this speech, Chubais was supposed to go straight back to Moscow. He turned to his aide and asked him whether the car and his ticket were ready yet. His aide replied: "I haven't got a ticket." "Did you say who I was?" said Chubais. The aide said: "I did, but they didn't give me a ticket anyway." And that was after what he'd said about having all the assets in Russia at his disposal! And it was immediately clear what the state's executive powers in the process of dividing up property were."

"When people criticize privatization, they usually talk about whether things were divided up fairly or not – who got too much, who didn't get enough," says Naytshul. "In the circumstances, with a weak executive, what happened was what was bound to happen: if people already had something, they were given what they had. Any citizen, incidentally, who had a nominal right to a state apartment, was given it as their own property, and that was a lot of money, particularly in Moscow.

As it happened, our version of privatization had some rather bigger flaws. Firstly: there was a massive amount of red tape in our privatization process, and it therefore led to a rapid strengthening of civil service control over the economy. After all, what sort of people were governors in 1991? There were no governors. The breaking up of the country into regions among the civil service grew off the back of privatization among the civil service, when local civil servants began deciding who could buy what. Generally speaking, post–Soviet bureaucracy – and not just regional bureaucracy – in many ways grew off the back of privatization, and it is now a mechanism which is holding back the development of a free market economy.

Secondly: property was privatized, but debts were not. If a factory's got debts, its new owner has to take the factory and all the debts into the bargain. The people's assets were put into private hands, and the people's debts were hung around the necks of the government."

When asked by a journalist what he had done with his own personal voucher, Vitaly Naytshul replied: "Nothing at all – I never picked mine up. And when voucher privatization came to an end, the vouchers were cut up, and I had a small fragment of voucher lying in my wallet for ages. I didn't have time for it... As everyone knows, the voucher wasn't worth much, that was why. The vouchers couldn't buy you anything in its entirety, just a set of additional rights which weren't enough to make you the outright owner. All property had de facto been confiscated, and that was why the vouchers proved to be so cheap in the end. And it wasn't just the vouchers, I might add – so too did all the state's efforts at privatization. When they began to privatize housing, for example, they tried to force people to pay for the state–owned apartments they were living in. It didn't work out: people were too smart to be hoodwinked; they knew that even without privatization they owned those apartments, and that someone had covered their operating costs. That's the sort of paradox you get with privatization..."

A pledge of prosperity

The second stage of privatization involved pledge auctions, in which shares were exchanged for loans. The state was in urgent need of funds with which to fill up the holes in the budget, and in 1995 a group of bankers led by Vladimir Potanin offered it loans secured against shares in companies owned by the state. The state agreed to the idea.

The Russian government undertook a lightning–quick operation which was radically to change the entire economic structure and political situation in the country. The shares–for–loans auctions were conducted in late November and early December 1995, and by the time they were completed, privately owned financial and industrial empires had been created in Russia, in no time at all, which could rival Western corporations in terms of sheer size. In return for the relatively modest sums that they paid, the owners of these empires – the so–called oligarchs – acquired not only the country's most promising companies: they also acquired unprecedented opportunities to exert influence on the decisions taken at the decisions being taken in Russia's White House.

The auctions for the right to lend money to the Russian government in exchange for shares in assets owned by the state were conducted in accordance with presidential directive No. 889 dated 31st August 1995, 'On the procedure for the pledging in 1995 of shares owned by the state'. A list of the companies put forward for shares–for–loans auctions was drawn up by the State Property Commission at the end of September. The sizes of the parcels of shares, the starting values of the loans, the deadlines by which the auctions had to be completed and the additional terms and conditions of the auctions were defined by a special auction commission which included representatives of the Ministry of Finance, the SPC, the Russian Federal Property Fund and a host of ministries in the sector.

In other words, a special auction commission containing representatives of the Ministry of Finance, the State Property Committee, the Russian Federal Property Fund and a host of ministries in the sector decided who its prospective members might be, what the starting price of parcels of shares would be and what the additional terms and conditions would be. People bidding for shares who satisfied all the formal requirements and were permitted to take part in the auction had to submit bids on the value of the loan to the auction commission. Whoever submitted the biggest bid won the auction. The winner signed the relevant contract with the Ministry of Finance, and in return for the loan received a pledge of shares and the right to vote at meetings of the shareholders.

For three weeks, during the auctions, the state transferred to private ownership companies worth a combined total of one fifth of the federal budget and employing a million people. Major parcels of shares in 29 privatized companies were put up for sale. The most famous and attractive of them were Norilsk Nickel, LUKOIL, SIDANKO, Surgutneftegaz and Yukos.

In exchange for "factories, newspapers and shipping," the oligarchs gave the government a guarantee of absolute political loyalty, swore to turn the old Soviet factories into competitive corporations following the Western model and promised that as a result they would pull the entire Russian economy out of the crisis like locomotives. Their confidence in the success of the undertaking was bolstered by the fact that the auctions, as it turned out, had been very carefully planned and unfolded like a real piece of theatre, in front of around fifty journalists.

And these auctions were in a league of their own in terms of the intensity of the emotions on display, the personalities of those involved, the number of accusations flying about and the gravity of them – in short, for sheer scandal and drama.

The behind–the–scenes preparations for the auctions had begun back in the summer. Bankers kept on calling the State Property Commission (SPC) asking how much money they were paying out for shares. That was how the starting prices were determined.

Alfa bank, Inkombank and Rossisky kredit did battle with Menatep bank in the auction for shares in the oil company Yukos. Norilsk Nickel fought with Oneksim bank and Rossisky kredit over shares in RJSC Norilsk Nickel. Oneksim ran out the winner. Rossisky kredit locked horns with Oneksim bank once again in the auction for shares in Sidanko; again, Oneksim was victorious. Inkombank was not allowed to take part in the auction of shares in Sibneft: the commission discovered discrepancies in its documents...

The director and protagonist of this whole affair was the acting chairman of the SPC, Alfred Kokh. From the outside looking in, it may have seemed as though, during the auctions, he was suffering the after–effects of intoxication. He kept pushing his chair away from the table, then pulling it back to where he started. Then he suddenly put his elbows on the table – and they immediately slid away to either side. And from time to time he simply rested his head on the table, as if he was about to drop off to sleep. But as soon as it came to the crunch, i.e. the opening of the envelopes, we witnessed a Kokh who was ready to do battle with anyone and everyone and was 100% sure of himself. He was quite capable of looking directly into the eyes of any of the bidders and telling them their bid was being removed from the auction purely on the grounds that "that's how it has to be". And he didn't shy away from doing so...

People who knew Kokh later said that the SPC director's 'intoxication' and apparent self–assuredness in the matter in hand signified that he was extremely nervous. Because he knew just how much was at stake. It was perhaps for precisely this reason that everyone involved – the civil servants, the bankers and the journalists – had such serious expressions on their faces. Let's take a look at proceedings. Another sealed bid is opened. Firm X, which no–one has heard of, wants to acquire a huge oil company. Straight away there is a rustling in the hall: what sort of structure is it? Who owns it? Which bank is it affiliated to? What does its envelope look like? And which end of it is the auctioneer going to open?

All this seems absurd now, but at the time there was much serious talk even about such things as the internal design of the envelopes – that was how high the stakes were. For example, when Norilsk Nickel was up for grabs, the starting price was set at $170 million. Bids were submitted by Oneksim bank, which bid $170.1 million, and Rossisky kredit, which bid $355 million. Oneksim, admittedly, had been put in charge of conducting the auction, and was therefore in a position to be able to reject a bid made by someone else. Sure enough, it did so. Rumour had it, however, that the envelope containing Oneksim bank's bid was not just any old envelope, but was dual–bottomed, and that inside the concealed base there was a bid for $355.1 million...

This was probably no more than fanciful speculation. Yet without such incidents, this eye–catching spectacle would have been transformed into nothing more than a run–of–the–mill reading out of the government's decisions. Instead, it was genuinely dramatic. A short time later, incidentally, it emerged that there certain people who had known the outcome in advance. Vladimir Potanin, for example, made barely any effort to conceal the fact that even before the auctions he had "agreed everything with Oleg Nikolaevich" (he was referring to Oleg Nikolaevich Soskovets, who at the time was first vice–premier and the most influential state civil servant). So the competing parties might as well have submitted bids in triple–bottomed envelopes, for all the chance they had of getting their hands on Norilsk Nickel.

The other people who ended up on the winning side after the shares–for–loans auctions in 1995 were Boris Berezovsky (of LogoVAZ), Mikhail Khodorkovsky (Menatep) and Vladimir Bogdanov (Surgutneftegaz). Later the list of oligarchs was extended to include a few other businessmen who had been given assets of one kind or another as a form of protection for the government, but at that time the White House's main favourites were those four.

And aside from Rem Vyakhirev, who at that particular time no longer had any need for auctions, because Gazprom had been privatized in accordance with a special timeline, it was these businessmen who would go on to become the first so–called oligarchs, i.e. owners of huge assets who were on special terms with the government.

The essence of the auctions, however, was not about giving out gifts to individual companies at all. The shares–for–loans auctions of 1995 were the result of a fundamental politico–economic agreement between the president and the government and a group of businessmen. On the eve of the presidential elections in 1996, there was an urgent need for some firm guarantees that it would be impossible for the Communists to gain revenge. At a time when Yeltsin's ratings were practically zero, there was practically no alternative available whatsoever. Aside, that is, from cancelling the elections altogether and establishing a dictatorship along the lines of the Chilean or South Korean model. Yeltsin decided otherwise, however, and put his faith in money and entrepreneurs' natural urge to preserve their own property. If you give them the best assets in the country, the president reasoned, they'll bend over backwards to hold onto it. And he was spot on. "Take us, or Menatep, for example: losing assets is the last thing we would ever agree to," Vladimir Potanin once admitted to journalists in Moscow.

In other words, the deal suited both parties.

In late November a joint press–conference was held at the Moscow hotel the Slavyansk, for the directors of Alfa bank, Rossisky kredit and Inkombank. The press–conference was held in order that the banks could make a joint announcement. They proposed calling a temporary halt to investment tenders and shares–for–loans auctions of shares in "strategically important companies". In their opinion, it was essential to set up a commission which could draw up the terms under which the auctions and tenders could be conducted.

The president of Inkombank, Vladimir Vinogradov, emphasized that the group of three banks had nothing against the idea of shares–for–loans auctions or investment tenders per se. He said that what the banks were against were the unequal terms which had been set up for those taking part in the current stage of privatization. By way of example the banks referred to the situation that had arisen in regard to shares in the oil company Yukos. The president of Inkombank declared that Menatep had enjoyed advantageous terms by comparison with those faced by the other banks – it was both conducting the auction and participating in it at the same time. Vladimir Vinogradov insisted, however, that Menatep intended to use funds from the Ministry of Finance during the tender and the Yukos auction. Three banks also accused Menatep of taking on obligations during the investment tenders which were far in excess of its own net worth. In connection with this, the president of Rossisky kredit, Vitaly Malkin, put forward a proposal on behalf of all three banks that an 'authorized commission' be set up including representatives of the RFFI, the State Duma, Menatep itself or other banks, to check how the banks were performing their investment obligations.

Some experts felt that the joint declaration was an attempt by those banks which did not have enough money to take part in the auctions and tenders to postpone the dividing up of the most attractive Russian companies. In response to this, Mikhail Fridman said that none of the banks had the kind of ready cash on their balance sheets required in order for a pledge to be made. This was not to say, however, that the banks didn't have any money – it was just that the money they had was invested in other assets. The banker maintained that the total assets, main capital and profits of the three banks was several times greater than those of Menatep. Mikhail Fridman made an interesting observation, however. He said that in order to free up funds so as to take part in the auctions, the banks would be forced to sell the SPC, and that this would affect both the state securities markets and the currency markets in a way that was far from ideal. In conclusion, Fridman made an important announcement: he said that the *troika* intended to form a 'united front' at the shares–for–loans auction for Yukos.

In early December 1995 an interview with Mikhail Khodorkovsky was published in the newspaper Kommersant. He revealed that the *troika* had entered into a 'gentlemen's agreement' with Menatep: "I had personally agreed with Fridman that although we could not see eye to eye with one another on absolutely everything, we would act within the acceptable limits of decency, and refrain from trying to blacken each other's name in the mass media. We kept to this agreement: we didn't refer to Alfa bank in a single article or a single declaration. We also had a verbal agreement with Vinogradov <…> under which Menatep would sell its shares in the Babaevskaya factory to Inkombank, and Inkombank would behave in the right way when it came to the privatization projects, and that if our interests ever came into conflict at any point, he would reciprocate – and give way."

The conflict between the banks touched on other interests as well. First and foremost among them were the interests of the State Property Commission. Its director Alfred Kokh was categorically against any postponement of the shares–for–loans auctions, maintaining that his very life depended on their results. In response to the consortium's proposal that Menatep's investment activity be looked into, the vice–premier Anatoly Chubais announced that the behaviour of all four of the banks would need to be examined. But the presidential aide Alexander Livshits announced that the 'war of the banks' was producing a "painful impression". Each of the rival parties, according to Livshits, had "found the time to make their case both at the Kremlin and at the government White House."

Postponing the auctions would not have been in the interests of Oneksimbank, either. Oneksimbank had, at the behest of the State Property Commission, conducted the majority of the auctions. This had been not only a prestigious role but a profitable one: after all, it was Oneksimbank that held the funds of most of those taking part in the auctions, which had been transferred to it as a form of deposit.

All manner of rumours circulated among the bankers about how the bank had managed to obtain this status. And the bankers never shied away from discussing, behind the scenes, the excessively close links between some of their colleagues and individual representatives of the state bodies. They said that a comfortable seat had been prepared for Koch either at the bank itself or at the finance–and–industry group Interros, which was 'on good terms' with it. Admittedly, Oneksimbank categorically denied this.

Soon people started referring to the conflict between the banks as a war. The bankers themselves strove to avoid using this word. And indeed there was barely cause for describing as a war the accusations that were flying around – even the bitterest of them – or the threats of legal action. There was one particular circumstance, however, that justified talk – regardless of the actual term applied – of a threat of serious failure in the process of bringing stability to Russian statehood. A brutal, open struggle had begun for the right to obtain control over the most attractive state–owned assets. The first few moves had been made.

And then suddenly everything fell quiet. Society and the media lost all interest in the auctions. And 1st September 1996 – the formal deadline for the pledges – went by completely unnoticed. None of those involved in the rows wanted to be plunged back into the atmosphere of the autumn of 1995, even for a second. None of the figures with most influence over public opinion raised the issue of what the future might bring for the state property that had been mortgaged. None of the economists made any attempt to explain the outcomes, or the chances of combining advanced financial management with the Soviet tradition of management. Society simply chose to ignore altogether the supposedly fateful day when, under the presidential directive 'On the deadlines for the sale of shares which were federally owned and transferred by way of pledges in 1995', the state assets which had been pledged were due to be redeemed.

And it became clear beyond any doubt that what had taken place had been nothing more than a show right from the very start. And the plot of this show was not particularly complicated. After the presidential elections, Vladimir Potanin, the chief ideologue behind the government's mortgaging of the state's parcels of shares – became the first vice–premier, and as for the first deputy chairman of the SPC, Alfred Kokh, he announced on 4th September 1996, without seeming overly embarrassed: the redemption period had expired, and the pledge holders were free to do whatever they wanted with the shares.

So what had been the reason for the silence regarding the pledged shares? Perhaps it was the fact that both sides in the deal realised they had been defeated? Some believe this was precisely what happened.

"These guys don't know what's going on, and just what a quagmire they've fallen into," said the then minister of fuel and energy, Yuri Shafranik. The clash between old–style production management and the Western financial model did not seem to him to be at the root of the problem. Far more serious for the economy were the long–term consequences of this clash and the resulting slowdown in the speed at which companies were getting back to financial health: "They will realize very soon that without the state they will be unable to lift a company that is in a state of crisis out of that condition." But who was suggesting that the banks intended to manage companies without support from the state? By all accounts they had agreed on this support right from the outset.

Meanwhile, judging by the scale of the support that was required, the state genuinely seemed to be caught in a trap. By transferring parcels of state–owned shares, it had formally received itself of the burden of having to keep a host of its companies afloat. And yet it was forced, as it had been in the past, to bring in various programmes of state support, because without that there could be no talk of stabilizing companies' financial position. For example, the amount owed to the state by RJSC Norilsk Nickel, the state's parcel of shares in which had been acquired by Oneksim bank, reached 13 trillion roubles and was continuing to grow rapidly as a result of financial penalties. However large the bank may have been, it was not in a position to be able to pay that kind of money. Things were not much better at Sibneft, which owned the famous Varieranneftegaz: at least $2 billion was needed in order to save it from bankruptcy.

However that may have been, there was an alternative point of view: neither the banks nor the state were any the worse off after the deal.

The banks had known from the start what they were in for. Even if they had been unable accurately to assess the scale of the problems related to the companies in which they had taken shares in the form of collateral, they nonetheless benefited from a range of advantages. Firstly, right at the start of the auctions nasty rumours were circulating (and are still circulated to this day) to the effect that the people most likely to give loans to the government used the state's money rather than their own money. There may have been some truth to this. Banks which had brought in various programmes on behalf of the Ministry of Finance and which held its funds may well, for instance, have handed out loans to companies which took part in the auctions on their behalf. And they in turn gave them back to the Ministry of Finance, secured against shares. Secondly, it is extremely significant that the banks serviced the accounts of the companies, shares in which they held on pledge. These were big companies with big account balances, such that when the banks launched them (as banks are required to do), they could earn quite a tidy profit. Thirdly, the company shares that had been pledged could be seen as investments for the future. For the companies involved were among the top companies in Russia. They merely needed a bit of work done on them. Specifically from a financial point of view: they needed to have their balance sheets cleaned up, their cash–flow and internal prices optimized, their debt to the state restructured and their management procedures fixed. If this had been done, the company would soon have started working. This would have immediately increased investors' interest in it. Fourthly, the banks obtained influence and political weight along with the shares. They now embodied not only themselves but the whole of Russian industry. And now they also embodied the Russian economy.

In other words, it was in the banks' interests to obtain pledged shares. But it was in the state's interests as well.

It should not be forgotten that the state decided its budgetary problems in no small measure with the help of bank loans. Moreover, the banks, forced to follow programmes of state support from "affiliated" companies, were now more closely attached to the state in their economic relations. And as a result they found themselves politically dependent on the ruling elite. Let's not forget that the terms and conditions of the shares–for–loans auctions contained a point about them being funded by the winners of investment programmes. At least the state managed to achieve investment in the real sector, albeit it in circumstances that were far from ideal.

4. The Scum. Embezzlers, Criminals and Bandits

Everything can be bought and sold

In the early nineties, even fortunes that were made lawfully seemed to be amassed with incredible ease, yet this was also a time when criminals of all kinds seemed to be making money out of thin air. The boundary between honest business and crime (and, at a more basic level, between honesty and dishonesty) had become so blurred, the people were so demoralized, and there were so many gaps in the legislation, that the embezzlers, bribe–takers, criminals, thieves and bandits felt utterly at home. Kaspirovsky, Chumak, Mavrodi, Sylvester, Kvantrishvili and their kind did not come from the outside: they were as much a product of their time as the people who suffered at their hands. And their victims, as has always been the way, often suffered through their own fault – because of their own greed, stupidity or love of getting something for nothing.

Fraudsters could make a quick buck out of almost anything at all. So there were problems with liquidity, and the clearance system for payments between companies kept breaking down? That meant there was an opportunity to make money using counterfeit promissory notes. So the people had found out what deposits and dividends were, but had not yet learned how to use them? That meant it was a good time to build Ponzi schemes. So the amount of anxiety in society was on the increase, and people felt confused and scared of change? Astrologers, druids and cult leaders were at their service. So the state was not up to the task of protecting the new class of private property owners? That meant there was fertile ground for racketeering and contract killings to flourish.

The number of zeros on the banknotes grew longer and longer, but the amount you could actually buy with that money grew ever smaller. The government struggled against inflation, but this struggle did not sit well with the requirements to finance agriculture, the delivery of goods to the north and other activities. With its other hand the government therefore turned on the printing press. By this time the primary national currency was the dollar. People had grown tired of carrying huge wads of roubles around with them, and dollars were accepted almost everywhere; there wasn't a single child who didn't know how the exchange rate for the dollar at any given moment.

It became a routine occurrence for salaries to go unpaid for months on end. Companies which had lost customers and had no turnover had nothing to pay them with, but the workers still turned up on the shop–floor out of habit, to tighten a few screws here and there or give something a fresh lick of paint. Later they became fed up with the situation and began to hold mass strikes and protest rallies.

And it was at that moment, amid the turmoil of the economic collapse, that president Yeltsin did something utterly unheard of: in November he signed a directive which gifted incredible tax breaks to the National Fund for Sport, which was run by Shamil Tarpischev, a tennis coach and a personal friend of his. All the goods imported via the NFS were exempted from the payment of customs dues, VAT and excise tax. At the same time, the NFS became one of the biggest commercial structures in the country. Up to 95% of all imports of tobacco and alcohol came through it and the firms that it helped to establish. As might be expected of any major player, the NFS would in later years be linked to a number of dramatic incidents – arrests, murders, assassination attempts, political rows...

The legendary commentator and former goalkeeper for the USSR's national team, Vladimir Maslachenko, described how rapidly those who found themselves 'close to the top' could climb the career ladder: he once went along to a football match between the Russian government (coached by Boris Nikolaevich Yeltsin) and the Moscow city government (coached by Yuri M. Luzhkov). He stood on the touchline and watched the game. "Well don't just stand there... go and get in goal!" Yeltsin shouted out to him. Maslachenko replied: "I mustn't, Boris Nikolaevich, I'm not allowed – I'm not a member of the government." Then coach Yeltsin shouted to one of his players, Gaidar: "Quick, write out a directive: Maslachenko is to be appointed an advisor to the RF government on sport." The directive was signed there and then, and Maslachenko joined in with the game. This may have been nothing more than a fable from a great commentator. But it conveys Yeltsin's style perfectly.

This was how issues were decided at the top. Is it any wonder that the people tried as hard as they could not to miss out on any opportunity that might come their way, going to whatever lengths were required? As early as in 1991, contentious issues could be resolved by means of the firm 21st century Association, which was run by the famous businessman Otari Kvantrishvili. Or alternatively by calling on the assistance of a private consultant who went by the nickname Sylvester. And in 1992 a law 'On the activities of private detectives and bodyguards' came into force. The first licensed security firms were established. And now a multitude of criminal gangs were given the opportunity to carry out their work on the basis of official documents.

In 1996 the newspaper *KommersantDaily* revealed that a group of bandits had threatened an FSB officer with dire consequences if he failed to repay a loan.

The officer requested protection from his bosses, but they all merely shrugged their shoulders indifferently. It was only through his own private connections that he was able to put together a team of gunmen, who arrived at the 'firing range' and gave the bandits what for.

A similar tale was told by a businessman who had once been in the government. He had once received a visit from a would-be *krysha*, or protector. He told an acquaintance of his from the security services about the incident. His acquaintance promised him protection in the form of one of the elite special ops units (for a fee, naturally). At a rendez-vous with the group of bandits, the businessman sat outside in the corridor, and the special ops commander popped his head round the door from time to time and said to him, with a worried look on his face: "You know, it's quite a bit more complicated than we thought. Our services are therefore going to be a little bit more expensive." After yet another hike in the cost of these 'services', the entrepreneur told his protectors where to go and went in to negotiate with the bandits on his own – and it worked out much cheaper.

A few more examples. In the mid-nineties the phrase 'the girls from Tverskaya' went into common parlance. Before long, numerous groups of girls – each roughly equivalent in size to a football team, or even a small demonstration – were regularly filling up not only Tverskaya Street but the whole of Leningradsky Prospekt, heading beyond the Ring Road to Khimki and even signalling at night-time drivers beyond Zelenograd. The same thing was taking place on the capital's other highways as well. The girls were literally embodying one of the principles of a market economy: the idea that "everything can be bought and sold".

The nineties were a wonderful time for all manner of hysterical individuals, clairvoyants, astrologers and the other crazy characters who thrived on the fertile ground of change. The general public energized water in front of their TV screens, following the instructions of the former journalist Alan Chumak. The astrologers Tamara and Pavel Globa sang songs to greet the dawn of the Age of Aquarius, which was destined to bring Russia untold good fortune. Anatoly Kashpirovsky continued to save the public from incontinence, and his group psychotherapy sessions led to him being put forward as a candidate for the State Duma by the LDPR, and even elected, on hearing of which he sent a fax from America saying he had no wish to be a member of parliament for the LDPR because Zhirinovsky was a racist and a war–monger.

But there were also others, besides him, with whom it was possible to engage in group psychotherapy: another former journalist and deputy, the wife of a former lecturer from the Knowledge society, Marina Tsvigun–Mamonova, who had assumed the title 'Messiah of the Age of Aquarius and Mother of the World Maria Devi Christos', created the 'Great white brotherhood YUSMALOS'. There were branches of this brotherhood in almost all the cities of the former USSR. During the preparations for the Last Judgement, which was due imminently and was to be crowned with an act of collective self–immolation, the Mother of the World was arrested along with her brethren and sentenced to four years behind bars.

The first half of the nineties was also marked by a procession into Russia of representatives of all manner of sects and pseudo–religious movements, many of which enjoyed support from the very highest echelons of power.

At the beginning of 1992 the Japanese sect Aum Shinrikyo appeared in Russia. According to Aum Shinrikyo's calculations, the end of the world was due to take place in 1997. Only the sect's followers would be saved. There were numerous reports in the media about its close ties to people within Russia's political establishment. The name of Oleg Lobov, the secretary of the Security Soviet and the first vice–premier in the government, came up with particular frequency. In 1992 Oleg Lobov was the president of the Russo–Japanese University, a charitable organization established in 1991 with the aim of enabling an expansion of ties with Japan in the fields of culture, economics and the environment. Aum Shinrikyo had a vast following in Russia. By 1995, when it was banned (in March 1995 Aum was responsible for a terrorist attack in the Tokyo metro involving the nerve gas sarin, as a result of which 12 people died and several thousand were poisoned), some reports suggested that the sect's Russian branch was eight times bigger than its Japanese one.

It was a boom period for religious sects and private occult organizations. And almost one in five Russians turned to them, losing considerable amounts of money in the process. The outright champions when it came to collecting donations were the Moonies. The sect's Korean founder, Sun Myung Moon, claimed that the second coming of Christ had already happened, that he himself was Christ, and that mankind must unite around him. The sect had some 2–3 million members. Unlike other sects which were accused of secretly milking money from their followers, the Moonies made no secret of their need for money: they maintained that in order to unite the planet's inhabitants around Moon, huge sums of money were required. In order to achieve their objectives, the sect's followers were allowed to deceive society. This also explained, incidentally, the huge number of organizations set up by Moon, which had no formal relationship to the sect (the International Women's Association, the Association of Professors for Peace throughout the world and the International Education Fund). The sect's activities in Russia began in 1990 following a meeting between Moon and Mikhail Gorbachev.

The Children of God sect was busying itself at this time, too. The sect's founder, David Berg, taught that God could be found through carnal love. After followers sprang up on every continent of the planet, Berg began publishing illustrated theological pamphlets which were deemed to be openly pornographic in some countries. After several notorious trials during which Berg himself and his followers were accused of paedophilia, the activities of the sect's communities in many countries were put under open police surveillance. In Russia the sect was known as the Union of Independent Christian Missionary Communities.

In 1989 the Mother of God Centre (the Community of the Church of the Mother of God) was established. This was practically the only sect that was purely Russian. At the heart of its doctrine were the 'revelations' of the Mother of God, as passed on to a prophet – a man named Bereslavsky (the visionary father John). The centre's leaders met Yazov (when he was Defence Minister of the USSR) and Rutski. Reports appeared in the media about representatives of the centre having meetings with Naina Yeltsina and Vladimir Zhirinovsky.

The Krishnaites have been active in Russia since 1990. The international society for Krishna Consciousness was formed in the USA and instantly achieved popularity on both sides of the Atlantic. The Mormons, the Jehovah's Witnesses and others also became active.

But the most powerful and destructive force of all was the Scientologists – the Church of Scientology, whose founder, Ron Hubbard, is reputed to have said that the best way to make money is to found your own religion. The sect has practically nothing religious whatsoever about it, besides unconditional faith in the wise teachings of 'commodore' Hubbard. During the course of its history the sect has found itself at the centre of attention on many occasions due to scandalous allegations about tax evasion, its brutal treatment of defectors and so on. In Russia the Scientologists acted not only under their official name but also through the organizations that they set up: Narconon, Hubbard College, the Moscow Dianetics Centre and so on. The Hubbard Centre, which was housed in a two–storey nursery school not far from the VDNKh metro station, looked like the office of a company which distributed Herbalife products. There were the same penetrating eyes of people with extraordinary strength of conviction, and the same points that could be earned by part–time staff, in lieu of money, by selling books and bringing in new believers. People would use these points to pay for professional training courses, after which they could become 'in–house' scientologists. Behind a glass frame and golden chain in the centre was a place known as Hubbard's Office, which was reminiscent of museum mock–ups of Lenin's office: it contained a leather armchair, a huge table made of expensive wood, bronze writing implements and a cupboard containing the works of the father of scientology. "We don't worship Hubbard like a god," the centre's staff hurried to reassure visitors, "for us he's a sort of symbol. And on top of that, it's a tradition: during his lifetime Ron Hubbard loved to travel to various scientology centres, and the centres were always ready for his visits, aware that he used to like doing a bit of work during his leisure time (in fact Hubbard did not think of himself as a god, but as Satan, particularly in the last few years of his life, when he was in a lunatic asylum). Whereas the members of other totalitarian sects generally tended to be people with psychiatric problems and teenagers, who could easily be talked into joining, the Scientologists used different tactics, attracting new members by means of courses, which supposedly helped people get through difficult situations and at which people learned how to behave and interact properly. As they took the tests, the sect's clients found out that they were far from being geniuses but had the potential to become exactly that. And that Scientology would help them get to that point.

The rank and file Scientologists worked in the name of an idea: for them, money was not important. And they quickly became fans. "I experienced it for myself," one of the victims tells us. "You become a sort of drug addict, i.e. you can't get by without completing more and more new courses, you want to get better and better, and you're constantly trying to scrape together enough money to pay for the lessons. As well as the various courses, they also make you write down your 'overts'. This is a procedure in which people have to write down all their negative actions. Then they check whether or not you're telling the truth using a lie detector. It felt as though I had travelled back in time to 1937 during all these procedures: every word I said was recorded. All this information is then stored in personal files. And then they can use this at a later time, to force people to work for the organization. For example, I hadn't done anything wrong in my life, but what if someone had once committed fraud or done something else that was illegal, and now the Scientologists knew all about it? There was a time when I wanted to steal the file they had on me, but I wasn't able to do it. Basically, they can try and drive people to do whatever they want – even to suicide. As for their attitude towards defectors, they both hate them and fear them at the same time. The ones who have left the organization or have doubts about its teachings are called PTS, or Potential Trouble Sources (Hubbard, incidentally, wrote that all Scientologists are entitled to cause harm of any kind to the organization's enemies: for example, by taking property from them or even physically destroying them. – Ed.). My own personal tale is quite revealing. Members of the sect went as far as to force my husband to divorce me...I had met him while doing the courses, and we had later married. Dima is a doctor, a neuropathologist, and, unlike me, he was strongly under the influence of the sect. At first the Scientologists tried to persuade me not to marry him: it seems they could tell that I was influencing Dima and might take him out of the sect. But I went ahead with the wedding. Six months later, though, my husband filed for divorce, stating our "different objectives in life" as the grounds.

In addition, the Scientology organization Narconon, which claimed to be able to liberate people from drug and alcohol addictions without the use of medication, was operating in Moscow. The organization handed out vitamins B1 and B6 to drug addicts. Staff at the centre also claimed that people could be freed from the inevitable withdrawal symptoms, too: "The key thing is strength of conviction." Incidentally, in the USA this 'programme' failed to obtain a license, and in this country it was banned by a directive from the health minister in 1996.

According to experts on the study of sects, the sect of scientology had a considerable influence on Russian politics. The sect first made contact with Russian politicians in 1989. Galina

Krylova, a legal advisor to Yuri Luzhkov, the mayor of Moscow, was the most important legal representative of international sects in Russia and was also a member of the board of trustees of the Citizens Commission on Human Rights in the USA. This is an organization run by the scientology sect, whose goal is to "cleanse the world of psychiatrists". For several years Krylova represented sects from all over the world in all the major court cases, ending up on the losing side in most of them. In 1995 she represented the Japanese sect Aum Shinrikyo after it carried out a gas attack in the Tokyo underground network, and she also represented the Moonies, the Hare Krishnas and the Jehovah's Witnesses. Krylova's most important task, however, was the work she did with the scientologists, where her duties went beyond the remit of a legal advisor. The scientologists invited her to join the board of trustees of the Citizens Commission on Human Rights. When photos of the "fighters against psychiatry" were published in 1997 in the newspaper Scientology News, there was a picture of Krylova in the front row.

And in March 1998 the Berliner Zeitung published the news that the Russian Prime Minister Sergei Kirienko had once taken a course in scientology.

The Chechen promissory notes

One of the first cases of fraud which resonated throughout the entire country was the machinations involving the so–called 'Chechen promissory notes'. In 1992, tens of billions of roubles were stolen from the Central Bank with astonishing ease.

In the early '90s the market–based financial system, which was in its infancy, was suffering from systematic delays in payments. The regional payment processing centres were unable to cope with the processing of the documents coming in from the commercial banks, particularly the promissory notes, based on which the amount written on them was paid into banks' correspondent accounts. Staff at the Main Financial Settlements Centre (MFSC) were unable to sort through the hundreds of bags containing payment documents which had accumulated at the MFSC's offices. Moreover, in accordance with a directive from the Central Bank, the consolidated promissory note which was sent by one regional MFSC to another was accompanied by the payment documents from all the banks involved. In the event that one of the documents was missing, the whole package was posted back to the settlement centre that had sent it. There it would lie around waiting to be processed, and would have the required documents added to it, which as a rule were not easy to find.

In May 1992, therefore, the Central Bank made yet another attempt to speed up settlements between commercial banks. To this end the system of wired settlements between regional MFSCs was abolished. Henceforward, commercial banks situated in Russia were able to send payment documents directly to one another. And in June 1992 Russia's commercial banks received a telegram from the Central Bank of Russia banning them from making payments based on payment documents coming into Russia from Chechnya, without special confirmation from the Chechen side. The reason for these restrictions was the appearance at the Moscow payments settlement centre of false promissory notes amounting to around 30 billion roubles, issued in the name of Chechen banks. At the beginning of June 1992, the Central Bank ordered that blocks be placed on several Moscow banks through which these fictitious sums of money had been moved.

The scheme for the use of false promissory notes was fairly straightforward: a 'courier' would arrive at a firm in Moscow with a blank note and offer, in return for a particular percentage in cash, to send far bigger sums to the company's bank account by cashless transfer. Of course the Chechen 'financiers' generally tried to target the clients of banks which had the capacity to operate with substantial amounts of cash.

By April 1993 the flow of fictional promissory notes had slowed, but the police were trying to track down the people who had sent the old counterfeits. And just as they had previously, the police were still stubbornly accusing Chechens of having committed such crimes. This prejudice on the part of the police is explained by the fact that the Chechens were the first to turn a form of bank fraud which had been known since the 1970s into a successful money–making operation.

In June 1993 word got out that agencies within the Ministry of Internal Affairs had arrested five senior directors at the Central Bank, led by the director of the central operational directorate Ravil Sitdikov. The charges brought against them were serious to say the least: manipulation of promissory notes and bribery in connection with the issuing of centralized loans to banks. 100 criminal investigations were opened, related to extremely serious defrauding of banks using the fake promissory notes.

In the case of the false promissory notes, charges were brought against some civil servants in very senior positions. In bankers' circles, however, it was said that the investigation may have been aiming even higher. Many financiers admitted that the counterfeit documents (the first of them, at any rate) could not have come to light without the involvement of people with considerable influence in banking circles, who, thanks to the position they were in, already knew about the counterfeit promissory notes and had access to the Central Bank's activities. Rumour had it that the cunning plan to make money out of fake promissory notes had been devised by experienced financiers and even someone with a PhD in economics.

The crafty Vlastilina

1993 brought the nasty whiff of financial pyramids to the country, for the first time. This was the year when Valentina Solovieva, a cashier at a hairdresser's, registered a company called

Vlastilina in Podolsk. The firm had money put into it by old ladies, but also by civil servants, soldiers and crooks (the total amount put in was half a trillion roubles and $2.6 million).

Rumours about a company in Podolsk which was settling accounts with its customers using cars, without breaking the law, began to emerge in the spring of 1994. The stories told by friends and strangers alike set the pulse racing, and many began to entertain the thought: "Why not risk it?" The firm did indeed exist, and for some time was even able to fulfil its obligations to its investors as far as the provision of cars was concerned.

The CEO of Vlastilina was Valentina Ivanovna Solovieva. She was born in 1951 and had completed a technical secondary school. She was officially registered as residing on Ryazansky prospekt, in Moscow, but in fact she lived in Podolsk. The pyramid got going in 1994. Vlastilina began to become popular thanks to an ad in the newspapers. The advertising campaign was relatively small, but when the first customers of Vlastilina took the ads at their word and paid in $2000 in one month for an *Oka* and $4000 for a *Zhiguli*, and actually received the cars, mile–long queues began to form in Podolsk. Customers would pay roughly 30–40% of the normal asking price for each car. In cases when the firm was unable to give an investor a car on time, it would pay out a cash sum that was enough to buy the model requested from the nearest car showroom (there were several showrooms in Podolsk). Those who had failed to spot the ad in the papers soon heard about the wonders that were taking place from their neighbours. A love of cars and faith in the miracle of Podolsk encouraged ordinary labourers, businessmen, policemen and even members of the Federal Counter–espionage Service to queue up to pay into the system.

Valentina Solovieva signed contracts with three major automobile manufacturers – AZLK, AvtoVAZ and GAZ – and soon began selling *Moskviches*, *Volgas* and *Zhigulis*, at a loss. On top of this, she took out loans from Podolsk Commercial

Land Bank, the Podolsk branch of Unikombank and Moscow's Russo–Slavonic Commercial Bank.

By the end of the summer Valentina Solovieva had put money into residential construction and provided full investment for several extremely lucrative projects. Vlastilina then began taking deposits for the acquisition, on six–month mortgages, of apartments in Zhulebino, Butovo and Mitino. The prices charged for these apartments, which were barely a quarter of their actual value, attracted a new wave of depositors.

Among the first to find out about this were the police. In particular, senior staff from Moscow's Regional Organized Crime Section put their subordinates' money into Vlastilina. This form of collaboration created a sort of 'police protection' for the firm for a while, and served as an effective bait for other clients.

But this ideal situation did not last long. The first alarm bell sounded in 1994, when the car manufacturing plants hiked up car prices. Again, the police were the first to find out about the rise in prices for cars. And they decided to get their deposits back before they matured – with interest. At 12 noon, several officers from the Organized Crime Section of the Moscow Internal Affairs Department arrived at the grounds of the Podolsk Electromechanical Works, where Vlastilina rented premises patrolled by guards. From what they said it was clear that they intended to retrieve the money they had handed over in expectation of receiving *Oka* cars. An ugly brawl ensued.

After this, Vlastilina began offering interest bearing deposits only, with 100% interest charged each month on deposits of 50 million roubles and above. When the firm began taking deposits at 200% a month, customers literally came flooding into the offices of the sole proprietorship. All manner of people brought their money along, from ordinary citizens to members of criminal gangs. Centralized collections were even organized at the prosecutor's office, the Ministry of Internal Affairs, the FSB, the tax offices and the government departments.

In September 1994 Vlastilina failed to pay dividends to its depositors for the first time, but only one of them (who had paid in 68 million roubles) reported this to the police. The others took Solovieva at her word when she cited "temporary complications" as the reason for the delay. As for the police, they only opened a criminal investigation when the company's office was suddenly abandoned at the end of October...Valentina Solovieva had disappeared. Police officers found no trace of her either at her private apartment (at 45 Ryazanskoye Shosse, Moscow) or at the apartment she had been renting in Podolsk. It became clear that the pyramid had collapsed. A warrant was put out for Valentina Solovieva's arrest.

At the beginning of November 1994, the Vlastilina affair came to the attention of the wider public. The firm's clients organized a mass demonstration (in which over a thousand people were involved) from Vlastilina's office to the town administration building in Podolsk. A rally was then held and a message was sent to the city's authorities demanding that Solovieva be arrested and that their money be repaid. By mid–November 1994 more than 5000 of the firm's former customers had reported what had befallen them to the police.

By the time she disappeared, Valentina Solovieva had managed to make somewhere between 10 and 20 trillion roubles depending on whose estimates you believed – money which vanished without trace.

And a whole year went by before she was arrested, in July 1995.

Valentina Solovieva was charged with fraud under article 147 of the Criminal Code of the Russian Federation, which at that time read as follows: "Fraud shall be defined as the acquisition of the private property of citizens or the acquisition of rights to their property by means of deceit or the abuse of trust. Fraud which causes substantial losses to the victim...shall be punishable with imprisonment for a term of between three and ten years, accompanied by confiscation of property.

Solovieva was well aware that the investors who had been duped were interested less in seeing her punished for what she had done than in getting their money back. And she promised to pay them back in full as soon as she was released. Since there were a lot of influential public figures among Vlastilina's clients and partners, the story was exploited by politicians right from the outset. The elections were fast approaching. Based on previous experience of election campaigns, it was well known that wherever there is big money and a huge number of potential voters, someone will always come along who is keen to make political capital out of the situation. And sure enough the public soon heard about a request made by Zhirinovsky to the general procurator, Ilyushenko, asking that Solovieva be released.

Back in July, when Valentina Solovieva was arrested, she had announced that any investigation into her firm's activities might prove damaging to certain people. The entrepreneur, who had always maintained that there were a fair few 'big cheeses' among her clients, had refused to name any names up until that point. But now she underwent a transformation, from a woman in debt to the whole nation to a woman who was accusing all and sundry.

The 'investors' she named included dozens of high–ranking members of the presidential staff, government bodies and law enforcement agencies. Only seven or eight names were made known to the general public, however. Journalists from *Kommersant* managed to get their hands on some exclusive documents which mentioned 23 names – names which made Minister of Internal Affairs Anatoly Kulikov's hair "stand on end". Two names stood out in particular. The first was the deputy prime minister of Russia, Oleg Soskovets (200 billion roubles in 1993 prices). The second was the chairman of the Federation Council, Vladimir Shumeiko.

Valentina Solovieva had even gone so far as to plan an election campaign. The professional union of entrepreneurs for the Moscow region put her forward as a prospective candidate for the State Duma. Solovieva intended to stand for election in the 112th district of the town of Podolsk. She was busily collecting signatures. Amusingly, she could have been up against the mayor of Podolsk himself, Nikulin – one of the people on the list of 'senior' clients who, according to Solovieva, had obtained two Volgas from Vlastilina by posing as a miner with an assumed name.

Valentina Solovieva was sentenced to seven years' imprisonment for defrauding almost 17,000 investors. But in 2000, three years after her arrest, she was released early for good behaviour.

Solovieva was not the only one to build a 'pyramid'. Volgograd had two pyramids – Khopyorinvest and Russky dom Selenga. And Moscow had the Joint–Stock Company MMM. The ad for MMM, which featured a butterfly and the slogan "Flying from the darkness into the light", was put up in every metro station and became pretty much the most instantly recognisable ad in the country. There was almost a year to go until shares in MMM were put on sale to the public.

MMM – *for a problem-free life!*

On 31st July 1991, a short time before the August putsch, many Soviet citizens (for they were still Soviets back then) – not just Muscovites but also those who watched a special report on the news – first heard the name of a certain co–op, "that one with the three letters", which had paid for a day's free travel on the metro, and the surname Mavrodi. And there were undoubtedly millions who fell for the ad. It was followed by ads featuring Lenya Golubkov and "lonely Marina Sergeyevna", advertising hoardings with the slogan "Flying out of the darkness into the light..." and long queues outside 26, Varshavskoye Shosse.

The founding father of MMM, Sergei Mavrodi, was born in 1955 into an ordinary Moscow family: his father was a builder and his mother was an economist. The only thing that marked him out from his peers in any way was his exceptional gift for the applied sciences. It is hardly surprising, therefore, that after finishing school he enrolled at the faculty of applied mathematics at the Moscow Institute of Electronic Engineering, graduating from it in 1978. He did not remain in his chosen profession for very long, though: he had a job as an engineer and mathematician at one of the research institutes in the capital but quit it in 1981. After leaving the institute, the budding entrepreneur began manufacturing and selling cassettes and videos. And in order to avoid being jailed for parasitism, he also took on a job as a night watchman. He was arrested for the first time in 1983, accused of private entrepreneurial activity, the punishment for which was extremely severe in those days. He was released after just ten days, however, and warned that he ought to 'wind down' his small–scale business. He was apparently helped by a resolution of the CPSU's Central Committee, which condemned recent 'excesses' in the struggle against illegal income.

It is not clear whether or not the shady businessman heeded what the police officers said, or became more careful, but he was not arrested again before the start of perestroika. It was only when the first co–ops appeared in the USSR that Sergei Mavrodi's talent was really able to shine through. By then he had formed a partnership with his younger brother, Vyacheslav. At first they got involved in anything that might make them a profit, and in 1988 they were even arrested on suspicion of embezzlement (or as some sources have it, for unlawfully converting money into cash). Yet again, however, things turned out well for Mavrodi: the brothers' guilt could not be proven, and they were released. Both brothers brought their involvement in dubious operations to an end and got involved in the most lucrative business of all at the time: buying and selling imported computer parts. And they set up MMM.

Prior to 1991, the MMM co–op was involved in a wide range of retail activity, and did not cooperate with any other companies in the alternative sector of the economy. In 1991, however, when it came up against the problem of converting money into cash, the co–op created a network of subsidiaries. Some of them had already existed previously but came under MMM's wing in 1991. Others were created by the co–op itself. Thanks to the organizational skills of the co–op's founder, Sergei Mavrodi, in the early '90s MMM, later known as Joint–Stock Company MMM, became widely recognized as the market leader. It boasted more than 30 branches throughout the USSR and over 300 firms of various kinds (including small companies and co–ops). MMM's success was also helped by the fact that it had managed to secure loans from commercial banks without any difficulties.

And it would all have been plain sailing, were it not for the fact that in January 1992 officers from the tax inspectorate turned up at the association's head office at 10, Gazgoldernaya Street, accompanied by armed men from the Ministry of Internal Affairs. They went in and seized all the company's financial documents. Six weeks later, staff from the Organized Crime Section of the MIA seized documents from six banks with which JSC MMM had had dealings. The up–to–no–good agencies described their actions as a routine inspection.

The inspections continued until the end of the year. A host of serious violations of the laws on tax and economic discipline on the part of MMM's directors were uncovered. According to officers from the tax inspectorate, prior to 1992 only the MMM co–op had conducted any form of practical activity, whilst the fifty or so other companies that were in the association had merely received money and withdrawn it from their accounts. What had happened to that money thereafter was anyone's guess. As the tax inspectorate saw it, the main objective that MMM's directors had been pursuing when they set up such a wide–ranging network of companies had been the ability to convert large amounts of money into cash in as short a time as possible. During their inspection, the tax inspectors also discovered the existence of a company that was far from typical of the Russian economy in those days – MMM bank. At the time of the inspection, the only client it had, besides the MMM association, was a single small company – i.e. the bank had in effect been created by MMM to service its own needs. Another original way of doing things that had been thought up by MMM's directors was the following financial operation: the association took out loans from Sberbank, the savings bank of the RSFSR, and invested the money in the capital of other banks. According to tax officers, the association owned over half the capital of several major banks, and MMM had racked up millions of dollars of debt on the loans.

After the documents had been examined, there followed a statement to the effect that the association was guilty of tax evasion. A block was placed on its account at MMM bank.

As a result, MMM bank ceased to exist, and no–one was prepared to lend money to MMM any more. It may have been this particular circumstance that prompted MMM's director, Sergei Mavrodi, to switch from trading operations to financial ones. Initially, MMM offered Russian investors American securities. Later it got involved in voucher privatization, enjoying considerable success. It set up its own cheque investment fund (CIF), MMMInvest. In February 1993 MMM began exchanging its shares for privatization cheques. Local residents, most of whom were unaware of the problems MMM had had to face, willingly invested their vouchers in the fund. During the course of privatization, MMMInvest acquired fairly large packages of shares in AO AvtoVAZ (more than 8%), the Tomsk Petrochemicals Combine (18.5%), Ulyanovsk, Automobile Plant (17%), OJSC Kosmos Hotel Complex (201,000 shares) and others.

In 1993, MMM began trying to raise money from the general public. It promised investors annual returns of between 1000% and 3000% on shares and tickets in MMM. The so–called MMM tickets, incidentally, came about thanks to the relentlessly high demand for shares in MMM when the company had reached the height of its success, each of which was worth 25,000 roubles. Not everyone could afford to buy shares at that price, and MMM's directors felt it would be acceptable to issue papers with a lower face value – 'tickets'. No register was kept of the tickets issued or of the ticket–holders, and it was far from easy to tell the difference between shares and tickets. It transpired that the concept of face value did not really apply to the tickets, because nobody ever traded a single ticket. Initially the notes were issued in the form of 'certificates' for 50, 100, 500 or 1000 tickets each.

What was more, Sergei Mavrodi was not afraid to splash out on advertising. The marketing stunt involving a day's free travel on the Moscow metro was the first step towards creating "the image of a reliable firm". The second step was his foray into the world of show–business: he put money into the making of new TV shows, such as 'Contacts, contacts', 'The last peep' and 'Under the sign of the Zodiac' (an arty show featuring celebrities having parties). As the association's directors saw it, MMM's image was to be enhanced less through direct advertising of its services than via the creation of a favourable impression by means of the programme itself, and the effect of MMM's 'tangential presence' on the screen. Soon the protagonists of MMM's TV ads, such as Lenya Golubkov and 'lonely Marina Sergeyevna', were among the Russian people's favourite stars.

And the people invested their money: according to the former director of the State Tax Service, Vladimir Gusev, sales of shares in MMM yielded 4 billion roubles a day in the first six months of 1994. The firm saw a dramatic upturn in performance, and by 1994 estimates of the number of people who had invested in it ranged from 2 million to 50 million.

It was at this point that it began having problems with the tax inspectorate. The police began to suspect that the reason Mavrodi was paying MMM's shareholders annual returns of 1000% was that he wasn't paying his taxes. They discovered non–payment of taxes at one company only – the MMM firm AOZT

Investconsulting. But the tax inspections had the desired effect. The fund market grew anxious, and MMM's share price began to yo–yo. At the end of July 1994, MMM's directors, citing problems with cash collection, called a temporary halt to the acceptance of shares, and Mavrodi devalued all the shares by a factor of 125. It was not known how many investors lost out as a result, but according to data from the Ministry of Finance, printing companies had manufactured a total of 2.8 million certificate forms, for approximately 27 million shares in MMM, as well as 72 million MMM tickets. And the total damage done by MMM's activity, according to the most conservative estimates, was 100 trillion roubles.

A nervous–sounding message from the company's president, Mavrodi, was published. The case he put forward was as follows: he had supposedly invented a *perpetuum mobile*, i.e. a self–sustaining economic mechanism which made it possible not only to increase the value of its stake several times over in the space of a month, but to do so again and again, *ad infinitum*. Mavrodi maintained that this *perpetuum mobile* would have kept going until kingdom come, had the tax inspectorate not broken it. In retaliation the mechanism's founder threatened to put into effect "the most effective and radical method of solving all its problems – a nationwide referendum," the outcomes of which "carry the greatest possible legal weight." With this ace up his sleeve, Mavrodi announced: "We are seeing the emergence in Russia of a new political force, one which is so powerful that it is highly unlikely there is anything that can stop it." He was referring to himself and MMM's stakeholders.

It is not clear, admittedly, which question Mavrodi wanted the referendum to be about: plebiscites on issues which directly affect the vested interests of voters are prohibited by law. Even if they had been permitted, it was still an empty threat. The way the question was posed – "Do you want a situation in which, without doing anything, you double your wealth every single month until the end of your life?" – was clearly idiotic. And the more modestly phrased question: "Do you want to get your investments back?" was clearly nonsense. At the end of the day, most of the population chose not to play the MMM game, and it is highly unlikely that those who didn't play the game would have voted in favour of having to cover the victims' losses out of their own pockets. The way the question about reimbursement was phrased signified that there was no money in MMM's coffers, i.e. the man who had been behind the idea of the referendum was openly declaring himself to be a fraudster. The whole appeal had been the suggestion that thanks to Mavrodi's wizardry, the gold coming out of the sky would last forever. Now that this shower of gold was no longer in prospect, the shareholders couldn't care less about what happened to Mavrodi himself – but saving his own skin was precisely what this had all been about for the wizard.

On 29th July 1994 the president of JSC MMM, Sergei Mavrodi, informed his shareholders that as of 29th July, "in order to stabilize the situation", the official rate for the sale of shares in the JSC would be set at 1000 roubles, whilst the rate at which they would be sold would be set at 950 roubles. As might well have been expected, the pyramid collapsed.

After taking time out to think things over, the authorities decided to arrest the president of MMM. And on 4th August 1994 special ops officers abseiled into his apartment, entering through the balcony, and took Mavrodi away to the tax inspectorate.

Mavrodi's arrest caused much indignation among those who had invested in MMM and gave politicians the opportunity to show what they could do in front of the electorate. Various campaigns and events were soon organized. Investors in JSC MMM picketed the Criminal Investigation Department of the Interior Ministry at 38 Petrovka Street. They demanded that they "get their hands off Sergei Mavrodi". Nine of them were wearing signs that said "shareholders in JSC MMM to go on hunger strike from 10 am on 7th August. A Union of MMM shareholders was set up. The union's members sent an appeal to a representative of the Russian government apparatus. In their appeal the investors demanded that the government not make any unofficial statements concerning JSC MMM in the media, to avoid panic among the shareholders. Moreover, the union's members called on the government not to interfere in JSC MMM's debt obligations to its investors, who still had faith in Sergei Mavrodi.

From his cell in Matrosskaya Tishina (Sailor's Rest) prison, Sergei Mavrodi registered in the 109th Mytischinsk district as a prospective candidate for the State Duma. The two months that Mavrodi had spent in jail had strengthened the people's faith in JSC MMM. Many felt that it was only the actions of the law enforcement agencies that were preventing him from giving the investors their money back. The desired result was achieved: on 30th October 1994 Mavrodi was elected a member of parliament. In connection with this he was released from custody, and the investigation into him was closed.

The long–awaited day came – 10 million shareholders in JSC MMM had waited impatiently for 1st November 1994. The newly–elected deputy had, it seemed, kept his promise: exchange points for shares in MMM opened that day. Once again, however, Mavrodi had a trick up his sleeve: the new points had no intention whatsoever of buying up old shares and notes in JSC MMM. It was proposed that they be forgotten about until the following January, when somone was going to determine the price of these shares and tickets. The outlets dealt exclusively in new papers.

The shareholders (though it was impossible to describe them as such in any meaningful sense) were being asked to play a new game, the object of which was supposed to be a new violet–coloured MMM ticket. The new colour was the only distinctive feature of these new tickets. Shares and old tickets were not accepted for buy–back.

In response to this, the shareholders threatened hunger–strikes and self–immolation in order to frighten Mavrodi into action. One of them threw himself from a 6th floor window. Others decided that rather than sacrifice themselves, they would file a lawsuit against JSC MMM, but the company's press secretary Sergei Taranov assured everyone that "the shareholders' lawsuits are bound to fail", because JSC MMM had no obligations whatsoever to its investors. And the people's favourite benefactor, Mavrodi, began to see his fan club dwindle in size. A man from Novosibirsk who had the misfortune of being the spitting image of Sergei Mavrodi was even beaten up by investors in MMM at Barnaul railway station. This doppelganger had barely stepped down from the train when he was 'recognized' and set upon by a group of enraged locals who had entrusted MMM with their savings. The victim said, incidentally, that he could fully understand where his attackers were coming from, and asked the police not to take the matter any further.

The state agencies decided to wash their hands of all responsibility for the crisis unfolding at MMM. In November the tax inspectorate's press service published the sensational news that in July, senior managers at the Moscow offices of the State Bank had allowed JSC MMM to withdraw 142 billion roubles in cash in order to settle accounts with investors. This money would have been enough to buy up all the registered shares at 125,000 roubles and even some of the tickets. But MMM didn't even give the money to those on low incomes, although it had promised to do so. MMM's chairman gave people a simple explanation for everything: "We spent the money on exactly what we had received it for."

In the summer of 1995 Mavrodi suddenly decided to find out exactly how many of his followers were "partners, as opposed to free–loaders". And to line them up in strict, almost military ranks. His objective in doing so was a deputy's seat in the new State Duma. All those who held MMM papers were invited to get actively involved in storming the stronghold. The incentive for the soldiers in Mavrodi's campaign army was the same as ever: that the money they had put into MMM's pyramids would be returned to them. The date on which the money was to start being paid back was fixed for 16th November 1995.

But just when Mavrodi was probably imagining that he was through the worst of it, there was a bolt from the blue. In October 1995 the issue of his immunity from prosecution was raised at a meeting of parliament. This was by now the third attempt to deprive Mavrodi of the immunity he enjoyed as a deputy. The first two attempts had ended successfully from his point of view: his colleagues had refused to give him up, and the investigation was stopped. But on 6th October 1995, at the third request (in a rare show of unanimity – 303 votes for and one abstention) his immunity was removed.

The investigation into the Mavrodi affair was resumed in the same month, October 1995. A further charge – of embezzlement – was added to the previous one (failure to pay taxes). Sergei Mavrodi was not arrested this time, however, nor was he even summoned for interrogation. Key to this was probably the fact that the case against Invest–consulting for non–payment of taxes had little chance of being successful, and the law enforcement agencies could not make up their minds to bring it to court. As regards the embezzlement, that was hardly an open–and–shut case, either: the lawyers might be able to persuade the court that the case of MMM and its investors was a matter for the civil courts.

In 1996 the director of MMM once again made headlines by attempting to stand for president of Russia. The electoral commission rejected a substantial proportion of the signature sheets supporting him, however, and refused to register him as a candidate. A short time later Sergei Mavrodi went underground.

The criminal investigation against Mavrodi was re–opened, then closed again...in January 1996 the investigation into non–payment of taxes was renewed. But in March it was brought to a halt on the grounds that there was no proof that Mavrodi himself had taken part in committing any crimes. Seized funds and property were returned to Mavrodi on 4th May 1996, to the tune of more than 800 million roubles. In January 1997 an additional investigation began, on the orders of the general prosecutor Yuri Skuratov, into the affairs of JSC MMM and Sergei Mavrodi, but the prospect of these cases having any success in the courts were not good.

In September 1997 the arbitration court of Moscow declared JSC MMM bankrupt in connection with its inability to satisfy the demands of its creditors and an excess of liabilities with regard to its assets. This was the result of the efforts of several investors who owned notes and shares which had not been redeemed by Sergei Mavrodi. The process of declaring MMM bankrupt passed off without any great fuss or demonstrations. The court's judgement simply declared MMM bankrupt. Sergei Mavrodi himself was already on the run by this time, and his brother Vyacheslav was continuing to collect payments from the public. In 1998 a federal arrest warrant was put out for the elder Mavrodi brother, and this was later followed (when news broke that he was in Greece) by an international arrest warrant. It was later reported, incidentally, that he was in hiding and safely ensconced in the Moscow suburb of Zhukovka 3 (he was regularly spotted at the high–class Tsar's Hunt restaurant). Mavrodi didn't just sit about twiddling his thumbs whilst he was on the run. According to law enforcement agencies in the USA, in early 1998 the former head of MMM created a new financial pyramid along with his cousin Oksana Pavlyuchenko, using the Internet. A website appeared for a company called Stock Generation Ltd, which was a virtual stock exchange. The site featured quotations for shares in non–existent companies, and recommendations on which ones to buy. The stock exchange lasted about two years, and some sources estimate that 20,000 people in the US and Europe fell victim to it (others claim that more than 275,000 people were conned by it). The victims began to send in complaints to the US Securities and Exchange Commission, and the Stock Generation website was blocked.

Sergei Mavrodi avoided arrest until 2003. On 31st January he was detained in Moscow. He left a signed note for the detectives who arrested him: "A souvenir for the criminal investigation department."

The criminal branch of power

In 1994, Anatoly Bykov's business group tightened its grip on the Krasnoyarsk Aluminium Plant (KAP). Bykov joined the plant's board of directors and deleted from the register 17% of the shares belonging to the Chorny brothers' Trans World Group, thereby triggering the 'first aluminium war'. The same processes were under way in other regions, too.

The criminality wasn't just on the streets: it was also, just like the general sense of disarray, in people's heads. As time passed, the criminal 'brothers' and new Russians became the butt of jokes, but the lawless way of life took firm root among the people: there was far more prestige associated with looking like a hooligan than an out–and–out loser.

And whilst the crooks were picking one another off, perfecting their shakedown technique and mastering the slang of the 'new Russians', whilst also watching the new Tarantino flick Pulp Fiction (the irony in which was completely lost on them), there was indeed a 'love story' of some sort unfolding between the business world and the criminal community.

In 1995 analysts first started suggesting that wild, free–market capitalism might be replaced by a civilized way of doing business. But along with this new–found civilized approach, an element of criminality also forced its way into the economy, and to all intents and purposes became a branch of power in its own right. The year 1995 began to the sound of gunfire, and there was no let–up for the rest of the year. And the violence was not confined to Chechnya, where federal forces had been trying to take the presidential palace in Grozny for over a month, since new year's eve. Things were kicking off all over Russia, particularly in Moscow, where some of the most notorious murders of the last twenty years took place that year.

On 1st March the journalist Vladislav Listev was shot outside the door to his apartment building. Swathes of bankers met an untimely demise as well. At the end of the year *KommersantDaily* catalogued all the bankers who had been killed – there were more than ten of them. Most notorious of all were the murders of the director of the Yugorsky bank, Oleg Kantor, and the director of Rosbusiness Bank, Ivan Kivelidi. A short time before he was killed, he told friends: "I'm a slave to my bodyguards." He seemed downcast and had some presentiment of his fate. Kantor's death was arranged with fastidious brutality: his entire security team was slaughtered at his dacha, and he himself was butchered in the style of a ritual killing.

Things were somewhat different with Kivelidi. Whereas Kantor had expressed an interest in shares in the Krasnoyarsk Aluminium Plant, Kivelidi was not treading on anyone's toes. He was poisoned by heavy metals inserted into his telephone receiver. No–one ever found out what the motive was.

The business community began to panic. Everyone had realized the extent to which crime had permeated the business world. The head of the NIPEK corporation and the company Biotechnologiya, Kakha Bendukidze, who went on to be the Economics Minister in Georgia, told a reporter from the Kommersant publishing house: "Criminal gangs have a radically different ideology about state–building. A liberal–democratic method of running the state and a free market are not the only alternative. There are also examples of market–oligarchic methods: Paraguay, pre–war Japan. There are cases in which the state is a hostage to the world of crime (Columbia), when the state and the criminal clans are equally strong. I am sick of hearing that it was supposedly just like that in America once, and that it all went away!

It hasn't gone away in Paraguay...we are already aware of members of parliament at various levels who are linked to armed gangs. And it may prove to be the case that after a year or two the situation gets out of hand, because a substantial amount of power will end up in the hands of people who are linked to organized crime in some shape or form."

When asked "What, in your opinion, does the criminalization of the state signify?" he replied: "Let's say all the members of the Duma and heads of administration in a particular city are crooks. They are in charge of transport and municipal services, and bring their own particular order to the city – and they do all this with the help of criminals. In a situation like that, there's no easy way out. The next round of elections either won't take place at all or will be rigged to suit the interests of the criminals. And over the next two years this process is going to take place in most of the regions, and then the fate of these areas will be sealed for a long time to come."

The people who still maintained that the country's future would be tied to capitalism were waiting patiently for the emergence of "the invisible hand of the market". They would have loved to give this powerful hand a shake, but were simply unable to do so: utterly unseen and unheard, it slipped inside people's pockets and into bins throughout the country.

In 1996 the Russian market continued to be plagued by scandal. On 2nd November the American co–owner of the Radisson Slavyanskaya hotel, Paul Tatum, told reporters from Kommersant about a conflict that had arisen between him and his business partners. The next day he was shot dead in an underpass. Tatum's favourite dictum had been: "Invest in Russia and perish."

In 1996 turnover at Luzhniki, the country's most important market, reached its peak and then plummeted.

This was a unique concept and time, when all of the trading that went on in the country was concentrated in a single place. The well–known entrepreneur Yevgeny Chichvarkin, incidentally, came out of that environment.

Andrei Renard, the president of the consulting company EMS, recalls: "It was the marketing centre for the whole of Russia, and you could track the progress of the whole of the Russian market by studying it. I think they ought to put up a monument to the shuttle traders there. They used to fly to China from the military airbase of Chkalovsky and land at a military airbase in the south of Beijing. And it was impossible to identify the business owners. There were approximately 40–50 monopolies on various groups of products – even the sales assistants in the stalls didn't know who they were working for, but the prices were co–ordinated and the firms used to reach detailed agreements about the competition. Then this monopoly model shifted to the Russian market as a whole. Today, the whole country, with its state capitalism – it's one gigantic Luzhniki. It took us a long time to track down the owners – they didn't respond to our letters or promotional literature. We had to use live bait to catch them – we opened a stall and put our products on display at knock–down prices. The other day a sales assistant called and said that some guys had come and "tried it on" aggressively. That same day we met up with them and they suggested that we reach an agreement. That was how we found out who was in charge."

No–one really knew who owned the market, but it was thought that it belonged to JSC Luzhniki (whose CEO was Vladimir Aleshin). There were also rumours that it was controlled by the Solntsevo mafia gang.

In fact there were a lot of people who wanted to make an honest living. V. Gendlin, a journalist from the Kommersant publishing house, writes that an entrepreneur he knew who had been involved in an illegal business – converting non–cash funds into cash – had tried to get back on the straight and narrow. In 1996 he approached a well–known international law firm and asked them to devise a system for him which would enable him to pay all his taxes legally. The lawyers looked into his business and shook their heads: "Sorry, but you were operating in the shadows, and you're going to have to stay in the shadows." To ease his conscience he had to organize his own charitable programme, helping elderly ladies in the apartment block where he lived. The reason he did this, as the businessman put it in his own words, was that "no–one told Mum when they should have done that I had been smoking behind the bike–sheds."

5. THE MASTERS OF LIFE: OLIGARCHS AND ORDINARY RICH PEOPLE

The burden of possibility

A question that was often asked in the nineties was: "If you're so clever, how come you're so poor?" And sure enough there was so much money floating around, literally right under people's noses, that it seemed as if you could just reach out and grab armfuls of the stuff. So why on earth didn't everyone do that?

The stats tell us that the proportion of entrepreneurs – i.e. people who "make money" – is roughly the same in every country – around 30%. Everyone else is either unable or unwilling to do so. The 'unable' include those who lack ability or are unfit for work; the 'unwilling' include those who simply have no interest in making money, because their interests lie somewhere else entirely: they would far rather cure the sick, teach the young, devote themselves to academic studies or join the army. Entrepreneurs are important to the state, because without them the country would descend into idiocy and weakness and die a death.

It's a good thing when a nation contains the following groups: the well off, the rich, the super rich and the fabulously wealthy.

It's a bad state of affairs when the only thing stopping teachers, doctors, academics and servicemen from becoming 'masters of life' is that the state is neither willing nor able to pay them the kinds of salaries they deserve.

It's a good thing for the rich to have the ability to be considered masters of life.

It's not good when only the rich can aspire to have this status. All the more so when it suddenly transpires that they weren't masters at all, and that they were in the lap of the gods: some were blown up in their own cars, others were killed in the entrance–way to their own buildings to the apartment blocks where they lived.

It's a good thing that life itself does not, in fact, have any masters at all.

Capitalism in Russia was developing at blistering speed. Advertisements offered 'European standard' interior design services and 'satisfaction of the most refined tastes', 'elite' apartments complete with jacuzzis, the first tourist packages and private casinos and clubs. The society pages of the newspapers were filled with reports about an unending stream of presentations, opening ceremonies and performances.

In 1993 a new must–have accessory came into being without which no–one would step out in the evening: the mobile telephone. These early models were gigantic and cost between $5000 and $6000 each, and it was *de rigeur* to be seen holding one as you emerged from your Mercedes and headed towards the doors of the restaurant, so that everyone could see that you'd got...no, not a Mercedes, but a satellite phone. Admittedly, there was no network to speak of as yet in Moscow: whereas in St Petersburg the telecoms company Delta Telecom had got going back in 1991, in Moscow Vympelkom and MTS were still trying to secure licenses in 1993, and the first large–scale networks were not built until the following year. Another highly desirable means of communication was the pager: in the summer of 1993 the companies RadioPage, Mobil Telecom, VessoLink and InformExcom came into being one after the other.

In 1994 the gulf between the various classes in society led to an open and demonstrative breaking away from the broader masses by a rich layer at the top. And this new class gleefully set about the tasks of management, consumption and entertainment.

In 1994 the first Seventh Continent supermarket opened

its doors. The Kalinka–Stockman chain had been around since 1989, it must be said, but its shops were not quite so up–market. Whilst 99% of the population (including quite a number who were reasonably well off) did their shopping at dirty markets, Seventh Continent was a shop people could go to if they wanted to get a real sense of just how entitled they were. The security staff used to ask customers who were not quite sufficiently well turned out: "Were you after something?" What they really meant was: "Aren't you forgetting something?"

The 'closed', 'elite' nature of these shops was a fashionable marketing ploy. Presentations for a select few were held not only at clubs and restaurants, but also by the manufacturers of run–of–the–mill consumer products. A private presentation by a world–famous manufacturer of saucepans took place in the apartment of a famous Russian actress. They were incredibly thorough on the door – they had everything but passport checks. There were only ten or twelve people present – those who, in the firm's opinion, deserved to be within touching distance of these unparalelled saucepans.

The Harlequin Club had its own leopards. There were famous artistes at every elite institution. Games most people had never heard of before, such as baccarat and chemin–de–fer, began to be played in special 'private' rooms, entrance to which was restricted to only the most 'elite' guests.

All this nonsense seems ridiculous now, but one can see where the new class of property owners was emerging from: just a short time earlier the nation's citizens had all been *tovarischy* ('comrades'), often fairly uncouth and unsophisticated. The ones who had made a bit of money imagined, quite naturally, that they had earned themselves the right to live a more wholesome life, to be more selective in their circle of friends and to spend their leisure time in a more sophisticated way than all those yobs in their tracksuits. The easiest way to stick out from the crowd in 1994 was to wear a club jacket, but the 'maroon blazer set', as they came to be known, were not so very far removed from those 'comrades' of old. And the owners of the clubs were willing to indulge their tastes.

Nowadays, when people tell of the horrors of the 'wild nineties', they try to contrast the 'stability' we have today with the 'complete lawlessness' that was the order of the day then. The truth is that it was quite a fun time to be alive – a time of enormous opportunities.

In 1995 there were grounds for optimism as regards the economic outlook. Manufacturing picked up in several areas, and the rouble suddenly gained ground in relation to the dollar. No-one had the faintest idea how the rouble had suddenly managed to get so much stronger: some attributed it to the influx of capital coming in to the treasury bills market; others felt it was because of the Central Bank's policy, which had become more independent. It reached the point where, in the summer of 1995, a 'currency corridor' was introduced, and this was maintained right up until the default in 1998.

Big business began to take shape, as well. Prior to this point, the business environment had been reminiscent of the random Brownian motion of stars, which were extinguished after their very first bright flash; now everyone could see exactly where capital and influence were concentrated.

At that time all hopes rested on big business. For everyone understood the situation: once this phase – the initial accumulation of capital – was complete, the big banks would inevitably start investing money in manufacturing. Among the banks deemed to be the biggest were Menatep, Oneksim, MostBank, Inkombank, 'Natsionalny kredit' and Stolichny.

It was pushing it to describe them as big banks, however – for they were all dwarfed by Sberbank. At the time, however, it was very hard to assess in real terms the weight, influence and wealth of the individuals who would later become known as the oligarchs. This may have been the reason why there was such a proliferation of various kinds of services, which took it upon themselves to compile rankings of the top entrepreneurs, in order to list them in order of their degree of influence or the size of their fortunes. Since there were no reliable ways of estimating people's actual wealth back then, none of these rankings were worth the paper they were written on. Even run–of–the–mill entrepreneurs now had the chance to be featured in expensive catalogues full of photographs of the elite along with sycophantic accompanying blurb. But they had to pay through the nose for the privilege. As a result, alongside glossy pictures of Mikhail Khodorkovsky, Vladimir Vinogradov, Oleg Boiko, Andrei Rapport, Vladimir Gusinsky and Alexander Smolensky, pages that were equally glossy and luxurious were dedicated to 'almighty' companies which offered apartment rental services or toilet repairs.

It was a time when oligarchs were still relatively accessible. On the night of 31st December 1994, when federal troops began storming Grozny, shots were fired at the bohemian White Cockroach club as well. When armed police arrived, they treated the revellers brutally. They were very democratic in the way they went about it: even the influential banker Oleg Boiko, who owned OLBI and the bank Natsionalny kredit, got caught up in the mêlée. Boiko was seen at many an A–list party. Nine months before the incident at the White Cockroach he had attended a party marking 1st April at Tabula rasa. On that occasion it was not Boiko who had set the tone, but a group of men from the LDPR and the trust company GMM. GMM was engaged in collecting money from the public, and few people remember it today. At the time, though, it had almost as noisy a presence in TV ads as MMM: its director, Anton Nenakhov – a thick–set, well turned–out man – sat ensconced in his throne looking like Louis XIV in full 'Empire' style, and promised savers riches and prosperity. Another character in that particular series of ads was a young shoe–shine who was transformed into a millionaire after he found out about GMM.

Interesting things started happening in business. The strengthening of the rouble, the fact that there was now more competition and the concentration of capital had all noticeably altered the way the business world operated, and called for a completely different type of professionalism.

Prior to that, business had looked more like a scrappy game of football in the yard. The pricing policy in the 'boutiques' had been organized roughly along these lines: the lady running the show, as she pulled out from a bag some cloths brought back in rowing boats from Poland and Turkey, would say to her assistant: "Right then, that one's going to cost $100, that one – $75, and that one...well, let's say $250." When you visited other countries, such as Poland or Germany, you could buy up a product that was unheard of in Russia, such as beer mugs featuring borders to keep drinkers' moustaches out of the way (in those days, all Western products were pretty much unheard of in Russia), and distribute them for resale at five times the price. If you couldn't shift the goods, you could always call on a few friends to simulate feverish demand, so that by your next visit the retailer was willing to give you half the money up front. If the product started to sell well, everyone rushed to fill this niche in the market and spent quite a long time skimming off the cream.

In 1995, however, the profit margin on retail operations fell to between 3% and 5%. The ready availability of computers (which it had previously been possible to sell to state bodies at a profit margin of 200%) and electronic goods led to deep and widespread price cuts. The same thing could be seen in other sectors too: foodstuffs, apartments and cars ceased to provide the sort of profits that meant you could get rich through a single transaction.

Businesses which had a finger in lots of pies began to come up against difficulties. At first, business would consume anything. SAVVA traded in snakes and apartments, laid on VIP taxis and promoted Zippo lighters in the Russian market. IVK sold computer parts, computers assembled in Russia (dubbed 'red–assembly' models), and one day found itself mining coal in the Kuzbass and even building a railway so that it could transport this coal to China. Mikrodin (which soon merged with the Interros financial and industrial group) tried its hand at pretty much everything too, as did OLBI (Oleg Boiko Investment).

All this came to an end in 1995. In January Anton Nenakhov, the director of GMM, fled the country. He was followed by the director of Moscow city bank, Anton Dolgov. Then the director of the Erlan retail centre fled the country, and the LLD group went bankrupt. In August Oleg Boiko's bank IndustriaServis went bankrupt, soon after merging with his other bank, Natsionalny kredit. None of them had been able to cope with the side–effects of growth: falling margins, the rapidly growing scale of business, and lack of experience in matters such as cost–cutting, mergers and acquisitions and financial management. In other cases this was supplemented by petty theft or simply a desire on the part of the owners to cash in on the business, i.e. to strip it of its assets. Some were simply swallowed up by their *krysha*.

As for Erlan, it was a retail centre that was typical of its day. It had been set up in 1991 by five founder members who dealt in screen filters, television sets, calculators, Goesser and Heineken beer, furniture and up–market residential properties. The adverts for all this featured a bearded chap called Mr Erlan, who wore an expensive suit. To enhance its image, the company bought two Rolls Royces and a Bentley (though none of these cars ran). Remembering that the devil was in the detail, however, did not prove as effective as splashing the cash. In 1994 the company bought 20 elite villas in Moscow at a cost of $700,000 each, which it intended to sell on for $1.5 million. In order to fund the venture it took out loans. Towards the end of the year Erlan spent $120,000 on a corporate party at the Harlequin Club. But at the start of 1996 all five of the company's founders travelled to Inkombank to sort out the problems they were having with the loans (on the initial loan of $6 million alone, Inkombank made a tidy profit of $36 million). Whilst *en route*, however, they took fright, sensing their lives might be in danger, and they were never seen again. All that was left of Erlan was its bare bones:

its chief accountant, Irina Arutyunova, who was handed a long prison sentence, and Mr Erlan from the ads, who ended up in a lunatic asylum.

Some converted the newfound opportunities that arose after 1991 into money, but others (using that same money) converted them into power.

One man whose name would be remembered by the public was the scandal–hit entrepreneur Vladimir Bryntsalov, who stood for the Duma for the first time in 1993, although less in the guise of a politician than as a pharmacist seeking to sell a brand of vodka which he had named after himself. In 1995 his fortune was estimated to be worth $2 billion.

This was one of the most dramatic incidents of the time: the case of *White Eagle* vodka (the ad was created by the British advertising agency Young & Rubicam). Just like the vodka *Kremlin de luxe*, it was produced by the joint enterprise Russkaya Amerika, which had been founded in 1991 by three men from Odessa who had emigrated to the USA – Yakov Tilipman, Mark Nudel and Leonid Baranchuk. The following year *Kremlin* vodka was ranked fourth in the world based on sales, knocking *Absolut* into fifth place. But in 1996 the National Fund for Sport, through which these brands had been sold, had its presidential tax breaks cut, and the vodka producers went bankrupt. In late 1996 Mark Nudel was detained and taken away by unidentified men who introduced themselves as FSB agents. His body was found in the Moscow River. Yakov Tilipman was shot in 2002 at his dacha in Opalikh. The pop group White Eagle took its name from this gruesome tale of instant wealth followed by destruction.

Key figures

In the nineties, everyone knew who owned Russia: the oligarchs. But who were the oligarchs, exactly? The term 'oligarch' went into common parlance in Russia on 13th October 1992. That was the day when Menatep bank announced that it intended to create a body that would provide banking services for the "financial and industrial oligarchy" – clients with a personal fortune of at least $10 million, in relation to whom an "exclusive approach" was required due to their degree of influence and the nature of their requirements.

And in 1996 the so–called 'letter of the thirteen' sent shock–waves reverberating throughout the country: on 27th April a letter from 13 oligarchs was published – the first manifesto from the ruling elite of those with big money, later to become known as the 'Seven Bankers' Cabal', by means of which it publicly announced its existence to the world. "Those who seek to infringe on Russian statehood, putting their energy into ideological revanchism and social confrontation, must understand that Russian entrepreneurs have all the resources and will–power required in order to influence both the politicians who are too unscrupulous and the ones who are too uncompromising." These days it beggars belief that this passage was written by Mikhail Khodorkovsky, along with Leonid Nevzliny, Boris Berezovsky and Vladimir Gusinsky. But precisely such a threat was included at the end of a letter addressed to President Boris Yeltsin and the main contender to succeed him, the leader of the CPRF Gennady Zyuganov. Given the context at the time, the 'letter of the thirteen' had a subtext which went something like this: "Dear candidates! Without us neither you, Mr Yeltsin, nor you, Mr Zyuganov, will have a controlling stake in power. The time has come to decide whether or not you can reckon with the power we hold."

In November 1996, Boris Berezovsky, who at the time was the deputy secretary of the Russian Security Council, told an interviewer from the Financial Times the names of seven people whom he claimed controlled more than half of the Russian economy. The list, which would later be referred to using the term 'Seven Bankers' Cabal', included the president of the commercial bank Stolichny, Alexander Smolensky, the president of Oneksim bank, Vladimir Potanin, the founder of the Menatep group, Mikhail Khodorkovsky, the president of MostBank, Vladimir Gusinsky, the chairman of the board of directors of the Alfa Group consortium, Mikhail Fridman, the president of Alfa bank, Pyotr Aven, and Berezovsky himself, who was the director of LogoVAZ and Obyedinenny Bank.

What happened next is common knowledge. Just one month later, Boris Yeltsin acknowledged that the 'Seven Bankers' Cabal' and its members were a legitimate institute of power and a constituent part of the ruling executive; in 2000, his successor, Vladimir Putin, excluded it from power; and thereafter some of the signatories to the 'letter of thirteen' suffered oppression on purely political grounds, and some of them joined the Russian Union of Industrialists and Entrepreneurs (RUIE), which to this day is still trying to thrash out its attitude towards the regime.

Boris Berezovsky left for the United Kingdom. In August 2002 the General Prosecutor opened up a case against him for embezzling money from LovoVAZ. In September 2003 Berezovsky was granted asylum in the UK. In September 2004 he was charged by the prosecutor's office of the Moscow Region, in absentia, with stealing a state–owned Dacha in the suburbs of Moscow, and in January 2006 he was accused by the Procurator General of "activities aimed at seizing power by force".

Vladimir Gusinsky, the chairman of the board of directors of the Most group, signed an agreement on the sale of MediaMost to Gazprom and left the country. In September 2000 he refused to fulfil his obligations under the agreement, and the Procurator General charged him with fraud. In December 2000 Gusinsky was arrested in Spain, but Russia's request that he be extradited was rejected. In August 2003 he was arrested in Greece, and once again the Greek authorities refused to extradite him to Russia. In March 2005 Gusinsky was interviewed by Israeli police in connection with money–laundering at the Hapoalim bank.

Mikhail Khodorkovsky, the chairman of the board of directors at Menatep bank, was arrested on 23rd October 2003 and charged with the fraudulent acquisition of shares in AJSC Apatit and tax evasion.

Leonid Nevzlin left for Israel in the summer of 2003, where he was granted Israeli citizenship. On 15th January 2004 an international warrant was issued for his arrest, in connection with charges of financial fraud and tax evasion.

In October 2004 Alexander Smolensky gave up business for good and in 2006 he co–wrote a political thriller called *The Hostage* with Edward Krasnyansky. Aleksei Nikolaev retired on his 67th birthday, on 31st January 2002. Viktor Gorodilov retired on grounds of poor health on 14th November 1997. Sergei Muravlenko was elected a deputy in the State Duma in December 2003, representing the CPRF. Vladimir Potanin, Mikhail Fridman and the others are still going strong today.

But the problem of the relationship between business and power continues to cause consternation in Russian society to this day. In an interview he gave to E. Drankina, a journalist from the Kommersant publishing house, in 2011, Pyotr Mostovoi asserts that the idea that the oligarchs must be distanced from power is perverse: "This idea directly contradicts the idea of capitalism. Capitalism presupposes that you have capital, and you have capitalists, and both of these things exert a tangible influence on the life of society and the state of the economy. And now we get to the heart of the matter of why we don't have capitalism in this country. It has become common for people to claim that all Russian companies are undervalued. The fact that companies' assets are undervalued signifies that they have not been converted into capital. They are nothing more than property that is lying there as a dead weight. In a capitalist society, capitalists are key figures. But in this country people don't tend to be capitalists. The practice of the state weeding out the shoots of entrepreneurialism is now a regular occurrence, a constant in any given part of the country. The moment a green shoot pokes its head through this half–withered grass, it finds itself at the centre of heightened levels of attention. And either it withers, like everything else, or it gets weeded out. On the whole, society's attitude toward capitalists is negative: people want to be rich for the sake of consumption, but don't want to be capitalists – they don't want to be producers. The policy adopted in the country isn't dependent on capitalists, and their ability to have much impact is extremely limited.

If it was the capitalists that decided on the state's policy, it would be a good thing for society: if capitalism's what we've got, then that's how it ought to be. If we've got something else, then let there be some other group of people, called something different, who determine our policy. There are capitalists in China, for example, but they don't play a role in society at all. Over there, prominent capitalists join the party and subordinate themselves to the party's decisions. But at least there you can identify who the decision–makers are, and work out how decisions are taken. The decision–making procedure over there is far from straightforward, but you can nonetheless make sense of it and work with it. In Russia, just like in the Strugatsky brothers' novel *Prisoners of Power*, the state is managed by 'unknown fathers' – it's impossible to say who the decision–makers are.

The problem with our country is that we don't have a ruling class. And bureaucracy grew stronger precisely because of the deficit in power. In normal states, the individual in power is not at the same level as the government apparatus, but stands above it. Historically, the individual in power was the tsar. In most modern states, power is not embodied by a single man: they have a sort of collective tsar, who has been moulded over the course of history, and this group of people sets the coordinates of power."

The 'masters of life' consisted primarily of bankers, but also included men who owned large companies and people from the upper echelons of power. Vagit Alekperov, Vladimir Bogdanov, Rem Vyakhirev, Viktor Chernomyrdin, Vladimir Potanin, Vyacheslav Sheremet, Anatoly Chubais, Leonid Melamed, Alexander Khloponin, Roman Abramovich, Aleksei

Mordashov...the people in power wanted money and the people who had money wanted power.

In 2001 journalists from the Kommersant publishing house tried to analyse their own personal contribution to the emergence of this group of protagonists. Their study was based on the frequency with which their names had been mentioned in Kommersant over a period of 10 years.

The study demonstrated that the oligarchs were wealthy individuals first and foremost, as might well be expected. The man on the list who proved most popular among journalists was the former prime minister of Russia, Viktor Chernomyrdin. The height of Chernomyrdin's popularity came in 1994: that year his name was mentioned in almost 1000 publications by the Kommersant publishing house (he was referred to in three articles per issue of the newspaper, on average). Some distance behind him came Anatoly Chubais (639 mentions in 1997) and Boris Berezovsky (336 mentions in 1999). The oligarchs who were not involved in public politics were mentioned on the pages of Kommersant's publications between 20 and 50 times a year. Thus oligarchs could be characterized as people whose activities were written about in Kommersant at least once every three weeks (if they were written about less often it meant they had not yet become an oligarch or had temporarily ceased to be one).

In order to give a business newspaper sufficient cause to write about them that many times, the protagonists of these articles had to: a) have serious amounts of capital in banks or in industry; b) have the desire to multiply this capital – any actions taken to this end (mergers and acquisitions, the securing of exemptions, success in shares–for–loans auctions etc.) provide substantive grounds for an article; c) have a network of connections broad enough for them to be able to influence the state's economic policy or successfully overcome the negative effect of this policy on their business. In a state with an economy that was undergoing reform, it would be impossible to fulfil condition 'b' without adhering to condition 'c'.

An oligarch was also a public figure. It is worth noting the guise in which oligarchs first crop up in the pages of the newspaper. Some of them first appear as active, second–rate businessmen who go about solving specific issues related to their business, such as Boris Berezovsky, who traded in Russian–made cars. Others are first mentioned when they have already become magnates with considerable influence in political circles. The very first reference to Mikhail Khodorkovsky, for example, was as follows: "The CEO of the inter–bank association Menatep, Mikhail Khodorkovsky, has been given an office on the third floor of Russia's Soviet of Ministers…" The simplest explanation for this is that a wealthy and influential person had to undertake public action of some description, and thereby come out of the shadows so that the newspapers paid attention to him. In other words, oligarchs are entrepreneurs and politicians who consent to being thought of as oligarchs.

Furthermore, oligarchs are interesting people. The study revealed an interesting trend: the years in which most articles were published about oligarchs in the nineties were 1995 and 1997, i.e. years which in Russia are generally seen as periods of relative wealth and stability. What is the explanation for this? Firstly, in times of crisis the mass consciousness is too preoccupied with answering the question "What is to be done?". The business press therefore spends most of its time covering stories of a practical nature: how to rescue your savings from a bank that has gone bust, whether or not the time has come to move to a more stable country, etc. In years when there is more stability, readers have more time to ponder questions such as "Who is to blame?" and "What exactly is going on in this country?" And at times like these the business media are willing to devote column inches to describing the life and times of prominent entrepreneurs. In other words, the oligarchs are influential businessmen whose activities provide interesting reading matter for the public.

On top of this, oligarchs are resilient, crafty types. The second explanation for the correlation between periods of stability and an upturn in the publicity given to oligarchs is as follows: in years of instability (financial crises, attempted coups, presidential elections etc.), the weakest politicians and entrepreneurs exit stage left. The stronger ones survive, and the strongest and shrewdest of all are even able to exploit the crisis and turn it to their advantage in some way. Thus oligarchs must be resilient and crafty enough to be able to emerge victorious from any crisis, no matter how serious.

Last but not least, oligarchs are market economy men. In other words they are people who not only have money but have the ability to make money (in very large quantities). Given that you can only make money in Russia when the state gives its tacit approval, oligarchs by definition must be close to those in power, and the few exceptions only serve to prove the rule.

The final point that seems pertinent is this: the oligarch's place at the table is never left vacant. If one suffers a dip in fortunes, others see their business prosper. For example, Kommersant wrote about Viktor Chernomyrdin 283 times in 1999 but mentioned Rem Vyakhirev on only 61 occasions. The following year, in 2000, Chernomyrdin was mentioned 114 times whilst Vyakhirev received 152 mentions. The conclusion to be drawn from this is as follows: the names that feature in the lists of wealthy oligarchs may change as the years pass, but the lists themselves are not going anywhere. For the simple reason, apart from anything else, that the presence of major entrepreneurs in this country, who are not afraid of the public eye and lobby on behalf of their interests in the corridors of power, is a natural consequence of having a market economy.

Interestingly, the mayor of Moscow, Yuri Luzhkov, was not included in this 'study'. The height of his 'oligarchhood' came later, in the 2000s, although in the nineties he was the capital's genuine and all–powerful master, providing one of the most eye–catching examples of all of the accretion of power and money.

6. THE END OF AN ERA: THE CRISIS

The illusion of developed capitalism

In 1998 it transpired that everything had to be paid for. It became clear that if money could be made out of thin air, sooner or later it would be turned back into thin air again. And that if the country was dependent on oil, a fall in oil prices might lead to a disaster. Integration in the global economy at a time when the domestic market had not yet reached maturity would leave the country vulnerable in the event of a fall in the global markets. And as for the dependency on the dollar and an influx of external capital – that had the potential to bankrupt the country.

And then we would have a crisis on our hands – crisis being the Greek word for judgement. Payback time.

Because there is no free lunch.

In 1997 half the companies in the country were in ruins, but the banks succeeded in making money out of money – in the interbank loans market and on speculative transactions. One can understand why the financial sector began expanding at such a rapid rate – this 'blood circulation system' was vital in order to resuscitate an economic organism which was suffering from paralysis. It looked, however, as though the business of 'blood transfusion' had turned into an end in itself, and this threatened to turn the economy into a bubble (as was to happen a year later, when all the financial empires which had seemed so powerful suddenly collapsed like a house of cards).

It is not easy to characterize an economy in which journalists are paid high salaries and TV presenters can earn millions, whilst miners and metal workers go for months without being paid, as healthy. In March the professional unions held a nationwide demonstration, and there were stormy strikes and demonstrations the length and breadth of the country. On 1st May the miners stopped delivering coal to the Primorye power station, causing an extremely serious energy crisis.

Yet there were signs of improvement in the Russian economy in 1997. GDP stopped falling and in some sectors began to rise. Inflation fell to just 10%. This enabled companies to invest in the development of manufacturing. At the start of the year work began on the construction of the Taganrog Car Plant, which could churn out 120,000 cars a year (the amount invested in the project was $320 million – a gigantic sum in those days).

Thanks to their decent credit rating, Russian companies were able to borrow money on the external market. In 1997 several credit organizations – Alfa bank, SBS Agro, Oneksim, Vneshtorgbank and Rossisky kredit – issued three–year bonds worth a combined total of $1.025 billion. Tatneft, MGTS, Mosenergo, Irkutskenergo and Sibneft took out loans in Euros worth a total of a billion. Admittedly this came back to bite them after the default in 1998.

In August President Yeltsin issued a directive on redenomination: three zeros were to be taken off banknotes as of 1st January of the following year. Labels showing both prices – the old one and the new one – were attached to products on the shelves, to help customers who had difficulty grasping the changes. A joke did the rounds: "So does this mean my Mercedes 600 is going to be converted into a Lada model 6?"

But the year's most important trend was that business began to show a keen interest in professionals. Journalists weren't the only ones in demand. Management, marketing, branding, advertising, PR – all these words which used to make the 'filibusters of business' frown, in the early nineties, became incredibly popular. The abbreviation MBA – Master of Business Administration – acquired considerable weight. In the past people had thought that experts from the West didn't understand the first thing about Russian business. Now they were going to the opposite extreme: getting an overseas education became the 'in thing' to do. The news that Interros had hired two young Harvard graduates as lawyers caused quite a stir in the market: the group paid each of them $200,000 a year. They wouldn't have been able to earn that kind of money anywhere in the West (Harvard's own statistics suggest that the average starting salary of a Harvard graduate was around $120,000).

Whereas in the past staff had been poached from international companies for no real reason other than to provide valuable lists of wholesalers and suppliers, employers were now consciously calculating that ex–pats might be able to introduce Western management technologies or product promotion strategies.

Talk of marketing and branding was of particular interest to them. In the past marketing had been founded on plain and simple deception of customers. For example, a product of some kind would be imported from a remote corner of South–East Asia and hyped up as a world–famous brand, although no–one had ever heard of it outside Russia. The TV manufacturers Shivaki and Funai were presented as "legendary, world–famous brands", as were charlatan counterfeit brands such as Pawasonic, Panasunaic, Akaiwa and others whose strategy was to make their name sound very similar to that of a well–known brand. For many years Russian consumers were under the illusion that Mars and Snickers were the bitterest of foes – that says it all! Similarly, customers naively assumed, in 1995, that the refreshing drink Hershi had made its way to us from some enlightened European country, and that WimmBillDann juice came from somewhere exotic and sunny. The pretence that Russian products had been made in the West paid dividends during the early stages, however. In 1995 a ladieswear collection by a famous designer saw a huge boost in sales after the product started being supplied from Germany. People had far more trust in the brand name Slava Zaitsev when they saw it written in Latin letters than when it was written in Cyrillic.

As Russian business grew up, however, all this began to change rapidly. The consumers themselves changed, too. And in 1997 it felt as if we were entering an age of developed capitalism. No–one was fooled any longer by the so–called 'suckers' brands', and Russians suddenly began to feel nostalgic about home–grown Russian products and brands.

One of the pioneers when it came to exposing a product's true identity was WimmBillDann, which in 1995 began to think long and hard about its own nationality, and then decided to change it. A publicity stunt was held in Izmailovsky Park, during which clowns dressed as little WimmBillDann creatures revealed the truth, saying: we WimmBillDanns are every bit as Russian as you. Carbon copies, indeed!

And in 1997 there was an even more startling revelation: it emerged that Tom Klaim (a fashion label) wasn't the brother of America's Calvin Klein at all, indeed wasn't even related to him – he was Anatoly Klimin, a man as ordinary as they come, a Russian entrepreneur who had been a black marketeer and underground businessman in Soviet times. His pret–a–porter clothing range was hugely successful, despite the notoriety of his 'suits for secretaries': their garish colours and provocative cuts were somewhat at odds with generally accepted notions about how middle–class women ought to look. Be that as it may, in 1997 Anatoly Klimin won the Viktoria award for 'Designer of the Year'.

1997 can also be described as the year that marked the start of the Internet era in Russia. One of the notes in the November edition of Kommersant Money began with the line: "Right now there seem to be people talking about the Internet at every turn." The deputy prime minister, Vladimir Bulgak, declared that there were already half a million people using the Internet in Russia. Most of these, admittedly, were people who worked for major companies – there were very few people using the Internet on their own personal computers. The Internet was mostly used to send and receive emails back then.

But compared to previous years, it was clear that progress had been made: whereas in the past those looking at pornographic websites had had to spend five minutes waiting for the girl on the screen to get her kit off, so that they felt like giving up and curtailing the whole cheap spectacle, it was now possible to watch short video clips.

By the middle of the year it began to seem as though after all the destruction that had taken place, the conflicts between the various branches of power and all the contract killings, life was gradually starting to return to normal. Shopkeepers learned the art of smiling sincerely at customers, and even got into the habit of putting their shopping in bags which they let them have free of charge. Car mechanics stopped being rude and adopted a mellow, soothing tone of voice. People acknowledged the role played by competition, and even began to derive pleasure from the experience of interacting with customers. Civil servants began talking to visitors in a respectful manner – they did not feel particularly sure of themselves when they did so, but their visitors, by contrast, soon grew accustomed to having a sense of their own value.

As all these encouraging external changes were taking effect, some barely noticeable yet important processes were unfolding inside the country. Admittedly, there was the so–called 'writers' union' affair, when five authors, led by Anatoly Chubais, were accused of pocketing $90,000 for a book called *A history of privatization in Russia*, which they never wrote. This was directly related to the conflict surrounding Svyazinvest, when Boris Berezovsky and Vladimir Gusinsky, who had once been enemies, joined forces in the struggle against Chubais. Gusinsky and Berezovsky wanted to get their hands on Svyazinvest for a starting price of $1.18 billion. A meeting was held in France where the bankers tried to reach an agreement and divide up Russia's

87 biggest telephone companies, a quarter of the entire Russian network. But Chubais backed a proposal by the director of the Oneksim group, Vladimir Potanin, who later teamed up with George Soros's fund Mustcom and bought up a blocking stake (25% plus a single share) for the record sum of $1,875,040,000, roughly equal to the amount of money coming into Russia's state budget each month. This was the biggest scandal to hit the news in 1997.

The unskilled labourers in the stock market got on with their routine, buying up companies that were little–known but important. It was a golden age for the stock market. An army of unknown soldiers of fortune plundered all the hidden backwaters of their homeland clutching attaché cases containing millions of dollars, to buy up shares in factories and power stations. Their fingers grew black and swollen as a result of constantly having to count out banknotes. Often they were acting on the orders of strategic investors (if they were operating on the over–the-counter market) – a broker would receive an order and the broker would send out a gang of buyers to simulate competition. Otherwise it would have become clear that an order had been placed and prices would have rocketed. Sometimes, on the other hand, a different group of actors would deliberately stir up a lot of fuss about a company and go halves with its directors, so as to then offload shares to the investors who had been enticed in. Several small towns in the middle of nowhere were transformed almost overnight into millionaires' villages. The town of Zeya in the Amur Region is a case in point: there were no roads going beyond the town and the nearest railway station was 400 km away, but this was the site chosen for the Zeya hydro–electric power station. At one time, visitors to the town were buying up 2.5 billion roubles' worth of shares a day. The locals ran across the town square from one buyer's office to another, sold their shares, bought cars and TV sets and couldn't believe their luck. Then they started to worry that they had sold their shares too cheaply. Others flew into a rage because they had held on to their shares, only to see their value plummet. It was all quite fun until the default of 1998 came along to spoil the party.

1998

At first 1998 seemed to be a year that oozed well–being and prosperity. Russian capitalism continued to derive pleasure from the trends of the previous year. Just as before, the people with the best salaries were the ones in the professions that were hardest to understand: financiers, auditors, journalists, designers, brand managers, PR experts, marketers and experts on branding. Marketing and branding were in the driving seat, just as they had been in the past. In the food shops the Dovgan brand reigned supreme (it made vodka, mayonnaise and other useful products), whilst in the supermarkets the Russian brands Carlo Pazolini and TJ Collection (Timur and Yulia, who had settled in South Africa, presented their fairly high–quality goods as having been manufactured in London), Faberlic, Gloria Jeans from Rostov and other Russian labels with foreign names.

Foreign investors were now being joined by ordinary Russian citizens in playing the treasury bonds game, and these people felt a deep sense of satisfaction as they cashed in their coupons in order to receive dividends.

The nature and scale of the problems with the economy were markedly different from what had gone before. On 20th June Moscow was hit by strong winds and heavy rain, and on the morning of the 21st it emerged that a hurricane had caused 11 fatalities, wounded around 200 people and brought down some 45,000 trees. Public transport was brought to a standstill, the rooftops of the Bolshoi Theatre and the Great Palace in the Kremlin were damaged, twelve of the Kremlin's ramparts were broken and crosses had been blown off the Novodevichy Monastery. An estimated 1 billion roubles' worth of damage had been done. It was the most destructive natural disaster to have hit Moscow since 1904.

In the middle of the year the Committee to Welcome the Third Millennium was set up. It was comprised of all the most colourful characters from the ruling elite: Kakha Bendukidze, president of the NIPEK corporation; Sergei Karaganov, a member of the Presidential Council; Yury Milyukov, the co-chairman of the "Business of Russia' Round Table'; Alexander Oslon, president of the 'Public opinion' foundation; Gleb Pavlovsky, president of the Fund for Effective Policy; Professor Sergei Kapitsa; Fyodor Shelov–Kovedyaev, director of the Institute of Contemporary Politics and Economics; Leonid Parfyonov, chief producer at NTV; Konstantin Ernst, general producer of ORT; the writer Vladimir Sorokin; and Marat Gelman, to name but a few.

On the whole everything seemed to be going smoothly. On 17th July the remains of the Tsar and his family were buried in the Petropavlovsk Cathedral in St Petersburg, 80 years to the day after their murder. It was a stiflingly hot day and the only thing most office workers were bothered by was the fact that their bosses weren't letting them wear shorts to work. People who knew a thing or two about economics were expecting a crash – but who could be bothered to listen?

One of the few economists who said that a default was inevitable was Andrei Illarionov, a former economic adviser to Yeltsin. In 2011 he revealed, when interviewed by a journalist from the Kommersant publishing house: "The official data left me in no doubt as to what was taking place in the economy. The conclusions I reached, to the effect that a fall in the value of the rouble was inevitable, were based on an analysis of the statistics – primarily those that concerned the finances and the budget. The unambiguous message coming from this data was that a devaluation was inevitable; the question was not if, but when. On the basis of this information I began to talk about an impending crisis. Yegor Gaidar, Anatoly Chubais and Sergei Dubinin spoke out against me in public. On 2nd August 1998, Dubinin called a press conference at the White House which was attended by about 300 journalists. The main issue was the devaluation of the rouble – was it going to happen or not? Dubinin claimed that I wanted the rouble to collapse so that I could make money from the Chicago Currency Exchange through my relatives...the Russian authorities were assisted in their efforts to convince the public that no crisis would materialize by a promise of financial support made by the IMF, and then by the arrival of this financial aid. When unrest about the impending disaster began to grow among representatives of Russia's business community in the spring of 1998, they paid a visit to Yeltsin and said that in the circumstances, only a huge loan from the IMF could rescue the economy. In June Chubais, after being appointed by Yeltsin as the president's special representative for relations with the international financial organizations, flew to Washington for talks with the IMF and the American authorities. In mid–June he secured a special package of aid worth $24 billion. This aid took the form of new loans – in addition to the $23 billion of extra external debt which Russia had acquired during the first half of 1998.

The first tranche of it – $4.6 billion – was handed over. By my calculations, this portion of the loan might have delayed the onset of the crisis for one–and–a–half months at most. But the IMF transferred this money not to the Ministry of Finance, as it usually did, but to the Central Bank. There was not enough income in the federal budget to service treasury bills, the nominal interest rates on which had risen from 20% to 160%. Each new weekly interest payment required the issuing of new bills and the securing of additional funding to the tune of approximately $1 billion.

For the sake of objectivity it should be noted that the policy which led to the crisis was one that was advocated by Stanley Fischer, who was no ordinary man. This highly respected economist and high–ranking civil servant ensured that recommendations on so–called exchange rate–based stabilization were adopted as the IMF's official position. This was a policy of financial stabilization based on a fixed or quasi–fixed exchange rate. The IMF issued similar recommendations to many major countries which had had difficulty balancing their finances.

In practically all the places where this policy was pursued for any sustained period of time, it led to an extremely grave financial crisis: this was the case in Mexico, Thailand, South Korea, Indonesia, Russia and Brazil. It is not easy to think of any other economic policy that has caused such phenomenal collapses over the course of a single decade. Chubais and Gaidar were on good terms with Fischer and adopted his proposals in full. As for the practical form that Fischer's recommendations took in reality – the so–called currency corridor – that was Chubais's brainchild."

Incidentally, no trace of the first tranche of that first loan from the IMF has been discovered to this day – it simply vanished into thin air...

What we do know is that in August Russia faced the most turbulent time it had experienced in the 1990s since the putsch. And just like the putsch, these troubles are seen as having come like a bolt from the blue, although in actual fact they were entirely to be expected.

Andrei Illarionov takes up the story: "On 14th August, a Friday, Boris Yeltsin flew to Veliky Novgorod in the afternoon. Having been force–fed the false assertions of his team of economists, he announced that there would be no devaluation and that everything was under control. The next day, on 15th August, Kirienko, Dubinin, Aleksashenko, Zadornov, Chubais and Gaidar set about discussing the manner in which the forthcoming devaluation would take place...on Sunday 16th August they invited the directors of the commercial banks to come and see them, and Aleksashenko said to them triumphantly: "Had your fun, have you?" In response to which one of the bankers said: "We aren't the ones who've had our fun.

You are." The next morning Kirienko and Dubinin announced that the borders of the currency corridor were going to be changed and a moratorium was going to be introduced on the servicing of external debt, i.e. on a devaluation of the rouble and a default on the external debt."

Sergei Kirienko shared the blame for the default with Anatoly Chubais, Sergei Dubinin and Mikhail Zadornov, and was soon dismissed. But in his subsequent career there were signs that he was a man of considerable political flexibility. He was one of the founders and co–chairmen of the Union of Right Forces Party, but rather than pursue a career as a member of the opposition he opted to help build the vertical system of power and became the President's plenipotentiary in the Povolzhe region.

The events of 17th August 1998 might have seemed like just the latest banana skin for the government (in April Viktor Chernomyrdin had been replaced as prime minister by Sergei Kirienko). But when salaries for the month of September went unpaid and entire product lines started disappearing from the shops, it became clear that things were serious this time and that the problem wasn't going to go away any time soon. As Vladimir Potanin put it, "a considerable portion of the Russian economy started sinking to the bottom, because we spent years bringing in unrealistic and terrible budgets, whilst the role played by the financial crises in Asia and the rest of the world can hardly be seen as playing a decisive role in the circumstances in which we found ourselves." Alexander Lebed observed: "The international currency fund and the World Bank found themselves in a delicate situation in Russia, because for six years they had been giving out money and issuing advice, yet the majority of the population were still living in abject poverty."

Although the announcement of the default on 17th August caused consternation for many, most ordinary citizens were indifferent about it at first. Several institutions where people had grown used to spending their leisure time had to be shut down. Then the exchange rate for the dollar went up fourfold, from 6 roubles to 24 roubles. It became clear that this was a crash. And so the struggle to stave off the crisis began...

This struggle was expressed in other ways in Russia, besides the non–payment of salaries. A huge number of businesses found that they owed money to their partners, whom they had formerly trusted. It was simply not enough to take a hard line in such circumstances – there was no choice but to seek compromises. Some people chose to bring down prices. Others decided to restructure their business. Creditors seeking to have their loans repaid tried to foist projects on the companies that owed them money. One particular firm – a leather haberdashery – put all its money into real estate and ended up staying in this new line of work for good. Others shifted their focus to Russian suppliers – it transpired that many of our companies were more than capable of replacing imports with home-grown manufacturing. Even western companies learned how to be flexible. Japan Tobacco International, which had bought up all of RJR Reynolds Tobacco's international business for $8 billion, began to work directly with retailers after a number of distributors left the market: merchants would load up their vehicles with boxes themselves, and take the products to the sales outlets. In addition, the company decided to support distributors who didn't 'sit on the goods', and brought in a currency corridor for them. The supplier would set its own dollar exchange rate for distributors for a period of two weeks, at somewhere between 8.5 and 9.5 roubles.

A debt market soon formed. Ads began to appear in the newspapers and online: 'We'll buy the balance in your bank account'. The balances of accounts held at Toribank and SBSAgro were immediately dubbed 'toriks' and 'agriks'. It turned out that even accounts which had been frozen could sometimes be brought back into play. One way of doing this was to transfer them to one of the banks which were not considered problematic – i.e. they were neither too big nor too small, and had not got caught up in the whole treasury bills fiasco. Savers soon caught on to the fact that even frozen funds could sometimes be returned once enough time had elapsed, although perhaps not necessarily in full, and that if they never came back they could at least be earned once again.

In chronic condition

In 1999 the crisis was stabilized, so to speak. It was an everyday occurrence to see businesses in their death throes. The ones which were able to continue paying salaries were considered to be flourishing. Banks which had once been big names fell into oblivion: Menatep, Oneksim, SBSAgro, Rossisky kredit, Inkombank. The owner of Inkombank, Vladimir Vinogradov, who had fought hard for all the juiciest morsels among the industrial assets and was a veteran of the wars of information, had had problems with his health in the past. Three years later he passed away quietly in his rented apartment in the commuter belt in the south of Moscow, and a number of bankers – his former friends and rivals – chipped in to cover the cost of the funeral.

The most important lesson to take away from that year, as one expert put it at the time, was that "more can be achieved with people than with money." As importers regrouped, Russian manufacturers were growing in confidence and growing their share of the market. The most eye–catching and at the same time paradoxical event of that time was the sudden appearance of Korkunov sweets. Against a backdrop of depression on all sides, a premium–class line of products had suddenly sprung up impudently...and was enjoying considerable success. Some analysts perceived this as some sort of incredibly crafty move, the devilishly clever calculation of a market genius. But the reality was far simpler: as Andrei Korkunov later recalled, he had started work on his factory in Odintsovo before the crisis even began, along with an Italian business partner who jumped ship, leaving the entrepreneur in an extremely difficult position. He was left with two alternatives: drop everything and cut his losses, or ramp up the risk factor dramatically and see the project through. The former soldier went for broke and emerged triumphant.

Another phenomenon that made headlines was the success enjoyed in the Russian market by the Ukrainian vodka Nemiroff, with its two flavours – 'Special' and 'Honey and pepper'. Yakov Gribov, who was in charge of the company at the time, followed Andrei Korkunov's lead: he refused to jump into the mass market and instead put his faith in high–quality products at middle–of–the–road prices. He ended up victorious, too.

On the whole, though, the 'downward trend' prevailed. The supermarkets Seventh Continent and Crossroads gave up their high–falutin' image and brought their prices into line with reality, becoming shops that catered 'for all'. The demands made by highly–skilled professionals also became more realistic: with unemployment high, they had to endure a two–fold or three–fold reduction in their salaries. One event that sticks in the mind was a mock demonstration by financiers and brokers on the Arbat, as they protested against unemployment and delays in the payment of their salaries.

Mobile communications became accessible to the masses, too – it was in the year after the crisis that mobile phones that were affordable to the masses first appeared on the shelves. It did not take long for Russian tourists visiting other countries to grow used to seeing homeless people merrily chatting away on mobile phones.

The Angarsk petrochemicals works found an original way to draw attention to itself, by launching a washing powder called 'Ordinary'. This was a witty attempt to poke fun at Procter & Gamble, whose TV ads for their Ariel washing powder invariably featured comparisons with a certain 'ordinary powder'. Now Angarsk's 'Ordinary' powder could kill two birds with one stone: accuse the rest of the world's manufacturers of making unfair comparisons, causing them loss of earnings, psychological harm and so on; and at the same time they could also piggy–back on someone else's mass advertising campaigns.

The entertainment world got a little bit cheaper, too. Foreign visitors went crazy about Moscow and all that it had to offer – especially the night–life. But in March 1999 the nightclub that had come to define an entire era, the Hungry Duck, was closed down. This extremely popular haven of debauchery inside the Entertainers' Centre was notorious among the authorities but hugely popular among ex–pats and also young women, who on Ladies' Nights were able to enjoy free drinks and were allowed to indulge in a bit of topless – and occasionally bottomless – dancing on the bar.

The club was managed by a Canadian named Doug Steele, who had gone into business with an odd group of Chechen–Kalmyk businessmen – they provided the *krysha*, or protection. Before long Doug had an in–depth knowledge of Russian business: threats, 'peaceful resolutions' which were not so peaceful, and attempted kidnappings and murders became part of his daily routine in business. After the Duck closed down, Doug recalled that four of his initial partners had soon met an untimely demise. The last of these, a Chechen named Roman, died right after arranging a 'peaceful resolution' with Steele. Fearing for his life, Doug took a contingent of Special Forces along to the meeting with him. But the next day a policeman told him he no longer needed to worry, because Roman had... suffered a sudden heart attack.

But whereas the criminals failed in their mission to destroy the business, this task proved well within the powers of the veteran ballerina Olga Lepeshinskaya, who was on the board of the Entertainers' Centre. After the shameless dancing on the bar came up for discussion at the State Duma, she managed to terminate the lease agreement with the club, and the *kryshas* – the Special Forces included – were powerless to do anything about it.

Here are some of the facts and figures which Doug Steele listed in his memoirs as he reflected on what had gone on at the Duck over the years: "8 shots fired in the bar; 5 bullets lodged in the floor, 3 in the ceiling. Over a million pints of beer drunk and more than 1.5 million customers. 256 criminal inquiries made by the police in connection with the club. More than 2000 passports reported lost at the bar. Three bomb threats. One attempt to kidnap the owner, five death threats. More than 250 fights recorded in the bar. More than 40 ambulances called out to tend to customers who had fallen off the bar. One visit to the club by Mrs. Yeltsin, who was accompanied by two Orthodox priests (they refrained from dancing on the bar)."

...And yet, curiously, there was a strange feeling of relief after the crisis. Imagine yourself ditching all your responsibilities, casting off your clothes and shoes and dispensing with the briefcase containing your ID papers and your money – and pressing ahead stark naked.

The default of 1998 gave the Russian economy the deep clean that it needed. The word on the street was that there would at last be an end to excessive salaries, inflated mark–ups and the obsession with imports. And so it proved: imports cleared out of the market for a long time, salaries fell by two or three times and business itself began to change radically, for the better.

II

A POLICY OF INTERFERENCE

7. "THE BIGGEST GEOPOLITICAL CATASTROPHE IN HISTORY." HOW THE USSR BECAME RUSSIA

Halfway to collapse

Russian dictionaries define the word *likhoi* as 'evil' or 'heavy' – in the sense of 'burdensome' – on the one hand, and 'brave', 'hot–headed', 'devil–may–care' and 'adroit' on the other. It would be futile to try to work out which of the two dominated in the 1990s – evil or bravery. For the fact is there was a bit of both. The nineties were wild in every possible sense of the word. And this wildness was displayed right from the outset, and in full measure.

The Soviet Union was creaking at the seams. The 'brotherhood of peoples' was writhing and falling apart. Cracks had appeared in the monolith that the USSR had once been (or had seemed to be), and from these cracks blood, of the most natural kind, was no longer trickling but gushing out.   The first time it had begun to show signs of cracking was back in 1989, in Tblisi. In April of that year, the Republic's leaders failed to take control of a rally attended by many thousands of people, organized by the leaders of the nationalist movement. The rally moved quickly and inexorably from the subject of the conflict in Georgia and

Abkhazia to issues which were openly anti–Soviet and anti–Communist. Troops were sent into the city and the rally was broken up. 16 of those taking part were killed on the spot, and a further three died later of their wounds in hospital.

Not even the commission set up by the Assembly of National Deputies of the USSR, headed by Anatoly Sobchak, was able to establish who had "started it", or who had ordered the troops to break up the rally. The General Secretary of the Supreme Soviet of the USSR and the Chairman of the Praesidium of the SC USSR, Mikhail Gorbachev, refused to accept responsibility for the way events unfolded at the rally, and said that the blame for the loss of life lay entirely with the army. The man who would go on to be the USSR's first (and last) president would later demonstrate this approach to politics – a sort of side–stepping of tough decisions, accompanied by a small amount of scorn – on a number of occasions.

As Valery Boldin, the head of the president of the USSR's administration from 1990–1991, recalled: "Gorbachev loved having other people do things for him. During the planning for the events that took place in Tblisi, Vilnius and Riga, he gave Yazov verbal instructions. Yazov said: "I need an order in writing." But Gorbachev replied: "My word is sufficient."

Before that there was Kazakhstan, Nagorny Karabakh, Pridnestrovie...

In January 1990 the uprisings in Baku began (or rather, continued). It all happened in exactly the same way as it had in Tblisi: the conflict around Karabakh suddenly intensified, and the party in charge in Azerbaijan lost control of the situation in the republic. On January 11, for example, a Soviet troop formation was overthrown in the city of Lenkoran. On January 13 pogroms against Armenians began in Baku, resulting in the deaths of 56 Armenians. They were not brought to an end until January 15.

By that time the Nationalist Front of Azerbaijan (NFA) had taken *de facto* control of most of the Republic, having clearly decided not to wait until the spring elections for the Supreme

Soviet, in which it might well have been able to win a decisive victory, without any blood being spilt.

On January 15, Yevgeny Primakov, who at that time was a member of the Politburo of the CC CPSU, had stated during a meeting with NFA leaders that "the leadership of the country has no plans to announce a state of emergency in Baku." On January 18, while speaking at an NFA rally attended by many thousands of people, he once again denied the "rumours" that troops were going to be deployed in Baku. By the evening of January 19, however, the whole of Azerbaijan's government had left their offices and moved to the headquarters of the North Caucasus Military District.

At midnight, units from the Tula paramilitary division, under the command of Alexander Lebed, the Alpha group and reservists who had been specially conscripted – a total of about 9000 soldiers – entered Baku. As a result of this night–time operation, 137 people in the city died and over 700 were wounded.

The troops opened fire, broke through the picket–lines on Airport Highway and other roads leading into the city, and blockaded the barracks, where the bloodiest battles of all were fought. The following day, notices were put up on the building of the Central Committee: "Down with the Soviet Empire!", "Down with the CPSU!", "The Soviet Army is a fascist army". Numerous signs and leaflets levelled criticism at the head of state, in offensive language. Pictures of him were defaced in public.

Ten years on from the events which came to be known as 'Black January', Mikhail Gorbachev, true to form, accused the NFA of opening fire first, but the USSR's Defence Minister, Dmitry Yazov, who was in personal charge of the operation in Baku (along with the Minister of Internal Affairs, Vladimir Bakatiny), explained the aim of the operation with military precision: "to destroy the structures of the NFA and not to allow the opposition to be victorious.

As for the means by which constitutional order was restored in a country that was falling apart, the General Secretary did not seem to have had any qualms about it. And there was probably no other method that he – or anyone else, for that matter – could have come up with. When Lithuania declared itself an independent republic in March 1990, the authorities chose not to send in the army because they had something else entirely on their minds: the extraordinary III Congress of People's Deputies of the USSR (they would go on to send in the army in 1991). Among the items on the agenda was the cancellation of the "role of the CPSU as director and leader" (the 6th clause of the Constitution of the USSR), the introduction of the position of president of the USSR and, accordingly, the election of one.

The first and the last

One of the instigators of the campaign to abolish the 6th clause of the Constitution of the USSR was Andrei Dmitrievich Sakharov. After being named one of the co–chairmen of the Inter–Regional Deputy Group (the radical wing of the pro–perestroika group, whose other leading figures were Yury Afanasiev, Gavriil Popov, Boris Yeltsin and Viktor Palm), it was Sakharov who insisted that a call for the abolition of the 6th clause should be included in the Inter–Regional Group's manifesto.

The abolition of the 6th clause later became known as 'Deputy Sakharov's amendment'.

At the III Congress the 6th clause was not abolished, but amended: in its new form, in addition to recognising the CPSU, it acknowledged the possibility that "other political parties, as well as professional unions, youth organizations and other charitable organizations and movements with mass popular support" could have a role to play in the way the state was governed."

At the same time, the party–based government managed

to preserve, within the text of the main law, the Communist party's exclusive status as the first and most prominent political organization in the country. Mikhail Gorbachev was elected president of the USSR and remained General Secretary of the Central Committee of the CPSU, which in effect meant that the Communist Party had won the battle for the presidency – without a general election having been held. It is worth noting, however, that one and a half thousand deputies voted against the idea of the roles of president and general secretary being combined – a telling figure.

The collapse of the country continued in the parliamentary sphere as well. The fragile alliance between the Inter–Regional Deputy Group (the IDG), which was referred to at the time as the 'left–wing opposition' (but which would be dismissed as a bunch of 'wishy–washy liberals' today), and the deputies from the republics began to splinter during the voting for the position of Chairman of the Supreme Soviet. This position, which after 1977 was the most senior position in the Soviet Union, became something akin to the position of speaker in parliament after the III Congress. It was held by Anatoly Lukyanov, while the more authoritative figures from the IDG, who had already been around for some time, suffered a dramatic loss in popularity after changing their minds so quickly on the issue of how the president should be elected. New leaders, with youth and enthusiasm on their side, came to the forefront: whereas Anatoly Sobchak won just 77 votes, Konstantin Lubenchenko secured 377.

As for the issue of Lithuania in effect breaking away from the USSR, Mikhail Gorbachev declared in his speech at the congress that he was categorically against any bilateral negotiations with Lithuania as a sovereign foreign state, and the congress adopted a decree declaring the decision of the Supreme Soviet of Lithuania illegal. But less than a month later, when, as president of the USSR, he hosted Endel Lippmaa, the Estonian 'minister without portfolio' (the Supreme Soviet of the Estonian Soviet Socialist Republic had declared the Estonian Republic reinstated on March 30) – Mikhail Gorbachev had far more to say on the matter. Mr Lippmaa interpreted what he heard from Mr Gorbachev as: "When you start seeing inter–state conflicts, and presidential governance is introduced – then you'll find out what it means to be an occupied state."

Whether by design or by accident, Mikhail Gorbachev had demonstrated that presidential power was turning into a powerful instrument for managing the system, capable of provoking outbursts of national and political passion but unable to remove the causes of them. In order for some other form of power to exist, which could be constructive in some small degree at least, and act as a uniting force, trust was absolutely essential for the man in power. And as the magazine 'Power' observed, commenting on the III Congress of People's Deputies, "neither the procedure nor the atmosphere of the presidential elections at the congress inspired this kind of trust."

The Union continued to fall apart. The Republics openly protested against what the president of Kazakhstan, Nazarbayev, referred to as the "crazy policy of the centre", and rumours about a military coup could be heard on a daily basis. The "parade of sovereign states" was gaining momentum. Georgia declared its independence in April. Latvia and Estonia followed suit in May. In June it was the turn of Uzbekistan and Moldova. The stand–off between the Russian leadership and the Soviet leadership intensified. On August 6th, 1990, the head of the Supreme Soviet of the RSFSR, Boris Yeltsin, declared, in Ufa: "Take as much sovereignty as you can swallow." Less than a month before this he left the CPSU.

The central authorities continued to behave like an instrument of power, offering "discipline and order" as a panacea and making sure that the army and the secret police got increasingly involved in the political and economic life of the country. The battle in the Fergana Valley between the Uzbeks and the Kyrgyz in the first few days of June could only be brought to a halt by bringing in Armenian units. According to an investigative group from the office of the public procurator of the USSR, approximately 300 people died in the 'Osh riots'. Unofficial sources put the death toll far higher.

Gorbachev, who had spent his whole life governing amorphous 'masses', now had to try and find his place in the civil society that was emerging. At the same time, he was himself gradually turning into a burden for all the players in the political game: the 'leftists' thought that from now on he was going to stand firmly in the way of all liberal reforms; as for those on the right, the only use he had in their eyes was as a smokescreen for the "restoration of order": by no means was he their recognised leader for the future.

Describing the relations between Gorbachev and the political authorities in the early 1990s, Maksim Sokolov, a columnist at the newspaper *Vlast*, observed that "prior to the summer of 1990, both the leftists and Gorbachev had a common goal: to take party–based power out of the picture. The XXVIII Congress of the CPSU, to all intents and purposes, had buried the former CPSU, and the trough of power had been transferred to the coalition between the military and the secret police, which attempted to halt the accelerating collapse with an iron first and – in the long–run – planned to use this self–same iron fist to make great technological advances which would restore to the country its former status as a superpower.

The concessions Gorbachev made to the conservatives (his refusal to accept the '500 days' programme, the departures of Bakatin and Shevardnadze, a harsher stance with regard to the republics, the *de facto* presidential veto imposed on Russian agricultural reforms) only served to whet the appetite of those in favour of "core values".

The centrism that the president of the USSR was attempting to display began to look more and more like a policy of "sitting on the fence". Gorbachev's amorphous position was in line with the amorphous state of society at the time, as has been well–documented. In 1990 proto–parties (including 'Union' and 'Democratic Russia') began to take shape with incredible speed, as did proto–states (the former Republics in the Union), and various classes in society began to take a harsher line with regard to their own interests (trade and industry, the military, the working classes, agricultural labourers etc.); as for Gorbachev's position, it was best described as the complete absence of a position. And yet the proposal by the CPSU deputy Sazha Umalatova that a vote of no confidence in the president be held was supported by just 426 deputies at the IV congress. None of the political powers were able to put forward a leader with the 'technical know–how', administrative qualifications, tactical artistry or intuition that Gorbachev had. Gorbachev remained the only politician who was seen by both the administration and the liberals as to some extent "one of us".

Some people saw things differently, it must be said. During a demonstration on Red Square in November to mark the anniversary of the October Revolution, Aleksandr Shmonov, a locksmith from Leningrad, attempted to assassinate Gorbachev. His attempt failed, but it was clear that Shmonov's actions reflected the way many people in society felt. As journalist Vladimir Gendlin recalled: "As she poured me some vodka to go with my cabbage soup, my grandmother uttered her verdict: "Gorbachev ought to be shot! Yeltsin ought to be shot! Gaidar ought to be shot!"

Towards the end of 1990 Gorbachev appointed Gennady Yanayev, an activist from the youth professional union, vice-president. The new vice–president kept the deputies amused with his risqué jokes. As he told the congress: "I've got all the afflictions that real men suffer from," the second most powerful man in the country parried questions about current policies from politicians and reporters. And the young contender's next *bon mot*, pronounced with the gusto of a junior member of the Komsomol, delighted the public even more: "I certainly intend to turn my attentions to women's issues – as long as my wife doesn't mind too much, of course." At long last they were going to have a *bona fide* good–time Charlie, to make up for those gloomy moralists Rasputin and Gubenko.

The Russian parliament led by Boris Yeltsin stepped out of line again, as it could be relied upon to do: yet again it ceased to provide funding for the Union of Soviet Socialist Republics. In response to this *Kommersant*, with no small degree of irony, commented that from now on "the union's minister of finance, Valentin Pavlov, would find it easier to explain to the deputies where all the budget finances were going. Under the previous system, in which all the money went towards the centre, no–one – not even the deputies in the Union's parliament – had been able to get full and accurate information from Pavlov about those 'black holes' in the budget."

The country was in a gloomy mood as it saw in the New Year, 1991. There was hardly anyone left who held out much hope for the future: the liberals were afraid of having "order restored", whilst those in favour of tough power feared "anarchy and a separatist orgy", not to mention the "rejection of socialist values". The 'progressives' feared revenge on the part of the Communists, whilst their opponents worried about a conspiracy between the Jews and the masons and an American invasion. This public feeling found its expression in demonstrations attended by hundreds of thousands of people, and it was impossible to walk around the centre of Moscow due to the police cordons and endless processions.

Gorbachev's high command, after ridding itself of the liberals and the waverers, decided that the empire must be saved at any cost (with the possible exception of mass killings of innocent people). The tools required to do this were created, in the form of laws governing any potential referendum, a set of emergency presidential powers and a strengthening of domestic forces by means of the transfer to them of four army divisions.

One possible outcome predicted by *Vlast* magazine was that a form of 'barracks capitalism' might be created, in which relatively free entrepreneurial activity would be combined with high taxes, tough sanctions for failures to abide by contractual obligations and 'control of the relationship between labour and consumption'. All this combined, of course, with limits on political freedoms and 'the strong arm of power'. We shall leave it to readers to make up their own minds as to the extent to which this prediction came true in 1991, and the extent to which it is true today.

But one thing's for sure: there was never a dull moment. Right from the start of the year there were some gripping TV shows on the box: 'Desert Storm'; the storming of the television centre in Vilnius, led by the future separatist Aslan Maskhadov; Prince Narodom Sianuk's return to Cambodia; *The rich cry too*; the war in South Ossetia; a programme made by St Petersburg TV which claimed that Lenin had been a mushroom; Winnie Mandela's conviction for kidnapping and the subsequent reforms in South Africa; the intervention by Soviet troops in the Nagorno–Karabakh War; Zviad Gamsakhurdia's presidency and his war against the Mkhedrioni, with their dark glasses – a group founded by the writer, director and 'thief in law' Jaba Ioseliani; Dzhokhar Dudayev's election as president of Ichkeria; Pridnestrovie's declaration of independence and all manner of other declarations, referenda and independences...

The final attempt to save the Union was the referendum held in March. The citizens of the republics which agreed to hold the referendum (it had been completely ignored by the Baltic Republics, Georgia, Armenia and Moldova) were asked the following question: "Do you consider it essential that the Union of Soviet Socialist Republics be preserved as a modernized federation of sovereign republics of equal standing, in which the rights and freedoms of people of all nationalities are guaranteed?" – that was how the Supreme Soviet decided to phrase the question. But even in the republics in which the referendum was held, the question was rephrased, or else additional questions were added. In Kazakhstan, for example, people were asked to vote for 'A union of sovereign states'. The people of the RSFSR voted on whether the post of president of the RSFSR should be brought in. So for these people the referendum had an impact on the latest round of the confrontation between Gorbachev and Yeltsin, too.

This 'battle of the titans' ended with the two men neck and neck: 71% voted for Gorbachev (the percentage of the population who voted to keep the USSR) and 70% for Yeltsin (the percentage who voted in favour of the new post being established in Russia). This forced the rivals to step up to a whole new level of Socialist competition, which grew into a pre–election campaign before people's very eyes. In other words, the great masses of the population, to whom the leaders had been forced to appeal, had demonstrated a high degree of unanimity in their good intentions: the majority had expressed their support both for the Union and for Russia. The stalemate continued.

Despite the fact that over 75% of the people of the Soviet Union had voted in favour of the Union being preserved, those in power were not encouraging people to be under any illusions. As Konstantin Lubenchenko, the deputy chairman of the Legislative Committee of the Supreme Soviet of the USSR, put it: "When you have 70 million people out of a total electorate of 182 million against the union, and six federal subjects refusing to recognise the referendum – there's no way you can call that a victory."

The confrontation between Yeltsin and Gorbachev ended, as one might have expected, with troops being sent into Moscow. To begin with, 29 people's deputies of the RSFSR complained to the president of the USSR about the people of Moscow (for supporting Boris Yeltsin) and demanded that they be protected from them. Their complaint did not fall on deaf ears: On March 27, 1991, the premier, Pavlov, effectively introduced a state of siege in Moscow and said to the people: "Are we really going to put the people on the edge of a precipice beyond which there may be disasters that none of us can predict?" Troops were sent into the city, and the pro–Yeltsin demonstration planned by the democrats was outlawed. The Congress of people's deputies of the RSFSR, which had opened on March 28, was cancelled by a directive from the Union cabinet office. The demonstration, which was attended by 100,000 people, including deputies in the first few rows, began.

Soldiers and protesters stood side by side, peacefully. A group of jazz musicians played a rag–time tune beside the TsUM shopping centre. Some security police, who were standing nearby, listened to the music, ice cream cones in their hands. It was as if the officers and soldiers were themselves at a loss as to why there was any need for them to be out on the streets. Some cadets from the air force school, in response to a journalist who asked: "What are you doing here?" answered gloomily: "We're flying high." Jokes about Gorbachev and Pavlov did the rounds, causing merriment among both the demonstrators and the troops in equal measure.

Ultimately, it was abundantly clear what was going on. The soldiers were not there to maintain order or protect law–abiding citizens. They were there with the specific objective of protecting the president, who had been left behind in the empty circle of the Garden Ring, from the people in the city. In the end it was quite awkward...

On the day before the demonstration, Mikhail Gorbachev had declared, on television: "If any violence breaks out, it will signify my political death." The day passed off without any violence, thank goodness, and there was no political death. Instead there was a clinical death in the political arena. On March 29 the city centre began to live a moribund existence, which was essentially caused by the lack of any meaningful opportunities whatsoever to have any effect on what happened in politics. As it transpired, on March 28 a chain of military lorries clearly marked out the borders of Gorbachev's territory: the Boulevard Ring in Moscow. And if there was anyone who cottoned on to the fact that March was merely a dress rehearsal for August, they chose not to let on.

Mikhail Gorbachev was busy with his 'Novo–oragarevsky process' – the preparations for a new agreement on union, which both prolonged the death throes somewhat, and at the same time brought the end within sight. In the summer Boris Yeltsin became president of Russia, whilst Gavriil Popov and Anatoly Sobchak were elected mayors of Moscow and Leningrad. *Soviet Russia* published an open letter entitled *To the people*, calling on them to "halt the domino effect of the mortal collapse of the state, its economy, its identity, so as to enable the strengthening of Soviet power, and the transformation of it into a governing power which genuinely represents the people, rather than a feeding–trough for the grasping nouveaux riches, prepared to sell anything and everything for the sake of their insatiable appetites; so as not to allow the fire of inter–ethnic hatred and civil war to break out." Among the signatories were Lyudmila Zykina and Gennady Zyuganov, Alexander Prokhanov and Valentin Varennikov, Valentin Rasputin and Yury Bondarev...

"You're all pricks, the lot of you!"

The putsch began on August 18, and by the morning of August 21 it had turned into a hopeless parody of a *coup d'etat*. Those involved had provided more evidence of the 'first law of treason': a conspiracy must be successful in its first three hours, else it is destined to fail.

According to statements released by the information agencies, Saddam Hussein, on hearing of the putsch in Moscow, described it as a "well executed affair". According to the people's deputy of the RSFSR, Vladimir Lysenko, on the evening of August 18 Gorbachev ended a conversation with Kryuchkov, Baklanov and General Varennikov with the line: "You're all pricks, the lot of you!" Saddam Hussein had been wrong. Gorbachev, as it turned out, had been right.

The tanks entered the city on the morning of the 19th. And they simply stayed there in the streets. It transpired that the tank drivers under the command of General Lebed, who had surrounded the White House, had no intention of killing anyone at all. The telephones and the international lines continued to work as normal. No arrests were made. No curfew was declared, either: cars rushed around the city all night long, as usual, and no–one made much of an effort to prevent anyone going about their business. There were no military patrols.

Groups of citizens had gathered in Moscow, including some *agents provocateurs* from the KGB. They either encouraged people to smash in shop–windows or demonstrated in favour of those behind the putsch. But as it turned out there was a surprisingly large number of law–abiding, optimistic people, given that the country was so ill–at–ease, who simply went to the White House and set up barricades.

Vladimir Gendlin, a journalist at *Kommersant*, recalled that on the critical night of August 19th–20th the journalist Alexander Politkovsky used a loud–hailer to tell those assembled about the brutal actions of a group of soldiers who had killed people defending the tunnel in Smolensk Square. "I remember that people were dipping their handkerchiefs in puddles in case of gas attacks, and were taking bets on who would come to storm our offices – 'Alfa' or 'Vympel'. At that point everyone thought that what they were doing was for the best, because no–one wanted to live the way we had been living before. People longed for *liberté, egalité, fraternité*. It was probably on August 20th that it became clear that we weren't going to be stormed, and that the putsch had failed, and it must be said we felt a certain sense of romanticism and hope...One of my friends who had stood outside the White House became a deputy in the State Duma ten years later. And the first thing he did was call me and request that a female colleague of mine at *Kommersant* stop writing bad things about his region – "or else it'll come to a head..."

Nowadays the people who defended the White House, or some of them at least, recall these events – just as Vladimir Gendlin did – with a mixture of healthy cynicism and a certain sense of irritation, and have become resigned to the nickname 'YEBelDoSy' (Yeltsin – *Bely Dom* (the White House) – *Svoboda* ('freedom')). The man who coined this nickname has long been forgotten, as have twenty–three year–old Dmitry Komar, twenty–eight year–old Ilya Krichevsky and thirty–seven year–old Vladimir Usov, who for a while were considered heroes. The circumstances of their death can be interpreted equally as either heroism or as screaming incompetence, a farce that suffered from poor stage direction and even worse acting. These were the words of another journalist – Mikhail Kamensky – in his live report as the events unfolded: "A group of people managed to throw a tarpaulin over the safety glass of the armoured tanks, so that the crew were unsighted. Their task was made more difficult by a blonde woman who was clearly under the influence of alcohol, and who kept running around the vehicle, trying to throw herself under its caterpillar tracks. At one point, when she was standing directly behind the vehicle, it suddenly reversed, and the woman stepped towards it with clear suicidal intent.

A man who was standing nearby pushed her out of harm's way, tripped and was himself crushed by the caterpillar tracks; the vehicle moved forwards and then reversed again, crushing him again. The only part of him that was left intact was his legs, which the police took away once the fighting was over..."

In their first insurrection the men behind the putsch made no secret of their attachment to the ideals of a great empire – and it was this, it would seem, that was to prove their downfall. Their incantations about the "unity of the Fatherland" were not mere demagoguery (which is without question an essential component of any putsch): they also reflected the conspirators' genuine belief that such a thing as a unified empire actually existed in reality. Judging by the reaction of Marshall Yazov, at least, who exclaimed, on being arrested: "What? What's this all about?" the conspirators were entirely unaware that what they had done amounted to a betrayal of the state: for seventy years acts such as these had been referred to as a change of leadership in the USSR.

Clearly it was their belief in the importance of classical templates that had induced the instigators of the putsch to make a glaring error: after successfully isolating Gorbachev and sending a series of messages and proclamations, they proceeded to rest on their laurels. The senior authorities in Russia remained untouched, the Government building of the RSFSR was not seized, and Yeltsin had earned himself some precious breathing space.

By the night of August 20–21 it had become clear that the members of the State Committee on the State of Emergency (SCSE) were mainly concerned with how to avoid the criminal sanctions set out in article 64 of the Criminal Code of the RSFSR: Yanayev was "puffing and wheezing", Yazov either tendered his resignation or allowed rumours to that effect to circulate, and the others said nothing. The final stage – the flight of the members of the SCSE – not only turned these men themselves into a 'final warning' of sorts, but also dramatically altered the positions of the individuals who did not play a full part in events: Pugo's deputy Boris Gromov, the head of the General Staff Mikhail Moiseev, and to some extent even the Chairman of the Supreme Soviet of the USSR, Anatoly Lukyanov. They were also united by the fact that they all "came back from their holidays and knew absolutely nothing", and therefore had no stains on their reputations.

So Gorbachev had every right to refer to these people, in that expressive manner of his, as "the saviours of the state".

He found that he had even more reason for doing so after his return to Moscow. The president of the USSR had gone from being in the hands of Bolshevik revolutionaries to being in the hands of anti–Bolshevik revolutionaries. He had nobody on whom he could rely. As early as August 22 Gorbachev attempted to stop the avalanche somehow, but by the 23rd, at a meeting with Russian deputies, realising that it would be no good trying to swim against the tide, he effectively gave his consent to the new coup – a genuine one this time – that was taking place before his very eyes, offering the sole proviso that "everything should be kept strictly above board". There followed concession after concession: on the evening of the 24th Gorbachev dismissed the Union's cabinet of ministers and declined to accept the post of General Secretary of the CPSU, while the Central Committee of the CPSU declared its own disbandment. The CC's building in Staraya Ploshchad was sealed off, property that belonged to the party was nationalized and the KGB building was emasculated: the statue of 'Iron Felix' outside the Lubyanka was taken down. The "mind, honour and conscience of our age" had decided to risk everything – and had lost. Perestroika had come to an end, and an age of 'politics minus the fools' had begun.

According to surveys conducted by the 'Sociological opinion' foundation in 2001, 61% of respondents were unable to name any of the members of the SCSE. Only 16% could remember at least one name; 4% were able to name the leader of the putsch, Gennady Yanayev. For some time the public was intrigued by the thought that Gorbachev himself might have been behind the attempted putsch. The members of the SCSE maintain that he not only initiated it himself, but that he was also trying to secure political capital for himself, regardless of how events unfolded.

As Valery Boldin recalled: "Sensing that he was losing one of the supports that were propping him up, in early 1990 Gorbachev invited a group of members of the Politburo and the Security Council to his office – all those who were later members of the SCSE (among them were Kryuchkov, Yazov and Baklanov) – and raised the issue of introducing a state of emergency...In the end Gorbachev realised that Yeltsin's separate negotiations with the leaders of the republics would lead to him being cut off from power once and for all, and he set the wheels in motion so that the intelligence agencies would announce a state of emergency."

This is what Oleg Baklanov, who in August 1991 had been Secretary of the CC of the CPSU and deputy chairman of the USSR's Defence Council, had to say on the matter: "As regards the events of that August specifically, the need to create the SCSE arose after one of the newspapers printed material on either August 17 or 18 from the Novo–ogarevsk camp, where, essentially, Gorbachev, Yeltsin *et al* drew up the document which confirmed that the Soviet Union was being disbanded. Moreover, Gorbachev was willing to sign it as early as the 21st...In the end there was a fairly coarse exchange (at the presidential dacha in Foros), after which Gorbachev said: "Very well. Take action yourselves." He was effectively giving his 'seal of approval'..."

The regional leaders behaved in different ways during the putsch, as might have been expected. Some of the republics condemned the actions of its instigators and refused to obey their orders in the first few hours, whilst others preferred to play a waiting game and see what happened. Still others (initially at least) supported the SCSE. Or rather, as far as they were concerned no coup ever took place. All the businesses, organizations and institutions functioned as normal, and the leaders of the republics restricted themselves to calling for discipline and order. They carried out all the decrees issued by the SCSE, although not all of them officially recognized it.

The putsch was broken up by the signing of a new Union agreement, and the republics began, one after another, to declare that they were leaving the Union: on August 20 – Estonia, on the 21st – Latvia, on the 24th – Ukraine, on the 27th – Moldova, and then Azerbaijan, Uzbekistan and Kyrgizia, and in the autumn the remaining republics. Not one of them had carried out all of the procedures prescribed by the law of the USSR dated April 3, 1990 'On the procedure for deciding issues related to the withdrawal of a Republic in the Union from the USSR'.

And on September 5, 1991, the Congress of people's deputies effectively declared its own disbandment, thereby bringing an end to the USSR's seventy–plus years of existence. As he disbanded the congress once and for all, Gorbachev had his photo taken alongside members of the Inter–regional Group of Deputies, for old time's sake.

Anatoly Sobchak even suggested, on the spur of the moment, that the body of V.I. Ulyanov–Lenin be buried, but the ceremony was postponed: the remains of V.I. Ulyanov–Lenin could wait, whereas the remains of the former Union of Soviet Socialist Republics were in rather more urgent need of attention. "We find ourselves in an unforeseen situation" – that was Gorbachev's take on all these goings–on. The tactical calculations made by those who drew up the declaration on the break–up of the Union, which was read out by the president of Kazakhstan, Nazarbayev, were founded on three points.

Firstly, a state of emergency must be declared in the assembly immediately. There was a gloomy, 'do or die' decisiveness etched on Gorbachev's face, which is entirely understandable: the president and the provincial princes were seriously concerned that the assembly, which was composed mainly of people who had lost everything over the last two weeks, would resort to desperate measures, and that the team of '10 + 1' would decide to strike first.

Secondly, it should be made clear that things were not as awful as it might seem, and that good behaviour would not go unrewarded. It was decided that the deputies would be able to keep their status (i.e. sinecures and the immunity from prosecution) up until 1994.

Thirdly, at the decisive moment (on the morning of September 5th), Gorbachev threatened to walk out of the congress and leave it alone with a country in turmoil. Everyone got the hint, and the vote passed off without a hitch. By 13.00 the congress had given up its powers to the State Council and the new Supreme Soviet, which had not yet been formed. Gorbachev headed off to have his photo taken with the IDG, after rejecting complaints from those assembled, who wanted the meeting to last a little longer:

"You intervened during a period of transition! That was before the new era; the new era has now arrived."

It was an era that was to become known for expropriation. In August 1991, a comissar from the democratic powers in the RSFSR walked into the office of the chairman of the State Bank of the USSR on Neglinnaya Street and demanded the keys to the repository. Viktor Geraschenko didn't have any such keys in his possession – all he had was the key to a safe containing some personal belongings, and Viktor Vladimirovich decided against giving the commissar *that* key: instead, he walked out, and at that moment the idea that one year later those self–same democratic authorities would ask him to return to his old office in Neglinnaya Street was no doubt the furthest thing from his mind: somehow it just wasn't working out without Geraschenko.

What happened next has been fairly well documented. On 8th December, 1991, the heads of state of Belarus, Russia and Ukraine acknowledged, in the Belovezhskaya Pushcha National Park, that the days of the USSR were over, declared that it was out of the question for a Union of Soviet States to be formed and signed an Agreement on the establishment of the Commonwealth of Independent States (CIS). The regrets expressed later by Boris Yeltsin and Leonid Kravchuk (in 1996 and 2007, respectively) came far too late in the day to alter any of this.

And to many people it was as though some sort of new life was beginning. The new protagonists of the stories in the newspapers and on the TV looked like more than mere protagonists: they literally looked like new life–forms.

Everything that has fed our existence over the last 20 years, and that feeds our existence today, was contained within that one year, 1991. And it was not just about the SCSE and the collapse of the USSR. The Internet and the Linux operating system were invented that year. The USA's first attempts to take on Saddam Hussein (operation 'Desert Storm') began in 1991, too. It was in 1991 that Bill Clinton declared his intention to run for president of the USA. The regional conflicts that are still simmering today either began in 1991 or reached their climax that year: South Ossetia, Nagorno–Karabakh, Pridnestrovie, Chechnya. Even the 'vertical system of power' and 'tandemocracy' – for what is the institute of the vice–presidency, if not an attempt to create a tandem governing the country? – have their origins in that particular year. The collapse of Yugoslavia began at that time as well. So did the end of apartheid in South Africa.

And at the same time the old Communist *nomenklatura* was replaced by those whose task was to become the new *nomenklatura* – whether they liked it or not.

The Stalinist–democrat

Anatoly Sobchak, a democrat in the Gorbachev mould and a man who denounced totalitarianism with a passion, declared, a year before his death, that in his opinion Russia needed a new Stalin, someone who would be less bloodthirsty but equally stern and uncompromising. He had clearly come to the conclusion, over the preceding few years, that democracy had its downsides.

Sobchak's political star had risen in 1989, when he was elected a national deputy of the USSR. Rumour had it that his friendship with Mikhail Gorbachev, which went back a long way, had played a considerable part in this. In the 1960s Sobchak was a member of the Stavropolsk Regional College of Advocates.

The first cohort of democrats marched to power defiantly and without a moment's hesitation, intoxicated by the incredible good fortune that had come their way. Sobchak spent just two years as a deputy before leaving on a practical assignment: his task was to restore Leningrad to its former glory. After a hands–down victory in the mayoral elections (he secured 66.25% of the vote), he decided to rechristen the city with its historic name, St Petersburg. This would go down as one of his biggest achievements in Russia's Northern capital. Sobchak backed

Gorbachev in August 1991 and Yeltsin in October 1993. In the critical days of the Russian putsches he managed to maintain his grip on power in the city. After the uprising in October he became one of the main authors of the new Russian Constitution.

But after 1993, relations between Sobchak and the Kremlin gradually began to sour. The mayor of St Petersburg failed to heed the advice of his counterpart in Moscow, Gavriil Popov, who not only gave up the post of mayor of the capital of his own accord, but also tried to persuade Sobchak to do likewise.

As for Sobchak, those who were involved in the events of that time characterize him as being too independent and self–assured, and add that he was rather too fond of the high life. He liked the fact that he was always on the TV. He loved to host prominent figures from the West in the city. He invited Rostropovich and Vishnevsky for tea, and made sure the TV cameras were on hand to capture the moment. As one of Sobchak's colleagues in the democratic movement remarked acerbically, "he tried to come across as some sort of Danton among the reformers". For this reason Sobchak was unpopular among civil servants both in St Petersburg and in Moscow.

When the presidential elections drew nearer, the Kremlin, quite naturally, began to suspect the mayor of St Petersburg of having designs on the presidency. Sobchak's enemies used this to their advantage with considerable skill: an opposition was formed in his mould which received active backing from Moscow (specifically Yury Luzhkov and Oleg Soskovets, who was still an influential figure). Sobchak refused to admit defeat until the very last moment. But lose he did – following the sort of democratic elections for which he had himself campaigned ever since 1989.

And it was immediately after this that Sobchak began to be hounded openly. St Petersburg's former mayor was forced to flee to France, in fear of reprisals. It was whilst he was there, in Paris, that he took time out to reflect on Stalin. In the spring of 1999 he told 'Gazeta.ru': "Sad to say, but Russia needs that sort of man. Someone less bloodthirsty but equally stern and uncompromising, who would be able to get the people working again."

After returning from Paris and losing out in the elections for the State Duma, Sobchak refused to give up his desire to return to the political scene in Russia in a leading role. He was appointed Vladimir Putin's authorized representative in St Petersburg, and took charge of the Political Consultation Board for democratic parties and movements.

Sobchak was probably hoping that under Putin's presidency he would be able to pull himself out of the political mire into which many of the first wave of democrats had fallen. He did not live to see this ambition become a reality. On February 20, 2000, during a pre–election visit to the Kaliningrad Region (he made the journey as one of Vladimir Putin's authorized spokespeople), Anatoly Alexandrovich Sobchak died.

The capitalist governor

Konstantin Titov was as influential a figure in Samara as Sobchak had been in St Petersburg. Under his guidance the region became one of the most successful in the country, whilst he himself became one of Russia's most famous governors.

In November 1989, when the city was still known as Kuibishev, people were preparing to elect the chair of the city's Council of people's deputies. Several of the democrats, who were beginning to be a force to be reckoned with, had put themselves forward for the role, but the city committee of the CPSU was having problems with its candidates. Demonstrations were organized in Kuibyshev by the public, who were inclined towards democracy, on almost a weekly basis, and neither the regional committee nor the city committee could do anything to stop them. Given this backdrop, putting forward a poor candidate with a party membership card in his pocket would be tantamount to suicide.

According to witnesses and those who were directly involved in what took place, it was a head of division on the city committee of the CPSU, Olga Galtsova, who had the idea of putting forward Konstantin Titov as the communists' candidate.

It was an inspired move: Titov was a communist, but he had reached the stage of standing to be a deputy not via the party list but from his position as a laboratory head at the Kuibishev Institute of Aviation. Unlike the tongue–tied party functionaries, he was an eloquent and animated speaker, and never bothered with notes. All of this meant that Kostya, as Titov was referred to by his rivals and subordinates, both at the time and in later years, when he was not present – was the very man to take the fight to the democrats in the city council. There was another important factor too, and it proved decisive: Kostya himself made no objection. He was unable to "take the higher ground" at the first attempt, however, although the CPSU city committee's candidate secured more votes than anyone else. A second round was required, prior to which Olga Galtsova managed to persuade one of the democratic candidates to send his votes Kostya's way.

The events of August 1991 were to play a decisive role in Titov's career. Rumour had it that for the first two days of the putsch the chairman of the Samara State Council was at his dacha, and was unwell. However that may be, a different person appeared before the public at the time: the chairman of the Kuibishev Regional Council and Executive Committee, Viktor Tarkhov. According to his version of events, he had set himself the task of maintaining law and order in the region. It was certainly no easy task, especially given that the troops in the Volga military region were under the command of general Makashov, a well–known figure who was even alleged to have ordered armoured tanks to be taken onto the streets. But that never happened. On August 21 it suddenly transpired that two letters had been delivered to Boris Yeltsin, who by then had practically secured victory, allegedly signed by the chairman of the city council, Titov. One contained a detailed description of

Tarkhov's actions during the putsch, whilst the other contained a few words of encouragement from Boris Yeltsin. It is said, moreover, that the second letter was dated August 19.

The response was not slow in coming: on August 31, under a directive sent by Boris Yeltsin, Konstantin Titov was appointed head of the administration of the Samara Region, and Viktor Tarkhov was relieved of his duties as chair of the Executive Committee. He was to stay on as head of the regional council right up until the end of 1992, and would never forget the 'surprise' he had been served up during the putsch.

At that stage, in order to prop up the regional budgets in some shape or form, the federal authorities had brought in a policy of so–called territorial orders. The governors were permitted to sell as much as 10% of the total output produced by local businesses in the region's best interests. For the Samara Region, which boasted the Volga automobile plant and an oil industry – and these sectors accounted, in total, for as much as 78% of the income in the regional budget – Klondike was precisely this sort of solution.

In order to sell products produced as part of the territorial order, the Samara Trade House (STH) was founded in the region, headed by a graduate of the Kuibyshev Aviation Institute, Lev Khasis (who until recently was the chairman of the board of directors at the X5 Retail Group N.V.). The system that was put in place was ingeniously simple: the STH would receive a consignment of cars from the AvtoVAZ at the government rate and would sell them at the market rate via the trade exchange. This business arrangement proved incredibly profitable. By way of example, the cost of a 'Number 9' manufactured by VAZ at the time was 27,000 roubles, but on the free market such a car could easily fetch 240,000.

It was not that Titov was particularly zealous in the way he directed all the processes taking place in the region. He simply put the right market tools in place, and stood back to allow entrepreneurial activity to develop. For example, in one of the leaner years in the Volga Region, when the heads of the neighbouring regions had shut off their borders to prevent manufacturers exporting bread to other regions, Titov simply increased the purchase prices. In the end the Samara Region was left in a strong position thanks to these market mechanisms, filling up its grain elevators with produce from other regions.

In the mid–1990s several ambitious agricultural and industrial projects commenced at the same time in the Samara Region, once again at the governor's instigation (although it is said that certain closely associated commercial structures with vested interests also played a supporting role). Titov's political opponents maintain that all these projects were primarily aimed at lining the governor's own pockets and those of his close associates, but for all that the Samara Region in the 1990s was consistently in the top three or five in most ratings of the Federation's subjects, demonstrating the highest rates of growth in terms of socio–economic development.

Things would have continued in the same vein if only Konstantin Titov had stuck exclusively to the recommendations of Milton Friedman and the other famous economists whom he loved to quote in the early stages of his administrative career. But the governor of Samara was a politician as well as an economist.

He could not help but make a bid for the highest position of all. The entire logic behind the development of Titov's policy prior to that point dictated that he do so. The overwhelming majority of the governors appointed during Yeltsin's tenure were 'multi–party men': during the 1990s they changed parties and movements several times, as they bid to become the party of power. But Titov stole a march on many of them in this regard, too. He was a member of the Association in Support of Reform (the ASR), 'Demvybory Rossii' and the NDR. Later he had his own 'Voice of Russia', which merged into the SPS, the Party of Social Democracy, which became part of the Social democratic party, and – only later – United Russia.

But whereas in the early days membership of one or other of the parties of power was the standard approach, in the late 1990s, when, following Viktor Chernomyrdin's retirement from the post of prime minister, 'Our house is Russia' slowly began to go under, Titov set up his own party. The split with Chernomyrdin, who was replaced in the party by Titov, did not pass off without incident. In the post–default September 1998 he spoke at the Council of the Federation against the recommendation that the Duma confirm Viktor Chernomyrdin in the post of prime minister, saying something along the lines of "we're fed up with Chernomyrdin and those bald patches of his." At that time Chernomyrdin rebuked his former deputy in public, saying that his – Chernomyrdin's – high temples looked as they did because "you [Titov – Ed.] did such a good job of licking them clean."

There are plenty of people who remember this particular story in Samara. But politics is politics, and the governor of Samara survived this too, and emerged into calmer waters. Moreover Boris Yeltsin favoured him, and Titov's personal political views (at that time, at least) were considered quite liberal. The association 'Voice of Russia', which had been created by the governor, was successfully transferred to a position of leadership in the Union of right–wing powers. It was at that precise moment that Irina Khakamada, Boris Nemtsov and Sergei Kirienko began to be seen increasingly frequently in Samara. The latter, incidentally, said at the time to journalists, off the record: "You've got a good governor, he's a clever man. The only thing is, when you talk to him you get the impression he's standing on a stool."

At those elections, the *Soyuz pravykh sil* (Union of Right–wing Forces) in the Samara Region picked up about 20% of the votes, and clearly inspired by this Konstantin Titov resorted to the most reckless step he had ever taken in his life. He decided to stand for president, in spite of the fact that Boris Yeltsin, in an address about his retirement made on New Year's Eve, had given a clear indication that his successor was to be Vladimir

Putin. This risky initiative on the part of the governor of Samara was not greeted with any real enthusiasm by his political allies from the SPS, or by the governing elite. The leaders of the SPS publicly refused to back Titov, whilst the elite and the local oligarchs simply moved quietly into the shadows, refraining from taking on the honourable duty of sponsoring the governor's new assault on power.

There was no miracle, and the governor of Samara secured about 1.5% of the votes and ended up in a situation that was clearly worse than the one in which he had found himself prior to the presidential campaign.

People in Samara are convinced to this day that if Titov had not stood for president in 2000, Samara, rather than Nizhny Novgorod, would now be the capital of the Volga Federal District.

Stepanych

No gallery of the Russian politicians who, in the 1990s, shaped the country we see today, would be complete without a portrait of Viktor Chernomyrdin.

Nobody can quite put their finger on what exactly it was that Chernomyrdin did to enable Russia to flourish. But many people will forever remember that "*that* prime minister" wore knitted cardigans and loved to play the bayan, ride a jet–ski and drive a combine harvester.

No–one (or hardly anyone) remembers – and it would be very strange if they did – what exactly it was that Viktor Stepanovich Chernomyrdin achieved during his visit to America, where he met the vice–president Al Gore as part of the Gore–Chernomyrdin Commission. But there are plenty of people who remember that once upon a time, on a winter's day in the Yaroslavl Region, the former prime minister of the Russian government killed two bear–cubs and their mother during a hunting expedition.

There is not a single publishing house that would contemplate publishing Chernomyrdin's speeches: they all lost their meaning as soon as the microphone was switched off. But it will be a long time before the country forgets the aphorisms he coined, such as the famous, though hackneyed, "we were hoping for the best, but ended up with the usual."

The country joined him in his calls for the Chechen terrorist Basayev to "raise his voice". Along with Stepanych, who was "in favour not of a bazaar, but of a market", the country found out about the fundamental elements of a capitalist economy. He taught the Russian people about the new economic landscape: "We don't need bankers in Yakutia, we need people who can dig." He let us in on some of the most precious state secrets of all: "We're the government – we're not supposed to think." Like him, there were many who "unfortunately, didn't read books": "if only I had time to read through the documents I have signed". Or who grew accustomed to repeating: "This is all absurd, but I've got no choice but to do it." Something else he said comes to mind, too: "I can't think of an occasion when we've needed something and it hasn't worked out."

In short, he was a hair's breadth from nationwide glory: he would either go on to become president or the butt of many a joke.

Appointed prime minister in 1992, Viktor Chernomyrdin somehow managed to please everyone. Chernomyrdin had no clearly defined political position whatsoever, and he meticulously performed all the essential rituals involved in expressing personal loyalty. For the leftist opposition, attempting to harbour a dislike of Chernomyrdin was simply absurd: the former instructor of the CPSU's Central Committee and Minister in the Union could inspire only admiration on the part of representatives of the left with his various antics. The 'pro–market' (or, if you prefer, pro–Western) groups within the Russian elite had even more reason to see this 'Russian Rockefeller', as the Russian press dubbed Chernomyrdin in 1992, as one of their own.

The course on which Chernomyrdin intended to set Russia was one that he had formed more or less immediately after he was appointed: "The market is exactly the thing I am in favour of. As for the idea that we want to clog up our nation with shop–fronts and thereby save the economy and improve our wealth into the bargain – I don't think that is ever going to happen." In the first two days of his presidency, Chernomyrdin made more promises about his commitment to the market than Gaidar had done in a whole year.

At the same time he always remained a principled conduit for the party line, an ideal executioner, a 'strong manager'. Even the political projects of which he took charge were organized more like projects run by the nomenklatura. The first of these was 'Our home is Russia'.

'Chernomyrdin's party' was christened right from the outset not only as the 'party of power' but also as the 'party of the Fuel and energy complex of Russia'. The premier, naturally, rejected such a restrictive definition, just as he rejected the even more restrictive name by which some people referred to his party: 'Our home is Gazprom'.

He outlined the key tasks more in the manner of a prime minister than a politician: stabilizing people's living standards, a program of measures to tackle inflation (we'll get 1.5–2% growth in prices a month, and the investment will come"), stimulating an increase in national capital, and monitoring the activities of natural monopolies ("that means both ensuring normal competition, and tackling inflation in costs"). "For me, the functions of the state, in its participation in the course of economic processes, are determined by the requirement to resolve these top–priority questions. The forms they take, and the resources put in, are prescribed by Russia's economic life itself."

The elections to the Duma were held on December 17, 1995. And they ended (at least in part) sensationally. In first place, with almost double the number of votes secured by their nearest rival (the LDPR), was the CPRF, which picked up 22.3% of the votes. The NDR could only secure just over 10% of the vote.

But this failure had practically no impact on Chernomyrdin's personal political authority. This authority, which relied on the backing of Boris Yeltsin, among others, enabled Chernomyrdin to win back the Duma with ease in the summer of 1995, when the deputies decided to hold a vote of no confidence in him. Boris Yeltsin chose to ignore the move by the Duma members altogether, but Viktor Chernomyrdin opted for a different tack. By posing the question of confidence in the government in the lower chamber the very next day after the vote of no confidence had been announced, the premier wrested back the initiative from the Duma. The deputies had 10 days in which to make up their minds.

By voting to express confidence in the government immediately after merciless criticism of the direction he had chosen and the declaration of a vote of no confidence, the deputies would have been displaying a complete lack of principle, which they would never be able to live down. By confirming their verdict, the people's elected representatives saved face to a certain extent, but found themselves in an extremely deep political hole: a vote of no confidence in the government would mean the dissolution of the Duma.

The idea of giving the deputies a Hobson's choice such as this was the brainchild of the deputy prime minister Sergei Shakhrayu. As a result, the deputies' victory, much to their chagrin, was quickly replaced by the prospect, for parliament, of an impending, destructive, shattering and above all humiliating defeat.

Viktor Chernomyrdin demonstrated his personal loyalty to Boris Yeltsin in 1996, when he declined to put himself forward for the presidency on a technicality. The prime minister, to whom people had grown accustomed as if he was stability personified, was prevented from taking a decisive step by the very same qualities which had made him an acceptable and, in all likelihood, potentially successful candidate for president: restraint, solidity, the ability to reason and the ability to unite his supporters. It is rare for a person with his qualities to have a lust for power, and people lacking in *Wille zur Macht**, don't usually strive hard enough for the crown. In the past it seemed as though Russia's woes could be put down to the lust for power with which its leading politicians were afflicted; now it was becoming clear that a shortage of that same quality might lead to problems too.

In April, Viktor Chernomyrdin, speaking at the opening of the III congress of the movement 'Our home is Russia', called on people to take stock of the movement's capabilities "without any complacency" and mobilize all the powers at its disposal in order to make sure Boris Yeltsin won the presidential elections. It was probably the only speech he made in public as a politician: during the run–up to the elections, and whilst they were taking place, he performed the role of prime minister – "nothing more than that."

Chernomyrdin always demonstrated an amazing ability to get out of seemingly hopeless situations at the very last minute. The first deputy prime minister, Oleg Soskovets, who had usurped his boss's role on several occasions, had designs on his position. And yet each time he got close to it, it slipped out of his grasp literally at the very last moment. Chernomyrdin, moreover, as a result of both his own past and his mentality, was much closer to the leaders of Russia's federal subjects than Anatoly Chubais, Aleksei Kudrin or the man standing in the shadow of those two, Vladimir Potanin. They saw him as one of their own, even in the midst of the thrill of the chase.

Another of Chernomyrdin's strong suits was the unvoiced support given to him by the left–wing majority in the Duma. By comparison with Anatoly Chubais, Chernomyrdin no longer seemed such a brutal monetarist, gas baron and the "puppet of

---

* 'Will to power' in German. – Ed.

the comprador bourgeoisie". In 1997, all these negative monikers were used to describe Chubais, with the exception of 'gas baron'.

Chernomyrdin's strength was that he satisfied all the criteria imposed on those who sought to obtain, in Boris Yeltsin's eyes, the right to immortality within the administration. Chernomyrdin, like Yeltsin, had undergone a tough period of training in the union's administrative school, and was always careful to abide by all the unwritten rules of the game that are obligatory for senior figures in the nomenklatura. He hid the extent of his own intellect and kept his distance from the head of state, playing the role of the ideal 'number two'; he took great care when selecting his entourage and only put his trust in a small circle of advisers, whose personal loyalty he had tested many times over. He acted as the second most powerful focal point in the administration after Yeltsin, and he was aided in this by the colossal capabilities of the financial group that had formed around Gazprom and the Central Bank.

Chernomyrdin suited both the left and the right. He was referred to affectionately as Stepanych, when he was not present, both in the White House and in the Duma; both at Gazprom and in the Moscow mayor's office.

This went on right up until March 23, 1998. That day, an event was to occur in the political and economic life of the country which went a long way towards determining the direction of Russia's future development. Viktor Chernomyrdin, who had long been considered the most likely candidate for the role of head of state, was fired, along with his entire government. And although he would still be required to perform the duties of the premier for a while, his political career was, to all intents and purposes, over.

Commentators wrote at the time that the events that had unfolded in relation to Chernomyrdin's sacking left no room to doubt that the president would never let him back into the structures of power again, if only because of the fact that by the spring of 1998 Chernomyrdin had become more than just a prime minister.

The system of state government created during the head of state's lengthy illness had rendered the president himself almost obsolete – in the premier's eyes, at any rate. The premier had begun, with increasing frequency, to make statements which under normal circumstances were supposed to be made by the president. It appears that for Boris Yeltsin, the final straw came when he found out about a secret, informal meeting which had taken place between Viktor Chernomyrdin and Al Gore, during which the deputy heads of state of the USA and Russia had discussed their vision of how they were each going to go about becoming head of state. It may well be that Chernomyrdin looked on this meeting with Al Gore as the most important thing to come out of his trip to America.

Chernomyrdin's sacking had two consequences: it meant that the former premier had practically zero chance of ever following in Yeltsin's footsteps; and it meant that the president's entourage, the so–called 'Family' consisting of Boris Berezovsky, Tatiana Dyachenko and Valentin Yumashev, along with the closely associated group comprised of Vladimir Gusinsky, Mikhail Khodorkovsky and Alexander Smolensky, was transformed into the most powerful political group in Russia.

In August 1998, after sacking Sergei Kirienko, Boris Yeltsin once again appointed Chernomyrdin to the post of deputy prime minister. Chernomyrdin was given carte–blanche to do as he pleased and, as he told the president's press–secretary Sergei Yastrzhembsky, "the full confidence of the president with regard to preparing the government's manifesto and recruiting staff." Viktor Chernomyrdin had thus been given a chance to haul himself back from the political abyss into which he had been thrown by Boris Yeltsin in March. But within two weeks he had let this opportunity slip.

Had Yeltsin not effectively appointed Chernomyrdin his successor, everything would have been far more straightforward.

But he could not go back on something that the entire country had heard him say.

It was at that point, at the end of 1998, that Viktor Chernomyrdin called time on his eventful political career by turning down the opportunity to stand for election to the Duma.

There were not too many politicians who were able to boast the advantages with which Viktor Chernomyrdin had been blessed. He had resources within the corridors of power, administrative resources and financial resources at his disposal. From the very outset he had the backing of the regions, and he was respected by the 'ordinary' electorate.

He may perhaps have lacked the charisma of a leader – although he certainly had the charisma that came with being seen as "one of us" and yet at the same time a "strong organizer". Perhaps he had insufficient experience in the field of political warfare – although he clearly had plenty of experience of doing battle within the administration. He even had international backing. But such is the nature of politics in Russia.

Viktor Chernomyrdin said as much himself, giving a gloomy assessment of the nature of the way parties were set up in Russia, and of the results of his own career as a politician: "You can set up any party you want – you will still end up with the CPSU."

8. THE MASTERS OF THOUGHT. FROM SOLZHENITSYN TO THE ENTERTAINMENT INDUSTRY

Live not by lies

The symbol of the 1990s – or of the first half of the decade, at least – was, in some ways, Alexander Solzhenitsyn – or rather, his return to Russia. As Solzhenitsyn himself once said, the sense that he would one day return to his homeland had never left him: the key thing to understand is that he predicted the fall of communism.

The preparations that were made for his return were extremely thorough. At the first signs that censorship was going to be lifted, every effort was made to ensure that Solzhenitsyn's books were published in Russia. It was no easy task, and as usual, a large number of people were required in order to make it happen. And it was significant that the writer began his return "in book form", at *Novy Mir*: it's important to rise up again at the very spot where you fell down. What followed was an ultimatum to the people and to the country's leaders: 'How are we to furnish Russia with what she needs', 22 million copies of which were published as a supplement in a special edition of *Komsomolskaya Pravda*. These 'powerful reflections', admittedly, turned out to be a sort of digest of the emigrant works published by Solzhenitsyn and the *Red wheel*.

The liberals were probably overjoyed to see that Solzhenitsyn had not written anything that expressed support for Russian national socialism. The 'patriots' probably took issue with his harshly expressed rejection of "thinking in terms of a vast state, the imperialist drug", which, according to Solzhenitsyn, was essentially "a devoted form of support for communism as we lie dying."

The wide audience that Solzhenitsyn, judging by his choice of publication, wished to address, was, for the most part, slightly shocked, not to say a little bit frightened by the writer's florid style, which was quite difficult to read. Moreover, judging by the tone and scope of the recommendations he was making, Alexander Solzhenitsyn's call to 'furnish Russia with what she needs' was directed not at the general public, but at a leader. As for which leader he had in mind, he didn't say.

The publication date of this text, which advocated the establishment in Russia of an authoritarian class, coincided with the draft edict from the Supreme Soviet of the USSR on the allocation of emergency powers to Gorbachev. The day after he was given these powers, Gorbachev, disassociating himself from the pro–monarchy tendencies shown by Solzhenitsyn, said to the deputies: "He is stuck in the past, the Russia of old, the monarchy. I see myself as a democrat with radical views."

Perhaps, though, Gorbachev and Solzhenitsyn simply did not share the same ideas about what was the best form of authoritarianism. Whereas the 'president' advocated by Solzhenitsyn was merely a pseudonym for the 'Tsar of all the Russias', Gorbachev was apparently inclined to preserve an empire of an altogether different kind. With his counsel that Russia ought to rid itself of its "Central Asian underbelly" and the phrase he used, "The Union of Socialist Soviets will collapse in any case", this advice from 'the monarchist of Vermont' was likely to do the president more harm than good.

Yeltsin, too, felt that Solzhenitsyn's message was not particularly helpful. A rejection of parliamentary principles, set against the backdrop of the actions taken by the union's leaders, would have spelt political disaster for Yeltsin. The request from Vermont for an "unequivocal refutation of a blind and malignant

Marxist–Leninist utopia," and the calls to "give full voice to healthy private initiative" were an area of common ground at that particular moment in time.

You got the feeling that Russia – in no small part thanks to Solzhenitsyn – had emerged into a new, bourgeois–democratic era, whilst he had remained stuck in his own era, in the past.

The process of his return went at a pace of its own, however. The next phase of it was a TV interview that was broadcast to the nation. The interviewer he chose was not Eldar Ryazanov, the comedian, but Stanislav Govorukhin, a writer of adventure novels. Finally, in an interview on his birthday, Solzhenitsyn declared that he was not going to join the party but that he would remain an impartial observer, and would try to teach everyone how to reason properly.

Solzhenitsyn went to Russia, where everyone was already expecting some sort of change at government level, but was not sure what precise form this change might take. In this sense he had chosen exactly the right moment for his arrival, and everyone set about trying to work out whose side he would be on, confidently predicting what they thought the writer himself was going to say. When the initial fuss died down, it transpired that Solzhenitsyn – who had appeared to arrive at such a convenient moment – was in fact of no use to anyone: nobody had any real intention of using either the man himself, his ideas, or even his image in politics. All the more so given that some of his ideas (such as the view that he expressed in 1992 to Yeltsin, that the Kuril Islands should be handed back to Japan) had made no impact at all on Kozyrev's understanding of foreign policy, which was later roundly condemned as defeatist.

After travelling right across Russia from Vladivostok to Moscow, Alexander Solzhenitsyn stopped off at the Duma in order to express once again his unprejudiced views on the men of the Duma and on parliamentarians in general.

The speech that Solzhenitsyn made in the Duma did not really contain any surprises. Declarations to the effect that the reforms were being implemented in the worst possible way and that the people were in a state of poverty and despair (cue applause from the left) were interspersed with reminders that the country's current woes were the result of the Communists having been in charge for seventy years (cue applause from the right).

The only thing that was to some extent new was the fact that the writer, who in the past had referred only to a union of three Slavic republics and the need to rid ourselves of the 'Asian underbelly', was now admonishing Russia's leaders for their scorn for that self–same underbelly. There was another innovation, too: after announcing that "in that Duma there were 30 genuine peasants for whom tilling the land was in their blood", the writer caused consternation among the agricultural men present, who could only conclude that it was not something that was in *their* blood.

His reasons for giving this speech, and the precise meaning of it, were not altogether clear. Solzhenitsyn had given such a detailed description of the irresponsible behaviour, narrow party–based egotism and alienation from the country's needs that were inherent to previous generations of Duma deputies, and had gone to such lengths to explain the harm that would be done by both the multi–party system that was breaking up the nation, and of the 'four–pronged' electoral system (a universal, direct, equal and secret vote), that his speech to the Duma, with its multiplicity of parties, and whose members were elected based on precisely that 'four–pronged' system, looked pretty strange: why address people who were not only tainted by individual sins, but who, moreover, had been elected based on a principle that was flawed from the outset?

The writer himself allowed for the contradiction, stating that he made the speech by popular demand: thousands of people had asked him to express the people's needs to those in power, i.e. the 'Letter to the leaders No.2' was read out in the Duma (or rather, No.3 – the *Kommersant* columnist Maksim Sokolov had described Solzhenitsyn's article 'How are we to furnish Russia with what she needs' as the 'Second letter to the leaders').

From the point of view of parliamentary tradition, what happened was an entirely run–of–the–mill event: a scheduled speech by a distinguished and respected foreign guest – an everyday affair in Western parliaments. By choosing this method of communicating with the authorities, Solzhenitsyn had involuntarily made himself appear to be a foreigner with expert knowledge.

And it was in that capacity that he remained, leading not so much the life of a recluse, but certainly not the life of an enlightened individual (still less that of a public political figure), at a dacha given to him by Yeltsin. His only venture of note into public life occurred towards the end of 1998, in connection with his birthday – or rather, in connection with an award related to his birthday.

After finding out in advance that he was going to be given some sort of award, the writer sent a written request to the president asking him not to do so. The president paid no attention, and awarded Solzhenitsyn the Order of Saint Andrew the Apostle the First–Called. Solzhenitsyn thanked Boris Yeltsin for his wishes through his spokesman, Oleg Sysuev, but declined to accept the medal. "I cannot accept an award from the powers that have brought Russia to its current moribund condition," the writer declared, adding that "perhaps, in time" his sons would accept the award on his behalf.

There was not much of a row about the matter – Solzhenitsyn's popularity rating in the country was already so low that this decision went practically unnoticed by the general public. Yet he was certainly popular enough to remain – against his own will, perhaps – a hero of the nineties.

It is pertinent that the writer made the speech in which he declined to accept the award at the Theatre on the Taganka, where Yury Lyubimov's play 'Sharashka', based on the novel *In the first circle*, was being put on to mark his 80th birthday.

Solzehnitsyn chose to celebrate his birthday with those whom he considered his former lifetime companions in the USSR.

The conscience of the nation

On September 30, 1999, the academic Dmitry Likhachev passed away in a hospital in St Petersburg. Strictly speaking, to call him a hero of the '90s is to underplay his significance in terms of Russia's history, culture and spiritual life dramatically. His life fitted neatly into the 20th century, taking up almost all of it. He was born after the first Russian revolution and lived through all the events that followed it, including the war and a prison sentence. Among those who survived the war there were plenty of people who lived to a ripe old age – this was not because they had been hardened by the labour camps, but because only the toughest had survived the labour camps. There were plenty of men among them who were recognised for their wisdom – once again, this was not down to their experiences in prison but because prison had sifted out the idiots.

Likhachev was blessed with both longevity and wisdom, but Dmitry Sergeyevich proved to be essential to the country, as could clearly be seen in the last decade – less as a wise patriarch than as someone who preserved ideas about the correct way to behave – ideas which society had come very close to losing.

His role as a guarantor of spirituality and a symbol of Russian culture was determined right back in 1986, when he took charge of the Culture Foundation, which had been set up a short time earlier. This had no relation to his spell in prison, his academic work, Pushkin House, Russian literature, his 'A word about the leader Igorev' or the poetics of Russian gardens. From that point on he performed the role of the officially appointed conscience of the nation – the very role that the writer Solzhenitsyn, or, to a lesser extent, the physicist Sakharov might have been able to assume. For objective reasons, however, Gorbachev and his coterie opted instead for the diplomatic, intelligent and presentable philologist from Leningrad. It was at this point that he became the man he was when he died: Likhachev the Academic, a man who was able to 'speak truth to power', and who was the very embodiment of human virtue.

He coped with this incredibly thankless task – one that could have destroyed even the strongest of natures – with extraordinary dignity.

He managed to establish a rapport with his fellow prisoners – it was no coincidence that his first academic work was about the origins of underground slang, which he had mastered while imprisoned at the Solovetsky camps. His later works were about the ecology of culture, and, in turn, created the very same cult slang in which even criminals find it so easy to express themselves today. He could have worn both the gold star of a Hero of Socialist Labour and the medal of the Order of Saint Andrew the Apostle the First–Called on his professorial jacket at one and the same time. On his passing, the president sent his condolences to his family.

On Dmitry Likhachev's death the newspaper *Kommersant* published something akin to his political testament.

Some of his views, which had formulated at various times in his life, are quite relevant even today. There is every chance they will remain so in the future as well.

On the idea of common nationhood he said: "The idea of common nationhood as a panacea that will cure all our ills is not only plain stupid, it's an incredibly dangerous bit of stupidity!"

On the "path to power" he said: "We ought to adopt a Constitution that sets out, in precise terms, extremely exacting and demanding requirements on every individual who stands for election to the highest echelons of power." Peter the Great introduced something similar – look at his 'Table of ranks', for example. A person ought to serve the requisite time (hold office for a fairly lengthy, set period of time) before progressing to the next rank and the next title. But we failed to grasp this. We thought this was bureaucracy, plain and simple. But it's far from being bureaucracy. It is simply caution."

On land reform: "It is my firmly held conviction that given the desperate situation in which our country finds itself, the thing that might rescue the country – the whole nation – would be to give title to the land to the labourers, immediately."

On the presidential elections: "We ought to change the format of the voting slips for the forthcoming presidential elections in Russia: we should put a plus sign and a minus sign next to each candidate's name, 'for' and 'against', and then subtract the total number of votes 'against' from the total number of votes 'for' each candidate."

On the struggle against crime: "For many criminals, a sizeable fine, leaving the criminal free to fulfil the obligations he has to his family, would be more effective than keeping him locked up in an overcrowded prison, at the taxpayer's expense, and relieving him of his familial obligations."

On the death penalty: "If we were to replace the death penalty with life imprisonment, with no hope of parole, for particularly inhumane crimes, we might be able to protect society from criminals and from our own mistakes in the law courts."

On limiting the amount of violence and pornography in the media: "The fines imposed on the programmes that include this kind of footage must be imposed after the film has been shown, and must be so high as to prevent anyone from wanting to show such films again. It would be dangerous to reinstate censorship: from moral censorship it is only a small step to political and ideological censorship, the abolition of which was one of the most significant achievements in Russia in the latter stages of the 20th century."

On the Russian language: "First of all, we ought to copy what the French have done, and form a Committee for the Russian language headed up by the president. Secondly, we ought to organize a Russian language telephone service. It need not even be a free service – it can't be that hard to arrange. Some of our linguists, with their dictionaries at the ready, would be on hand to answer the first phone call from a deputy from the State Duma, for example (the deputies seem to have serious problems with their native tongue), or from whoever it might be, and to explain how a word should be written or pronounced, or where to put the stress in a particular word."

On the problem of urbanization: "This problem is particularly pertinent at the moment – all sorts of restrictions have been removed, and registration in your place of residence is about to be abolished – St Petersburg and Moscow could soon grow to unheard of proportions. The influx of refugees is huge: 25 million Russians from our closest neighbours. Sooner or later they are going to come pouring into Russia, and most of them will head straight for Moscow or St Petersburg. It is essential that we create some medium–sized cities, and different types of cities."

Dmitry Likhachev led an extremely long life, and for that reason he was able to adopt a philosophical view of a reality that did not look good. He even managed to show loyalty to it. It was this world–view that was the key to the Academic's wisdom: after all, he had seen and lived through a time that was far, far worse; he understood that the transition away from damnable, Soviet power was never going to be easy, and he was even able to forgive those rescuing the country from Soviet power for the fact that they often turned out to be far more destructive than those whom they had replaced.

After becoming, with the authorities' consent, something rather like a national elder or, if you will, the Kremlin's official spiritual voice, he used his influence carefully and to good effect. On a few occasions his opinion was put forward as the opinion of the Russian intelligentsia as a whole. He managed, for example, to persuade Boris Yeltsin to travel to St Petersburg to attend the burial ceremony for Nicholas II. This was all the more difficult given that the church was in no hurry to acknowledge the authenticity of the remains, and Likhachev believed in God and respected the church. In this instance, Likhachev's advice carried more weight than the patriarch's official opinion.

The path to the temple

Towards the end of the 1990s, even the secular authority of patriarch Aleksei II – not to mention his practically indisputable authority within the church – was impressive. The most holy patriarch Aleksei II became the fifteenth Primate of the Russian Orthodox Church in 1990, replacing patriarch Pimen in the role. He was elected on the eve of the collapse of the USSR: Aleksei II was the first patriarch to be elected without any interference by the state at all, and this in itself represented a breakthrough in relations between the church and the secular authorities. Aleksei, meanwhile, also became the first member of the clergy to bring together, as far as was possible, not only those representing religious authority and secular authority, but also the interests of these two groups.

The archbishop Mark provided a concise description of the patriarch's role: "Aleksei II led the Russian church out of its Babylonian imprisonment, i.e. out of the Soviet Union, to a new life."

After the fall of Soviet society the patriarch managed to iron out relations with the country's rulers. President Boris Yeltsin, who had formerly kept his distance from the church, was the first post–Soviet leader to enter a church. Russia's first president saw it as his duty to congratulate the patriarch at his residency on his birthday and enthronement day, and the head of the Russian Orthodox Church, in turn, never missed the festivities marking the president's birthday. Moreover, the patriarch was one of the few men who was in attendance at the hand–over of power in the country: on his last day at work, as he handed over his responsibilities to Vladimir Putin, Boris Yeltsin invited Aleksei II to the Kremlin.

The fact that the making of modern Russian statehood took place in parallel to that of Russian orthodoxy meant that the patriarch's involvement in political life was unavoidable. In 1993, Aleksei II adopted the role of peacemaker during confrontations between the president and the Supreme Council.

The fact that contacts were established with the secular authorities during Aleksei II's reign meant that the ROC was able to make a number of acquisitions. There was not a complete restitution of the property that the church had had before the revolution, but those churches that had remained intact were handed over to the church free of charge, and the Church of Christ the Saviour was constructed with substantial funding from the state.

In the mid–1990s, administrative structures related to the ROC received tax relief from the Russian government for the importing of alcohol and tobacco, and this led to widespread abuse and an extremely unpleasant row. The row was quelled after the tax relief was cancelled at the personal request of Aleksei II.

The well-known theologian, deacon Andrei Kuraev, declared that the patriarch's greatest achievement was the fact that he had "managed to avoid the collapse of the orthodox world": "He became patriarch at a time when there was a parade of sovereignties, when everyone expected that processes such as this were going to begin in the church, but today, 20 years on, we can go to church without having to ask: "Do you support the reds or the whites?""

The fourth estate

One of most significant results of Aleksei II's activity during the 1990s was the rebirth of interest in orthodoxy within society. Even the creator and main presenter of the hard–hitting news programme *600 seconds*, which had a cult following, started to touch on orthodoxy in his reports. Admittedly, he touched on such subjects in the context of a fairly radical form of Russian nationalism – and they were broadcast alongside reports full of brutal realism, accompanied by the use of coarse language, nudity, dismemberment and so on.

After making his name as a TV reporter for whom no subject was off limits in the late 1980s, Nevzorov remained true to himself in the 1990s. If mainstream political life held any interest for him at all, it was only to the extent that it enabled him fervently to set out his own point of view, which could be described as ultra–patriotic. He approved unconditionally of the actions of the armed police in the Baltic states, campaigned for general Makashov in the run–up to the presidential elections in 1991, and played a slow–motion video explaining to viewers how to vote in the referendum on whether or not to preserve the USSR.

The authorities tried to shut down *600 seconds* back in 1991. On November 28, the director of St Petersburg TV, Viktor Yugin (who chaired the Committee on the Media within the SC RSFSR, a 'democratizer', who had replaced one of the 'old guard', Boris Petrov, in this role) banned *600 seconds* from being broadcast, and the doors of the programme's offices were locked. Rumour had it that the previous day Yugin had given a stern warning to Nevzorov that he must refrain altogether from any form of "criticism and baseless accusations". Nevzorov, however, opted to ignore his boss's instructions – on the contrary, he began explaining to viewers that Yugin and the other ruling democrats were no more than members of the nomenklatura of yesteryear.

A second attempt to shut down the programme was made in 1993 by Bella Kurkova, who by now was the General Director of the Federal Television Service, but once again it was unsuccessful. The team behind *600 seconds* responded with a letter to the president of the Russian Federation in which they didn't mince their words, and called the directors of the FTS lackeys, cowards and scoundrels, "just like their president".

In a sense, Alexander Nevzorov and his programme can be seen as a predecessor of Mikhail Leontev and his programme *And yet* (which Maxim Sokolov spent some time working on as well, as "one of the founders of the modern style of Russian journalism", which he had honed at *Kommersant*), and the 'TV killer' of the late 1990s, Sergei Dorenko. Nevzorov gradually moved into mainstream politics and feature–length TV journalism, and other big names came in to replace him.

One of these big names was Alexander Minkin. In 1997, the magazine *Vlast* named him as the singer of the new Russia, its true servant, the protector of the interests that had been inspired by the new times and at the same time one of the most opportunistic and scandalous journalists of his day.

Minkin declared on several occasions that he was leaving mainstream journalism – almost in the same way as Moscow's mayor Gavriil Popov had announced his retirement. On the eve of the elections in 1996 he swore that if Zyuganov won he would have to live in Kolyma, and that if Yeltsin won he would go back to being a theatre critic.

Minkin's greatest professional achievement was the departure of Chubais from his role as Finance Minister in November 1997. In January, Minkin had told the public about the incredibly high taxes that Chubais was paying; in August he conducted an investigation into the bonuses paid to Chubais's closest rival Alfred Kokh; and then in November 1997 he initiated the "literary affair", which was followed by a cabinet reshuffle.

In the jargon of the security services, writers like Minkin are referred to as "channels for the authorized leaking of information". As it happened, the journalist himself was philosophical about all this: "If you write about something that is damaging to one person's interests, there will always be someone else who stands to benefit. What should you do in such cases? Not write anything? I will always write something if it coincides with my views." As a precaution, he never fully explained his views.

The puppet–masters

In the mid–1990s it began to seem as though society, which was as seriously engaged in politics as it had been in the past, was nevertheless starting to relate to it with an increasing degree of light–hearted cynicism. The reason for this may have been an idea that was gaining currency in society – the notion that, as Maxim Sokolov so aptly put it, "the extreme stupidity of the opposition was only matched by the stupidity of those in power."

Politics had begun to be transformed into a form of entertainment, a spectacle. And political satire was becoming something of a farce (the fact that it had emerged from a farce perhaps seemed sufficient grounds for sending it straight back there). The only TV programme in this genre, which speaks volumes, was *Puppets*, for which the satirist Viktor Shenderovich was one of the screenwriters and the inspiration. After a torturous search for some suitable material in Russian public life for a programme along the same lines as the French TV show *Les Guignols de l'info*, the programme's makers hit upon matching parody versions of classic characters, plots and texts with individuals who were "an un–literary as they come". It proved a stroke of genius.

The ironic exaggeration of the characters made it all the more effective when they were turned on their heads. The fact that the literary prototypes had features that were so obviously different in size, and had been so clearly distorted, undermined the unfounded complaints of the people parodied: the essence of any comic effect is in the disproportional relationship between image and essence.

Before long, however, the programme's makers became fixated by one particular topic: the favouritism shown by Yeltsin. This subject featured Yeltsin, surrounded by his favourites (such as Korzhakov and Grachev), and reflecting on what role to give to so–and–so, and on who to form an alliance with; after this, in strict order, the following came before him: Gaidar, followed by Zhirinovsky, Yavlinsky and Zyuganov – and with all these candidates he engaged in witty banter to varying degrees. Every Saturday viewers were shown the same thing, and in order to make up for the monotony of the subject matter the puppets were dressed up in costumes from an array of well–known literary works (Hamlet, Faust, Robinson Crusoe etc.), and all the characters' most noteworthy speeches (Gaidar's speech on reform and monetarization, Zhirinovsky's speech on the race to the South) were also "dressed up" linguistically – the protagonists spoke partly in flowery language taken from the literary works depicted.

But *Puppets* was a very popular show. A popular joke in the late 1990s was: "You know things aren't going well when the president comes across better in *Puppets* than he does in the news." Society was prepared to forgive the satirists for being so low–brow, for the programme was performing quite an important function. Each week it flattered society, and revealed the true root of Russia's ills: cronyism, born of the wicked nature of the strong of this world, rather than the state of Russian society as a whole.

As for this society itself, it was gradually coming to the realization that the "real politics" was being done by someone else – and not at the very top, but somewhere on the sidelines, in the shadows. To begin with it was Boris Berezovsky, and then, in the second half of the 1990s, this niche was filled by others. And they were referred to as political strategists. One of the worst of the political strategists was Gleb Pavlovsky. The *Daily Telegraph* referred to him as "a myth and a hero of our time", "the most influential person with a dissident background in Russia" and "the black sheep of any family".

The most in–depth study of Gleb Pavlovsky's rise was written by the publicists Dmitry Bykov and Ivan Izmailov in *Moskovskaya Komsomolka*. Here are a few excerpts from their tale.

Pavlovsky "never directly denies his involvement in any project, whether it has succeeded or failed. He merely smiles, mysteriously and trustingly, in response. For he knows full well: the more the rumours circulate, the more respect, fear and, ultimately, money, there will be.

For that reason, in the history of modern Russia there are virtually no events in which, as far as public opinion was concerned, Pavlovsky did not play a part. Chubais's next rise to the top (in 1996), Yeltsin's triumph and, later, his retirement, Stepashin's retirement, the appointment of Putin as the successor, the heavy defeat of Luzhkov and Primakov, the end of the second Chechen War, the creation of the 'Edinstvo' (Unity) party..."

"As he once said himself, in a frank interview: "There is a great demand in society for a global conspiracy, for there to be someone with absolute power, pulling all the strings." In a different article, in which he was even more open, Pavlovsky went so far as to reveal the reason for this demand: people's suspicion that they were being manipulated was in fact suspicion of how prone they themselves were to being manipulated. The people who go looking for conspiracies are the ones who are willing to become part of them themselves...and he played on this, encouraging, in every way he could think of, his own reputation as someone Great and Terrible to flourish.

"Pavlovsky doesn't actually organize anything in practice – he simply doesn't have the tools at his disposal to be able to do so. He merely predicts what is going to happen, and occasionally he is spot on. So Russia is indeed developing in the way he predicted it would back in the late 1970s. The fact that Pavlovsky did not tie this to it, but predicted it, is a different matter altogether. And only one thing was required in order for him to make this prediction: a sufficient degree of freedom from intellectual prejudices. Equally alien to both party men and dissidents [when he was arrested, he confessed his guilt, thereby avoiding a prison sentence, and was sentenced only to exile. "I respect those who acted differently, but that is the only thing about them that I have any respect for," he sniggered], Gleb Olegovich turned out to be the only person who predicted what lay in store for Russia: from an age of empire through a decade–long collapse, and into a new state structure and a new imperial ideology."

His new image consisted of showy cynicism and intellectual shock tactics – Pavlovsky made the firm decision to become a 'person close to power' ..." When the 36–year–old historian undertook the publication of the independent magazine '*The 20th century and the world*', the dissidents, with one voice, described this as machinations on the part of the KGB. They said the same thing again a little later when the information agency PostFaktum appeared (in 1988) along with Limited Liability Partnership Fact (directed by Vladimir Yakovlev), which provided the information required for money. Later, when the bill for all these Limited Liability Partnerships, Limited Liability Companies, "analytical" and "information" centres had long been lost, it became clear that the reason for all this was not "the hand of the security organs" but the boundless energy of Pavlovsky himself, who was carving out a niche for himself within society. When the Soviet Union collapsed, it seemed to him, as it did to many others, that nothing was beyond the bounds of possibility. The turbulent atmosphere of those years was recreated by Viktor Pelevin in his novel *Generation P*, one of whose characters is based on Pavlovsky – the secretive and extremely important figure Farseikin.

Pavlovsky got involved in the politics of protest for a while due to a sense of inertia, but soon gave this up. Pavlovsky himself professes that he did this not out of his dislike of the masses, who were "in the grip of a nasty idea, and were all rushing in the same direction, like a herd of bison". Even at that stage Pavlovsky sought to prove (in the pages of his journal and elsewhere) that *perestroika* could not be begun without a new concept of statehood: if it went ahead armed with nothing but the idea of freedom, it would be suicide. Particularly in a country such as Russia, which is always "on the brink of descending into chaos". Gleb Olegovich considered himself a statist through and through and was sharply critical of the actions of Yeltsin's "anti–people regime" – particularly the attack on parliament in 1993. At that stage he attempted to unite his fellow ideologues under the slogan "We're not on your side, you bastards". When this failed, he left PostFaktum. It seemed to many that he was going to end up among the unreconcilable opposition, but suddenly the whole situation changed.

Pavlovsky later gave the following explanation for what happened: "When I caught wind of the fact that our intelligent society was turning its back on Yeltsinism and was turning toward its antithesis, anti–Yeltsinism, I immediately reacted against it: you won't find me following the crowd, not on your life."

"In 1995 Pavlovsky set up the Foundation for effective policy, and to begin with began consulting the party led by General Lebed, the 'Congress of Russian communities' in the elections for the Duma. The party suffered a heavy defeat, but the consultant's assurance was noted, as were his unusual campaigns, featuring the age–old Russian tendency to be provocative. Incidentally, it was at precisely that moment that Pavlovsky came up with his slogan, which later became famous: "There is such a man. And you know him" (essentially this was plagiarised directly from the famous joke about the Chukchi man who suddenly sees the person for whose benefit everything is done). This slogan later served Lebed well in Krasnoyarsk.

Back in 1994 Pavlovsky had let the cat out of the bag in the media about a coup that was allegedly being prepared by a group close to Yeltsin. This "theory No. 1", which was invented in order to drum up some hype about the 'Common newspaper', caused quite a stir, and Gleb Olegovich very nearly ended up behind bars for libel. Soon, however, the talents of this creator of all manner of "theories" were called for right at the very top. In 1996 the Pavlovsky Foundation, with the involvement of Igor Malashenko, was asked to create a "positive image" of president

Yeltsin. The things Pavlovsky did while in this role soon became known as "black PR". In addition to some invaluable experience, the election campaign also gave Gleb Olegovich the opportunity to fall in with the right sort of people, including Tatiana Dyachenko and Mikhail Lesiny. "Back then, at the end of 1995, there were two people who believed Yeltsin was electable, and very electable at that: Chubais and myself," he later commented.

"Soon Gleb Olegovich's fame grew rapidly – in part thanks to his furious activity in the burgeoning world of Russian online journalism. Pavlovsky had been personally involved in setting up Vesti.ru; he was the founder and editor in chief of the online publication Russian journal; and he was a patron of Strana.ru, on which misinformation is forever appearing in subtle forms – he was a key figure on the Russian internet. Orders came flooding in to his foundation. "Anyone can create a bit of hype if they've got the money to do so," Pavlovsky used to say, "but to be elected you need to be the one whose vector is pointing in the same direction as that of the country." As has already been noted, Pavlovsky had a particularly strong feel for this vector. In 1999, on Dyachenko's advice, the successful political strategist was hired for a new election campaign. The Kremlin needed people who had no intellectual complexes."

"At that point Pavlovsky made a move that took many people by surprise: right from the outset he tried to persuade the Family that Yeltsin ought to step out of the election campaign, and cede his place to Prime Minister Putin. Pavlovsky went all–in – and lost. Many people even ascribed the plan for the successful military campaign in Chechnya to him, not to mention the brilliantly executed campaigns against the Primakov–Luzhkov faction."

The authoritative deceased

To the average citizen looking on from the outside at the criminal gangs of the day and their tit–for–tat violence, the contract killers, *bratky*, 'new Russians' and other such heroes of the age probably seemed like mythical characters, figures invented to suit a particular style, characters from jokes or templates based on which they could model their behaviour. Yet they were all too real.

One of the most scandalous events of the '90s took place in Moscow on 5th April, 1994. The shadows were lengthening. At 5.40pm, Otari Kvantrishvili, one of the most authoritative people in the country – an athlete, decorated coach, respected businessman, benefactor and budding politician (and one of Russia's biggest mafiosi, to boot) – walked out of the bath houses in Krasnopresnenskaya and headed towards the bus stop. Along the way he stopped to have a swig of *Borzhomi* from a bottle. At that moment several shots rang out. Otari Kvantishvili was killed. The Lev Yashin Foundation for the Social Security of Athletes, which supported three orphanages in Moscow, had just lost its director.

Otari Kvantrishvili's involvement in criminal business dealings dated back to the mid–1970s. Back then, he and his brother Amiran received money from an underground sweepstakes and from professional card–sharps.

The Kvantrishvili brothers gained increasing influence through their broad network of connections in the world of sport, and thanks to the personal qualities of Amiran (he was killed on August 6, 1993). One of the professional card players who worked for the Kvantrishvili brothers at the time – they were his *krysha* (protectors) – said that "Amiran himself" had stuck up for him when he lost a huge sum to a cheat and refused to pay up. According to the card–player, Amiran said something along the lines of: "You lost, and you've gotta pay up. But if you take the money," Amiran said, turning now to the cheat, "you'll have me to deal with."

The firm '21st century Association', which was run by Otari Kvantrishvili, engaged quite openly in "dispute resolution" – i.e. it acted as a protector, arbiter or middle–man between businessmen and criminals. In its office, on the 20th floor of the Intourist hotel, there was every chance you might bump into some of the most famous people in the country, such as Joseph Kobzon, the people's artist of the USSR, a man loved by so many.

Otari Kvantrishvili continued his coaching work in wrestling in his spare time, and as time passed, and several of his proteges became world champions, his fame as a coach became quite considerable. Various former wrestlers and people who had engaged in other strength–based sports disciplines came under his wing. Gradually, prominent figures from the criminal underworld started to try and get the measure of him.

In the mid–1980s he was given the opportunity partially to legalize his business. The first time Moscow was divided up between the representatives of the criminal structures was in 1988, in Dagomys. The Chechens did not show up for the summit, declaring that they would overrun Moscow just as the Sicilians had overrun New York and Chicago. Kvantrishvili wasn't there either.

Through the agency of Otari Kvantrishvili, the capital's first hard–currency casino, *Gabriella*, was opened, using money siphoned off from various official sports organizations. This casino paved the way for hotels, alcohol production plants, wood processing firms, oil production plants and retail centres, and supported various federations of professional unions. A substantial share of the proceeds from the casino went to charity: helping sports schools for children and disabled athletes via the Lev Yashin Foundation for the Social Security of Athletes.

These same connections, along with Kvantrishvili's work as a coach, helped him to create an entire network of professional sports organizations. First and foremost these were open associations of representatives of the combat sports – boxers and wrestlers.

But in Autumn 1992, articles about Otari Kvantrishvili's criminal activities first started to appear in print. Almost all the representatives of the law enforcement agencies were of the same opinion in their unofficial comments: Kvantrishvili was a senior figure in the mafia. But he would never do time because he never got his hands dirty. Instead he would probably be killed. It was said that he might be killed not so much (or not only) because of any criminal conflicts, but also because of politics – after the events of October 1993 Kvantrishvili started to put money into politics. Using his popularity in the world of sport, he managed to set up a party called *Athletes of Russia*.

Many years after Kvantrishvili's death it transpired that the man who had organized the hit on him was a well–known "big cheese" from the Orekhovskaya organized crime group nicknamed Silvester (aka Sergei Timofeyev), who outlived his victim by just over five months. This same man, incidentally, was involved in the notorious attempt on the life of Boris Berezovsky, in the same year – 1994 – which prompted Boris Yeltsin to talk of the "boundless criminality in Russia".

Kvantrishvili's funeral procession was attended by almost the entire board of the State Committee on Sport, the Russian National Sports Foundation, sports organizations and individual athletes. The newspaper *Kommersant* observed – seeming somewhat puzzled – that "no representatives of the government of Russia and Moscow attended the funeral".

The funeral was attended by over a hundred prominent figures. They included a large number of famous people who had come to see Kvantrishvili off as he passed into the next world: Shota Mamalashvili, Igor Kochnevsky, Boris Khmelnitsky, Valery Vasiliev, Alexander Tikhonov. Joseph Kobzon flew back from the USA so that he could be there. The face of Alexander Yakushev was glimpsed fleetingly among the huddled crowd. Bogdan Titomir hovered somewhere in the background.

The coffin was placed in the ground in silence, alongside that of Amiran Kvantrishvili. Once the ceremony was over, Alexander Rozenbaum said: "The country has lost – I'll make so bold as to say it – a leader."

In almost the same way, in 2009, a similar crowd – this time consisting of Josif Kobzon, Alla Pugacheva, Vladimir Vinokur, Lev Leschenko, Nikolai Baskov, Maxim Galkin, Alexander Rozenbaum, Igor Krutoi, Stanislav Govorukhin, the deputy Aleksei Mitrofanov, the president of the Russian Basketball Federation (RBF) Sergei Chernov, the director in chief of the TV channel Sport, Vasily Kiknadze, and the head coach of Russia's women's national team, Valery Tikhonenko – would pay their respects to another hero of the 1990s, of almost legendary status: Shabtai Kalmanovich, who by that time had added an aristocratic–sounding 'von' to his surname.

The spy, international adventurer, 'diamond king' and international rogue Shabtai Kalmanovich saw in the 1990s in an Israeli prison. The KGB agent had ended up there after being arrested in 1987 in London, on suspicion of fraud involving precious stones and sending fake banknotes to banks in the USA.

As for how he spent his time in prison – that is quite another matter. It was from prison that he began a medicine business which, upon his release, was to make a rich man of him in Russia. He found a good job in his Moscow–based company for the son of the chief prison warden – a shy Moroccan jew – in exchange for which the boy's grateful father made sure his benefactor was able to enjoy the highest possible standard of living: air conditioning in his cell, furniture, food from a local restaurant, the latest newspapers every day, telephone calls...

On one occasion Kalmanovich called Vladimir Vinokury, who was on tour in Israel, and the latter started imitating Gorbachev's voice. All the telephone calls made from the prison were of course recorded. The next morning, the prison authorities demanded to know how the prisoner had managed to get through to the president of the USSR. This case was soon resolved. But as for the fact that the chief prison warden let Kalmanovich use his private toilet to enjoy intimate moments with a young female soldier, who was regularly allowed into the prison to see him – they were unable to forgive him for that. When Kalmanovich was released (after a petition was put forward by Kobzon and vice–president Rutski), the chief prison warden was forced to move into the cell himself – this time in the capacity of a prisoner.

After serving his time Kalmanovich moved back to Russia, where, along with Josif Kobzon, he opened the pharmaceuticals firm LiatNatali, which was engaged in the importing and wholesale trade of medicines. In 1996 the partners sold the firm, but Kalmanovich stayed in the pharmaceuticals business. He was also the director of Tishinka: he rebuilt it, it is said, largely using state funds, and then sold it. He then moved into a different market – Dorogomilovsky.

Another aspect of Kalmanovich's business activities was the work he did as a producer. In the late 1990s he helped his wife Anastasia set up the company VIPconcert, which produced Zemfira. Kalmanovich put on concerts in Russia by Liza Minelli, José Carreras and various other stars from the West.

Basketball was the business for which Kalmanovich was best–known, and also his biggest industry in terms of turnover – admittedly, just like his work as a producer, it was not particularly profitable. He got into the business in 1996.

"Arvidas Sabonis, Misha Krichevsky and myself set up the Joint–stock company Sabonis Basketball Club 'Zhalgiris' so that people would stop popping up demanding that old debts be paid back, Kalmanovich recollected. "We chased out all the alcoholics and built a school that has 800 students today; we brought in Kazlauskas – he was God's gift to coaching, and we were the first in this country to sign black players. In 1998 we won the Saporta Cup, and in 1999 we were European champions. Lithuania went into raptures. A 30,000–strong crowd was shouting my name at the airport; the Lithuanian president held a reception for us, and presented us with an award..."

It was thanks to that victory by Zhalgiris that Kalmanovich was given a Lithuanian title and the prefix 'von' before his surname: in addition to the order of Prince Gediminas and his officer's cross, he was also given – as he himself put it – a lordly title. The newly titled baron accepted all these marks of honour, then left the club. "In business nothing must ever be permanent" – that was how Kalmanovich explained his departure from Zhalgiris...

Kalmanovich had a finger in yet another pie, too: admittedly one that is not acknowledged so much in Russia as "from the side", and which is illustrated by official documents from the American federal institutions. This had to do with a special report by the FBI, drawn up back in 1996 and dedicated entirely to "the criminal organization led by Semyon Mogilevich". Special attention was set aside for Shabtai Kalmanovich in the document. Among his partners, in addition to Mogilevich, was Sergei Mikhailov, better known as Mikhas, and Viktor Averin, who was mentioned in police reports as Avera senior.

Despite the FBI's suspicions, the Americans never made any official accusations against Kalmanovich.

The Russian law enforcement agencies were indeed aware of Kalmanovich's relations with the Solntsevskaya organized crime group. "The people who worked in external intelligence gathering were often forced to get things done, to practise the dark arts," a source close to those in charge of the Ministry of Internal Affairs told a journalist from the magazine Ogoniok. "Naturally, they had links to certain circles. It is quite possible that Kalmanovich worked with members of the Solntsevskaya group.

"Kalmanovich had dozens of businesses – people in high places helped him to get them going," the source added. "He built up financial schemes and business schemes. A structure as big as the Solntsevskaya organized crime group has its own legal firms, too. They need to work, bring in a profit and keep up a good image. But at the same time you need to understand something: you don't just walk away from these sorts of relations and take your pension. If you're someone with a bit of authority, that authority stays with you your whole life."

Kalmanovich was often used as a middle–man not only in criminal issues but in political ones too: rumour had it that he often dealt with delicate requests from the Ministry of Transport in the Baltics, and helped Lithuania to resolve the problems in its relations with the Kaliningrad Region. Kalmanovich himself once confessed to journalists: "I was asked to work in the President's Administration as an advisor in the Baltics... What we're doing is in both countries' interests. We are doing some big things, some good things..."

Contract killings

The ties between the criminal world and the burgeoning entertainment industry in the 1990s were incredibly strong. The greatest music producer between 1991 and 1994, Yury Aisenshpis, who won two national *Ovation* awards for his achievements in the industry, is also famous for having spent almost twenty years 'inside'. Money and music were the two things for which he was known – at different periods in his life and with varying degrees of success.

Within the music scene Yury Aisenshpis was known simply as Shpis, for the sake of brevity and convenience. But in due course the man who became known as 'Russia's first music producer' was able to leave the public in no doubt as to how his name was spelt. Aisenshpis was the man who introduced the concept of the "music producer" into the lexicon of Russian showbusiness. He thought of the production of stars as simply another branch of the domestic economy, like heavy metallurgy or the manufacturing of suspenders.

He had a sense of what people were going to listen to, and what was worth 'hyping up'. His business was founded on intuition and sound knowledge of market trends. His resources were his personal contacts, backed up by investment. And the tools of his trade were his four phones, which never stopped ringing.

He was capable of causing a stir with a risqué statement, and of amazing the public with his external appearance (his jacket, the design of which looked like a jungle–fire, became the stuff of legend for some time); at times he could be wheedling and demonstrate a brutal nature. For him, each new project was a "life–long affair". The technical tricks that have become classic ploys in the "conveyor–belt of stars" can be attributed to him: flooding the airwaves with an artist's hit and then taking the artist on tour all over the country.

He was able to adopt an approach that bordered on the absurd but which was in fact "the supreme art of being a professional producer" and "a lifelong dream": to turn a complete nobody into a star.

After spending 10 years behind bars for financial fraud, he was let out...only to be locked up once again for a further seven years and eight months. For this he would later be granted an official pardon by the authorities and paid compensation to the tune of 42 roubles for every month spent behind bars. The last place in which Aisenshpis was detained was known as 'the meat–grinder', and had the dubious honour of having the highest mortality rate of all the prisons in the USSR. "What helped me survive and stay healthy was my ability to see eye to eye with people, and my belief in the fact that there was still some justice in this world, despite what had happened," Aisenshpis said of his ordeal.

He was released early thanks to an accident of fate. His mother had been born in the same village as the Chairman of the Supreme Soviet, the Foreign Minister Andrey Gromyko. Moreover, she herself held a position within the party. She jumped through all the bureaucratic hoops and managed to secure a meeting with the minister. In 90% of cases, appeals made by individuals were upheld.

Yury Aisenshpis said that March 30, 1998, the day of his release, was the happiest day of his life. Rather than become a vengeful, latter–day Count of Monte Cristo, he chose to look on the years he had spent behind bars as merely another chapter of his life. But it had been a different life. It had had nothing to do with music.

Shortly after his release, Aisenshpis was introduced to Viktor Tsoi in the gardens at the Hermitage. It was a brush with fame – for both of them! The motif of the star played a central role in much of Viktor Tsoi's artistic output. Aisenshpis had his own, distinctive definition of what a 'star' was, however: "When we first met, not only were they not stars: the band's name, *Kino*, didn't even feature in the Ministry of Culture's official lists of artists and performers."

Whether Aisenshpis's sixth sense and feel for market trends came to the fore, or whether by some happy coincidence, the alliance that they formed resulted in the ideal combination of commercial success and great music. The producer did not interfere with the creative process, whilst the musicians were provided with everything they needed in order to make that process work.

Kino – the first Russian band to fill Luzhniki

With their new–found authority and the almost complete lack of competition, the band found that moving forward on the crest of this new wave was, if not easy, then certainly not too troublesome. In addition to *Kino*, the private production company with the uncomplicated title 'YuA', which Aisenshpis founded, was also involved in putting on concerts between 1988 and 1990. It staged about a hundred of them in all.

The artists ranged from *Alisa* and *DDT* to Muromov and Zhenya Belousov. Carried away by this wind of change blowing through their smoky kitchens, the people had a thirst for big spectacles, and sell–out crowds in the concert halls became as common a sight as the queues for smoked sausage had been not long beforehand. It was a boom period.

A short while after Tsoi's death, as if guided by his new recruits' slogan, "press the button and you'll get what you want," Aisenshpis took charge of the band *Technologiya*. He certainly knew which buttons to press. Popular songs in the style of Depeche Mode, almost daily air–time on the TV and the radio, and within four months *Technologiya* was the country's biggest band. And the light of this new star began to provide warm rays, in the shape of the proceeds from the concerts.

Aisenshpis also helped to create a buzz around *Moralny Kodeks*, helping to make up for the shortage in the "guitar wave". As for *Young Guns*, both the band's style and its name were inviting comparisons with *Guns 'n' Roses*.

Whenever there was a disagreement on a point of principle, Aisenshpis gave a clear demonstration of how much he brought to the table. As soon as the first signs started coming that *Technologiya* had let their fame get to their heads, Aisenshpis abandoned them. It did not take long for the consequences to make themselves felt: the ratings fell overnight and the before long the band had split up.

At one of the *Young Guns'* concerts, Aisenshpis heard Vlad Stashevsky tinkering on a grand piano backstage, playing a piece by Shufutinsky.

Even Aisenshpis's colleagues and friends were sceptical about this particular artist's ability. But the line from Alyona Apina's hit song, '*I blinded him with what I had,*' encapsulated the ideology and machinery of Russian show–business. Anyone could become a star. Or rather, you could turn anyone into a star. The secret was that not everyone had the knack of being able to do so.

Aisenshpis certainly had it. Under his guidance, Vlad Stashevsky went through every stage of the rise to fame: 'up–and–coming artist in Moscow', 'young singer from Moscow', 'rising star', 'the biggest hope of the year', and finally the nomination for 'discovery of the year'...

"For the time being, show–business is a costly game to be in, and most of the time it is unprofitable," Yury Aisenshpis used to say at the time. "I have secured investment not from sponsors, but from patrons. Stashevsky has started to make some money from the clubs, of course, but these amounts are nothing to speak of, and are nowhere near as high as the costs, so my profits are much lower than you might imagine."

"We have spent about $800,000 publicizing Stashevsky," Aisenshpis continued, and the music video for *Love no longer lives here*, which made him famous, has been shown about a thousand times on various TV channels. Making the record on a phonogram cost $85,000; the two music videos cost $50,000 and $35,000 to shoot; and the music for the song, which was ordered by the composer, cost between $1000 and $3000. I had just two projects that were commercially successful in my lifetime: *Kino* and *Technologiya*."

As for his own wealth, Aisenshpis was rather scornful about it, saying that in the end he had made as much as he needed to provide for his family and pay his phone bill – he conducted negotiations over the telephone. It is worth noting, however, that he managed to get his hands on two new cars to replace a Volvo of his that was stolen: a Pontiac Bonneville and a Ford Explorer.

Of the three million cassettes of Stashevsky's music that were in circulation, only 5% were originals. Aisenshpis had a whole display of some of the pirate copies adorning his shelves at home (numbering about twenty). Cassettes were the most popular medium on which to listen to music at the time, and they cost a dollar each. In the West they cost 8–10 dollars. CDs cost about

10 dollars in Russia, and 15–20 dollars in the West. In Russia, a release of 20,000 CDs was quite something. For stars in the western hemisphere, a release of 100,000 was par for the course.

When it came to creating a buzz around stars, Aisenshpis reached the stratosphere in his profession. And this despite the fact that he was operating in stone age conditions. The stone age made way for the 'platinum' age.

In 1996, the head of the advertising group Premier SV, Vladimir Zhechkov, who was passionate about singing, hired the songwriters Dobronravov and Matetsky and recorded three albums. When it came to deciding on a name for the band, the name *White eagle* popped into his head. That was the name of a vodka made by one of his clients, for whom Yury Grymov had filmed a TV commercial. Even today *White eagle* is associated not with the bloody millions made by the founders of the company but with the heart–rending line 'How captivating they are, the evenings in Russia!'"

There was another famous singer who made his mark in business: Georgy Vasiliev, a bard and member of the duo *Ivasi*. An idol among young people and students, he and his workmate Aleksei Ivaschenko broke through onto the nation's television screens with the song '*Come to me, Glafira*'. But not many people knew at the time that he was also the chairman of the October Executive Committee of the District Soviet of People's Deputies for Moscow (where almost all the capital's co–operatives were registered). And in 1991 he took charge of the Moscow Trade Exchange. Thereafter his career followed a strange trajectory: after three years he became the chairman of the board of directors at Vympelkom, and in 2001 he presented the first musical ever composed in Russia, which was entitled NordOst. Exactly one year later he would go on to spend three days in a building seized by terrorists in Dubrovka; he survived this ordeal and, after a series of unsuccessful attempts to get NordOst going again, he moved into the cartoon industry.

Incidentally, in the summer of 1996 a meeting took place between the head of the tax ministry, Alexander Pochinok, and various stars of the stage: Alla Pugacheva, Igor Nikolaev, Alyona Apina, Alexander Malinin, Natalia Korolyova, Nikolai Rastorguev and Oleg Gazmanov, at which he called on them to set an example to the nation of good practice and obedience as regards to the payment of taxes. The stars agreed to do so.

And in 1997 a radio station came on air that adopted a risky policy: it played nothing but Russian songs. But *Russkoye Radio* was soon a huge success. At first this had less to do with the songs than with the jokes of Nikolai Fomenko, which were broadcast before and after the ad breaks. After a while these jokes were shared on the Internet, and lists of them were printed out and distributed to all those who were still living in the dark ages (the vast majority) and did not have access to the Internet.

The most important art form of all

Sergei Bodrov, Jr. got into the film industry thanks to his father and namesake, the famous director. He got into it not by greasing anyone's palm, but by a happy coincidence – via the boiler room of cinematic production. Bodrovstarshy couldn't find a partner for the ultra–professional Oleg Menshikov in *The Caucasian Prisoner*, and decided to give the job to his son, who was an amateur actor. He turned out to be tailor–made for the role, and Alexei Balabanov's next screen appearance in *Brat* (*Brother*) transformed him overnight from a debutant into a national star.

This star had suddenly emerged on the horizon of a film industry that was moribund. There were still some good actors in Russian cinema, but none of them enjoyed symbolic status. None of the film stars in their fifties, or slightly older, can claim to be recognisable to all, or to embody the 'spirit of a generation': the expression itself seems old–fashioned and almost forgotten.

Sergei Bodrov, however, who was twenty years younger, managed to become someone who fitted that mould. The fact that he had never had professional training as an actor suggested that fate had chosen him for the role.

This intelligent lad from Moscow embodied the complexes and neuroses of people from the provinces who had the good fortune and misfortune to live in the new Russia. Not in a Russia in which "people could live a normal life in a normal country". But in a Russia where there was extreme poverty, social inequality, the cult of the fire–arm, crime and Chechnya. A country in which Danila Bagrov (the hero of *Brother*) is "a brother to us all", and in which we take the slogan "Strength doesn't come from money, it comes from the truth" over to America, which has sold out – and we take a bit of xenophobia and racism with us as well. If this metaphor had not already been used, we might have been able to say that Bodrov's character became a new hero in an 'age without heroes'.

But although Danila and "our brother" are everything we hold dear – i.e. the fruit of our absurd reality, Sergei Bodrov managed from the very outset to show maturity beyond his years, and to distance himself from his image and from the character he had played. This ability to distance himself from his image as a celebrity, to avoid letting his fame go to his head and remain a normal person, is something that is extremely rare among film actors.

He was transformed into a symbol once and for all, and irrevocably, by the Kolka rock ice slide, which left Sergey Bodrov Jr. and the rest of his film crew buried in the Karmadon Gorge in September 2002. When news of the tragedy broke, one young critic, who was the same age as Bodrov, said: "If the worst happens, we will have our very own James Dean." And he added: "Would that we had never got one."

Aleksei Balabanov – the director who made Sergei a star and turned Danila Bagrov into a cult character – could himself lay claim to being the biggest big–screen hero of the 1990s. He managed to produce both a polished "cinema for a select few" and a more refined version of pop. The author of the art–house film *Of Freaks and Men* (which was filmed after *Brother*) amazed those who had looked down on the mass popular success of *Brother 2* by willingly seeking to restore the terminology of the cold war and anti–Americanism. One thing's for sure: Stalin would have liked the film. The more generously disposed of Russia's intellectuals, meanwhile, went crazy about the collectivism inspired by *Brother*. One female critic confessed that although it was a fascist film (the first *Brother* had been described as 'fascist', too), it had left her all a–quiver on the inside. Another smart–alec declared that Russia's new cinematic mythology had its origins in the two *Brother* films.

Incidentally, Balabanov was up against a highly competent rival in the shape of Alexander Rogozhin. When the film *The peculiarities of hunting in this country* was released in 1995, the critics declared, as one, that it was destined to become a cult classic. Rogozhkin acquired a reputation, meanwhile – starting with the films *The Guard* and *The Secret Service Agent* – as a gloomy voyeur obsessed with brutality and violence. *Life with an idiot* added two further ingredients to the mix: russophobia and sexual pathology.

Those who knew the director, incidentally, maintained that he scorned all perversions, including intellectual ones, and loved spending time with the 'brotherhood' from the Lenin Film Studio – they may even have gone hunting together. It was when he was in the midst of this group that he first had the idea for a film entitled *The peculiarities of hunting in this country in the autumn*. It is probably impossible to say with any certainty, now, who it was that had the good idea of trying to persuade Rogozhkin to return to comedy (a genre in which he had at one time made a not altogether successful debut). But whoever that person was, the role played by the film's producer, Alexander Golutva, must not be underestimated.

The film was an instant hit. Firstly, it was professionally made in all the most important respects (with the exception of the soundtrack, which was poorly put together) – from the dramatization to the acting. Secondly, Rogozhkin's humour, with all its national flavour, proved to be very accessible to incidental viewers: they identified keenly with the young Finn who had found himself among a group of thrill–seekers.

Everyone in Russia is aware that 'hunting' and 'fishing' are no more than euphemisms for a chaste little boy in the great outdoors, and an alibi for men, all of whom have a little of General Buldakov and a little of the Russian Buddhist Kuzmich in their DNA. It was for that reason that the sudden appearance of so many parodies of Rogozhkin's film, riding the wave of its success, such as Aleksei Rudakov's *The peculiarities of the Russian banya, or Fucked–up Stories* (1999) and *The peculiarities of banya politics, or Banya 2, or Fucked–up stories* (2000) didn't come as a shock to anyone. After all, going to the *banya* in Russia can sometimes be a euphemism, too: "I went to the *banya* – and had a good old scrub while I was there."

The film seemed to play on the various stereotypes of Russia effortlessly (hunting with dogs, bears, the *banya*, vodka), and also a reality which proved to be extremely exotic. A reality which could see you loading a cow onto a bomber in exchange for a couple of bottles of vodka, or bumping into a hunter meditating in a Japanese garden – who, if you sing him a song, turns into an outstanding chauffeur and starts speaking in Finnish. Or you might come across a taciturn general with a cigar forever in his mouth and the appearance of General Lebed (the inimitable Aleksei Buldakov stood out, even among the exalted company of the rest of the cast).

In theory, it was possible to find, in *The peculiarities of hunting in this country*, something resembling a national idea. None of the great cataclysms that the country had been through were depicted on the screen, but in the context of the film traces of these events could certainly be seen, in the choice of social templates that were depicted.

The other thing that made *Hunting* such a uniquely Russin phenomenon was the fact that this group portrait of Russian society in the great outdoors, which was followed by the far less successful *Operation 'Happy New Year'* (1996), *The peculiarities of fishing in this country* (1998) and *The peculiarities of hunting in this country in winter* (2000), had no paralells in world cinema.

There would be a need to explain that Rogozhkin succeeded in rehabilitating physical reality (to spite that other reality – the virtual one) – had the director not expressed his intentions a little more precisely himself, stating that the idea was to bring to the screen a short course in unscientific communism. In this rehabilitation process, Rogozhkin crashed a few rocks together and set off an avalanche. The words of the film's title instantly became more than just a flowery turn of phrase. In the combination of the words 'peculiarities' and 'national', the psyche of the general public seemed to see some sort of universal key, the explanation of and justification for all the pitfalls and peculiarities of Russian life.

It hardly needs saying that this turn of phrase, ultimately, explained absolutely nothing. And the role of national guru was the last thing Rogozhkin was seeking to take on. But a quick search on the Internet throws up hundreds of links to books, articles, audio–visual files and even video games which all play on the title of this legendary film in some shape or form. It transpires that the following all contain national peculiarities relevant to Russia, in some shape or form: army service, speculation, dawn raids, domestic servants, missiles, oncology, OSAGO, rap music, divorce, motivation, Internet statistics and love. As do dharma, barricades, natural disasters and tears. A line from *The peculiarities…* is even quoted in the tag–line for Nikita Mikhalkov's movie *The Barber of Siberia* (1997): "He's Russian, and that explains a lot."

Against the backdrop of post–modernist thought like this, however (and Pelevin was by no means the only person who advocated it), the public demanded something that was a little more familiar, and that made more sense. And nostalgia for the Soviet Union ticked both of those boxes. In the run–up to the new year, 1994, the show 'Song of the year', featuring Angelina Vovk and Yevgeny Menshov, returned to Channel One, and went on to become one of the most odious symbols of *homo Sovieticus*, who refused to be killed off, on Russian television – alongside Yevgeny Petrosyan's show 'Hit song'. Nobody was too shocked or upset by this quiet revenge on the part of *homo Sovieticus*, and *Song of the year* continued as the nationwide symbol of TV variety until the middle of the 'noughties' under Putin, before disappearing as quietly as it had returned, after being digested by the invisible stomach of the market.

The idea that the new stars of TV were singing old songs with new feeling can be ruled out. The first to start singing old songs were those who, cherishing their individuality, hardly ever turned on the television. Those who felt like vomiting when they heard the ardent, revolutionary phrase, 'the period of early perestroika'. Those who were not accustomed to marching in line, and had no intention of growing accustomed to doing so even in a democratic movement, and had no intention of cutting themselves off from the old Soviet world at a time when the majority of the people in this rapidly disintegrating state were decrying it with one voice, with frightening enthusiasm.

The first to start singing in their kitchens about mud–huts and the eagle of the steppes were art critics of a radical persuasion, artists, journalist–intellectuals and popular TV producers. One of the first to start singing in the great Stalinist style was the clever film director Ivan Dykhovichy, in *Bottomless pit*, which was idolized by film critics with an eye for the aesthetic. The film's plot did not have anything good to say about that era, but who cared about the plot when Stalinist Moscow came across as such a great and magnificent city on film!

The film critics immediately started to mourn the great days of Soviet cinematography, which would never be recaptured. The art critics, inspired by a serious of major overseas exhibitions about totalitarian art, set about trying to demonstrate that Stalin's Empire style was not the whim of a tyrant but a visible embodiment of the national vision of the beautiful, our own version of Disneyland. And we would not part company with this past for anything in the world – it was part of our DNA. The Russian museum responded with a huge exhibition of Socialist Realist art entitled *Agitating for happiness*. At the time it did not achieve nationwide popularity. The trendy gallery Roza Azora organized a nostalgic carnival on November 7, to which its enlightened regulars came along, disguised in the Soviet way. That same winter, NTV released a special New Year show in which Gazmanov sang instead of Zykina. The ratings soared. And it all kicked off...

Commercial advertisements began using images from revolutionary propaganda in their posters, and promoting the might of Western domestic appliances with the help of much–loved episodes from the soulful world of Soviet cinematography. The Krasny Oktyabr factory started to manufacture teddy bears. Real estate agents decided to build new high–end apartment buildings in faux Stalinist style. Television producers started to put touching programmes on the conveyor belt about our shared past, and gave screen–time to the masters of Russia's 'Golden generation', rather than to Oscar–winning actors. The authorities jumped on the bandwagon, too: a lugubrious song from the post–war years was chosen as the capital's new anthem. And before long even Luzhkov and Chernomyrdin were declaring in public that they had lived "in mud–huts, in trenches and in the taiga." By that time, when the masters of popular art and the upper echelons of the civil service had begun actively promoting the inventions of the jokers of elite art, the population was ripe for the consumption of nostalgic products. In the collective memory, the Motherland was now associated first and foremost not with the unpleasant physiognomy of the secretary of the party committee, but with the plump visage of an accountant who regularly paid out what was owed.

The whole of this tremulous intellectual and artistic Bohemia, and other citizens who were always inclined to go against the majority, began to make people feel quite nauseous. And, in a fresh fit of non–conformism, they continued to make their way along their chosen path – or rather, to sing their way along it. In his album *Songs from Mitkov*, Butusov sang not only the harmless *Over the seas and the waves* but also the out–and–out prison song *Vaninsky port*. Shenderovich's puppets brought the house down at the Taganka theatre on New Year's Eve. A new wave of nostalgia had begun, this time based on the tough brotherhood of the penal institutions.

Sex and the word

Whatever Roman Viktyuk dreams up from now on, he will never be able to match the effect produced by the work that made him famous: a production of Jean Genet's *The Maids* at the Satirikon theatre. That was the moment when the director became a public figure. He had been a stubborn youth from the provinces, who had travelled to Moscow to complete his studies: the Russian Academy of Theatre Arts, staging plays in the provinces, shared housing, directorial work at the circus school. But he became the trendsetter of theatrical fashion, in his ever–present colourful jacket with the sleeves rolled up: a man who sang of sin and of passion, the favourite of high society and quite a find for the TV cameras.

If there is a woman on stage, she will probably appear dressed as a man at some point; and the male actor will play the role of a woman, prancing around in high–heels, with a feather boa around his neck and his legs in stockings. Or else he will show off his gleaming torso to the audience, and flutter the angel–wings attached to his costume. The actors will go from whispering phrases into the microphone to shouting out something taken straight from the director's library: Wilde, Burgess, Missima, or little–known Italian playwrights, either discovered or invented. Sin. Love. Blood. Sex. Passion. All with a capital letter.

Viktyuk's success in the early 1990s was undeniable. There were packed audiences at the Mossovet Theatre, the Vakhtangov Theatre and the Satirikon – all Moscow was desperate to see one of the rebel's plays. Sex (homosexual sex in particular) was heavily censored in Soviet society, and Viktyuk presented it as an aesthetic, societal value. To many this was a way of resolving deep personal fears and self–imposed bans, but the director had assured himself of universal curiosity. And Roman Viktyuk did not flatter to deceive. Whichever playwright he chose, his interpretations always had the Viktyuk stamp all over them. Whichever subject the director dealt with, it always came back to sex.

Some ventured to suggest that Viktyuk was Russia's answer to Oscar Wilde. Viktyuk himself said on numerous occasions that the only similarities between him and Wilde were to be found in his art. A sworn Epicurean, Wilde always said that in order to find fulfilment the artist's lot was to make the world he portrayed a mirror of his own feelings. And as time passed it became clear that Viktyuk, whilst declaring his love for the art of the theatre, was simply admiring his own unchanging reflection.

When asked what sort of people came to see his plays, the director used to reply: "We don't just have any old people turning up to our theatre."

Viktyuk's plays always belonged to him, and no–one else: in them the director reigned supreme. It therefore seemed as though one couldn't watch Viktyuk's plays without having a passionate love of the director and strong faith in him. Slowly but surely, an extremely comforting symbiotic relationship began to form, between a director who could not live without the adoration of the public, and audiences who had grown used to worshipping "their master". These reserves of love and faith became the very thing that severed Roman Viktyuk's theatre from the life that was going on outside its walls.

Several other theatres operate using similar introverted systems as well. As for the success of Viktyuk's theatre with the public, and his ability to stay afloat, this can probably be explained by those very same social reasons, namely our people's deeply ingrained shyness, which can only be breached on 'cultural' grounds. In other words, the people who went to see Viktyuk's plays were upstanding citizens who would never be seen in a gay club, but who would go to the theatre at the drop of a hat.

"I hardly ever talk to people in literary circles," Viktor Pelevin said in 1997. "And my friends don't take much of an interest in literature. One of them might come round to visit in a black SAAB, and I would show him a Japanese book that I was reading, and he would say: "Viktor, when are you going to start doing something serious?" I like writing but I don't like being a writer. I am only a writer when I am actually in the process of writing something."

Pelevin enjoyed playing with his "target audience", and messing with their heads. His main subject – to use a definition taken from one of his own works – is "the means of existence of protein bodies in the fourth age of power". In other words, life itself, which, as Zhuang Zi – Pelevin's most avid reader in China – maintains, is no more than a dream.

Later, *Kommersant* managed to extract from Pelevin, in an extremely rare interview with the writer, a few thoughts about literature in general and about Pelevin the writer in particular. His thoughts could be characterized roughly like this: "In a culture regulated by market principles, the plethora of things on offer can quickly be summarized in just three or four supermarket shelves labelled 'murder mysteries', 'thrillers', 'erotica' and 'children's books'. Writers stop producing anything else because everything else takes a lot of effort that goes unrewarded...

On the other hand, if we were to organize culture along any other lines, we would soon see such scum crawling out of the cellars – the things we would see happening...If you ask me, far better the faceless vulgarity of the market than the personal vulgarity of a mass of specific people from the subsidized cultural establishment, i.e. the mafia. Good books will appear come what may, because there are a lot of other laws at play in this world, other than the law of supply and demand. In the past, good books appeared in spite of highly developed socialism; now they are going to appear in spite of the market, that's all there is to it...

Writers are responsible for the text they write, not for their readers or critics. For that reason it is a very lonely occupation. Moreover, I never try to take anyone anywhere: I simply write the kinds of books for others that I would find entertaining myself. In fact, they entertain me too, because I am the first person to read them. I don't take myself very seriously – far from it. And 'nowhere' is not a place that you can take people to, or indeed bring people back from. We all share this home right from the start, whether we realise it or not. Ivan Susanin was a great charlatan..."

9. WITH A FEW KIND WORDS AND A GUN. SECURITY AGENTS, TERRORISTS AND PEACEMAKERS.

The bodyguard

In modern Russia, Vladimir Putin was by no means the first person with a background in the security services to move into politics. When he did so he was treading a well–trodden path. The trailblazer in this regard was Alexander Korzhakov, whose fall was no less fantastical than his eleven–year term in office – the whole of which was spent on an upward curve – initially in the backround behind the president, and then alongside him. After going largely unnoticed and being 'added on' from 'the group of nine' in 1985, in 1996 experts rated him the second most influential man in the country, behind Boris Yeltsin. Yeltsin merely laughed this off – he had no doubt that one word from him would be enough to make the head of the PSS, who was one hundred percent loyal to him, come out of the shadows. Korzhakov laughed at it, too, feeling that his achievements over many years – the first time he made the front pages of the newspapers was probably the time he climbed onto a tank in front of the parliament building in August 1991 – meant that he had *carte blanche* to do as he pleased – or as good as.

One of the public actions taken by Korzhakov that attracted the most media coverage, during his tenure as head of the President's Security Service (PSS), was an operation involving the kidnapping of Vladimir Gusinsky's bodyguard outside the Moscow mayor's office. It was he that gave the order to go ahead with the operation. It will be known to posterity by its code–name, 'Face–down in the snow', which was dreamed up by his closest rival, Valery Streletsky.

On Friday, December 2, 1994, at the end of the working day, ordinary people going about their business in Moscow might have witnessed some thick–set men in stained uniforms and black masks, armed with state–of–the–art weapons, blocking off the approaches to the mayor's office and forcing a group of people to lie down with their faces in the snow. The latter were then dealt blows to the ribs and between the legs. The whole scene was reminiscent of TV images of hostages being seized by terrorists, or training exercises involving anti–terrorist units. The operation in front of the mayor's office lasted almost four hours: from 5 pm to 9 pm. It involved 24 automatic weapons.

Korzhakov later explained the reason for the attack on 'Most' in an interview, in simple terms: "We needed to show those guys what was what." Streletsky was rather more specific in the interview he gave: "This caused Gusinsky to leave Russia for six months. How else were we to stop him getting involved in politics?"

From the moment the PSS was created, Korzhakov and his subordinates adhered to a code that was kept secret, and which had been written for them alone. This code had been signed off by the president. It could be stretched, like a rubber band, in response to whatever situation they found themselves in. The first thing that happened to those in the service was that they were given a written guarantee of immunity.

The entirely lawful intervention in this armed incident in the city centre by members of Moscow's FSC cost Yevgeny Savostyanov, who was both the former chairman and the deputy chairman in Bolshaya Lubyanka Street. The foul–mouthed tirade to which he was subjected over the telephone by Korzhakov and Barsukov was followed, a couple of hours later, by a presidential directive stating that he was to be removed from his post. Only the man who had himself written the directive, and gone to request the president's signature in his own inimitable way, could have removed a director in such a lofty position from his position so quickly. And a man who had the complete trust of the president. The result of this action is well–documented, and serves to explain the reason. Gusinsky did indeed leave Moscow for London for six months and, by all accounts, had quite a fright. Moreover, during the course of the incident light was shone on his connections to various organizations and prominent circles to whom he had appealed for help, and these connections were cut off, temporarily at least.

But some time later the resourceful Luzhkov, reacting to the "signal" given by Korzhakov, publicly stated that he had no designs on the presidency whatsoever, and that the role of mayor suited him down to the ground. The financial relations between the mayor's office and the 'Most' group dragged on, and this affected Gusinsky the businessman more than anyone else.

This was the Chekist round in Korzhakov's battle, and, being a professional, he made sure that he won it. The law, and the defence, turned out to favour the stronger man. The interests of the state, or of security, had nothing whatsoever to do with this story, a fact which was indirectly attested to by the fact that during the presidential elections Korzhakov found himself surrounded by his own friends and enemies. And it was at that exact moment that he was tricked, as a political spin was put on what was no more than the latest demonstration of eagerness to serve.

On the same day that Yeltsin realized that he had underestimated Korzhakov, it became clear that Korzhakov had overestimated himself: this game of loyalty, just as in the incident involving Pavel Grachev, did not save him from the accurate appraisal: "I bit off more than I could chew…"

Prior to that, Boris Yeltsin had not been unduly bothered by the stories that were rolled out from time to time in the press, demonizing Alexander Korzhakov. He said almost nothing when, in 1994, Korzhakov's enemies handed to journalists a letter to the head of the PSS, Viktor Chernomyrdin, in which Korzhakov advised the head of the government how to handle special exporters and the economy in general. He remained silent when the mass media aligned itself firmly in Luzhkov's defence after 'Operation Face–down in the Snow'.

It was not until May 1996 that he publicly reprimanded the 'bodyguard', as Korzhakov liked to refer to himself. Back then, the latter gave an interview that was widely read to the British newspaper *The Observer*, and then to Interfax, declaring that it would be a good idea to postpone the presidential elections. The essence of Korzhakov's political thinking could be summarized as follows: "If the elections take place when they are scheduled to take place, we will be unable to prevent disorder. If Yeltsin wins, the radicals among the opposition will claim the results were falsified. If Zyuganov wins, then even if he tries to adopt a centrist approach, those same people will prevent him from doing so – and will again rise up."

Lieutenant–general Korzhakov's immediate supervisor reacted quickly and decisively. Yeltsin emphasized that he believed "in the wisdom of the Russian electorate, and therefore the elections will take place at the time they are scheduled to take place under the constitution," and he added, "I have already told Korzhakov to stay out of politics and not to make any more statements like that." By all accounts Yeltsin treated his subordinate very meanly.

Korzhakov understood the president's words in his own special way. Do whatever you think needs doing – but keep quiet about it. Sure enough, he did whatever his reason told him was best for Boris Yeltsin, and for Korzhakov and the rest of the country, by extension. It was only natural that his reasoning differed in many respects from the reasoning of the other members of the board of Boris Yeltsin's electoral team. The president, true to his experience over many years, had once again put the 'horse and the trembling doe' in the same stable. This method had proved to be successful over a long period of time: the men alongside the president, with their opposing views, balanced each other out. Their efforts to outmanoeuvre their internal rivals generated ideas, and Yeltsin then selected whichever ideas suited him best. But it transpired that when it was pushed to extremes, the system malfunctioned.

The final battle for the president's favour was a fight to the death. A strong position was not enough for either of the parties – they needed a decisive victory by the time the result of the elections was announced. The fact that a battle was taking place could be seen even in the small details: in the fact that both the liberals and the PSS had simultaneously set themselves the goal of making sure the first 'presidential' concert in Volgograd was a success; and in their attitude to the fact that the president's daughter, Tatiana, was involved in the campaign – the need to submit to the will of 'civilians', whoever they might be, irritated members of the PSS team beyond measure (this was the case in Tver, for example, where, with the elections around the corner, Tatiana Borisovna advised a close circle of security guards to take off their dark glasses, which made them look like members of the Tanton Macoute). The high point of all this (of the things that became known, of course) was an interview that Boris Yeltsin gave in Yekaterinburg, in which the president rejected a proposal by Anatoly Chubais that he return to a government of reformers along the lines of the government in 1991–1992. Alexander Korzhakov was one of the men who initiated that interview.

Korzhakov's joy at the president's statement that new men, rather than old men, would come in. This small victory over Chubais in Yekaterinburg turned into a heavy defeat: Lebed was brought in. He took his place alongside Yeltsin and immediately took on a great deal of responsibility. Unlike Korzhakov, however, he had a moral right to do so: 15% of those who turned out for the election voted for him. And that 15% counted for more than all Korzhakov's 11 years of service.

And, of course, the final straw was the detention of two members of the president's campaign team with a box of photocopies. Had this happened in the morning it could have been glossed over, explained away as a simple mistake; the President's Security Service and the FSB could have been cracked down on without anybody having to be fired. Korzhakov did not overstep the mark at night, when he was probably asleep. He did so the next day – at a meeting with Yeltsin, when he gave the latter an ultimatum. And this ultimatum was not accepted. Yeltsin weighed up the votes that could be secured by Korzhakov, Lebed and Chubais (who had Russia's biggest entrepreneurs behind him), and decided that Korzhakov's share weighed the least.

In any case, as paradoxical as it seemed, it was the elections that did for the head of the PSS. The very elections he had tried so hard to avoid...

Seeing in the New Year in Grozny

And yet everything had seemed so peaceful at first. The Chechen national congress, which was headed by the retired general Djokhar Dudayev, was referred to as 'pro–Yeltsin' as early as 1991. Shamil Basayev had helped protect the White House from the SCSE. Admittedly, Aslan Maskhadov had, in January of that year, been in command of some soldiers who, covered by Vilnius's armed police, stormed a TV centre, and was by all accounts an 'enemy of democracy'...

After Djokhar Dudayev's declaration that the Chechen Republic was an independent state, the allies' paths (were they ever really allies at all?) diverged once and for all. What followed was the war. It was a war which demonstrated that "there was no longer an army – i.e. a disciplined, hierarchical set of armed forces in Russia by the mid–1990s...The army (or rather the entity that bore this name) had gone from being the last support for the structure of the state, to representing the biggest threat to that state". If that assertion by the *Kommersant* columnist Maksim Sokolov seems unduly harsh, all we need do is list the major failures of the Russian armed forces in the 1990s and their consequences. All the official positions contained in the list are accurate as of September 1999.

1991–1992 – the armaments stores of the 14th Guards army in Pridnestrovie are robbed, as soldiers turn a blind eye. On June 28, 1992, army commander Yury Netkachev is transferred to command the army in the North Caucasus.

July 13, 1993 – 25 border guards are killed during an attack by mujaheddin from Tadjikistan on the 12th outpost of the Moscow border service. The outpost, left unprotected, is taken by the insurgents. The forces of the Federal Border Service were led by the commander of the border troops, Andrei Nikolayev, and the commander of the unit of border troops in Tajikistan, general–major Anatoly Chechulin.

December 31, 1994 – during an under–prepared storming of Grozny, federal forces lose over a thousand people. The minister of defence, Pavel Grachev, and the minister of the interior, Viktor Erin, were in overall charge of the operation. Separate groups involved in the storming of the city were under the command of generals Konstantin Pulikovsky, Anatoly Kvashnin, Lev Rokhlin (he was put forward for the title of Hero of Russia for the storming of Grozny, and declined to accept the award), and Ivan Babichev. No–one was reprimanded.

June 14, 1995 – the attack on Budyonnovsk by a unit led by Basayev; a large number of people are taken hostage. The unsuccessful operation to storm the hospital complex was led by the deputy minister of the MIA, Mikhail Yegorov, and the Minister of the Interior, Viktor Yerin. The actions of the federal forces were also directed by the defence minister Pavel Grachev and the head of the FSB Sergei Stepashin. The minister of internal affairs, Viktor Yerin, was sacked (he took up the role of deputy director of the External Intelligence Service), whilst the head of the FSB Sergei Stepashin tendered his resignation, as did the deputy prime minister Nikolai Yegorov (who was appointed an adviser to the president), the governor of the Stavropolsk Region, Evgeny Kuznetsov, and the heads of the regional FSB and Internal Affairs Division. Grachev stayed on as defence minister until June 18, 1996.

January 9, 1996 – the attack on Kizlyar and the village of Pervomaiskoye; civilians taken hostage by a unit led by Raduev. The storming of Pervomaiskoye, during which a large number of hostages died but most of the insurgents managed to get away, was directed by the director of the FSB, army general Mikhail Baruskov, the minister of internal affairs, army general Anatoly Kulikov, and the head of the General Staff, Colonel General Mikhail Kolesnikov. Nobody accepted responsibility.

March 6, 1996 – armed fighters take control of Grozny. In September 1996, the Chief military prosecutor's office opened a criminal investigation in relation to the former commander of the Chechnya, general–major Andrievsky. He was accused of negligence in the performance of his official duties with regard to protecting Grozny. Andrievsky himself described the opening of a criminal investigation as "an attempt to discredit the leadership of the Ministry of Internal Affairs of the Russian Federation". Nothing is known about the investigation into this matter.

April 16, 1996 – the 245th Motor Rifle Regiment comes under attack in a ravine near Yaryshmardy whilst advancing without the required military column. According to official data, 73 servicemen died and 52 were wounded; six armoured vehicles, one tank, one armoured reconnaissance and patrol vehicle and 11 cars were destroyed. The main military prosecutor's office opened a criminal case against the commander of the 245th regiment, and he was removed from his post whilst the investigation was ongoing. Lieutenant–general Rokhlin and chief military prosecutor Panichev later named General Major Kondratiev, Colonels Romanikhin and Tunilev, Lieutenant–Colonels

Vodolaev and Nerkovsky, the head of Central Command in Chechya, Andrievsky, the Minister of Internal Affairs in Chechnya, Taranov, Lieutenant–General Pulikovsky and the commander of the interior forces of the MIA RF, Rybakov, among those responsible for the loss of the column. There was no word about any punishments being imposed on any of them.

August 6, 1996 – Grozny is stormed by mujahideen, Ministry of Defence troops are caught unawares and the MIA RF suffers considerable losses (around 250 killed and 1000 wounded). A few days before the city was taken, a unit of special forces had been taken out of the city and the checkpoints on many routes were taken down. At that moment, Russia's first deputy minister of internal affairs, colonel–general Pavel Golubets, took charge of the MIA of Russia's coordination centre in Chechnya. According to accounts from witnesses, when the storming of the city began Golubets, finding himself blocked up in a government complex in the city centre, hid in a bunker rather than try to oversee the defence of the city. The other people in charge of the defence of the city were the commander of the Associated group of federal forces in Chechnya, lieutenant–general Pulikovsky, and the commandant of Grozny, Anrievsky. There is no data available about any punishments being meted out to officials guilty of failing to prevent the city from being taken by insurgents.

22nd December, 1997 – insurgents attack the 4th barrack town in the village of Gerali (a suburb of Buynaksk), where units within the 136th Motor Rifle Division were stationed. Three soldiers were killed and 13 were wounded; in addition, two T72 tanks were destroyed, as well as three cars and two fuel tankers. The commander of the temporary rapid–response group in the interior forces in the North Caucasus, major–general Andrievsky, and the commander of the North Caucasus Military District, colonel–general Kazantsev, were responsible for the situation. At the beginning of January 1998 Andrievsky was removed from his position.

The dark fascination of Budyonnovsk

By the summer of 1995 Chechnya was gradually coming under the control of Russian troops. Most of the Chechen insurgents had managed to evade capture, however. In an interview that he gave to a correspondent from ITAR/TASS, Djokhar Dudayev said: "The fighting is not yet over, it is merely assuming new forms."

The first to feel the impact of these "new forms of war" were the people of Stavropol. At around midday on June 14, 1995, a group of insurgents under the command of Shamil Basayev seized the city of Budyonnovsk. After taking the local hospital, the terrorists demanded a cessation to military operations in Chechnya, the withdrawal of troops and direct negotiations between Yeltsin and Dudayev, and threatened to kill the hostages they had taken – some 2000 people, including hospital staff, patients and children.

The director of the FSB, Sergei Stepashin, Russia's Interior Minister Viktor Yerin and his deputy Mikhail Yegorov flew out to the scene, and began talks with the terrorists. All the senior figures in charge of the country spoke about the terrorist attack, including President Yeltsin. Yeltsin, however, clearly deciding that it did not befit the president of a great nation to cancel state visits because of a bunch of terrorists, set off for Halifax for a G8 summit. Before leaving he told journalists that it had taken him a long time to make up his mind to go, but ultimately decided that the prime minister and the minister of the interior would be able to deal with the Chechens without his help. He, on the other hand, would take advantage of this opportunity to explain to his western colleagues once again what Dudayev's regime was all about, whilst at the same time discussing the measures that could be taken in the battle against terrorism.

In the space of three days, from June 16 to 19, 1995, federal special ops units made two attempts to storm the hospital in

Budyonnovsk (during one of them they managed to free 61 hostages); contact was established between the leader of the terrorists, Shamil Basayev, and Viktor Chernomyrdin, over the telephone; there were telephone conferences between the head of the terrorists and members of the Russian government in Buddenovsk; and, in the end, most of the hostages were freed and the terrorists left in buses that were provided for them. Millions of TV viewers witnessed the unprecedented, desperate public diplomacy of Viktor Chernomyrdin, who was attempting to do more than merely rescue the hostages. He had put his own political future on the line.

The prime minister took the initiative in demonstrative fashion: he opened the emergency negotiations at night. He promised to bring an end to the war, which had dragged on for many months. He ordered the commander–in–chief – who was flying overhead from Canada to Moscow – to cease military operations. As for Yeltsin, he made threats from Halifax against the bandits, with whom "there could be no negotiations". He revealed openly that he had agreed the terms of the storm in advance with Yerin. His words were echoed in Russia by Grachev, who by all accounts insisted on using force to resolve the crisis.

The two attempts to storm the building both failed. According to the Russian soldiers, during the first storm they took control of the ground floor of the main building of the hospital and could have taken the entire block, but were suddenly ordered to stand down. The order was given by Chernomyrdin.

The general public and the mass media in Russia had a strong case of Stockholm syndrome. The media were able to convey all the horror to which Basayev's victims had been subjected – they had been forced to identify with their executioner. But, making use of all the resources at the disposal of "TV reality" to show one side of the stand–off – "we must rescue these people", the media said nothing at all about the other side of it – "we must rescue the thing without which it will be impossible to rescue people in the future, i.e. the state, whose hand must not be forced by a bunch of absolute scoundrels."

One got the impression that the authorities' determination was not down to the fact that the situation was so hopeless, but was no more than a foolish stubbornness or, worse still, a blood—lust that they had been born with.

In the eyes of the general public, the only person who came out of the direct broadcast from the Budyonnovsk hospital with any credit was Viktor Chernomyrdin, who had entered into dialogue with Shamil Basayev. At that point the prime minister made a decision that was utterly humane, and which everyone could understand: he had the opportunity to act, and he took it. The TV viewers didn't have that opportunity, and, as they looked at the faces of the hostages in Budyonnovsk, it is unlikely any of them was able to reason coldly about whether any self—respecting state figure ought to negotiate with terrorists. That said, it is not clear which purpose the broadcast did more to serve: the successful rescue of the people or the glory of Shamil Basayev.

In spite of Chernomyrdin's peacemaking 129 people died in the terrorist attack in Buddenovsk, and 415 were wounded. No—one will ever know what might have been if Chernomyrdin had not stopped the rescue team, which was already in place on the ground floor of the hospital, awaiting its final order. But the order was not the one they had been expecting at all. As it moved out, 'Alpha' lost more men than it had lost while seizing the hospital.

"Shamil Basayev, raise your voice!" – Viktor Chernomyrdin's words to the Chechen terrorist in the summer of 1995 resonated throughout the country. "Yes, because of the people. Two thousand people. Although it is not the precise figure that matters. Even if there had only been one person in there, and I could have done something to help, I would still have opened negotiations with the terrorist," he repeated in an interview three years later.

No—one had ever taken such open action before. As Russian tradition has it, politicians in the Chernomyrdin mould only choose to be as desperately open as he was when the behind—the—scenes (or cabinet—based) methods to which they are more accustomed are no longer working. When he gave personal guarantees – "as the prime minister" – to the terrorists, he could not be certain, it would seem, that the buses containing the hostages and the terrorists would not be shot at during the journey. It would take 'Alpha' group 4–6 seconds to take a bus of that kind...

And yet the prime minister took that step.

On June 20, Boris Yeltsin saw fit to remind the country that Viktor Chernomyrdin, who had gone to considerable lengths to resolve the crisis in Budyonnovsk, was acting under his – the president's – constant guidance. Firstly, he had maintained "constant contact" with the prime minister – "if not every half—hour, then every hour". Secondly, the president declared that he "could not see any mistakes" in the prime minister's actions.

It was clearly felt in the Kremlin that the situation had reached a point when, for starters, it was time to start talking about the medals that were going to be awarded, and secondly, to work out who had earnt one. Judging by the way the president busied himself (on the third day after his arrival from Halifax), he was not inclined to award a medal for rescuing the hostages to the prime minister alone.

Shamil Basayev's raid, meanwhile, ended with the terrorists returning to Chechnya. During the journey, the engine of one of the buses cut out, and the armoured personnel carrier accompanying the convoy hauled it onto the hard shoulder until the engine got going again. In Chechnya the road snaked into the mountains, and the other buses started to get into difficulties, with parts constantly breaking or malfunctioning. Occasionally the brakes failed, and the passengers in this strange convoy feared they might simply go hurtling into the abyss.

At last the buses arrived in Zandak, a large Chechen village where there were no traces of the war whatsoever. It was clear that these people had never been subjected to bombings or shootings. Geese and hens were scurrying along the streets, the buildings stood firm, and the local Chechens did not look poverty–stricken at all.

A stormy demonstration began in the square in the centre of the village. The Chechens greeted Basayev's men as if they were heroic freedom fighters. A short time before these events, Sergei Kovalev, who had been removed from his position as spokesman on human rights, and who had volunteered to accompany the convoy as a "human shield", had spoken to those assembled. After his speech the Chechens started cheering: "Kovalev! Kovalev!" Aslambek, one of Basayev's youngest commanders, then took the floor, saying: "We did this out of desperation, we wanted Russia to find out what the smell of blood was like, and with the minor blood–letting of Budyonnovsk we sought to prevent the major blood–letting of war!"

Amid the general chaos, Basayev disappeared. Soon his people, too, headed off reluctantly to their respective homes.

But another demonstration was taking place in Buddyonovsk. The people were demanding that the resources which had been set aside for the rebuilding of Chechnya be put towards the rebuilding of Budyonnovsk.

To many, Chernomyrdin's efforts to make peace in Budyonnovsk represented an act of supreme humanity: they were a feat that neither the head of state at the time, nor the current head of state, would have been capable of achieving, simply by dint of the fact that their role was exactly that – to be head of state. But Chernomyrdin, as the journalist Natalia Gevorkyan put it, was some sort of "prime minister who did things his way".

For the others, it would have been the strategy of someone who could not see the bigger picture, and was a weak leader; it would almost have been a betrayal. It would have been all the more shameful because it was carried out at a time when

the scales in the first Chechen War seemed to be tipping in
Russia's favour. The result of the prime minister's "untimely lack
of backbone" was that the terrorists were able to regroup, make
their plans and shift the course of events in their favour, both on
the field of battle and in the mass media. The terrorist attacks in
Kizlyar and Moscow were a direct consequence of Buddyonovsk,
as was...the shameful Khasavyurtovsk peace.

A never–before–published
interview with Djokhar Dudayev

Nowadays it is probably hard to comprehend the extent to
which Russian society was polarized by the war in Chechnya. It
may be that we will gain a clearer understanding of the extent of
the stand–off by studying excerpts from the last interview ever
given by Djokhar Dudayev [Dudayev was killed by a guided
missile following a special operation by the Russian security
services on April 21, 1996], which was recorded not long before
his death by a former correspondent from the TASS agency,
Sharip Asuev (the interview was prepared for publication by
Vladislav Dorofeyev). This interview has never been published
before.

On peace: "The war will end sooner or later. And we will
sign a peace accord. Not in Moscow – I'll never go there – and
not in Chechnya – we must let Russia save a bit of face. It (the
signing of a peace accord – Ed.) will take place in the Caucasus,
in Dagestan. Do you want me to tell you exactly where it's going
to happen? In a railway car. (Khasavyurt is indeed in Dagestan,
but the peace accord was signed inside a building.)

On Russia: "The Russian people and the Russian state have
lost the idea which held the country together. The deceptive
idea of Communism – of a wonderful future – has disappeared.
There is no getting away from that. And since there's no idea,
there's no politics. Without politics, there's no ideology. Without

an ideology, there are no motives. Without motives, there is no incentive. End of story. Nothing but emptiness...

What path can Russia take in the future? Adopt the dollar and worship at its altar? They're ready to do that even now. What will come of it? It will be suicide, the road to destruction.

There is no spirituality – no faith. There is a complete lack of spirituality, immorality, an absence of morals."

On the war: "We have seen a clash of two titanic forces: the satanic force and the moral force. A war is being waged between the believers and the unbelievers. And there is no man on this planet capable of bringing an end to this war, no–one who will be able to stop this war, whether they want to or not. Yeltsin's demands, which he has stated on three occasions, carry no weight. The commands given by Grachev and Chernomyrdin carry no weight. None of the people in power in Russia can put a stop to this war – because there are no real levers of influence."

On himself: "As God is my witness, I never wanted to put myself forward as president. I didn't want a position of authority in this republic, in this environment, which has been hopelessly spoilt, at all. I am afraid of this environment, to be frank – I shrank from it.

On the one hand, I have wanted to go home for a long time; on the other hand, this place was so far from my intellect and the level at which I belong, with all its luxury, arrogance and behind–the–scenes games. For me, this environment was wild and distant. But gradually, when I started to meet people – in towns and villages, and in remote parts of the country – I saw in the people a vast spiritual potential, which was unable to be fulfilled and which must be allowed to be released.

But when I saw in whom the Nakh people had entrusted their sovereignty, and their future, on my honour – I felt my skin crawl...

I looked on and shuddered with horror. The faith of the people – look whose hands it has been left in! It became clear that this would mean the end. That we would not follow the path that the people had wanted to follow. That they would literally pervert this idea (sovereignty – Ed.), chew it up and spit it out. And the people would be transformed into nothing.

That was what forced me to assume this heavy burden. Freedom is a very expensive thing. And if you want it you have to pay in many ways – including with blood. If you grasp freedom, then you must grasp it and be aware of what you are getting yourself into. If you decide not to grasp it, you must do so consciously. We grasped hold of it. And since we have done so... it's one thing to come up with fine words from the tribunes, but it's another matter entirely when you have to put the decision you have taken into effect."

On Chechen statehood: "Everyone was corrupt. We needed time to purge the highest echelons of power. One cabinet was replaced, then a second, then a third. And we purged the upper echelons, we managed to do that. In the past, people used to bring it (money – Ed.) to the senior figures in the higher echelons of power, and there was a particular tariff, whereas now the senior figures wouldn't even dream of that happening. And those who thought that whole thing up, they felt the sword of Damocles hanging over them, about to chop off their heads.

But at the lower level, corruption continued to exist with undiminished strength. And in spite of this we created our own model – from scratch – of a political state: from local government to the highest political authority. And yet we managed to construct a state of our own, with a set of laws in place. We created our own economic, social, spiritual and cultural programmes. And how effectively those processes had begun to work! Before the war production was on the up, and progressing in great leaps and bounds!"

On modern society: "Of course I would have liked to have done a lot of things differently. But I wasn't able to because of the environment I was in – a society which was not ready for democracy, not ready to abide by the standards of law. Did I not want to have talented, intelligent, intellectual, creative people alongside me, people who were loyal to the cause?! But instead it turned out that the people around me were misers, who were only interested in one thing: unbridled profit. The circle I was in turned out that way due to the circumstances; there was no other circle."

Djokhar Dudayev, in the eyes of many Chechens, became not so much a hero as a mythical figure, a symbol of the struggle for freedom.

The race for Pristina

Another consequence of the first Chechen War – albeit one that was not immediately felt – was that it helped to rally the Russian masses. Three years after Khasavyurt – for almost the first time in Russian history – the generals secretly planned a major campaign, and implemented it outside the country, about which neither the Minister of Foreign Affairs nor the Prime Minister knew anything. At least twenty fairly young (their average age was around 50), energetic and like–minded generals were found, who were capable, in top secret circumstances, of independently planning and carrying out not only a military plan but also a politico–military one.

In June 1999, whilst talks were ongoing at Russia's MFA about the situation in Kosovo, a tense operation was under way at Russia's military HQ: a plan was being prepared for a thunderous redeployment of 200 paratroopers from Bosnia to Kosovo and the capture of Slatin aerodrome in Kosovo's capital, Pristina (NATO forces had not bombed the city, counting on using it as a base for its military transport planes and a command centre for the British peacekeepers). In the long–term, under the generals' plan, this was supposed to be the site where Russian Il76 military transport planes were supposed to land, bringing with them several thousand paratroopers from Pskov, Ryazan and Ivanovo.

The idea of using peacekeepers from Bosnia was the brainchild of Colonel–General Viktor Zavarzin (he had been given this latest rank, incidentally, for his successes in the Kosovo operation), who represented Russia's Ministry of Defence at NATO.

Under the headquarters' plan, 'hour zero' was fixed at 11.30 am on June 11. At 11.00, the head of the general staff, General Anatoly Kvashnin made a personal call to the president, informed him about the plan and requested his approval. Boris Yeltsin approved the plan, deeming it to be "the correct course of action, and a strong move". Only after this did Kvashnin tell the Minister of Defence, Igor Sergeev, about it, and report that it had the president's backing.

At 11.30 on the dot, on June 11, a column of Russian soldiers – approximately 200 people in 15 armoured vehicles, 30 lorries and 5 UAZ vehicles (equipped with enough dry rations to last five days) – began to move out of the area where the peacekeeping team was based (not far from the Bosnian city of Tuzl), towards the border with Yugoslavia. An hour later, a column of Russian paratroopers with KFOR emblems on their uniforms (the soldiers had spent the night painting them on before departing) crossed the border and headed deep into the country, accompanied by Serb police.

At that time, units of the air and paramilitary force, numbering 1000, were already concentrated at the aerodromes of Ryazan, Ivanovo and Pskov, as well as six planes from military aviation, VVS Il76MD, which were ready to fly out to the Balkans at four hours' notice. They were supposed to land at one of the aerodromes in Pech or Pristina.

Four hours later, the column proceeded through Belgrade. The route through Belgrade added an extra 100 km to the journey, but there was a reason why it was chosen: the Serbs were overjoyed to see their 'Russian brothers', and that provided a superb boost for morale. At 4.30 on June 12, the Russian paratroopers, after making their way through Pristina, where they ran into a demonstration attended by many thousands of Serbs singing songs and playing music, arrived at the Slatin airbase. A high–ranking civil servant in the general staff declared: "Thanks specifically to the firm position and practical steps taken by the General staff, there has been a new development to the situation in Kosovo, which NATO must reckon with. We were the first to reach Pristina, just as we were once first to reach Berlin."

At the scene of these events, to onlookers, this sounded less emotional but equally dramatic.

"They made their way to the aerodrome and took up a defensive position. The bulk of the troops were accommodated in an army barracks which had been home to Yugoslav soldiers before they arrived. They arrived in time to meet these soldiers – and what a meeting it was! The last people the Serbs were expecting to see at the airbase were Russian paratroopers. The Serbs wept. They wept because they were leaving without battle having been joined, and because they had so unexpectedly come across people of their own kind – Russians.

The Serbs handed the barracks over in perfect condition, and two days later General Zavarzin decided to move the paratroopers closer to the airbase. There they found a hangar where some planes were being repaired, and that was where they stopped. The paratroopers spent a few more days cleaning out the hangar. And throughout this entire time no–one cancelled the shifts of the reserve groups, units or positions. There were not enough people there, of course, and the people there sensed that they were almost at breaking point.

At that point Zavarzin once again gave the order for everyone to be moved: he had found another site, next to the barracks which they had left at the outset. They would be right there, across the street – but it was like chalk and cheese compared to the last one. It was an old ruin. The paratroopers, to give them their due, managed to bring order to the site as best they could. As for the first barracks, the Albanians, who by that time had started to return to Kosovo from Macedonia, had dismantled it.

Warrant officer Dima Zaviralov and eight soldiers, all from Semirkhan, were given the task of guarding the entrance to the airbase and also holding the road to Pristina, and not letting anyone through in either direction, under any circumstances. And they carried out their instructions to the letter.

And how many people there were on that road! Journalists? Don't let them through. Russians – don't let them through. Americans and Brits – all the more so. A Bulgarian journalist arrived, and stood at the gates for a long time asking to be granted access. He wasn't let through either.

Then there was the situation with the British tanks – that was right at the start, much was written about it. Ranged against their tanks were two of our Armoured Personnel Carriers, and it is a fact well known: the British tanks did not get past staff sergeant Dima Zamiralov's checkpoint.

At one point a pleasant–looking, middle–aged Italian drove up to the checkpoint, an amiable smile on his face, and, on discovering that he was not going to be let through, reacted as if he was pleased to hear this, and shouted out: "Hello!" and generally seemed to be in good spirits.

It was not until two days later, when the paratroopers were warned that Italy's deputy defence minister was going to go through the checkpoint, and that he must be let through, that they recognized him as that same amiable Italian..."

The second phase of the plan, however – the deployment of reinforcements from Russia – was at risk of failing. Hungary and Bulgaria refused to provide airspace. This was an unexpected hitch for the general staff. In actual fact, permission had already been given for the planes containing the paratroopers to fly into Bosnia, but only for the purposes of a scheduled rotation. The generals decided to use this to their advantage. But in Sophia and Budapest it was observed, with good reason, that the situation had changed radically.

The Russian MFA sent a request to the Bulgaria on June 12. The Russian ambassador Leonid Kerestedzhiyants went so far as to have a face–to–face meeting with the country's prime minister, Ivan Kostov. The latter amicably advised Moscow to sort out the issue with Washington. Otherwise, the Bulgarians would have to act in accordance with their Constitution: the Russian planes' unauthorized flights into Bulgaria (and Hungary) would be deemed to be an incursion into the country's air–space.

Thus the Russian paratroopers in Slatin found themselves effectively caught in a trap. They only had enough supplies left for two days. But they were supposed to remain there at least until June 18, when the G8 summit was due to begin in Cologne.

And they did so. "Of course, we had neither water nor electricity. And there was nothing at all on that road. There was a half–destroyed little building – it had been bombed two months earlier.

"Would you look at that," Dima Zamiralov said, "that's what we're living with.

And they're having a bad time of it?! The house looked as good as new. Three bedrooms, a bathroom, a kitchen, a veranda overlooking the road and a British cabin. The power's on, everything's working, a pump is sending up water, and someone is taking a shower; the television, which has a video recorder underneath it, is switched on, and some of our lot are watching NATO planes landing at their airbases on the BBC news; there's even a piglet grunting somewhere...They've really made themselves at home!

The paratroopers are in luck – the Yugoslav army's stores turned out to be right next to their cabin: the NATO troops bombed them with particular ferocity. But a great deal has been left intact.

"Everything in that house is like a trophy," said Dima, still looking as embarrassed as ever.

"What do you mean by that?"

"Well, it comes from over there," – he gestured towards the destroyed buildings of the stores, in irritation.

First of all some diesel fuel was brought out of the stores. It was something that everyone needed: our airborne troops, the British, and the Albanians, who had begun to return from Macedonia. I don't know where the British had got the diesel fuel from, but our men and the Albanians had raided the depots, of course. Our men took the diesel fuel one way, and the Albanians took it the other – trying, of course, to avoid catching each other's eye. What can you do?

Then one of our paratroopers found a unit that was almost entirely intact, for pumping engine oil. They pulled the pump out of it straight away and it was installed in the building. So now we had a shower: water came pouring steadily out of the pump.

After this, a masking net was required. The high command said no to this request from the cabin, because it had nowhere to get one. And it didn't need to: they found one in the warehouse. And they found enough for both companies of peacekeepers, with enough left over for a third.

The paratrooper Dima Gagauz had a garage in Tula; Dima was a mechanic. He was the one who pointed out some clapped out Yugoslav vehicles. Thus a charming Iveko lorry, which was almost brand new, was brought into the world. Admittedly, the team adopted it for its own ends.

Yury Mikhailovich Luzhkov, the mayor of Moscow, on hearing how rapidly the paratroopers had reached the airbase, awarded each of them a special commander's watch. And he sent the deputy Nikolai Moskovchenko to carry out this mission.

Moskovchenko reached the peacekeepers and started to hand out the watches. They were quickly handed out. Along came some Serbs who had been hired to work at the airbase – and they too were given watches. He met some of the British officers – and this was enough for him.

"There aren't enough watches for the paratroopers, Kolya," lieutenant colonel Morozov observed warily.

"Don't worry," Moskovchenko said reassuringly. "There are

enough for everyone." If Luzhkov had said there were enough for all the paratroopers, then there were enough.

After this he gave another watch to a driver from the Ministry of Emergency Situations unit.

At that point, the watches ran out. They were 40 watches short.

"Well, what of it?" the deputy said, in a placatory tone. "So what? I'll send the rest as soon as I can. If Luzhkov makes a promise..."

There were of course a few conflicts with the European peacekeepers. But nothing too dramatic.

"Once the British managed to get through to the airbase, by telling all sorts of lies, they saw two flags on the airbase building: the Russian flag and the flag of the Russian Airborne Troops. There was no sign of the Union Jack, which upset them no end. They brought one over and began discussing who was going to crawl out onto the aluminium flagpole and solve this unexpected and important problem.

A volunteer was called in. Without a moment's hesitation, he began the ascent. But something disastrous was about to happen: the higher he climbed, the more the flagpole leaned over. On top of which the flagpole was very slippery. And the poor guy was hanging from it, about two thirds of the way up, gripping the national flag between his teeth; and after hanging in that position for what seemed like an age, he came crashing down, in what was a disgraceful incident.

And what made things worse was that our men, sensing deep down how this drama was going to end, had already run off to fetch a video camera and were taking great pains to record the whole thing.

But our flags were flying. It is said that under cover of night, the British tried a few more times to take possession of the flagpole: after all, it would be very annoying for them otherwise, there are things that they hold dear too, and to the British, the Union flag is clearly almost as dear as the flag of the Russian

Airborne Troops is to a Russian paratrooper. But they just couldn't do it. They were spurred on by the irritation they felt and their dark respect for Russian people. Their attempts failed.

And they were doomed to fail from the start. Because our guys, when they arrived in Slatina, had found some runway steps, put it next to the flagpole and tied the flag to it. Why lose your life trying to climb it, when there was a staircase to hand?"

From the point of view of external politics, the assault on Pristina didn't pay off for Moscow at all. Putting emotion to one side, the brilliant capture of Kosovo's only airbase, albeit for a short time, provoked the West into getting involved. It did not radically effect the balance of power in the region.

The West, after recovering from its sense of shock at what had happened, did not soften its position during talks with Moscow one iota, and once again proposed the same conditions as before on Russian involvement in the operation: there would be no separate sector for the Russians, and they were to be subordinate to the general command.

The assault by the Russian paratroopers didn't have any affect on the position of the Serbs in the region either. By June 11, units within the Serb army and police had left Kosovo, and the exodus of the Serb population began soon afterwards.

A significant portion of Russian society reacted extremely favourably to the generals' initiative, however – not to say ecstatically. And within the army, these generals became not just formal leaders but also informal leaders.

And suddenly it didn't matter so much how the operation in the Balkans turned out, and what the results of the talks between Moscow and the West were; whether Russia was going to get its own sector in Kosovo or not; whether or not the IMF was going to give us credit, and whether our debts were going to be restructured. All this was for the diplomats and the government to get worked up about. As for the generals, they had done their job. The assault on Kosovo had passed into legend. And it was also seen as revenge over Chechnya, in a strange sort of way.

The Russian peacekeepers, meanwhile, moved into their zone of responsibility inside the US sector. And relations with their rivals from across the ocean resumed their normal course.

People bearing a striking resemblance to the Procurator general

1997 was a year full of scandals involving the security services. Undoubtedly the ugliest one of all was when a film came to light showing the then justice minister, Valentin Kovalev, playing sex games with prostitutes in a sauna. It surfaced in the context of an incident involving the theft of $7 million which had belonged to the bank Edintsvo (Unity), which had gone bankrupt. The man accused of the theft was the chairman of the board of directors at Montazhspetsbank, Arkady Angelevich – Edinstvo had been run by a friend of his, Dmitry Bureichenko. After searching his home, the Ministry of Internal Affairs confiscated the ill–fated tape, among other things.

They handed the tape to the notorious journalist Larissa Kislinskaya. Kislinskaya immediately published a story about in the newspaper *Sovershenno Sekretno* (Top secret), complete with photographs that were apparently screen–shots of the video footage. Moreover, Kislinskaya maintained that the cassette she had been given by an Interior Ministry employee was merely a "castrated copy". Part of the original recording was withheld from her: she was told only that the remaining bit of film contained "the logical culmination of proceedings – group sex involving the minister and three prostitutes, plus a few other well–known individuals."

A colonel from the Ministry of Internal Affairs' information department, Leonid Golovnov, immediately accused Kislinsky officially of having received the tape from criminals in the Solntsevskaya group, and then let slip in a conversation with a correspondent from *KommersantDaily* that exactly the same sort of tape had been found among the possessions of a recently arrested criminal group. Yet he also admitted that he did not know where the journalist had got the tape from.

The material gave no indication as to who had filmed the footage and how the video–tape had come to be in the possession of an assistant to the head of the Ministry of Justice. The police maintained that Kovalev, like the other figures in high office listed above, had already shown himself, in the Angelevich affair, to be a good mediator on behalf of the accused.

It transpired that Angelevich had been collecting persuasive arguments (or to express it in simpler terms, compromising material) for anyone who might be able to be of assistance to him.

Valentin Kovalev declared that the tape had been mocked up: "I have no intention of defending myself. I have nothing to defend. And no reason to do so. Nevertheless, out of respect for public opinion, I consider it essential to put on record that I am going to defend my good name, honour and dignity using all the resources available to me under Russian legislation and international law."

Larissa Kislinskaya, meanwhile, defended her journalistic right to receive the information: "The position of justice minister is a public office. My private life involves my wife, perhaps even lovers, but certainly not group sex with prostitutes at a banya run by the Solntsevskaya gang. If that is the kind of private life *he* leads, then I have indeed intruded on it."

In the end, Yeltsin fired Kovalev from his post, and two years later a similar technique was used against Russia's Procurator general, Yury Skuratov. Yet another compromising tape involving naked girls caused a full–scale political crisis (yet again) in the country, and filled the media with images of "a man bearing a striking resemblance to the Procurator general".

Alexander Korzhakov woke from his political slumber and threw himself into the 'war on compromising material' with gusto. He had first promised to reveal the Yeltsins' financial secrets back in the summer of 1996, immediately after going into retirement. Following the release of his book, 'Boris Yeltsin: from dusk to dawn', the president's former bodyguard once again stated, in November 1998, that he was prepared to give details about the various sources of income of the president's family, and the property in his possession. Moreover, he decided to write a second book on the subject. But Korzhakov evidently lost his inspiration, and chose not to write anything, storing up the information he had for a more opportune occasion.

Korzhakov's hatred of Berezovsky forced his hand. The general decided to continue the campaign to expose the then executive secretary of the CIS – a campaign which had been begun by Viktor Ilyukhin. According to Korzhakov, the reason they had not done so earlier was simple: Berezovsky was blackmailing the Yeltsins, by threatening to reveal their financial secrets.

Korzhakov decided to take this ace away from Boris Berezovsky, and proposed that the journalists look into all money matters on their own. "Pick up a pen and start writing, I'll give you the name you're after...Roman Arkadievich Abramovich, from Sibneft. Ask him why he's known as the banker. Ask him where the Family's accounts and property are," Korzhakov baited reporters.

Realising that saying a few things about Abramovich would not be enough to 'bury' Berezovsky, Korzhakov decided to drag up all the things he had already talked about in the past. He revealed a video–tape that had been recorded immediately after the murder of Vladislav Listev. It showed Berezovsky complaining to Yeltsin that an attempt had been made on his life, too, which had led him to the following conclusion: "From somewhere underneath you, Boris Nikolaevich, people are killing the last people loyal to you." On the same tape, the president of the TV channel REN TV, Irena Lesnevskaya, accused the director of MostBank, Vladimir Gusinsky, and the mayor of

Moscow, Yury Luzhkov, of playing a role in the murder in order to stage a coup and replace Yeltsin with Luzhkov.

Korzhakov also mentioned in passing that Kirsan Ilyumzhinov's declaration that he intended to break away from Russia was also something that could be attributed to Berezovsky. Allegedly, this had been an attempt by the executive director of the CIS to get rid of the finance minister, Mikhail Zadornov.

Incidentally, little came of the revelations about the former "chief security guard" – and not because they were all, largely, an open secret already – by the end of the 1990s it had become clear that Boris Berezovsky would only leave the world of politics when Boris Yeltsin did so too. Or that he wouldn't leave it at all, if he managed to find someone different to "take a liking to".

At the rank of general

The arrest of Konstantin Kobets in May 1997 caused quite a stir. Never before in the new Russia had a military man of such high rank found himself behind bars. On top of everything else, Kobets, following the putsch in 1991, was seen as someone close to Boris Yeltsin. Yeltsin had even appointed him Defence Minister, and made him one of the first to be given the title of army general. Admittedly, Kobets only spent a month in this ministerial post, following which he took up the position of chief military inspector at the Ministry of Defence, in which he had more influence but far less responsibility.

His career fell apart just as quickly as it had begun. In the summer of 1996 general Lev Rokhlin read a sensational report to the State Duma, in which he accused general Kobets of corruption.

Kobets was put in solitary isolation at Lefortovo until February 1998, and was released following a sharp decline in the state of his health. During his time behind bars, Kobets had become category one disabled, lost 40 kg and suffered two heart attacks. After his release, doctors found that Kobest was suffering from several serious illnesses: ischemic heart disease, hypertonia, arterial sclerosis and damage to the arteries in the brain. "If he had stayed in prison the general might simply never have lived to see the court case," investigators admitted. Kobets's health was so bad that due to constant high blood pressure – 240/130 – he was not even able to familiarize himself with the case material.

He denied all the allegations against him, incidentally. "They are trying to prove that the house I bought is a bribe," Kobets said. "But I've got all the documents, they're all in order. I put my dacha, my apartment and my other property down as a guarantee at the bank and took out a loan, which went towards the construction of the house. The only reason I couldn't pay back the loan was that I was arrested. All I can say is this: at a certain point during the arguments about reform of the army, I became an inconvenience. The proposals I made and the actions I took went against Yeltsin's plans. And I was savagely removed."

The whole affair looked likely to end up being decided in courts, meanwhile. The amnesty declared in connection with the 55th anniversary of Victory Day got in the way. And Kobets, as a man who had won military awards, seized his chance. His exact words to investigators were: "I consent to an amnesty (in effect this was an admission of guilt), because I have neither the strength nor sufficiently good health to prove my innocence."

The staff of the prosecutor's office merely sighed with relief. "Imprisoning an army general – that's a step too far," an official from the Chief military prosecutor's office told a reporter from *Kommersant*.

By the end of the 1990s you might even have said there was a set formula for political success, for any Russian general with a bit of initiative. To achieve success in politics, a post–Soviet general had to satisfy four obligatory criteria.

Firstly, he had to have had a successful military career: if possible he ought to have spent time in a "hot spot".

Secondly, a good general must have experienced conflict with the authorities, and must have been made to suffer in the name of a just cause. The general public in Russia has a soft spot for the unfortunate and downtrodden.

Thirdly, both the successful career and the conflict with his superiors had to be turned into something that would appeal to the broader electorate. The general must be seen as someone who would be a welcome guest on a variety of TV shows, and interviews with him must have been published in the country's most widely read newspapers.

Fourthly, he must have the support of influential allies – either groups within the ruling political class, or influential opposition parties, or groups from the world of finance and industry. He was allowed to chop and change the exact personnel, but these allies were the only people who could guarantee the general's long–term future in politics, and provide him with a stable electorate.

Alexander Lebed, Lev Rokhlin and Alexander Nikolaev ticked all these boxes.

It would be no exaggeration to describe the military careers of this triumvirate as outstanding. And by the time they got into politics, they had exactly the right range of accomplishments under their belts.

The commander of the 14th Army, Alexander Lebed, had commanded a battalion in Afghanistan, led troops into Baku, defended the White House from the SCSE men and brought an end to the war in Moldova and Pridnestrovie.

Andrei Nikolaev, the director of the Federal Border Service, who at 44 years of age was the youngest armed forces minister, had restored order to Russia's borders and those of the entire CIS, effectively brought an end to large–scale military operations on the Tadjik and Afghan border, and resolved the funding crisis for border troops. Under his command, the border troops had become a symbol of how good things could be for all other soldiers.

Lev Rokhlin, who was a corps commander, had been through Afghanistan and the Nagorno–Karabakh war, and led troops out of Georgia under fire; in Chechnya he was just about the only general who, during the storming of Grozny, managed to carry out the mission he had been set on time: it was his units that took the presidential palace and routed Shamil Basayev's notorious battalion in Abkhazia.

Before getting into politics, all of them had felt as though they had outgrown their military duties. Lebed was a member of parliament in the Pridnevstrovian Moldovian Republic, and in effect was not subordinate to Moscow in rank. Nikolaev wrote down his own ideas about military reform, and sent them to the president (although no–one had asked him to do so). Rokhlin, on his return from Chechnya, undertook, to use the military expression, a pre–election operation in Volgograd, and was then, on Pavel Grachev's orders, added to the NDR's pre–election list of candidates. Consequently he took charge of the State Duma's defence committee, but at that time Rokhlin had not yet become a politician, but was instead working hard in the nomenklatura, whose role was to do the bidding of the Ministry of Defence.

But in order to emerge properly on the political stage, it turned out that a successful career was not enough. You needed a scandal as well. So they set about creating one.

Lebed declared war on his minister. In the summer of 1994, after receiving a directive from the General Staff to reorganize the way the 14th army was managed, he announced to the world that this decision had been illegal, announced his possible retirement and promised a new Balkan war – no more, no less. It must be said, Lebed's plan almost collapsed: Boris Yeltsin himself expressed his backing for it in public. But a year later the story repeated itself, the Kremlin decided not to support the commander, and Lebed arrived in Moscow as a conquering hero – suffering at the hands of Grachev was a matter of extreme honour.

Nikolaev did not manage to break into politics at his first attempt, either. In 1996, following the events in Kizlyar, he took umbrage when the president publicly declared that "the border guards must have been asleep", and tendered his resignation. At the same time, his press service released a clarification to the effect that the terrorists had not gone through the border guards' zone of responsibility. But the opportunity went begging – Yeltsin did not accept his resignation.

Nikolaev had a second shot at the presidency, towards the end of 1997, in protest at the government's decision to move the Upper Lars checkpoint, on the border between Russia and Georgia, deep into Russian territory. It was such a trifling motive that no–one was left in any doubt: Nikolaev had decided to go and was merely waiting for the right moment. Many in the media explained away his retirement by putting it down to the scheming of the Georgian 'spirit mafia' – a very nice turn of phrase indeed for a Russian politician in the early stages of his career.

Rokhlin got off to a flying start in his career. After defending the Ministry of Defence loyally and truly inside the State Duma for six months, the deputy, three weeks after Grachev's retirement in June 1996, levelled some extremely destructive criticism at the ex–minister and his entourage from the dispatch box. He made some political demands, too: he proposed that a host of high–ranking generals be fired, including the commander–in–chief of the land troops, Vladimir Semyonov, and the deputy Minister of Defence Konstantin Kobets, and that the director of the General Staff's academy, Igor Rodionov, be appointed Minister of Defence (all these requirements were later satisfied).

All three generals had prepared well for their campaigns.

They had all begun to work actively with the media – Lebed in Pridnestrovie, Nikolaev in Moscow and Rokhlin in Chechnya. They were always glad to host journalists in their offices and military dug–outs: they almost always agreed readily to be interviewed, and took the journalists on trips to meet the troops, or to the front–line. The corps commander's powerful fist, intelligent smile and cracked spectacles, held together with tape, left a lasting impression on all who met him.

As the scandals unfolded around them, therefore, they were guaranteed not only articles and material for video clips, but also a favourable attitude on the part of the journalists, who kept up their end of the bargain: the generals achieved the popularity they needed, to go along with their fame.

None of the generals had experience in politics, sufficient funds for a pre–election campaign and trips to the regions, or a movement of their own – essential props for anyone looking to become a politician at the national level. And the generals began the search for political protectors.

The first to solve this problem was Andrei Nikolaev: within literally a few weeks of his retirement word got out that the ex–director of the Federal Border Service had formed an alliance with the Mayor of Moscow, Yury Luzhkov. The city's mayor helped the general win in the elections for the State Duma.

At first, Lebed made an error of judgement in relation to his allies. After agreeing to be listed second on the pre–election list of the semi–marginal Congress of Russian Peoples (behind Yury Skokov), he suffered a fiasco: in the parliamentary elections in December 1995 the CRP failed to secured the 5% of votes it required, and did not win any seats in the Duma. The general was rescued by the fact that he had taken the precaution of putting himself forward as a candidate in the single–mandate district of Tula, as well, where he had been in charge of a division for two years.

Lebed's failure forced him to take more care when choosing his allies. In the presidential elections in 1996 he enlisted the support of the pre–election quarters of Boris Yeltsin. The result was that he secured his first success. The post of secretary of the Security Council was the highest–ranking position in politics to which Lebed could realistically aspire at the time. Admittedly, after securing such a high posting, Lebed marched onwards, soon lost his influential allies and, left to his own devices, fell victim, in September of that year, to a carefully hatched plot in the administration.

His first serious political defeat did not lead him to break away from the establishment and move to the fringes of politics, however. Working in his favour was the fact that the war in Chechnya had been halted, the fact that he seemed to have been fired without due cause and the interest shown in him by the press. Lebed's decision to reject radical political parties secured him some influential allies. Onexim bank (which owned Norilsk Nickel), Russian credit (which owned KrAZ) and Boris Berezovsky provided the general with financial and organizational backing during the elections for governor in the Krasnoyarsk Region. And the general won the elections.

The only person who failed to abide by his final, extremely important condition – not to enter into conflicts with the entire establishment or go against the ruling system of power – was Lev Rokhlin.

He initially backed the Minister of Defence, Igor Rodionov, but after Rodionov's departure he decided to act on his own. In June 1997 Rokhlin wrote an open letter to soldiers serving in the army, in which he called on them to "come together, and in each military unit hold officers' meetings at which legal requirements are to be drawn up, and send them to the president, the government, the Federal assembly and the Supreme and Constitutional Courts." At that time, many people thought that Rokhlin had been sent by the authorities to join the ranks of the opposition.

A month later, however, the former corps commander created the Movement for the support of the army, the defence industry and military science, which took a tough opposition line. At first Rokhlin received backing from the Communists, who at the time were highlighting their "constructive opposition". The CPRF even gave him permission to use the party infrastructure on–site – all the so–called regional divisions of the Movement for the Support of the Army were located in the Communist Party's district committees and city committees.

But the more radical Rokhlin's demands became – a call for a vote of no–confidence in the government, then in the president, then a call for both to be sacked, followed by a call for them to be overthrown using constitutional methods, and ultimately for an uprising – the cooler the Communists' attitude towards him became. Ultimately they turned their backs on him altogether, voting in favour of the general being removed from his position as head of the Defence Committee in the lower chamber.

Unlike Lebed and Nikolaev, Rokhlin crossed the thin boundary that separates the political mainstream, which the majority of society respects and looks on as dependable, from the scary, discredited political fringes, where political figures, parties and movements that are more exotic, but in which it is impossible to have much faith, reside.

It was for precisely this reason that Rokhlin did not have a future in politics. Because in Russia, just like everywhere else in the world, the centripetal force will always throw onto the sidelines anyone who has become an enemy of the political system as a whole. And he was destined to become an odious figure – for all his personal achievements, one–time popularity or even the strength of his convictions.

It is perhaps for this reason that the 'official' account of the general's murder on July 3, 1998, at his dacha outside Moscow, failed to satisfy not only his allies, who were still manifold, but also people who were not directly related to him. According to the official inquiry, the general was shot using a pistol with his name on it by his wife, Tamara – she was put on trial twice as a result. But it's unlikely even the courts have cleared up all the questions that remain unanswered about that murder.

The Rokhlin's neighbours all had similar things to say about them: "Right from the general's first day in the village everyone could see that he was one of us. He was always quick to say hello, and answered questions with a lot of goodwill. We didn't speak to him all that often, mind: when he took strolls in the area around his dacha, the general preferred isolated spots."

Lev and Tamara Rokhlin spent almost 30 years together. They had met in the early 1970s in Tashkent, where Lev was studying at the Combined Arms Academy. It was a typical 'serviceman's marriage'. In an interview, Tamara said that she fell for her future husband because of his will–power and his tough, masculine nature. He had had the nickname *Zhelezny* ('Iron') at college. She said that Rokhlin's favourite writer had been Jack London, and that he had modelled himself on the protagonists of London's stories. It was this that had inspired romantic feelings in Tamara's soul.

Together, they had rushed from garrison to garrison and from one flashpoint to the next. The general was awarded four medals for his military successes and was also made a Hero of the Soviet Union, but as it turned out, he was not made a hero: the idea got lost in an office somewhere. There were some who wished to see the general made a Hero of Russia on account of the battles he had won in Grozny, but he refused to accept this award or a handful of other military medals. "That was a civil war, and it's wrong to go looking for glory in a civil war," he said.

Lev Rokhlin was extremely popular in the army. One of the men who served alongside him said of the general: "He was one of those commanders who could be tough and brutal when questioning his soldiers, but, if the subordinate deserved it, he was quick to reward good service, too. As for those who were merely making up the numbers, he got rid of them mercilessly."

Rokhlin was the first military man to talk openly to the media about the losses that were actually suffered during the Chechen campaign, and to tell them that the federal forces were fighting a well–equipped and professional army, rather than isolated groups.

After Rokhlin returned from Chechnya to Volgograd in 1995, he was threatened with reprisals by insurgents on numerous occasions. And when Maskhadov took power, the Chechen procurator general opened criminal proceedings against Rokhlin for genocide and declared him a wanted man. Rokhlin was given bodyguards who worked for the FSB.

Throughout all this time Tamara helped her husband in whichever way she could. In Volgograd she got involved in charitable work: she sent warm clothing and food to the North Caucasus, for the soldiers and officers. She was often to be found at military hospitals, where she organised concerts and charitable evenings for the wounded.

1995 was a year that brought much change for the Rokhlins, for it was in that year that the general decided to get into politics. His radicalism left a lot of people cold: his rivals, those who shared his views in the Movement for the support of the army and even members of his own family. The general's brother–in–law Abakumov, for example, asked him on several occasions to tone down his zealous fervour, as it was damaging his business. "I have people coming to check up on me every day because of you," he complained.

In late 1997, Rokhlin gave a press–conference at which he told journalists that there were forces in the president's entourage who wanted to discredit him and even physically destroy him. The Chechen version of how the crime was committed must not be discounted, either: it is well known that no statute of limitations applies to vengeance in the Caucasus.

The general was asked on several occasions whether he feared reprisals. Rokhlin usually responded by saying: "I have looked death in the face on more than one occasion. But if I *am* killed, it will be clear to everyone straight away who was really behind the crime."

10. POLITICS AS A BUSINESS: REFORMERS, CONSERVATIVES, DEPUTIES AND CIVIL SERVANTS

Yeltsin versus Khasbulatov

Perhaps one of the greatest achievements of the 'SCSE–conquering' democracy was the emergence of politics as a profession in Russia. People from an array of backgrounds went into politics – sometimes, perhaps, to their own surprise: lab owners and editors, physicists and poets, former secret service agents, future terrorists and active dissidents, lawyers and co–operators, priests and bandits. The merest hint of a public demonstration could be interpreted (and often was interpreted) as a political event.

Prior to December 10, 1992, all the charm and beauty of the Russian parliament was that it made as many decisions as it possibly could, without ever being held accountable for anything, because it was the head of state's job to be held accountable. The president's departure from the congress meant that the deputies were required to go through the motions of conducting activity related to the state, and the options open to them were all as bad as each other. This prompted *Kommersant*'s political columnist Maksim Sokolov to predict a gradual "blossoming of populism, during the course of which both sides are going to try to be more popular than the other."

On December 10, 1992, Boris Yeltsin recycled one of Stolypin's speeches, made by the Tsar's prime minister on March 16, 1907 at the II State Duma: "I must state, and I wish that this statement could be heard far beyond the walls of this assembly, that here, by the will of the monarch, there are no judges and no accused, and that these benches (he pointed at the ministers' seats) are not the benches of the accused – they are the benches of the government. All your attacks are designed to paralyse the will and thought processes of power, and of the government; they can all be summarized in two words: "Hands up!" On hearing this, the government can only respond, quite calmly, and in full awareness of its rights, by saying: "Stop trying to scare us." Two and a half months later, on June 3, 1907, the Second Duma was dissolved, after becoming known for this Stolypin–esque reaction, so lovingly depicted in the film *The Russia we lost*.

The president concluded his tirade before the congress with an unambiguous hint at precisely such an outcome, by proposing that a national vote of confidence be held and calling on his supporters to walk out of the assembly.

The deputies deepened the crisis which had begun by blocking off the communication channel to the masses (the presence of which, generally speaking, indicates that a parliament is in office) with procedural innovations, specifically a secret vote on constitutional amendments which altered the power structures of the state. In order to leave the electorate in no doubt that their elected representatives had been completely cut off from their feedback, the congress also brought in an amendment to the law on the referendum, stating that the issue of confidence in the elected members could not be the subject of a plebiscite.

It very quickly became clear that the disinclination to reach a 'nice little agreement', which the deputies had uncovered, had left the congress with a difficult decision to make: either accept power in its entirety (which was unacceptable), or take a backward step and try to reach a compromise. Thus Yeltsin's declaration at the congress, which had seemed the height of recklessness to many, turned out to be an astute political play.

So astute, indeed, that some journalists even commented on what was taking place in playfully benevolent tones: "...

the fact that the president reacted to the crisis like a living being, and not a mummy, is something that is deeply positive and encouraging. After all, it really is nice to have a normal, living and breathing individual as president, whose spontaneity minimizes the likelihood of dirty tricks. He took offence, as any normal person would, and began to be resigned to it, as any normal person would, because as well as being spontaneous, he was also the president. But the national elected politicians, who fitted the image of boys who had grown up as 'one of us' (with the emphasis on *us* – *we* were the ones who decided we wanted them), with all their aggression and promiscuity, with all the insanity of their euphemistic 'clarifying of relations', were nonetheless able to persuade the public that they were striving to reach an agreement."

Moreover, convinced that Khasbulatov was resolute in his decision to turn the president into a kindly old grandfather, and rule on his own, Yeltsin realized that there were not very many options open to him. It was difficult to talk about trying to reach a compromise with Khasbulatov, because experience had shown that deals reached by means of bartering collapsed almost as soon as they were concluded. The deals being done behind the scenes with influential figures who were not at the congress (the structures of power, leading figures in the economy and regional leaders) came to an end before the congress had even begun. As ever, there was only one thing for it: 'tear it all up and start from scratch'. And to a certain extent, that proved possible. The president used his only chance to strengthen his grip on power, and not to put the country in the hands of the upper assembly.

The peak of this popularity contest was the nationwide vote of confidence in Boris Yeltsin that was held in April, more commonly known by the slogan 'Yes–Yes–No–Yes'. Before it took place, the congress managed to adopt and then cancel its decision to hold the referendum; Yeltsin gave a televised address on the introduction of a "special procedure for governance" (it became clear fairly soon that he had signed a different order, but the Constitutional Court, which had not yet been shown this order, declared it an unconstitutional act), and then the congress spoke again – and attempted (unsuccessfully) to impeach Yeltsin. It looked as if the congress was going all–in.

According to Mikhail Poltoranin, one of Yeltsin's closest associates at the time: "Khasbulatov and co. gradually began to test the president's power and authority and see how far it would go. Understandably, that drove the president to distraction. And when they tried to impeach him in March '93 and fell just a few votes short, Yeltsin sensed the wild danger of the situation. When you put him in a corner, he becomes wild and unpredictable. He sees the red mist of political blood before his eyes, and he throws himself into the attack like a battering ram. But since he can't count the options, he is liable to fail, too. It's just that he always got incredibly lucky."

After this attempt at impeachment, the referendum was initiated. During the preparations for it, the president's side managed to secure if not the support, then at least a position of neutrality on the part of the industrial elite. As a result of some costly procurement by the president – and at a time when Rutskoi had begun a decisive attack on the government – the "centrist bloc" suddenly fell silent, to all intents and purposes leaving the vice–president without any support at all. Yeltsin, during the course of the bartering taking place behind the scenes, the staff appointments (such as the new finance minister Oleg Lobov) and, most of all, the money coming in as a result of inflation, managed in part to drive a wedge between the centrists and the communists.

His opponents relied mostly on the methods of black PR, attempting to compromise their enemies (the expression 'black PR' had not yet entered most people's vocabulary at that stage). Rutskoi exposed ministers mired in corruption. According to the director of the Parliamentary Centre at the Supreme Soviet of the Russian Federation, Konstantin Lubenchenko, Sergei Shakhrai, who had spent some time in the US in 1989, borrowed a substantial sum of money from the Americans, without giving anything in return, and used it to buy up more audio and video goods than could be loaded into an aeroplane, after which he was expelled from law–abiding circles in disgrace. The press centre of the SC RF spread stories about a *coup d'etat* that was supposed to take place on the night of April 25–26. The director of the Front for the Rescue of the Nation, Ilya Konstantinov, accused Yeltsin of being a 'Catholic mason'.

As for Yeltsin's team, it focused on the modern approach of the Americans and, for the first time in Russian history, almost got the people's favourites involved in the propaganda campaign – cultural figures, rock stars, famous footballers and popular psychics. The fact that rock stars and Spartak fans, who were influential in levels of society which had traditionally been apolitical, signified that the president's position among undecided voters had been greatly strengthened. Moreover, on the eve of the vote, Yeltsin announced that it was not about trust in general, but about trust in the new, presidential, Constitution, the core principles and several articles of which had been published on the morning of the 24th, the day before the vote.

Although it was hard to state the result of the referendum unequivocally (58.7% of those who voted expressed confidence in Yeltsin, but only 41.2% of the total electorate voted in favour of an early election for national deputies – those were the questions posed in the referendum), Rutski's aide Andrei Fyodorov provided an exhaustive commentary on the results of the referendum in advance: "Whatever the actual results of the referendum turn out to be, of fundamental importance now are the questions of where and when the first interpretation of the results is going to be given and who is going to give it – and which specific steps are going to be taken after these assessments."

Sure enough, steps were taken following the announcement. On September 1st Boris Yeltsin removed Alexander Rutski from the post of vice–president, demonstrating once and for all that in political duos the 'other half' is never really on an equal footing. The Supreme Soviet's response could be described as 'symmetrical' – it sent a request to the Constitutional Court and halted the effect of the order. On September 21st Yeltsin signed order No. 1400, effectively disbanding the Supreme Soviet. The deputies decided not to give up without a fight (all the more so given that the CC had declared the president's actions unconstitutional) and made the first move, attacking the headquarters of the Association of Armed Forces of the CIS.

At the same time, incidentally, Yegor Gaidar returned to the government for a while. Initially he was the first deputy for the Chairman of the Council of Ministers, and thereafter he was the acting Finance Minister.

A few days later barbed wire was put up around the White House and it was inundated with armed insurgents. On October 3rd those on the side of the White House took the mayor's office and attempted to take the Ostankino TV tower. On October 4th Yeltsin ordered tanks to fire at the White House. According to official sources, over 150 people were killed. The observations of Veronika Kutsyllo, a special correspondent from Kommersant, and the conclusions that she drew, reflect badly on both sides: "October was crazy. And everyone was acting crazy: the deputies, Yeltsin, the citizens looking on with curiosity at this 'little war' in the centre of Moscow, and us journalists, who demanded firm action from Yeltsin in 1993 against parliament, which had been blocking reforms – and as a result found ourselves with a White House that was ablaze."

"Inside the White House it was strange to come to the realization that somewhere out there on the outside normal civilian life was going on – without any barbed wire or shots fired by tanks, without any hysterical deputies, without this general willingness to kill anyone who didn't see things the same way as you...

During the first few days the deputies carried gas–masks with them wherever they went, and then they just chucked them down on the floor: the gas attack they had expected never materialized.

Scare stories were circulating in the White House constantly. Achalov kept chasing the deputies away from the windows all the time, saying that a grenade might come flying through at any moment. It seemed as though those assembled would have been prepared to fire on the journalists themselves, if only there would be no firing from outside...

At around noon on Sunday the news came in: demonstrators had broken through to the House of Soviets. Everyone rushed to the windows. A euphoric mood broke out: Moscow had risen up! The deputies congratulated one another. After the breakthrough, a mass fraternization process began with those who had just arrived. It seemed as if everyone believed that it was now going to be really easy to take the mayor's office, the TV tower and even the Kremlin.

The women running the buffet inside the White House sighed with relief – they had had to spend the last few days in an extremely nervous state. At night they sat in almost complete darkness, in the candlelight, and shyly asked people they knew among the journalists to bring them tights and warm socks 'from out there' (the hot water and the heating had been turned off, as well as the lights). It seemed to them as though all this would soon be over and they would be able to go home at last...

They went off to seize the mayor's office. To all those watching this from the windows of the White House, the events taking place were reminiscent of scenes from an American action movie: the road blocked by a lorry, the firing at the windows, and the hurried, but not hasty, departure of the armed guards through the yards at the back. The mayor's office stayed silent and the insurgents knelt down to fire shots at the windows...

Then everyone began to wait for news from the TV tower – they waited with bated breath. Khasbulatov gathered the deputies together and officially deceived them: "Ostankino's been taken." He also said, "The Kremlin must be taken today."

Both statements were greeted with shouts of glee from those assembled...

Someone woke me up at five to seven on Monday – I was sleeping in the canteen on the 6th floor, on a pile of chairs. I could hear gunfire. I looked out of the window: there were armoured tanks near the building, firing shots: they were firing at the barricades, at the cars and at the tents made of tarpaulin, where the defenders of the parliament had slept the night before. You could see people lying in the square: some were wounded, others had been killed. One of them was dragged to the White House by the hands, and a bloody track was left behind him on the square. It was impossible to get to the others – they were lying there on the ground, and tracer fire was being shot directly over their heads. We got the impression the shooting was only coming from the outside. I walked along the corridors: you couldn't see anyone firing from the windows...

You could see stretchers being carried along the corridors, bearing the wounded and killed. It seemed as if there were more dead than wounded. One of the bodies lay for a long time next to the internal lift. And it was practically impossible to pass along the corridor without seeing dark bloodstains on the rug..."

Why was it that in the end Khasbulatov, who had boasted about his nickname 'Faithful Ruslan' and maintained that "Boris Nikolaevich simply did not have a more devoted ally in the Supreme Soviet", had got into this fight? Surely it cannot have been as inevitable as he was to write five years after the shooting at the White House: "Yeltsin, who was incapable of serious analysis, would fly into a rage and start hating anyone who told him the truth. And since this truth was more often than not spoken from the benches of the Supreme Soviet, his hatred was bound to come crashing down on the parliament. Sure enough, that was what happened. Back in August he had said: 'We'll storm it in September.'"

Other leaders of the parliamentary opposition had demonstrated willingness to get involved in conflict as well.

Albert Makashov: "The deputies were hoping that they would be able to remove Yeltsin from power using legitimate, constitutional means. But as a military man I realized something: nothing would come of this plan."

Even more importantly, the president's allies showed exactly the same willingness. Mikhail Poltoranin: "Generally speaking it was practically impossible to speak to Yeltsin on the phone during those few days. He had signed his order – and stepped to one side. He had taken himself out of the picture. And it was for others to deal with the consequences of what he had done. An emergency commission was set up at the Kremlin. It was headed by Viktor Stepanovich Chernomyrdin. There's a man whose role during those days has been completely overlooked. He knew full well that the congress that was due to take place in November would force him to retire. And he used that to put pressure on Yeltsin: there could be no dead–end scenarios. He was the one who was angling for a confrontation."

Not even the intervention of patriarch Aleksei II could save the situation. He called on the politicians not to allow a civil war to break out and attempted to act as a middle–man between the two conflicting parties, something he very nearly succeeded in doing – the only agreement that was not violated by the opposition practically instantaneously was achieved with his direct involvement. Yeltsin would never have forgiven anyone else for such a thing: at that time, anyone who wasn't 'with us' was 'against us'. But he felt some sort of inexplicable piety in relation to the patriarch. It was inexplicable because Yeltsin, though he was in the habit of attending the Christmas mass, was never a god–fearing individual. Incidentally, relations between the two men became fairly close and cordial as time went on. When his health allowed it, Yeltsin always personally congratulated the patriarch on public festivals, and when he handed affairs over to his successor at the Kremlin, he asked the patriarch to be in attendance as well – it is said that not even the patriarch was able to explain why. Be that as it may, the gesture came across as symbolic: on the one hand, the transfer of powers took place under the supervision of a priest, and on the other hand, along with the transfer of powers the first president seemed to hand over to the second a church that was separated from the state, as well. Moreover, immediately after the inauguration Aleksei II gave Vladimir Putin his blessing for the presidency inside the Cathedral of the Annunciation, at the Kremlin.

Once the smoke over the White House had dissipated, the two opposing sides did not neglect to defend their actions, heaping the blame on the other side or on the mess that surrounded them. Alexander Rutskoi: "People criticize me for having sent people to the Ostankino TV tower. But let's not forget how it all began. A big demonstration was taking place along Kalininsky Prospekt. Who was it that started firing on the demonstration with grenade–launchers from the mayoralty? I sent deputies to Ostankino to tell them that demonstrators had been fired on." Then they started praying for our unreliable allies, after they had driven their tanks over them." Rutskoi once again: "They were fighting for human rights... That same Tuleev faded away from there on September 24. "I went off," he said, "to make the miners rise up." And I never saw him again. On the 26th Zyuganov disappeared. He went off to make the miners of Tula and Orel rise up. We later found ourselves on plank beds, whilst they ended up in parliament." They had not forgotten about the historical link between 1993 and 1991, and a moment of foresight he had had. Albert Makashov: "I remembered how in 1991, when I had stood as a candidate for the Russian presidency, I had spoken to these deputies and told them what was in store for the country if Yeltsin won. And how they whistled while I was talking! And now they had really taken a hit from the man who had once been their idol. Both for the ratifying of the Belovezhsky agreements and for the break–up of the Union. But this was not a time for gloating. There was merely a sense of pain on behalf of the state, on behalf of the Constitution, and for the national deputies."

Generally speaking, Yeltsin had a stylistic advantage over his opponents: he was solidly built and sharp–witted, with a generous Russian spirit; he liked his drink and could make cutting remarks. He was a different proposition altogether from Ruslan Khasbulatov, with the latter's unprepossessing appearance and squeaky voice. Or Alexander Rutskoi, with his 11 suitcases of comprising material which turned out to contain documents that were used to support allegations against Rutskoi himself – allegations which centred around corrupt ties to the Swiss company Seabeko. Perhaps they had a particular truth that was all of their own. But in the mass popular consciousness, the conflict between the government and parliament looked like nothing more complicated than a power struggle. And when it came to deciding whose side to take, people made up their minds based on their own personal tastes. The fact that he was out of favour, and did not fall into the same category as those around him, made Yeltsin an idol to those who would later refer to themselves as democrats and liberals. It was considered trendy to like Yeltsin, and vulgar not to...

It is a well–known adage that history is written by the victors. In our case, it was not so much the history books that they wrote, as the Constitution. Boris Yeltsin made full use of the fruits of his triumph. With his decree, he practically imposed legislative functions on himself. He disbanded the Soviets at all levels. He effectively disbanded the Constitutional Court, by forcing its chairman Valery Zorkin to retire (he would return to the post in 2003). He signed the Constitution once again. The word 'Duma' returned to Russia's political vocabulary.

Three days after shots were fired at the White House, on October 7, position number one – the guard at Lenin's Mausoleum – was abolished. This was another way in which the authorities emphasized that there had been a rupture with the past. They did not, however, break from the past definitively (by burying Lenin's body) – the debate on this issue still goes on today, and we have no way of knowing what the outcome will be.

Yeltsin's victory was welcomed by the democratic intelligentsia, too – or rather, by a substantial section of it. The most active among them were commented on in 'letter 42', which was published in *Izvestiya* on October 5. In the letter, they stated that those who had been defeated were "ideological dinosaurs and political adventurers", "red–and–brown bastards" and "thick–headed scoundrels who respected nothing other than the use of force" and called for force to be applied. Among others, the writers Ales Adamovich, Viktor Astafiev and Vasil Bykov, the poets Bella Akhmadulina, Rimma Kazakova and Bulat Okudzhava, the journalist Yury Nagibin, the human rights campaigner Lev Razgon, and the outstanding philologist, who had been given the unspoken title of the 'conscience of the nation', Dmitry Likhachev, demanded that all communist and nationalist parties be banned, that newspapers and programmes which "incited hate...and were among the chief organizers and culprits behind the tragedy" be shut down (including 'Den', 'Literary gazette' and the programme '600 seconds'), and that a "genuine" tribunal be held, as opposed to the farce into which, as they saw it, the trial of the SCSE had been transformed.

The president had thus been given a sort of *carte blanche* from the intelligentsia, and the latter demonstrated that it was not going to change its spots, whoever happened to be in power – letters such as this had been written since long before this, and would continue to be written afterwards (a recent example is the 'letter of 50' in support of the sentence handed down to Mikhail Khodorkovsky, which was also published in *Izvestiya*).

Yeltsin's victory made a politician – definitively this time, with no going back – out of Yegor Gaidar; or rather, it was not the victory itself but Yegor Timurovich's participation in it that did this. He was extremely confident when, on October 3, 1993, he called on supporters of the president and of democracy to gather on Tverskaya Street to defend the country against the uprising at Presna by the Supreme Soviet. And at the end of his televised address he said: "Our future is in our hands. If we lose it, we will only have ourselves to blame. I believe in our courage. I believe in society's common sense. I believe that we cannot lose today."

The man who really ought to have been addressing the public was Boris Yeltsin himself, or at the very least the premier, Viktor Chernomyrdin. But that evening, at that particular moment, it was Yegor Gaidar – with his spirit, confidence in himself and belief in 'us' and in what was 'ours' – who was the right man for the job. And he was a man who was not renowned for his mastery of oratory. The story about his visit to the Gorky car plant became essential reading. He was asked during the visit whether or not he believed in God, and he replied: "You know, my friends, I would probably categorize myself as an agnostic," and with that one sentence he lost all hope of finding any common ground with those assembled.

A political mass meeting

In October 1993 Gaidar created and took charge of the first party in power – the movement *Vybor Rossii* ('Russia's Choice'). Campaign placards depicting Gaidar's image were accompanied by the slogan: "Everyone else talks the talk...he's the one walking the walk." In the Duma elections in 1993, the bloc came second in the vote in the party lists (15.51%) and was the leader in terms of single–mandate members, which made *Vybor Rossii* the biggest faction in the Duma.

In December 1994, *Vybor Rossii* was given the prefix *Demokraticbesky* ('Democratic'), and at practically the same time, with Gaidar as leader, effectively broke away to join the opposition to Boris Yeltsin because of the start of the war in Chechnya. In January 1996, in protest at the actions of the federal forces in Chechnya, Gaidar left the president's council as well.

In 1997–1998 Gaidar did not hold any official posts at all. But his influence on economic policy remained significant. He provided consultancy services for Kirienko's government and conducted negotiations with representatives of the IMF, whilst simultaneously trying not to allow information to be disclosed about the impending crisis, in order to avoid panic – that was what Andrei Illarionov, for one, accused him of doing. Like the fact that Gaidar himself was actively involved in the state short–term debt obligations market, which completely contradicd his reputation as a man not driven by money.

Yegor Gaidar's peacekeeping mission to Belgrade and the Vatican in March 1999 can probably be described as his last public political act. He suggested that John Paul II write a letter to Bill Clinton asking him to stop bombing Yugoslavia. It proved to be a futile mission...

By then, however, a series of larger–than–life individuals had come in to replace Gaidar.

Vladimir Zhirinovsky attracted considerable attention for the first time, thanks to his public support for the SCSE. But it was by no means this that made him a controversial figure: the SCSE was supported by far more famous people than one might think, both during the putsch and after it. Alexander Nevzorov, for example, publicly declared: "Every true citizen of Russia dreams about the SCSE in his heart of hearts, because the country is essentially in the grip of the enemy," i.e. the leadership of Gorbachev, Yeltsin and Sobchak. Alexander Nevzorov, incidentally, is the man who must take the credit for setting up the socio–political brand *Nashi* ('Our lot') – that was the name of the popular liberation movement he set up in 1991.

As for Zhirinovsky, his inimitable style of confrontational politics, avoiding all the unwritten rules and niceties, brought him a true sense of glory. He didn't just join the State Duma: he took it by storm. To everyone's surprise, his LDPR group won a majority in the parliamentary elections on December 12, 1993. Vladimir Volfovich exploited the weakness and inexperience of those in power (the State Automated System for 'Elections' was not set up until the following year).

His inner drive became his hallmark and the foundation for his political longevity. Vladimir Volfovich was unbridled and irrepressible in his political passions and in the way he expressed them. He was incapable of forgiving people, and did not like doing so. In 1994, the LDPR deputy Vladimir Borzyuk announced that he was leaving the party. Two of Zhirinovsky's bodyguards brought the recreant before the party leader. Uttering the command "Heel!", the leader grabbed the 'traitor' by the lapels of his jacket and started bashing him against the wall. Valery Borshchev, a member of the *Yabloko* party who happened to witness the incident, attempted to reason with the furious Zhirinovsky. In response, the latter threatened to "pull out that little beard of yours, one hair at a time."

Lawsuits on all manner of subjects became par for the course for Vladimir Volfovich. He filed lawsuits against the TV company Ostankino, Oleg Kalugin, VIP magazine, Anatoly Sobchak, the All–Russia State Television and Radio Broadcasting Company, Yegor Gaidar, the TV station NTV, Andrey Kozyrev and the newspapers *Kuranty* and *Moskovskiye novosti*. Here's a case in point: the journalist Alexander Minkin, who worked for *Moskovsky komsomolets*, called the LDPR leader an "idiot" in one of his articles, and described his letter to the president about the potential fates awaiting Russia as "paranoid drivel". This decision was to cost Minkin 1.5 million roubles – plus a retraction of the statement that Zhirinovsky was an idiot.

In the Duma, Zhirinovsky considered it standard practice to advise the chairman what to do and what to say regularly, from his place in the chamber. When the irritated deputies tried to exclude him, Zhirinovsky shouted, stomped his feet and called the police. He declared that he was not happy with the role of 'speaker–dispatcher' and, banging his fist on the despatch box, refused to accept the office, threatening his opponents with terrifying punishments as soon as he became president. He swore that Chubais would one day find himself locked up at Lefortovo.

His famous fight in the State Duma made headlines throughout the country. The deputy Nikolai Lysenko decided of his own accord to excommunicate Gleb Yakunin, taking away his cross. A brawl ensued. Zhirinovsky, in a loud voice, spurred his friend on: "Kolya, hit him, strangle him, rip his cassock!" When Tishkovskaya, a deputy from the provinces, tried to separate the two men, the LDPR's leader pulled her away by the hair. Tishkovskaya later said she wanted 100 million roubles in damages. Ultimately, however, she decided not to file a lawsuit.

The LDPR's leader was involved in a furore of equal proportions during the filming of the programme 'Head to head', in which he had been pitted against Boris Nemtsov. Unable to restrain himself, Zhirinovsky, with a shout of "Scumbag!" threw a glass of juice into Nemtsov's face. Nemtsov was the governor of the Nizhny Novgorod Region at the time. He responded in kind. At that point Zhirinovsky threw another glass over him. Off–camera, Nemtsov had a bottle of talcum powder thrown over him, too. And half–an–hour later, Vladimir Volfovich shouted out, over the shoulders of some security guards: "Lock him up in Butyrka prison! Lock him up in Lefortovo!" Such a precaution might well have served a purpose: during the broadcast, Nemtsov had a bottle of 'Governor' champagne, which he had brought along as a gift for Vladimir Volfovich, under the table.

Telman Gdlyan suffered at the hands of Vladimir Volfovich, too. On the night of December 13, 1993, in the State Kremlin Palace, Zhirinovsky publicly declared to Gdlyan that he was "arresting people without trial or investigation". He added, flaring up: "You'll answer for everything, you bastard!" and hit the investigator on the back of the head.

It must be said that by the end of the 20th century, Vladimir Volfovich, now a hardened veteran, became a more dependable and disciplined politician, although he was still liable to burst out with rage at a moment's notice, pick up a glass of water from the presidium and throw it over his political opponents. But he was incorrigible when it came to racking up punishments, in the form of being banned from taking the floor. On two occasions he managed to stay quiet from the first bell to the last. In December 1998 the CPRF faction felt the wrath of his righteous anger after supporting the ratification of the agreement on friendship with Ukraine, which, the leader of the LDPR was convinced, would lead to that country joining NATO. "A curse on you, Russia's 243 traitors!" he shouted. "And you can scrap the word 'communist'! A member of the CPRF party – spit in his face...!" But less than a year later, during a debate on the issue of sending conscripts who had served less than six months to Chechnya, Zhirinovsky was deprived of the right to speak for a day – for his fight with Alexaner Lotorev (from the 'Russian Regions'), who had called the LDPR leader a "phoney colonel", and then for a whole month – for attacking Nikolai Stolyarov, along with his colleague Alexander Lotorev.

Vladimir Volfovich was very fond of women, however. The former porn star Ilona Staller (Chicholina) was delighted by Zhirinovsky: "What a lovely creature he is. He was simply magnificent. He kissed a roast piglet! If you have creatures like that in your parliament, I'm all for it. Zhirinovsky came across as a mild–mannered, democratic person."

When he got married, incidentally, Zhirinovsky for some reason decided that he wanted to see his wife in the same monastery (Uglich monastery) as Raisa Maksimovna and Naina Iosifovna, "so that they don't distract their husbands from the job of running the state." Zhirinovsky was reckless and impulsive when it came to foreign policy. In a speech to the Belarussian parliament, he described several of the nationally elected deputies as "filthy", and promised to "turn them inside out and hang them up for 15 hours". Commenting on the USA's rocket attack on Iraq, Zhirinovsky said: "Clinton is worse than Hitler", and added that "his attempts to take control of the northern part of Iraq can be likened to B. Yeltsin's attempts to bring order to Chechnya." The leader of the LDPR called on the president of Kazakhstan, Nazarbayev, to spend less time "running around in short trousers", and promised to turn Kazakhstan into what would be not so much a Russian governorship as a provincial backwater.

For sheer colour and ardour, the "doctor of the working sciences" Vasily Shandybin, who resembled the brave soldier Shveik from Yaroslav Gashek's novel, was almost a match for Zhirinovsky. He took audiences by surprise on numerous occasions with outrageous gaffes from the fields of onomatics ("my surname consists of two roots, "shan" and "dyb", plus the prefix "in"), astronomy ("The Earth is flat, but fat!") and culturology – he described Jesus Christ as the first communist. He proposed that Israel become part of Russia, "so that those honest Jews can bring some order to our country." He charmed audiences with his naivety, as well (it was probably put on), and his logical reasoning, which was obscure but spot–on: "Cheating on your wife is tantamount to betraying the motherland!" He stood up for the honour of his party comrade Vladimir Semago against the independent deputy Sergei Yushenkov, who had called Semago a "political prostitute".

Sergei Yushenkov himself, incidentally, was also known for his statements, which bordered on outright boorishness. In January 1997 he proposed that the communist Viktor Ilyukhin, who had never spoken in favour of Boris Yeltsin being removed from his post on grounds of ill health, be appointed "chief doctor of the president of the Russian Federation". Ilyukhin agreed, on condition that Yushenkov join him "as a nurse". Speaker Seleznev declined to put this suggestion to a vote. "Very well, I'm prepared to withdraw my proposal," Yushenkov declared, "but only because of the fact that Mr Ilyukhin's sexual orientation came as a complete surprise to me." The agricultural man Nikolai Kharitonov immediately proposed that Yushenkov be banned from speaking in the Duma for a month due to his "constant sexual preoccupation": "Children are often brought along to watch us in session. What on earth will they go away thinking?"

By evening, however, this punishment, at the speaker's behest, had been replaced by a one–day ban on speaking in the chamber.

Galina Starovoitova came almost to embody Russia's political emancipation in the 1990s. A died–in–the–wool liberal and democrat, she inspired either genuine admiration or a hatred that was equally sincerely felt, both among colleagues in her own profession and on the part of "ordinary Russians". In order to achieve this, she didn't need to make any fiery public speeches: deputy Starovoitova spoke fairly rarely in the Duma and generally only talked about particularly important issues. The most memorable thing she said was probably the following statement: "Politicans should be changed as frequently as nappies, and – this is the crucial bit – for the same reason..." Her initiative regarding lustration (a ban on the profession) for employees of the CPSU party apparatus and full–time members of the security services would probably have been enough to make her famous. Admittedly, neither the Supreme Soviet of the RSFSR in 1992, nor the Duma in 1997 agreed to consider this law.

Her political career began in 1989 when she was elected a people's deputy of the USSR and took part in the creation of the Inter–regional deputy group. In February 1993 she was elected co–chairman of the Democratic Russia movement. Two years later, in 1995, she was elected a deputy of the State Duma for the Northern single–mandate district of St Petersburg. In 1996 she attempted to register as a candidate for president of Russia. Even as the head of a political party or bloc, Galina Starovoitova, in standing for parliament, stood for election for the single–mandate district and never on the party lists.

In addition to her work on laws, which mainly concerned citizens' rights and freedoms ('On the employment of the RF population', 'On the rehabilitation of witnesses of political repression', 'On the rights of national cultural associations', 'On alternative civil service', 'On freedom of conscience and religious associations', 'On the restoration and protection of the savings of RF citizens' and so on), she played an active role in protecting civil rights as well. She was involved in helping to free over 200 Russian soldiers from captivity in Chechnya. Thanks to her stubbornness, the first steps were taken in the creation of an institute for the rehabilitation of soldiers who had been involved in war or military conflicts.

Galina Starovoitova left her 'civil service' position as the president's adviser on international relations (she may have been sacked by Yeltsin) in November 1993 due to differences of opinion over Russia's policy in the Caucasus. Her aide, Ruslan Linkov, said that she did not let a single message that referred to the trampling of civil rights and freedoms by the authorities go unnoticed, whether it concerned allowances for people with disabilities going unpaid, Russian soldiers being taken prisoner in Chechnya or the squandering of budgetary resources. He said of her: "She was never indifferent to someone else's suffering, and at the same time she was capable of being tough and unbending whenever a decision that people needed had to be beaten out of the civil servants." He also described her as "the iron lady of perestroika".

She was seen (by public opinion, at any rate) as perhaps the only democrat in the first draft who had an unblemished reputation in the world of politics. The murder of Galina Starovoitova outside her apartment block on November 20, 1998 was perhaps the most scandalous political killing in Russia (the investigation into it is ongoing to this day, but the identity of the person who ordered the killing has not yet been revealed, although the perpetrators were brought before the courts), and caused genuine shock in society. "Starovoitova was working in a zoo in which the cages were left wide open," the Yabloko deputy Vladimir Lukin said at her funeral. "And it was the wild beasts that did for her." Viktor Chernomyrdin spoke next, without using any notes: "She spoke up to protect freedom, but remained unprotected herself."

A figure who was just as well–known and authoritative as Galina Starovoitova was Viktor Ilyukhin, a man whose political views were diametrically opposed to hers (but who could be accurately described as a carbon copy of her as regards having principles and being thorough).

He attempted to secure a criminal investigation into every single one of Dmitry Medvedev's predecessors in the post of president, including the president of the USSR Mikhail Gorbachev, for which he was fired from the agencies of the prosecutor's office immediately after he opened a criminal investigation against Mr Gorbachev over the collapse of the USSR (under the article on betraying the motherland). In all other regards Mr Ilyukhin was subjected to exactly the same amount of pressure from the authorities as any member of the opposition experiences in modern Russia.

His professional qualities as a lawyer enabled him to resist this pressure.

It may be that it was thanks to these qualities that he went into politics, although he had perhaps not intended to. However that may be, he found himself drawn into politics after getting involved (in 1987–1988) in the "cotton affair regarding the Uzbek mafia", which was being conducted by investigators from the General prosecutor's office of the USSR Telman Gdlyan and Nikolai Ivanov. Mr Ilyukhin was convinced that if he were to get involved he would restore justice and stop "these lawless men". Society, on the other hand, sympathized with the investigators, and Viktor Ilyukhin had the reputation of being the man who had had a hand in the "collapse of the cotton affair", thanks to which the senior leaders of the USSR avoided allegations of corruption.

His professional qualities as a lawyer made him one of the leading activists in the CPRF in the legislative process. Furthermore, in 1999 he was the main prosecutor in the impeachment procedures launched against the president of Russia, and made a speech before deputies in the State Duma setting out his accusations; the deputies who were against Yeltsin fell 17 votes short of securing an impeachment.

The communist party, which had rejected the "bourgeois democracy" that had developed within the country, had a practically irreplaceable critic of this democracy in the shape of Ilyukhin. Admittedly, as the journalist Viktor Khamraev saw it, the reason he was irreplaceable was that the communist Ilyukhin levelled criticism at the "bourgeois authorities" at times, and for certain initiatives, when it had taken a step back from the principles of "bourgeois democracy" and had trampled on "bourgeois freedoms". As the journalist observed, in the CPRF only a man who had made a career in politics without its help, and without the help of its predecessor, the CPSU, could allow himself to do such a thing.

The years that followed the shooting at the White House – for most Russians, at least – were more like a political 'jolly'. And it was not just the deputies that kept it going. In 1994, the Russian president had been unable to emerge from his plane to meet the prime minister of Ireland, and during an official visit to Germany he had tried to conduct an orchestra. On December 2 the country first heard the expression *maski–show* ('mask show'), when the Alexander Korzhakov Federal Guard Service of the Russian Federation put the security guards at MostBank "face down in the snow". This was a hint to the banker Gusinsky that federal power still existed in the country.

And the federal powers were gradually assuming the features, as the political columnist at *Kommersant* Maksim Sokolov observed, of "enlightened authoritarianism".

The year 1995 got under way to the accompaniment of shooting, and it did not stop for a moment all year. And the violence was not confined to Chechnya, where federal forces had been trying to take the presidential palace in Grozny for over a month, since New Year's Eve. Violence was kicking off all over Russia, particularly in Moscow, where some of the most notorious murders of the last twenty years took place that year.

On March 1, Vladislav Listev was shot outside the apartment block where he lived. Then numerous prominent figures in the media, business and politics declared that they "knew who had killed Listev": Konstantin Ernst, Irena Lesnevskaya, Boris Berezovsky, Sergei Lisovsky, Alexander Korzhakov...This situation, when everyone knew what had happened but said nothing, spoke volumes about the state the country was in from an ethical point of view.

The embodiment of this ill-health on the ethical front was Boris Berezovsky. It was not straight away that he came to be known as the most demonic figure in Russian politics. Prior to 1994 he was known to the wider public only as the CEO of LogoVAZ. He was one of a growing number of oligarchs – nothing more, nothing less. Of course, Berezovsky was going about his business using political methods even then, but this was all conducted behind the scenes. When his name was mentioned in the press at all, it was usually in connection with the automobile industry.

But in the summer of 1994 an attempt was made on Berezovsky's life. The event caused powerful shockwaves in the press and on the TV. At the time Yury Luzhkov went so far as to declare war on terrorism in Moscow, citing the outrageous incident involving Berezovsky. For almost the first time, the oligarchs gathered together and discussed what could be done to tackle contract killings.

It was probably at that precise moment that Berezovsky sensed that it was possible to play serious games not only from the shadows, and that contrary to the message contained in a certain well-known advertisement, image *is* everything. It was at this point that Berezovsky's big move into politics began. At the beginning of 1995 he created ORT, and in 1996, on the eve of the elections, he arranged the 'letter from the thirteen'.

The author of this message from Russia's biggest entrepreneurs to the general public, politicians and each other, which was entitled 'Turn back out of this dead-end!' and called for compromise and for action to prevent the communists winning the election, was the communist political strategist Sergei Kurginyan.

Thereafter, the pace quickened: in 1997 Berezovsky was the deputy secretary of the Security Council, in 1998 he was the executive secretary of the CIS and in 1999 he was a deputy in the State Duma. He took part in practically all the 'clear–up operations' that took place during the Yeltsin period: he decried Gusinsky along with Korzhakov, decried Potanin and Chubais along with Gusinsky, sang Yeltsin's praises along with all the oligarchs, and decried the communists practically on his own. His mobile phone was always at his ear. He was sometimes seen in public speaking into two phones at the same time, but it didn't even occur to anyone to suggest that he simply hang up on one of the calls and call the person back later. Everyone realized that Berezovsky was the key element in all these conversations, and that without his involvement nothing would get done.

This once almost all–powerful, and now fugitive, oligarch, manipulator, provocateur and schemer, Boris Berezovsky, was unquestionably a man with many strings to his bow. To such an extent that some journalists once said: "Berezovsky isn't a surname. It's a profession."

At first, he deliberately tried to create an image for himself as a man who was among the most senior authorities, and who was able to solve issues and advise people in power what to do in a given situation. Later there came a time when his image began to create him. Yet at the same time Boris Berezovsky always contrived not to be the man the general public thought he was.

He was only officially recognised as a politician after he became one of the deputies of the secretary of the Security Council – by no means the most important organ in the hierarchy of Russia's power structures. He was considered the ideal civil servant for tasks of particular importance. Negotiations with the Chechen leaders, the release of hostages in the North Caucasus, unofficial contact with communists in Moscow – this was his thing.

But it was only after he was sacked, amid much furore, in 1997 that the man himself, and others, began to talk about him as a public figure in politics. It was as if his self–restrained speeches in the south of the country, in the best popular tradition, had counted for nothing. His promise to secure permission from the federal government for Cossacks to carry weapons, alone, brought him more popularity than the prime minister's hour-long speeches.

To some extent, Boris Berezovsky was similar to Boris Yeltsin. The latter was unable to live an inert life, either – and would stir up situations. It was only at times like that he felt comfortable. In his position as deputy head of the President's Administration, Vladislav Surkov said that Berezovsky was a "man of conflict". This description was spot on. Yeltsin was a "man of conflict", too. Only the first president of Russia created conflicts with a view to routing someone, whereas Berezovsky got involved in someone else's conflict in order to protect his own interests – whether entrepreneurial or political. Unless he had a problem (whether real or created by his own hand) that needed solving, it was as if he simply got bored.

And in the heavy atmosphere of the mid–nineties, Berezovsky was in his element. At the time, even the most liberal liberals were upset by the helplessness of the government, which was incapable of dealing with the rebellious Chechnya. On January 9, insurgents led by Salman Raduev attacked the city of Kizlyar in Dagestan, where they captured a birth centre and took over three thousand hostages; ten days later, following a siege in the village of Pervomaiskoye, they managed to escape to Chechen territory. President Yeltsin, whose reputation was taking a beating, was a sorry sight as he spoke to the TV cameras about the "38 snipers" who were following the terrorists' every move.

It was a difficult year for Boris Yeltsin. Events in Chechnya had taken a terrible turn, despite the fact that the leader of the

Chechen resistance, Djokhar Dudayev, had been killed by a rocket in April during a satellite phone conversation with Konstantin Borov. He was forced to reach an agreement with a group of oligarchs who had promised to support him in the elections (the term 'Seven Bankers' Cabal' was coined by the former *Kommersant* journalist Andrei Fadin, who died in a plane crash a year later). The elections themselves were an extremely tense affair – Yeltsin won the first two rounds with a small majority over the leader of the communists, Gennady Zyuganov. The surprise of the elections was the emergence of a new politician – the retired general Alexander Lebed, who had been restrained during the putsch and decisive during the war in Pridnestrovie.

In the presidential elections in 1996, Lebed secured 14.52% in the first round, and thereafter he was appointed secretary of the Security Council of the Russian Federation; by the time the second round came along he was already in Yeltsin's team. On August 31 he signed the Khasavyurt Accord with Aslan Maskhadov, thereby bringing the first Chechen war to an end. General Lebed was incredibly charismatic and liked by large swathes of the population, and in the film *The peculiarities of hunting in this country*, which was released that year, everyone took pleasure in identifying a prototype for him in the shape of the general played by Aleksei Buldakov. Like all people with natural talents, however, General Lebed proved to be too inexperienced as a politician, and in October he was replaced in the post of secretary of the Security Committee.

The elections had not been entirely without benefit for Yeltsin, however. After the waltzes of the pre–election campaign, the president suffered a stroke. After that the media, for the first time in Russian history, delved deep into the intimate subject of the health of the nation's leader, when Boris Yeltsin was put on the operating table for a coronary artery bypass grafting. For the public, this was a sensational thriller featuring the surgeons Renat Akchurin and the American star Michael Debakey, although few were aware at the time that similar operations had recently been performed on the Prime Minister, Viktor Chernomyrdin, and the Secretary of the Security Council, Oleg Lobov – and also, a few years previously, on Bulat Okudzhava. Boris Nikolaevich lay in hospital next to the suitcase containing the nuclear codes, and the first thing he did when he came to was to cancel his order regarding the temporary transfer of power to Prime Minister Viktor Chernomyrdin.

'Auntie Lida's president'

The election in 1996 was one of those occasions when politics turned out to be a deeply personal matter for each individual voter. And this was something that everyone could sense. This was what the journalist Valery Panyushkin wrote about the situation: "When politicians talk to me they do so on behalf of a fifty–year–old woman; this woman is married, never went to university, and has kids...she never says anything and yet she plays a key role in the political life of this country. Let's call her Auntie Lida. The thing is, your average voter is a woman. Statistically speaking. It's a woman wherever you are in the world – and in Russia, it's a woman in her fifties, who's married, never went to university, and has kids. Auntie Lida. And whichever way Auntie Lida votes, that's the way the country votes. "I don't want to base my actions on what Auntie Lida does," we might hear from Konstantin Borovoy, with those limericks of his, or Grigory Yavlinsky, with his thick manifestos – and both end up losing...candidates running for president need to have Auntie Lida's approval.

But how are they to secure it? Yavlinsky writes a manifesto. Zhirinovsky offers her the role of prime minister. Gaidar says something clever. Bryntsalov promises money. All to no avail! Auntie Lida can't read Yavlinsky's weighty tome, and wouldn't know what to do as a chief accountant, let alone as prime minister. And when it comes to money, Auntie Lida deals in thousands of roubles, not millions of dollars...

Auntie Lida thinks about the candidates based on the roles they could play in the family.

Yeltsin is a father–figure. He likes his drink, of course – but having said that, his word is his bond and he always has a little something put aside for a rainy day, so that he can give a combine harvester to a Chechen village, for example. If something is going wrong somewhere in the country, it simply means that father wasn't aware of the situation, that's all. As soon as he hears about it, he'll make it right. And Zyuganov is wrong to insist on all sorts of medical check–ups. Papa has every right to get ill now and again. Auntie Lida is in her fifties, let's not forget, and her own papa is very elderly. And the reason papa's heart is aching is that he's pining for Auntie Lida.

Zyuganov is a nasty man, in any case. He's like an evil stepfather. He couldn't find happiness in his first family, so he's come over to join ours. He plays volleyball and spreads his legs wide apart when he walks – a sure sign that he doesn't have the right sort of masculinity for fatherhood. But if anything happens to the father figure, the stepfather has an undisputed right to be head of the family.

Although a better bet might be the eldest brother – Lebed. He's strong, he's a protector and he's got a lovely bass voice.

None of the others can even dream of getting Auntie Lida's blessing. Yavlinsky and Zhirinovsky, from Auntie Lida's point of view, are at roughly the same level. They're like brothers–in–law, one on the husband's side and one on the wife's. There's not much difference between the two. Yavlinsky, of course, would be a little more intelligent and affectionate, but there's absolutely no way of knowing what he wants, and he basically seems to live a life of his own. As for what Zhirinovsky wants, that's a little clearer, but he's too flashy, and that's all down to a flaw in his character: he's afraid of his father.

In the past there was Gaidar, too – he was the younger brother, a mathematician. When he was a child he was often sick, so he spent a lot of time studying. Auntie Lida might indeed cast her vote for him, out of pity – but he's always trying to be such a clever–clogs that sometimes you just want to wave your hand and say: "Be off with you..."

The ones Auntie Lida has no time for are Bryntsalov and Shakkum. Who are these men, when it comes down to it? They're not on our side! They come charging into your house, thrusting money at you and putting on airs and graces. No, you're being naughty...Auntie Lida's an honest woman: she won't be bought off, and she'll only vote for her favourites. Auntie Lida doesn't know the first thing about money: she is firmly convinced, for example, that Konstantin Borovoi is richer than Artyom Tarasov.

Many of the members of Auntie Lida's family have wives. And that's of no small significance. It's entirely within the bounds of possibility that Auntie Lida won't vote for Gorbachev because of his wife. After all, Gorbachev won't do as a dad. His wife's too young, too well–dressed...she's the same age as Auntie Lida. As Auntie Lida sees it, Gorbachev's under the thumb. And he loves his young wife...Auntie Lida is more than a little jealous. And on top of that, Auntie Lida cannot forgive Gorbachev for the fact that she waited for him on the square, after his exile in Foros, and he never showed up.

As for Yeltsin, on the other hand – his wife is a mum. Softly–spoken and kind, she irons his shirts and bakes nice pies. And she's got a well brought–up daughter – a sister figure, who helps out around the house.

Zyuganov hasn't got a wife – Auntie Lida is pretty sure of that. Although come to think of it, there *was* a woman in his life...that's right, he's divorced! Auntie Lida is one hundred percent sure: he's divorced.

Lebed's got a wife – she's quite young. He's a big strong man, he needs a young wife.

But as for Yavlinsky and Zhirinovsky – they don't have wives, do they? Has anyone ever seen them with a wife? Zhirinovsky's a real ladies' man. (Auntie Lida's words, not my own). They ought to get married first, before standing for president. Or else what will come of it? Kids being orphaned? Families with no fathers? Abortions?

Bryntsalov's got a wife, everyone's seen her. But do you remember what he said? He said she had demanded intercourse five times a week, and instead of that he had given her ten thousand dollars! Is that the key to happiness? Is that what he's promising us? Well he can keep it...!"

Of course, the differences between Zyuganov, the Communist, and Yeltsin, the liberal, were made manifest more at the symbolic level. It was probably a generational thing: the energetic younger generation associated Zyuganov with a return to a past that was already buried in moss, and Yeltsin with their hopes for a bright future. For the first time, the little word 'stabilization' started to be bandied about (although various wits soon thought up an ironic form of it, 'stabilizaster'). And at the same time there was the sense of a 'movement' of some kind in the air, and a certain degree of optimism.

But those who supported Gennady Zyuganov (among whom there were a lot of pensioners) saw something else: abject poverty, endemic corruption and the collapse of state power. And in many ways they were right. The sense of ambivalence about his political stance (in the Russia of the 1990s, remaining a Communist whilst being in power seemed somehow...ambiguous) did not prevent him from being able to keep a firm grip on his leadership of the CPRF. This, in turn, enabled journalists to become dab hands at making ironic remarks at his expense.

A. Kabakov and A. Grishkovets gave the following description of Gennady Zyuganov in an article entitled 'The history of the CPRF. A short course': "Gennady Zyuganov showed himself to be an outstanding practical dialectician, capable of uniting communist ideology and his day–job within a bourgeois parliament, battling against the regime whilst supporting all its criminal decisions, thanks to which those in power managed to demonstrate their true anti–people nature in all its glory.

And by 1972 the party had entrusted him with the responsible position of first secretary of the Orlov regional committee, in the komsomol. Not even Lenin or, let's say, Gaidar (Arkady Gaidar, who is known to have taken command of a regiment whilst he was a minor, thereby exempting him of responsibility) were in charge of the regional youth at that age. It stands to reason that comrade Zyuganov's career path thereafter was lined with victories: secretary and second secretary of the party's state committee, head of the propaganda department at the regional committee, instructor of the propaganda department at the CC CPSU (entitled to wear a musquash hat), and, finally, deputy head of the ideological department of the CC CPSU (i.e. the third most important figure in ideology behind Alexander N. Yakovlev, the architect of perestroika), member of the Politburo of the CC CP RSFSR (whereas B.N. Yeltsin was only a candidate to be a member of the Politburo of the Central Committee – the CC of the CPSU, that is)...

It was then that comrade Gennady Andreevich Zyuganov's genius, as a leader of a new type of Communists, unprecedented throughout history, showed itself: he became a patriot. As early as in February 1991 he had organized a conference entitled 'For a great, united Russia!', as a result of which he became chair of the coordination council of Popular–patriotic forces of Russia... And all the subsequent activity of this best friend to the Russian people, and doctor of philosophy (his academic career began in 1980 with a dissertation entitled 'The principles of planning the development of a Socialist way of life in the cities'), of this first–class performer in military triathlon, a husband, father and grandfather, wonderful volleyball player and disciplined worker, who respected the Labour Code of the Russian Federation (in August 1991 and October 1993 he was enjoying well–earned holidays), was to be distinguished by the unity of opposites – patriotism and communism, activity on behalf of the opposition and activity for the good of the state, materialism and orthodoxy, battling against the post of president yet striving to secure the position for himself...

The aforesaid enables us to identify, as we are supposed to do, the three sources of energy and three component parts of comrade Zyuganov. The three sources: love, the komsomol and spring. Love of the Russian people; the komsomol in general; and the spring of mankind – fully developed socialism. And the three component parts: patriotism (confirmed by his peers Makashov and Ilyukhin), communism (enough to satisfy the experienced party leader Ligachev and the ordinary worker Shandybin) and conformity (i.e. pure Russian parliamentarianism).

This was precisely the kind of person – and indeed the only kind of person – who could lead (he led them and still leads them) the new breed of Russian communists, who could lead them (and continue leading them) away from victory (at the parliamentary elections), towards victory (in the presidential ones, which were supported by people other than themselves). Conscientiously and insistently, comrade Zyuganov struggles against anti–communism – starting with his signing in 1991 of 'A word for the people', thanks to which he radically and in timely fashion dissociated himself from his perestroika bosses within the CC, and right up until the present, when he is putting monumental effort into the battle against a president who is not fit for purpose, and who is capable of one thing only: banning the CPRF. And he would ban it, were it not for the wise policy of comrade Zyuganov: "The cry 'Onwards!' merely means two steps back."

This is why comrade Zyuganov has been leading Russia's communists, for so many years, to the required destination: yet another set of elections for a majority in the Duma, the toppling of the existing constitutional structure by legitimate means, the restoration of the Soviet Union within the borders of countries that are now sovereign states, commonly owned property using uncompetitive production resources, collective–farm abundance and a planned, economizing economy. That is why comrade Zyuganov – and none other than he – was, is and shall remain the ideal and most talented leader of the communist party of this era, the era of the final phase in the transition from socialism to its supreme stage: a wild, comprador capitalism for robbers and bandits. Comrade Zyuganov remains true to his principles: the party line wavers along with him, just as the great Lenin taught him it would; the class struggle intensifies as the next round of elections draws nearer, as the great Stalin also taught him it would; just as in the past, it was easier to construct socialism within one particular country, because you would never be able to conquer every country...And because he is faithful, he is all–powerful: comrade Zyuganov is stronger than all those who are weaker than him."

Boris Nemtsov, who served as first deputy prime minister in 1997–1998, was once seen as the natural successor to Boris Yeltsin. He was the first to start referring to the first president as a 'tsar', almost to his face. Nemtsov did not do anything much to distinguish himself in the post of deputy prime minister. Memorably, he called for civil servants to be made to drive Russian–made cars; and the club jacket and white trousers in which Nemtsov met Gaidar Aliev, whilst the latter was making an official visit to Moscow, also stick in the mind. Admittedly, Nemtsov has managed, since then, to acquire some political weight, and has become one of the most colourful orators in the Duma. But this colour was probably his most prominent political characteristic.

The same was true of Irina Khakamada. In the mid–1990s she was a genuine star. High society and the world of academia, market liberalism and the wastefulness of the state, political glamour and an avid writer's awareness of mainstream culture: all these things were woven into her nature, came to life and at times conflicted with one another, in a truly Gogol–esque (or quintessentially female) unity and struggle.

With regard to politics, she was capable of the following kind of reasoning: "Elections are always a mass deception. Women want to be deceived individually! There's justice in that! And it's women themselves who are to blame. They don't express their will, or use their votes as a bargaining chip. A political battle is a battle for market share, like any other. There must be a product, supply and demand. But to date there has been no progress. There is no market for the female vote..." Or again: "Our version of politics has become utterly devoid of emotion. People can no longer bear to see politicians on their TV screens, saying things that they don't mean and yet expecting people to believe them. Honest politicians, if they want to have any effect on the hearts of the young, need to switch on their emotions. Music always helps." Or again: "I want to be a Tsaritsa. And give everyone what they need. Then the people would fall in love with me and I would be not so much elected as loved by everyone." In 1995, *Time* magazine named Irina Khakamad its 'Politician of the 21st century', in its list of the 100 most famous women in the world. Polls conducted in 1997–1999 resulted in her being named 'Woman of the year', and in 1999 she won this category hands down.

The Family

The era of the blossoming of young politicians coincided with the strengthening of the concept of 'the family' in the political jargon. People had first begun talking about familial ties in the mid–nineties, and back then they were referring not to a certain group of people as a political group, but to Boris Yeltsin's style of presidency: in his work, Russia's first president depended on a narrow circle of trusted individuals – a circle which outsiders could only enter, or so it seemed at the time, by order from above.

This circle contained an incredibly diverse range of people with extremely diverse interests and passions: it included, for example, the bodyguards and security agents Korzhakov and Baruskov, and the democrats and advisors Ilyushin and Kostikov. And nobody would ever have dreamt of putting those two in the same bracket. They were not so much stepbrothers and sisters as adopted siblings, who, by various circuitous routes, now found themselves in a historic stage in the immediate circle around the 'head of the family', whom the members of this circle, even then, referred to informally as 'grandpa' in their conversations with one another.

Boris Yeltsin's daughter, Tatiana Dyachenko, became part of her father's political 'family' a long time after this term went into common parlance. This happened at the beginning of 1996, when Boris Yeltsin's campaign team were working on his campaign strategy. But it was precisely at the time when Dyachenko moved into politics that the 'family' became a genuine Family, and dispensed with the quotation marks. The quotation marks can be removed not only because a blood relative of the 'head of the family' had joined the family, but also because it was from precisely that moment that it started to turn into a group of people who were united by common interests.

And as for those with whom its interests diverged, it seized hold of them ruthlessly, paying no heed to a shared past. When Alexander Korzhakov began to get in the way of the Family's interests – he was one of the few who had not abandoned Yeltsin when he was out of favour in the late eighties and early nineties – the Family consigned him to the rubbish dump of history. When the Family needed to sacrifice Boris Berezovsky – the man who in 1996 had chosen to back Tatiana Dyachenko, and effectively turned the family into 'the Family' – it sacrificed him, and on top of that played a direct role in the sacrificial act.

Here are a few arresting portraits of the people involved. Or rather, a single portrait: interior, with the Family.

Boris Yeltsin's daughter Tatiana Dyachenko and the journalist Valentin Yumashev were the people around whom this big Family gathered. The trust Yeltsin placed in his daughter, and in the man who, when he was out of favour, had helped the former president write his book *Confession on the set subject*, was absolute. This was what Boris Berezovsky was playing on, when, in the run–up to the presidential elections in 1996, he assembled a broad coalition of oligarchs in order to ensure that Boris Yeltsin was re–elected. 'Tanya and Valya' became the main means of influencing the president and those whom he considered his friends or allies (and their main friend and ally was Boris Berezovsky), not only during the election campaign but throughout President Yeltsin's entire second term.

It was not that he followed their advice blindly, but that they knew better than anyone else how to talk their obdurate would–be 'grandpa' into taking the decision that suited them. It is thought that in 1996 Berezovsky had the idea of turning Tatiana Dyachenko into a player in the political scene, and Yumashev had the idea of making Vladimir Putin president three years later, in exactly the same way. In the spring of 1999, Anatoly Chubais, who at the time was an ardent ally of the new president, somehow couldn't restrain himself from saying, in public: "You have to admit it, Valya's quite brilliant! This was all his idea!"

Yumashev had indeed played a blinder – he had backed the right man. Following Vladimir Putin's rise to power, Dyachenko and Yumashev quite justifiably considered their historical mission complete, and, unlike their "spiritual father" Berezovsky, never again tried to dictate their will to the new president, although they kept up their relations with those of their 'relatives' who remained in power. They began to do what they did best: build a family. In October 2001, Tatiana Dyachenko and Valentin Yumashev were married (Tatiana took her new husband's surname), and in April 2002 they had a daughter named Masha...

"Roman is very strong in his personal relations with people. His grasp of political strategy is not yet as good. He's young, and receptive to instruction. He's clever and, importantly, he has a clear idea of his own abilities." That was Boris Berezovsky's assessment of Roman Abramovich in 1999. By 1999, three years had already passed since an unknown oil trader had first begun to be considered not only 'the Family's wallet' (as Alexander Korzhakov referred to him), but also as someone who was almost more influential than the man who had brought him into big business, and then into the Family – Berezovsky. Abramovich knew full well on whom he ought to bestow his personal charm: Tatiana Dyachenko and Valentin Yumashev were very friendly towards him, and by the age of 34 he had become one of Russia's biggest oil and aluminium magnates. By the time Putin came to power, he had a much better grasp of political strategy as well. Abramovich not only showed absolute loyalty to the newly chosen path, but also did what he could to help the new president implement it: for example, by leading the fight against poverty in the Chukotsk region, and by buying shares in the TV channel ORT from Boris Berezovsky.

A crucial task was given to Mikhail Lesin, a former presenter on KVN and one of the founders of the huge advertising agency 'Video International', who had been welcomed into the Family in 1996: he was to organize a campaign to exert direct influence on the electorate. After the elections in 1996, he took control of the Department of community ties within the President's Administration, and introduced the idea of a weekly radio broadcast by the president. The idea died when Lesin left his post as the deputy chairman of the All–Russia State Television and Radio Broadcasting Company, where he had started to build up a state propaganda corporation.

In 1999 his experience was needed at a higher level. The latest war between the oligarchs was taking place in the media, and around the corner was the second war in Chechnya and not one but two election campaigns – one for the Duma and one for the presidency. Senior 'family' figures were trying at the time to construct a vertical structure of power within the country, and Lesin, in his position in charge of the Ministry of Printing, was supposed to build the media into it – first and foremost, of course, the TV channels. At that stage, he coped with his task fairly well on the whole, and afterwards he coped admirably with the new tasks he was given in connection with the struggle against media organizations which were insubordinate to the Kremlin: first a new regime was brought in at NTV, then TV6 was shut down; after this, the channel TVS was hurriedly set up, especially for the "unique journalist collective", which had turned itself into a symbol of freedom of speech. It died a death just a year after it first started broadcasting, not without the involvement of the Ministry of Print.

As for Boris Yeltsin, he was a bad head of the Family. He met many of its members only a handful of times, and openly disliked several of them, including Boris Berezovsky. Interestingly, the first articles to suggest that Berezovsky might face expulsion from Russia appeared back in the late nineties, before Putin emerged as Yeltsin's successor. Yeltsin himself was on close terms with the very people who were never part of, or had long ceased to be part of, his Family (with the obvious exception of Tatiana Dyachenko and Valentin Yumashev). It is well–documented, for example, that Yeltsin was in fact friends with Pavel Grachev and Shamil Tarpishchev. It speaks volumes that on the very next day following his retirement, he invited to his house "for some *pelmeni*", in addition to Putin's successor and the head of the Administrative Office they shared, Voloshin, the defence minister Igor Sergeev and his wife. One man who was never a member of Yeltsin's political Family was Vladimir Shevchenko – the man in charge of protocol, who for many years was his closest aide.

It may be that the scandals which occurred in 1999, involving his family's accounts and property, came completely out of the blue for Yeltsin, and it is unlikely he even realised what his political enemies were accusing him of. His professed belief that the family's main source of income had been the royalties it received from books was probably genuine. Incidentally, in Yeltsin's third book, *The Presidential Marathon*, which was published in the autumn of 2000, Valentin Yumashev, who wrote it, indulged in quite a bit of micky–taking on the subject of the family. The book's author (Boris Yeltsin) sort of gave his consent in the end to pulling back ever so slightly the veil of secrecy around the secret of his Family – and listed the ten people who had at various times worked within the President's Administration or for it, including Antoly Chubais, who, since 1997, had been the Family's chief political enemy.

From 1998 onwards, the alarming atmosphere of an absence of executive power had begun to make itself felt in the country. Boris Yeltsin decided not to interfere in the economy. Or rather, his Administration decided that the role of the only 'Constitutional guarantee' suited the president better. Even that proved impossible, however. The president confined himself to statements to that effect, without taking any action at all.

Luzhkov enters the fray

By the end of 1998, the Kremlin had declined to accept responsibility in all sorts of ways, and was attempting, moreover, to burden the government with the role of being the centre of power. And not just the centre of economic power, but of political power too. The first deputy head of the President's Administration, Oleg Sysuev, said directly: "The position of prime minister itself, as the second most senior figure in the state, compels whoever is in the role to think about his potential as a future president. We are obliged to think of him, and he is obliged to think of himself, as someone who might at any moment be required to take on the president's responsibilities." However, Primakov, who was the head of the government, had no wish to be at the centre of power either. He tried to get out of the situation to the best of his ability, attempting, like the Kremlin, to restrict himself to phrases that would keep everyone satisfied.

In the 'political vacuum' that had formed, the candidates for president included Viktor Chernomyrdin, who had fallen into disgrace because of this, and Evgeny Primakov, who cancelled an official meeting in Washington in response to the decision taken by the USA and its NATO allies to start a military campaign in Yugoslavia. One of the political consequences of this decision, incidentally, was that a story appeared on the front page of the newspaper *Kommersant* about Primakov's move, under the caustic headline 'Russia loses 15,000,000 dollars thanks to Primakov', and this was followed by a period of significant shocks to the workforce at the publishing house, leading ultimately to a change of ownership.

But the main candidate for the position of president of Russia was the mayor of Moscow, Yury Luzhkov. The political portrait of this genuine 'hero of the 90s', at the high–point of his career, deserves its own separate narrative.

On September 30, 1998, at the Labour party's 97th conference in Blackpool (UK), the mayor of Moscow, Yury Luzhkov, announced that he was going to stand for the post of president of Russia: "If it should appear to me that the few individuals who have a chance of being elected will not be capable of governing the country sensibly and properly, I will run for president." The only explanation as to why it was not immediately suggested to Luzhkov that he resign is the weakness of the federal authorities.

In spite of his popularity in Moscow, until that point Luzhkov, while he was still an 'unelected governor', had demonstrated his loyalty to Boris Yeltsin, and had barely said a word about the presidency. But after his resounding triumph in the mayoral elections on June 16, 1996, in which he picked up over 89% of the vote, Luzhkov for some reason stopped giving direct answers when asked whether or not he would stand in the elections in 2000.

At that time, the city authorities set about dealing with some over-arching issues: spreading Moscow's influence to the regions, transforming Luzhkov into a figure of influence of national and even international scale, and creating a political force that could be relied on.

Luzhkov was hard at it for two years. He helped the sailors of Sevastopol, befriended Belarus, rescued Russian manufacturers by means of agreements with Moscow, hosted the Youth Olympic Games, united Russia's mayors – in short, he earned himself some authority. At the same time, Luzhkov was engaged in helping to build up the party. Taking the former head of the Federal Border Service, Andrei Nikolaev, into the State Duma, he backed him as the leader of his own electoral movement. After mastering the role of deputy, Nikolaev created the 'Union of popular power and labour' movement and began preparing for the parliamentary elections.

Among the genuine candidates for the presidency, Yury Luzhkov probably had the most precise, thorough and original economic views of them all. Luzhkov did not of course consider himself an economist, but his economic ideology can easily be identified based on his numerous speeches, and simply by dint of what he did in Moscow.

It matters little whether Luzhkov actually understood the significance of Peter the Great's achievements or not. What is beyond doubt is that he was an admirer of the man who founded St Petersburg. And this can be explained by the similarity of their souls. At the heart of Peter's views was a very specific attitude towards the West. The Tsar did not understand the West at all, and had no wish to understand it. Peter was concerned with one thing only: the country he ruled, which was lagging behind, and had to be transformed as quickly as possible into a strong and wealthy nation.

Yury Luzhkov made no secret of his contempt for economic theories borrowed from the West. It was no accident that he poured such scorn on the "wild and reckless monetarism" of Anatoly Chubais. It was no accident that he refused to acknowledge people's right to own private property on land in the cities, leading people to understand that Russia's citizens were not yet ready to exercise their constitutional rights. But as for making Russia wealthy and powerful, he had probably always had this desire (in the same way that he had been so concerned with Moscow's wealth and influence, whilst he was mayor).

Moreover, he managed to prevent politicians from the provinces from rising up against him, too, although the sphere of financial interests of the Moscow mayor's office stretched far beyond the borders of Moscow. The governors felt the same way about the Moscow mayor as nephews might feel about a rich uncle: he wouldn't be leaving them an inheritance, of course, but he might just decide to leave them enough to make a living. They genuinely considered him to be "Moscow's greatest city mayor of all times and all peoples". Not even the lavish celebrations marking the 850th anniversary of the founding of Moscow caused irritation in the provinces – "he's having a ball, but he's footing the bill himself."

In the last few months of summer 1998, Luzhkov's preparations for his presidential campaign entered their final stage. All the political forces that were favourable to him (Svyatoslav Fyodorov's 'Party of self–governance by the workers', Yury Petrov's 'Union of realists' etc.) entered into a union with Nikolaev's movement in some shape or form. The latter, in turn, began to set about his most important political task – "creating a left and centrist coalition", i.e. an association with the CPRF, which was sympathetic towards Luzhkov. This union would make Luzhkov the favourite in the pre–election race.

Nikolaev's efforts ended in success: he signed an agreement on mutual activity with Zyuganov. The leader of the communist party supported Luzhkov's idea of creating a 'left and centrist" union. Sensing his own strength, Luzhkov decided that the time had come to declare his pariticipation in the presidential election. All the more so given that one of his main obstacles – the possible involvement in the election of Boris Yeltsin – had practically been taken out of the equation. And on the day that Luzhkov made his declaration to the Labour party conference in Blackpool, the State Duma voted through amendments to the law on the presidential elections, proposed by deputies from the 'Yabloko' group. The essence of the amendments was that a single individual "could not be elected president of Russia more than twice in a row".

On October 1, 1998, Moscow's mayor confirmed once again that he was serious about making a bid for the presidency. On November 19, 1998, he announced that he had created a party. He held an assembly of the organizing committee for the new socio–political movement *Otechestvo* ('Fatherland'). His speech was reminiscent of the speech by the secretary general at the plenum of the CPSU. Yury Luzhkov blasted the reformers who had brought the country to collapse, and talked about capitalism's successes in Moscow, as a case in point. In order to "furnish Russia with what she needs" at last, the *Otechestvo* movement was created.

There is a simple reason as to why the mayor of Moscow decided to create a movement based on a coalition of tiny parties: it gave him an opportunity for endless manoeuvring and manipulation, thereby ensuring that his political platform was unsinkable. The authority of Luzhkov himself in Russian politics was by no means small. Moreover, Luzhkov had become a focal point around which politicians on the left and the right had hurriedly begun to align themselves. His presence altered the system of coordinates in the political landscape to such an extent that everyone else had to redefine their own place in it, this time in relation to Luzhkov.

Boris Yeltsin attempted to put this mettlesome candidate behind bars – by this time no–one doubted that Yury Luzhkov was going to put himself forward as a candidate in the elections – and at a meeting with the directors of Russia's leading TV channels on January 24, 1998, he hinted directly at his displeasure.

"It's very interesting to see which candidates have in effect declared themselves candidates – after all, the campaign has not yet begun, and yet there are a few people trying to get a head start on the rest of the field. I personally think that's a mistake, but on the other hand it's a good thing for people to get to know him better – they'll tear him to pieces," the president declared.

Naturally, Yeltsin preferred not to mention the name of this mysterious 'him', opting instead to hint at his identity: "Some of the candidates are so keen to get ahead of themselves that they forget what age they're living in – you can guess who I'm referring to." Lest anyone was still unsure, Yeltsin added: "There are still eighteen months to go until the elections, and he already considers himself president. Not only is that pretty unpleasant, it won't do him any good in the elections, either. Of that I have no doubt."

Yury Luzhkov demonstrated Olympian levels of calmness and had no intention of giving in. Everyone could understand that.

The former Prime Minister Viktor Chernomyrdin, who had initially reacted angrily and bitterly to news of the mayor of Moscow's presidential ambitions, had himself begun to look for ways of standing by the end of the year. On December 28, the leader of the 'Our home is Russia' movement set off to meet the capital's town planner in person. After a two–hour conversation with Luzhkov, Chernomyrdin acknowledged gloomily: "We looked at some political issues. We have plenty to work on, and *Otechestvo* has plenty to work on. We agreed to hold meetings more often."

Chernomyrdin also added that he was prepared to step aside and let *Otechestvo* have the title of "the party of power". And he added sadly that if Yury Luzhkov was to refrain from referring to the *Otechestvo* movement as the 'title of power', "that would be the height of class"...

A short time earlier, Sergei Kirienko had put out feelers to try and gauge his prospects as mayor of Moscow, distancing himself from Chubais and Gaidar. Negotiations on the creation of a political bloc went on throughout the last week of November 1998. Luzhkov was of particular interest to the former prime minister. He was the only young politician who might have been able to adjust and 'democratize' his image. A short time earlier, Luzhkov had attempted to reach an agreement on collaboration with Boris Nemtsov, but had been unable to do so.

At the start of 1999 the mayor continued to strengthen his coalition. He conducted negotiations with Gennady Zyuganov and Grigory Yavlinsky. The mayor explained his decision to bring in his political opposites as allies as follows: "There are only three strategic forces in the country: the CPRF (some people may not like it, but the CPRF is a serious and influential force), *Yabloko* and, if you'll forgive me saying it, *Otechestvo*." Of course, Yury Luzhkov had in mind both the dramatic strengthening of the position of Evgeny Primakov, and the fact that state power at the beginning of 1999 was on the edge of a precipice. In the spring, the mayor of Moscow began to talk about the 'death throes' of the Kremlin, and many of Yeltsin's allies privately admitted that the mayor had been spot on.

Usually the careful Luzhkov used to say only that "it is for the president to make up his own mind about his health." And he observed that terminally ill civil servants ought to resign from state service. The mayor never once explicitly accused Yeltsin of being terminally ill.

After Yeltsin's presidential address on New Year's Eve, which every politician declared would be his last, Luzhkov openly paid obeisance to him: "Why should that be his last New Year's address? Boris Nikolaevich will have an opportunity to do it again next year, too!"

"In the elections for the State Duma, whenever they are held – whether early or when scheduled, the Kremlin is going to have two main strategic tasks. The first is not to let the communists into the Duma. The second is to make sure there are as few deputies as possible from *Otechestvo*," a senior member of staff within the Kremlin administration told a correspondent from the Kommersant publishing house. President Yeltsin's entourage declared war on Luzhkov and his allies.

"The attitude towards Luzhkov in the Kremlin is the same as it was at the height of the government crisis in September 1998," the newspaper's source said in Staraya ploshchad. "Back then, during the clashes with Berezovsky, who had wanted to see Chernomyrdin made prime minister, Luzhkov was public enemy No.1 in the president's entourage."

But there was one major difference. The Kremlin did not simply intend to express quiet hatred of Luzhkov: it intended to destroy him – as mayor, as the leader of *Otechestvo* and as a politician. The pressure was unprecedented. The top priority was to debunk the myth of Luzhkov's glorious image as a model city mayor. As regards the methods used to achieve this aim, it was a case of anything goes – right up to pushing Moscow to default, something that many experts said there was a real danger of in the summer of 1999.

Yet the chances of preventing a Luzhkov victory in the mayoral elections were slim. It was therefore extremely important to the Kremlin not to allow the mayor's influence to grow in the regions. "The president's administration demanded that Shaimiev say no to Luzhkov. For that reason, none of the delegates at the 'All Russia' congress even hinted about a united bloc with *Otechestvo*, although this was seen pretty much as a done deal" – such were the views of the mayor's entourage.

The most successful attack made by the President's Administration was its struggle with the mayor of Moscow. Soon Luzhkov had none of his own people left, either at the

Kremlin or in the White House. He was fast losing the remnants of what little influence he had had in Primakov's government.

In response, Luzhkov's *Otechestvo* merged with Shaimiev's *Vsei Rossiyei*, and it seemed as though the Kremlin had lost everything there was to lose. And when Primakov agreed to take charge of the newly formed OVR, the answer to the question of who was going to be the next president seemed obvious. A new political reality had emerged in the country: instead of the win–win scenario, even with a weak Kremlin, in which Yeltsin was up against the CPRF, there was now a very dangerous scenario: Luzhkov and Primakov against Yeltsin. The powerful non–communist opposition might have been lethal for the president's circle.

But following the start of the mayoral election campaign in the capital, Yury Luzhkov gained a full appreciation of what it might cost him to try and have his cake and eat it.

First of all, the Luzhkov – Primakov alliance proved to be fairly flimsy. Those close to the mayor of Moscow made no secret of it: the decision had been made, and Luzhkov had no intention of giving way to anyone on the road to the Kremlin. Not even to Primakov. In behind–the–scenes conversations, the Moscow civil servants who had built the system emphasized that no–one ought to have any illusions about Primakov's status in the pre–election alliance: "The fact that they made him head of the OVR – that doesn't in any way signify that he has become our boss. In essence, we're going to have to give the academic a piggy–back to the Duma elections, because he's incapable of making his own way there. But that's only until December. After that, if he decides he wants to be president, he'll have to get off our shoulders and make his own way. With that radiculitis of his, and all!"

Secondly, there were enough powerful forces in the mayor's entourage itself who did not wish to let him out "from Moscow to the Kremlin". In order to make a decisive bid for the presidency, the mayor needed a powerful team at presidential level. Luhzkov attempted to create one, with the long–term goal of providing a Moscow *krysha* for the outlaws in the Kremlin – Yastrzhembsky, Kokoshin, Savostyanov and other politicians, who were not only familiar with how things worked in the Kremlin, but had first–hand knowledge of how power is built up at federal level.

In this setting, the terrorist war that came to Moscow dealt an extremely serious blow to the political prospects of the city's mayor. In light of this he was forced to work closely with the Kremlin and the government structures: when there's a war on, it's no time to be settling scores with others who are in the same trench as you.

The ideologues in the Kremlin were quick to take advantage of this. A message broadcast on the TV, which Boris Yeltsin had recorded in mid–September, included, with good reason, the following words: "We understand how difficult things must be at the moment for the mayor of Moscow, Yury Mikhailovich Luzhkov. I will provide him with all the assistance and support he needs during this difficult time."

For a while, Yeltsin's sincere words neutralized Luzhkov's anti–Kremlin rhetoric, on which his pre–election tactics had been based. The president had demonstrated that he was responsive and could be placated – how could anyone fight against that? And as for someone who, almost as if he was your own father, forgetting past insults, had provided you with "assistance at this difficult time" – all you could do was take your hat off to him.

The alliance between Luzhkov and Primakov, meanwhile, collapsed. The compromise proposed by Evgeny Primakov, under which there would be a power–share in the event of victory, if it helped at all, did not dramatically improve the situation. At the start of October, Primakov set out his concept of a new Constitution for Russia, consisting of seven points. The main proposal by the chairman of the Coordination council of the OVR block was that the post of vice–president should be introduced. The potential candidate for head of state gave the following explanation as to why it made sense to have this new position: "When I worked at the MFA, I saw how things worked: thirty ambassadors stood in line and handed diplomas to Yeltsin. We have to think about representative roles..."

Primakov did not specify who exactly was going to carry out these representative functions (he himself or Yury Luzhkov). But it was obvious that only the introduction of the post of vice–president would solve a problem which, after the elections to the Duma, might destroy the alliance between the former prime minister and the mayor of Moscow. The post of vice–president might well have satisfied these ambitions. In the end, Luzhkov, who had sat on the fence for a long time, pronounced the decisive phrase on November 26: "I am not aiming for the role of president."

But that came too late to rescue the situation. The political alliance between Yury Luzhkov and Evgeny Primakov and a host of influential governors (including the president of Tatarstan, Mintimer Shaimiev, the president of Bashkiria, Murtaza Rakhimov, and the governor of St Petersburg, Vladimir Yakovlev) suffered a crushing defeat in the elections to the Duma. On December 19, 1998, the *Otechestvo – Vsya Rossiya* movement came only 3rd, with 13.33% of the vote, a long way behind the president's *Edinstvo* party with 23.32% and the CPRF. As a result, the OVR was broken up.

Furthermore, even though he won the elections for mayor of Moscow, which were held at the same time as the elections to parliament, Luzhkov had lost more than 18% of the votes he won in the previous mayoral election. Admittedly, he still won in the first round, but the share of the vote that he secured (69.89%) was the worst performance in his career.

The net contribution of the political strategists

By the end of the nineties, the 'dirty tricks' used in the exotic world of advertising had been transformed into an everyday political reality. In the spring of 1999 the Duma unsuccessfully attempted to impeach Yeltsin. There was chaos in the government: in May, Yeltsin removed the prime minister, Evgeny Primakov, from his position, suspecting that he had designs on the presidency; in August, Sergei Stepashin was replaced by Vladimir Putin. There was also quite a saga involving the replacement of the procurator general, Yury Skuratov: he refused to leave his post, and on that very day a naked man bearing a striking resemblance to the procurator general appeared on the nation's TV screens, surrounded by some ladies who looked very much like prostitutes.

In response attacks were made against trusted individuals within the presidential Family. On July 12 billboards were put up in Moscow that read: "Roma is in the Family's thoughts. The Family is in Roma's thoughts. Congratulations! P. S. Roma chose a great job." Smiling down from them was a young man who had yet to become famous, and whom only the most well–informed could have recognized as the director of Sibneft, Roman Abramovich. The billboards were taken down that same day following a call from Sibneft. But the billboard war continued: within 10 days the city had been decorated with 20 advertising hoardings devoted to a different oligarch. These ones called on people to "uproot the boaBABs" (BAB was an acronym for Berezovsky's surname, first name and patronymic).

The response was not long in coming. Exactly one week later, an advertisement appeared in two newspapers: "CHAIRS FOR LUZHniKOV. Call now. Ask for Lena".

There was a rich tradition of billboard propaganda in Soviet history, going back to the time of Mayakovsky and the "Okon ROSTA". And thereafter the ability to kiss, or to lick with a rough tongue, a poster depicting either the latest general secretary, the beloved party, or the labouring masses, was a skill that was highly cherished. But here, for the first time in history, outdoor advertising was being used to settle scores between the various branches of power.

For the record it is worth pointing out that people had made their feelings clear in public both before and after 1999. In 1996, the director of the shoe company Vena Moda Austria, Alexander Sharapov, had hung up a portrait of his wife Svetlana on the streets of Moscow, with "I love you!" written on it. Pretty much the same thing, on a somewhat larger scale, had been done in 2000 by the former acting finance minister, Andrei Vavilov, one of the richest and most influential civil servants in the country, who had put up messages to his wife, the Lenkom actress Marianna Tsaregradskaya, that read: "Hi, Marianna" and "I love you".

Generally speaking, the second half of the 1990s was to some extent the age of the political strategists. At the time, many people felt that politics in Russia was conducted not by people in the Kremlin or the White House, but by unseen (so to speak) characters such as Marat Gelman or Gleb Pavlovsky. Admittedly, the all–powerful nature of the political strategists seems nonetheless to have been slightly exaggerated. In December 1999, the *Kommersant* correspondent Andrei Kolesnikov, who had joined the pre–campaign tour of Sergei Shoigu's team, had this to say about the work that they did: "...The other day, two psychologists were brought in especially for the pre–election campaign. "But they turned out to be, how can I put it kindly... theoreticians," I was told. "To give you an example, they made Karelin talk in public about neuro–linguistic programming. Then Karelin listened to a recording of himself, and Shoigu sent them packing. After that he had two more image–makers. They said that when Shoigu sat on a chair, the folds of his jacket gathered up on his back; they did a little role–play amongst themselves and two days later put down on the table several ways of solving this problem – for him to choose between. They were fired there and then."

Propaganda ideas of this nature are hardly likely to inspire anything other than amused bewilderment: "Aleksei Chesnokov, the director of the Institute of political affairs, who is always somewhere nearby, has suggested several times already that we take radical steps to liven up the trip.

'Let's arrange for Sergei Shoigu to have a car crash! But in reality no harm will have come to him, and he'll be alive and well! We'll tell his family that he's okay, but no–one else. Go on, do it! This one, I must admit, has already been used in various elections five or six times before, but that doesn't matter, I think it'll work." And he added, rubbing his hands: 'Victory shall be ours..."'

"Look, there's a wedding car!" shouted the political strategist Chesnokov, as we drove away from the airport. "A little bell, some baubles...I've got a brilliant idea. Let's have Shoigu going up and kissing the bride in front of everyone. That'll be great! I don't think anyone's pulled off a stunt like that before..."

"Yeah, he'll pull it off...and he'll get a punch in the face from the groom for his troubles."

It sometimes seemed as though Shoigu fared much better when the political strategists weren't around. He came across as more powerful, more vibrant. "Now they're asking him: 'Imagine that you're prime minister and there's some corruption in the government. What would you do about it?"

He stares at the person who asked the question. His press–secretary, Marina Ryklina, half–closes her eyes in dread at the answer he might give. Shoigu was going to come out with something, she thought, and there would be no way of rescuing the situation.

Shoigu's response was: "Imagine you're a cosmonaut and the seal of your spacesuit has broken. What's your next move?"

A different book

As for how the nineties ended, everyone remembers that well: after a series of explosions in Buinaksk, Moscow and Volgodonsk, troops were sent into Chechnya and the second

Chechen war began. The bloc 'Edintstvo' (*Unity*), set up by Boris Berezovsky, won the election, and then merged with Luzhkov and Primakov's bloc, 'Otechestvo – Vsya Rossiya' (*Our fatherland is all Russia*), and the party 'Edinaya Rossiya' (*United Russia*) was formed. And with less than 12 hours to go before the turn of the millennium, Boris Yeltsin apologized for everything to the Russian people. He then proceeded to present them with their new president – Vladimir Putin.

Thus the 'wild nineties' were replaced by the 'corpulent noughties' – but that was a different era altogether. And it calls for a different book altogether, too.

III

EVENTS AND CHARACTERS

11. A CHRONOLOGY

1987

January 13 – a directive is issued by the Presidium of the Supreme Soviet of the USSR 'On issues related to the creation on the territory of the USSR, and the activity of, joint enterprises, international associations and organizations, with the participation of Soviet and foreign organizations, firms and management bodies'; and the following decrees from the Soviet of Ministers of the USSR are adopted: No. 48 'On the procedure for the creation on the territory of the USSR and the activity of joint enterprises, international associations and organizations from the USSR and the other member states of Comecon, and their activity', and No. 49 'On the procedure for creating, on the territory of the USSR, joint enterprises with the participation of Soviet organizations and firms from capitalist and developing countries, and their activity'.

February 5 – the following directives are issued by the Soviet of Ministers of the USSR: Nos. 160, 161 and 162 – 'On the creation of cooperatives in the field of public catering', 'On the creation of cooperatives in the field of domestic services' and 'On the creation of cooperatives for the production of products consumed by the people'.

June 30 – the USSR law 'On the state enterprise (association)' is adopted, after which privatization begins in the country; the first stage of privatization takes place almost spontaneously.

The first cooperative (in essence, private) restaurant, Andrei Fyodorov's 'Kropotkinskaya, 36' opens its doors.

1988

May 26 – the law 'On cooperation in the USSR' is adopted.

The cooperative 'MMM' is registered (other sources state that this happened in 1989) (an abbreviation made up of the first letters of the founders' surnames – brothers Sergei and Vyacheslav Mavrodi and a woman named Muravieva).

November 16 – the parade of sovereignties begins: the Estonian SSR declares its sovereignty.

1989

January 3 – a commercial advertisement is printed in the newspaper *Izvestiya*.

March 26 – the first ever partially free and alternative parliamentary elections in the USSR are held (the election of delegates to the Congress of people's deputies of the USSR). The opposition candidates B.N. Yeltsin, A.D. Sakharov and others are elected deputies.

National conflicts intensify: the breaking up of a demonstration in Tblisi (in April), the Fergansk events (May), armed civil disorder in Sukhumi (July).

The following states declare their sovereignty: the Lithuanian SSR (in April), the Latvian SSR (in July), the Azerbaijanian SSR (in September).

May 21 – an opposition rally, attended by 150,000 people, is held at the Luzhniki stadium in Moscow; a series of demonstrations are held.

July 7 – at the I congress of people's deputies of the USSR, the first opposition group against the official leadership is formed – the Inter–regional deputy group.

July 11 – miners' strikes in the Kuzbass trigger strikes by miners all over the country.

August 15 – the state gas concern Gazprom is created. Viktor Chernomyrdin is appointed prime minister.

September 28 – 'Yeltsin falls off a bridge'.

October 9 – Anatoly Kashpirovsky's first seance on USSR Central Television.

The Alisa stock exchange is registered.

November 3 – the Baikal–Amur Mainline is commissioned. It stretches from Ust–Kut all the way to the Pacific Ocean.

December 12 – the Second Congress of People's Deputies of the Soviet Union is opened (only to close on December 24). Following a report by A.N. Yakovlev, the congress condemns the Molotov–Ribbentrop Pact (1939). The congress also condemns the invasion of Afghanistan by Soviet troops and and the use of military force in Tblisi on April 9, 1989.

December 13 – the Liberal Democratic Party of the Soviet Union is founded.

In December the business newspaper *Kommersant* goes on sale again.

The band *Nana* is formed.

December 31 – civil disorder in Nakhichevani; hundreds of kilometres of infrastructure destroyed on the Soviet–Iranian border.

1990

January 11 – a consignment of tanks, which the cooperative ANT was attempting to take across the border, is seized in Novorossiysk.

January 13 – 19 – pogroms against Armenians in Baku.

January 15 – Soviet troops are sent into Nagorny Karabakh in order to stop inter–ethnic clashes.

January 16 – Mikhail Gorbachev signs a decree from the Presidium of the Supreme Soviet 'On the restoration to citizenship of the USSR of M. L. Rostropovich and G.P. Vishnevskaya'.»

January 18 – the Azerbaijani SSR declares war on the Armenian SSR.

January 20 – 'black January': Soviet troops are sent into Baku; a state of emergency is declared in the city; 130 people die and around 700 are wounded.

January 31 – Russia's first Macdonald's outlet opens in Moscow's Pushkin Square.

February 4 – a rally in Moscow to express support for the route of reform attracts 200,000 people.

February 7 – the Communists' monopoly on political power is abolished. The Central Committee of the Communist Party of the Soviet Union (the CPSU) votes to abolish the 6th clause of the Constitution of the USSR, 'on the governing role of the CPSU'.

February 12–14 – mass civil disorder in Dushanbe, Tadjik SSR. 22 people die and 565 are injured.

February 26 – The Congress of People's Deputies of the USSR adopts the Law on private land–ownership in rural areas and the Law on the various forms of property.

March 6 – the law 'On property in the RSFSR' is adopted.

The following Republics declare their independence from the USSR: Lithuania (March 11), Georgia (April 9), Latvia (May 4), Estonia (May 8).

March 14 – the elections for president of the USSR take place at the Congress of People's Deputies of the USSR; the winner is M. S. Gorbachev, who duly becomes the first and last president of the USSR.

March 25 – tanks are sent into Vilnius in an effort to restore order as people agitate for Lithuania's exit from the USSR.

April 30 – the radio station 'Evropa plus' begins broadcasting in Moscow.

May 1 – immediately after the traditional May 1st parade of columns of workers, on Moscow's Red Square, an alternative display of democratic forces is held.

May 23 – Anatoly Sobchak is elected chairman of the Leningrad Council of People's Deputies.

May 24 – Nikolai Ryzhkov, the Chairman of the Council of Ministers of the USSR, proposes a plan for a phased transition "to a regular market economy". Panic breaks out in the consumer market. Regulation of the distribution of key food products is introduced.

May 27 – clashes in Yerevan between mobilized forces and divisions of the Soviet Army: 24 people die on the Armenian side.

May 29 – Boris Yeltsin is elected Chairman of the Supreme Soviet of the RSFSR, defeating the candidates proposed by M.S. Gorbachev.

June 2 – the first trade exchange in the USSR opens in Moscow.

June 4–6 – the Osh riots in Kirgyzia.

June 7 – the Local Council of the Russian Orthodox Church opens in Moscow, at which Aleksei II is elected Patriarch of Moscow and All the Russias (his enthronement ceremony took place on June 10).

The following declare their sovereignty: the Uzbek SSR (June 20), the Moldovan SSR (June 23), the Ukrainian SSR (July 16), the Belorussian SSR (July 27), the Turkmen SSR (August 22), the Armenian SSR (August 23), the Kazakh SSR (October 22) and the Kirgyz SSR (October 22).

June 24 – the last concert by Viktor Tsoi and the band Kino is held at Luzhniki.

KamAZ becomes a corporation in June. Nikolai Bekh, the director of the factory's casting division, is elected president of KamAZ. By decision of the government of the USSR, 38% of the shares revert to the property of the union, 13% become the property of Tatarstan, and the remaining securities are put up for sale.

July 13 – the Bank of Russia is established.

August 1 – the USSR Law on the media (ban on censorship, establishment of publication by the workforce) is adopted.

August 15 – the president of the USSR, Mikhail Gorbachev, signs an order restoring citizenship to dissidents exiled from the country, including Alexander Solzhenitsyn.

August 22 – the radio station 'Echo of Moscow' begins broadcasting.

August 30 – an agenda for the transition to a market economy, entitled '500 days', is published; it is never implemented.

September 2 – Pridnestrovie declares that it has broken away from the Moldavian SSR, but the act is not recognized.

September 18 – the newspaper *Komsomolskaya pravda* publishes an article by Alexander Solzhenitsyn entitled 'How are we to furnish Russia with what she needs?'

September 19 – a top–level national domain is registered for the Soviet Union – .su. The first ever website in Russia is the resource of the mathematics department at the Russian Academy of Sciences, ipsun.ac.msc.su.

October 15 – Mikhail Gorbachev is awarded the Nobel Peace Prize "In recognition of his leading role in the peace process, which is today an important component part of the life of the international community".

October 31 – the Supreme Soviet of the RSFSR adopts a law on the transfer of control over natural resources and the republic's industry to the authorities in the RSFSR.

November 7 – the last display and parade of military equipment on Red Square marking the anniversary of the October revolution, organized by the state. During the demonstration there is an assassination attempt against M. S. Gorbachev.

November 23 – the Supreme Soviet of the USSR provides

emergency powers to president Mikhail Gorbachev in order to maintain order in the USSR.

December 2–5 – mass civil disorder over nationality in the city of Namangan, in the Uzbek SSR. 5 reservists die, along with 3 of those who took part in the disorder.

December 11 – the chairman of the KGB of the USSR, Kryuchkov, gives a televised address in which he states that there has been a conspiracy by Western powers seeking the break–up of the USSR.

December 20 – Eduard Shevardnadze steps down as minister of foreign affairs of the USSR, declaring that there is a risk of a dictatorship being established in the country.

December 26 – the Cabinet of ministers of the USSR is set up, to replace the Council of Ministers of the USSR. Nikolai Ryzhkov tenders his resignation from the post of chairman of the Council of Ministers of the USSR on grounds of poor health.

The Moscow–Volokolamsk expressway, better known as the Novorizhskoe (or, colloquially, the *Nouveau–riche*) Highway, is opened.

1991

From January 1 onwards, *Nezavisimaya gazeta*, a newspaper founded by Mossovet, is published on a regular basis (three times a week).

As of January 1 a 5% tax on sales comes into effect in the USSR.

January – the bank Menatep, founded in 1988, begins selling its own shares.

January – Mikhail Fridman, who started out as a ticket tout buying and selling tickets to the Bolshoi Theatre, founds Alphabank and becomes chairman of its board of directors.

January 11 – a *coup d'etat* is attempted in Lithuania. The Committee for the rescue of the nation is created; it declares itself the only legitimate power in the republic.

January 14 – at one o'clock in the morning a special forces unit and the Alpha group storm the TV centre in Vilnius. The local populace puts up resistance. 15 people die as a result of the operation.

January 22 – the Cabinet of ministers of the USSR approves a directive 'On the cessation of the acceptance as legal tender by the State Bank of the USSR of money in 50 and 100 rouble denominations, minted in 1961, and the procedure for the exchange of said money and the restriction on the issuing of cash from citizens' savings accounts' (the Pavlovsk reform, named after the Prime Minister of the USSR Valentin Pavlov).

In January, the chairman of the board of directors of the bank Dialogue, the American Peter Derby, sets up the investment company Troika Dialogue, investing \$35,000 in it. A quarter of the students and graduates at Moscow State University, led by Ruben Vardanian, get involved in the business, and a year later Vardanian takes charge of the company.

At the start of the year Roslesbirzh is created; soon rivals emerge – the Forestry products exchange and other exchange structures. None of them meet with any success. Eventually people begin to trade export quotas for forestry products and timber on the exchanges, rather than forestry products; after the liberation of exports, they die out. For the forestry industry, the whole of 1991 passes under the slogan 'Those who can, export'.

In February, the first meeting of shareholders in JSC KamAZ is held.

March 1 – miners' strikes begin in the USSR: in addition to financial demands, they also put forward political demands, including a demand that Mikhail Gorbachev retire (the strikes continue until May).

March 17 – the All–union referendum on the preservation of the USSR – 6 republics boycott the referendum. In it, the electorate votes in favour of the plan proposed by Mikhail Gorbachev to create a renewed Federation of socialist sovereign republics.

March 27 – on the pretext of protecting the deputies of the RSFSR and preventing undesirable incidents, troops are sent into Moscow (they withdraw from the city later that day).

In March, the senior director of the Russian trade and raw materials exchange (RTRE), Konstantin Borovoi, and the director of the Central Research Institute, Vladimir Utkin, sign an agreement to cooperate on the creation of a Military–industrial exchange.

In April, in Nizhnevartovsk, one of the centres of oil production in Russia, Yugorsk bank is registered. Oleg Kantor is appointed as the bank's president. It was to have a colourful but short–lived existence. At first it concentrated on providing services to oil companies in Siberia. 'Yugorsky' reached the height of its achievements in 1993: it was listed 17th among Russia's biggest banks based on the total value of shares in it.

In June 1995 Oleg Kantor is stabbed to death at his dacha outside Moscow.

April 2 – a one–off hike in retail prices by 2–4 times. The measure is described as the second phase of the Pavlovsk reforms. The first phase was the exchange of vouchers which took place in January.

April 3 – the USSR law 'On the procedure for solving issues related to the departure of a republic in the union from the USSR' is adopted.

April 9 – the first trades on the Gosbank currency exchange. Ten commercial banks and a single financial organization take part in them.

April 10 – the former director of the Karagandinsky Metallurgical Combine, Oleg Soskovets, is appointed minister of metallurgy of the USSR. He is considered the chief benefactor of the group Trans Commodities (later renamed Trans World Group), owned by the Cherny brothers, which goes on to become the main exporter of Russian metals in the international markets.

April 23 – 9 republics and the union centre put pen to paper on a new union agreement in Novo–Ogaryovo.

May 13 – Russian television begins broadcasting on the second channel of the USSR's Central Television, and the first programme broadcast is *Vesti* (the news).

May 17 – the hoax documentary *Lenin was a mushroom* is broadcast on Leningrad Television.

May 20 – the Supreme Soviet of the USSR adopts the law 'On the procedure for leaving the Union of Soviet Socialist Republics and entering the Union of Soviet Socialist Republics for citizens of the USSR', which allowed citizens of the USSR to cross the country's borders (it came into force in January 1993).

May 22–25 – raids of customs points in Latvia and Lithuania by security forces from Riga and Vilnius.

In May Boris Berezovksy's company LogoVAZ is the first company in the USSR to be given the status of an official importer for MercedesBenz. In its first two months LogoVAZ sells approximately 60 cars. Most of these were cheap MercedesBenz 190s and the more reliable MercedesBenz 200D.

In May, the All–Russia State Television and Radio Broadcasting Company, which was founded in 1990, begins broadcasting.

June 12 – Boris Yeltsin is elected president of the RSFSR. Alexander Rutskoi is elected vice–president.

June 12 – Yury Luzhkov becomes mayor of Moscow, a post which he continues to hold until his retirement in August 2010. Anatoly Sobchak becomes mayor of Leningrad; his first act is to change the name of the city to St Petersburg.

In June, 400 companies from the USSR's metallurgy industry set up CJSC 'Metals Exchange'. The initial investment in it served as the starting capital for many of the trading structures operating today.

In June a number of major companies in the military and industrial complex establish the 'Conversion' trade exchange.

July 1 – the Supreme Soviet of the USSR adopts the law 'On

the core first steps towards denationalization and privatisation of enterprise'.

July 1 – official registration of the unemployed is launched in the USSR. Labour exchanges are opened in Moscow and other cities.

July 10 – Boris Yeltsin is sworn in as president of Russia.

July 17–18 – a meeting of the G8 is held in London, with the USSR in attendance.

July 31 – the US president, George Bush, and the president of the USSR, Mikhail Gorbachev, sign an Agreement on the reduction of strategic weapons stockpiling, under the terms of which both sides must cut their arsenals of long–distance rockets by a third.

August 19 – 22 – the August putsch in the USSR: the leaders of the USSR, headed by vice–president Gennady Yanayev, establish the State Committee on the State of Emergency and attempt to depose Mikhail Gorbachev whilst he is on holiday in the Crimea, but are themselves arrested less than 72 hours later; Gorbachev returns to Moscow.

The following announce their independence from the USSR: Estonia (August 20), Latvia (August 21), Ukraine (August 24), Belarus (August 25), Moldova (August 27), Azerbaijan (August 30), Kirgyzia (August 31), Uzbekistan (August 31), Tadjikistan (September 9), Armenia (September 21), Turkmenia (October 27), Kazakhstan (December 16).

In August, the broker of Russia's trade and raw materials exchange, Mikhail Zhivilo, and his brother set up CJSC 'Metallurgical investment company' (MIKOM). Rumour has it that the Zhivilo brothers are being assisted by their father, a senior civil servant at Minmetallurgy. MIKOM is allegedly being used as a vehicle for Western loans used to reshape companies in the sector.

September 2–5: the 5th congress of national deputies of the USSR takes place (it is an extraordinary meeting, and the last one ever held).

September 6 – separatists seize power in Chechnya. Armed insurgents from the NCCP expel deputies from the Supreme Soviet of the Chechen and Ingush SSR.

September – a mobile telecommunications network is set up in Russia for the first time. Russia's first network telecoms company, Delta Telecom, starts operating in St Petersburg. A joint enterprise consisting of the American company US West and the Leningrad regional telephone network begins selling mobile phones. The handsets are so heavy that they are dubbed 'bodybuilders'. Despite the outrageous cost of services at the time – a $60 subscriber fee and a charge of 60 cents a minute for calls, Delta Telecom signs up at least one new customer every day.

In September, Alexander Panikin creates the company Paninter, which rose out of the 'Chelnok' cooperative, which produced knitted goods. Its initial capital amounted to 2000 roubles and six second–hand sewing–machines.

September 16 – trade opens at the Moscow non–ferrous metals exchange, which intends to secure 45% of the global turnover of non–ferrous metals in the space of a year and 20% of global turnover of aluminium. This 'global giant' survives for a further three years.

September 26 – the first foreign currency Visa credit cards from a Russian commercial bank are unveiled. They are issued by Kredobank. The history of the plastic cards market in Russia can be traced to this moment.

September 27–28 – the XXII emergency congress of the Komsomol, which declares the role of the Komsomol in the past obsolete and breaks up the organization.

September 28 – the rock festival 'Monsters of rock' takes place in Moscow; estimates of the attendance range from 600,000 to 800,000.

The nightclub 'U Lissa' opens in September, along with the 'White cockroach' club on Karetny sidestreet, for the more bohemian crowd.

October 18 – the last meeting of the Praesidium of the Supreme Soviet of the USSR.

In October a presentation is made by JSC 'Military–industrial investment company' (MIIC), which was founded by several military–industrial companies in the RCE and the Military–Industrial Companies' exchange.

November 5 – Boris Yeltsin signs directive No. 1333 'On the transformation of the state gas concern 'Gazprom' into RAO 'Gazprom'. Only three Russian companies are given the abbreviation RAO – 'Unified energy systems', 'Norilsk nickel' and Gazprom. In accordance with the directive, extraction companies and transport companies in the gas sector are transformed into affiliates of the firm Gazprom, with one hundred percent control. Ancillary and service companies acquire the status of affiliates of the shareholder companies, with Gazprom's share standing at 51% of shares or more.

November 6 – Yeltsin takes charge of the government of reforms in Russia; Yegor Gaidar is appointed his deputy.

November 6 – the directive of the president of the Russian Federation, 'On the activity of the CPSU and the Communist party of the RSFSR', is published, banning their activity.

In November, by decree from the Council of Ministers of the USSR, the state oil concern 'Langepasuraikogalymneft' is set up, which incorporates three oil extraction firms – Langepasneftegaz, Uralneftegaz, Kogalymneftegaz – as well as the refinery companies of Permnefteorgsintez and the Volgograd and Novoufimsk oil refineries. Vagit Alekperov, the USSR's first deputy minister for the oil and gas industry, is appointed president of the concern. Hardly anyone now remembers the full name of the corporation: it became known almost immediately by the abbreviated title LUKOIL (this name was dreamt up by the company's vice president Ravil Maganov, for which he was awarded a prize of 300 roubles).

November 15 – Yeltsin signs a package of ten presidential directives and government orders related to Russia's transition to a market economy. They include the directive 'On the liberalization of external economic activity'. All management companies, regardless of their form of ownership, are entitled to undertake external economic activity.

November 27 – the fifth and final version of the Agreement on the Union of Sovereign States is published.

December 4 – the Vneshekonombank of the USSR announces to all of the world's banks and financial organizations that is going to stop paying out on the USSR's debts indefinitely. The bank resumes its activities three years later – after the release of the directive from the president of Russia 'On several issues related to the activity of the Bank of external economic activity of the USSR'. Under this directive, the bank officially became a state financial institution specializing exclusively in servicing the external debts and assets of the former USSR. Thus a major bank emerged in Russia which to this day does not hold a licence from the Central Bank.

December 8 – the Agreement to create the CIS is signed in Viskuli, Belarus.

December 12 – the Supreme Soviet of the RSFSR denounces the Agreement on the formation of the USSR in 1922 and ratifies the Belovezhsky agreement.

December 20 – the State bank of the USSR is liquidated. Its successor is the Bank of Russia, whose director is Georgy Matykhin.

December 25 – the RSFSR is renamed the Russian Federation, the Soviet flag atop the Kremlin is replaced with the three–coloured Russian flag, and Gorbachev announces that he is to stand down as president of the USSR.

December 26 – the USSR officially comes to an end; at the last assembly of the Supreme Soviet of the USSR, the disbandment of the USSR is officially announced.

December 27 – the law 'On mass information resources' is adopted. On the same day, the government, on the basis of the president's directive, establishes Russian state television and the radio company 'Ostankino', at USSR State television and radio.

In December a mobile telecommunications network is introduced in Moscow – the Joint Enterprise 'Moscow mobile network' is founded by the Moscow City Telephone Network (MGTS) and the American company US West.

In December a 23–year–old student from the physics faculty of Moscow State University, Oleg Deripaska, who prior to this had already worked as a broker at the Russian trade and raw materials exchange, founds and takes charge of the Limited Responsibility Cooperative 'Rosaluminprodukt'. The co–founder is the Military finance and investment company, where Deripaska had worked as director of finances.

In December, the advertising association PremierSV, founded by Sergei Lisovsky and Vladimir Zhechkov, is set up. It incorporates 12 advertising agencies, all listed as equal partners, including the Partnership Company 'Avrora', LISS and TISSA.

In 1991, the Chemical products exchange opens in Moscow, created by the biggest companies in the Ministry for the nuclear energy industry, the Ministry for the defence industry, the Ministry for the radio industry, and also by the Central Union, the Bank for the chemical industry and the External Trade Bank of the RSFSR. It fails to bring in any further profit for its founders and is closed in 1994 due to massive debts. Yet it was at this exchange that many of the companies which went on to play a major role as intermediaries in the sector, in the mid–nineties, earned their capital.

In 1991, the Swiss company Marc Rich organized its tolling operations at the Krasnoyarsk aluminium plant. As a result, the 'invention of tolling' would later be ascribed to Oleg Deripaska, Mikhail Chorny and Yury Shlyafshtein, but in fact it was Marc Rich who brought it to Russia.

In 1991, at the instigation of a former member of the KGB, Boris Smirnov, the Centre for ecological problems at the Academy of creativity of the USSR registers the small state enterprise 'P.A. Smirnov and sons in Moscow'. The business was created in order to produce 'Smirnov' vodka the way it was made before the Revolution.

In 1991, the new states of the CIS which have sea ports begin hastily dividing up the ships of the USSR's merchant fleet. Of the Soviet Union's 17 ships, 10 remain in Russia. The amount of maritime traffic is halved – from 163 million tonnes to 85 million tonnes. As a result, Russia falls out of the top ten states shipping goods by sea, and drops to 28th place. At the helm of Baltic Maritime Shipping (BMP), which owns 178 ships, is its new CEO Viktor Kharchenko. It signs the first agreement in post–Soviet history on the lease of ships by a private company. 15 ships owned by BMP are leased to the international charitable organization 'Global laboratory', directed by Andrei Filkinshtein, for $3.8 million. In later years, the directors of the Union of Russian ship owners (SOROSS) will refer to this deal as the 'first step on the road to the collapse of shipping'.

In 1991 the Ministry of textile industries of the RSFSR is transformed into the state concern Rostextile. At the time it is set up, the concern incorporates 350 companies in the sector, from 36 Russian regions.

In 1991 the 'Skorokhod' factory is privatized. Prior to this, several of its affiliates became independent, specifically 'Proletarskaya pobeda', which is renamed 'Viktoria'. The workforce become the new owner of the factory.

The company 1C is created in 1991.

Roman Viktyuk's theatre is opened in 1991.

1992

In January, the directive of the president of the RSFSR, 'On measures aimed at liberalizing prices', comes into force. At the end of the year, the value of the rouble falls by approximately 27 times. Russia becomes both the cheapest country for foreigners and the most expensive country for its own citizens. Nowhere else, not even in Africa, was it possible to get a meal for 10 cents (40 roubles), or buy a suit for $1 (400 roubles). Yet a basic monthly salary of 342 roubles would be enough to get you 1 kg of either cheese or smoked sausage at the market. Thus 'shock therapy' began.

On January 16, the directors of Coca Cola announce that they are setting up a joint–stock company called CocaCola Refreshments Moscow (CCRM) in order to construct a fizzy drinks production plant. By that time, Coca Cola's main rival – PepsiCo – already had quite a strong presence in our market. In the early 1970s the company had signed a deal with the USSR, under which it sold Stolichnaya vodka in the USA. In exchange, PepsiCo supplied concentrated Pepsi to Russia; this could then be poured neatly into 0.33 litre bottles at Russian companies.

In January, the first currency–related interventions are made by the Central Bank of the Russian Federation at the Moscow inter–bank currency exchange (MMVB). Moreover, on January 3, 1992, amendments are made to the Criminal Code of the Russian Federation, rendering invalid the clause, famous since the days of the USSR, entitled 'Violations of the rules on currency operations', which made cash transactions between citizens involving western currencies a crime.

January 29 – Boris Yeltsin issues directive No. 65 'On free trade'.

February 1 – the Russo–American declaration on the end of the Cold War is signed.

At the start of the year the Japanese chain 'Aum sinrikyo' appears in Moscow.

February 25 – the Russian Aerospace Agency is established.

February 29 – the prohibition law is repealed, along with the state monopoly on alcoholic drinks in Russia.

March 31 – a Federal agreement is signed at the Kremlin in Moscow, under which 89 subject entities become part of the Russian Federation.

April 15 – the Energetics Russian Company (ERC) is

registered; its founders are the Soviet state concern 'Energoatom', which had been rechristened 'Rosenergoatom' the previous day, eight nuclear power stations, industry–specific Scientific Research Institutes and the Brokinvset brokerage circuit.

April 28 – the first case of the sale of a Soviet foreign bank to a private bank is recorded. An assembly of the shareholders in OstWest Handelsbank, held in Frankfurt–Am–Main, decided to transfer 80.6% of the bank's capital to Tokobank.

The production company 'Video International' is registered in May. Its founders are Mikhail Lesin, Oganes Sobolev, Yury Zapol, Alexander Gurevich and Vladimir Perepelkin.

In May, the Ministry of fuel energy comes under the control of the head of the Gazprom concern, Viktor Chernomyrdin. He does not remain in the post for long – in December Chernomyrdin is appointed prime minister.

May 30 – Viktor Chernomyrdin hands over the reigns of command at Gazprom to his first deputy and former acquaintance from Orenburg, Rem Vyakhirev.

June 17 – during a visit to the USA, the Russian president Boris Yeltsin signs an agreement 'Of mutual understanding' with the US president George Bush. The agreement is the first stage in the signing of the START–II agreement (signed on January 3, 1993).

June 22 – two skeletons discovered outside Ekaterinburg are identified as the remains of Nikolai II and Alexandra Fyodorovna.

In June, a state privatization programme is accepted in Russia, involving the issuing of vouchers to citizens.

July 16 – the director of the Bank of Russia, Georgy Matyukhin, signs a declaration to the effect that he is retiring. Viktor Geraschenko is appointed acting chairman of the CB. His first move is to implement a bilateral cancellation of the companies' debts, accelerate the growth in the money supply by two or three times and reduce interventions in the internal currency market, enabling the exchange rate for the rouble to fall. As a result, the real–terms money supply doubled, the scale of the non–payment crisis is reduced significantly, and the commercial banks make and seldom used monetary savings.

In July, Boris Yeltsin signs a directive on the privatisation of the Sukhoi OKB design bureau.

In July, the Aeroflot group submits an application for the company to be privatized. The request was not satisfied until 1995.

On August 14, the president's directive 'On the introduction of a system of privatized cheques in the Russian Federation'.

August 21 – the Joint–stock Moscow company (JSMO) ZIL is registered. The company's workforce vote for a version of privatization under which they will receive 25% of the company's preferred shares for free and will be able to buy ordinary shares at a 30% discount.

In September the Russian academic Dmitry Zimin founds the company Vympelkom. The company incorporates Commercial Bank 'Impulse', the Mints Radiotechnical institute and a host of other businesses.

October 1 – the first trades of vouchers take place on the Russian trade and raw materials exchange (RTSB).

October 9 – Russia's first currency exchange point run by All–Union Joint–Stock Company Intourist opens, for operations involving foreign currency in cash. Prior to this, the only place in Russia where dollars were converted into roubles and vice versa was on the black market. The saying "There's no money, just 'greenbacks'" began to be widely used. Many Russian banks grew out of currency exchange points like this one.

October 13 – the term 'oligarch' first appears in official everyday usage. This was the day Menatep bank announced that it intended to create a body that would provide banking services for the "financial and industrial oligarchy" – clients who had amassed fortunes of $10 million or more, in relation to whom an "exclusive approach" was required due to the extent of their influence and requirements.

In October, the Kommersant publishing house (which started life as the Fakt cooperative, founded in 1988) begins publishing the daily newspaper *KommersantDaily*. The first issue contains: an article about the trial of Sergey Parfenov, a member of the emergency police, who stood accused of trading data with Russian reconnaissance satellites, and a short guide entitled 'How to read Daily."

In October, in accordance with the state privatization programme which was adopted in June, privatization cheques – vouchers – were put into circulation. The face value of the securities is 10,000 roubles, whilst the entire property of the country is estimated to be worth 1.4 trillion roubles.

In October Boris Yeltsin signed a directive 'On the specific characteristics of the privatization of the manufacturing association 'Volga car plant'.'

On November 17 directives were published regarding the creation of the oil concerns Yukos and Surgutneftegaz.

In November and the first half of December a whole series of government decrees regarding the privatization of arms companies, but when Viktor Chernomyrdin was appointed prime minister the privatization process at VPK came to a halt.

In November, Boris Yeltsin signed a decree on the privatization of the Manufacturing association GAZ, whilst in December Joint–stock Company 'GAZ' was registered.

In December, the state enterprise AOOT Rostelekom was created by order of the State Property Committee.

December 8 – the order of the president of the RF 'On the federal treasury' is issued. Thus began a struggle that was to last many years for the transfer of budget accounts from commercial banks to the treasury. Many major Russian banks evolved from the organizations that serviced these accounts.

December 14 – Viktor Chernomyrdin becomes prime minister.

December 17 – the government announces the privatization

of Russian Joint–Stock Company 'EAS of Russia'. The first package of shares (20%) is presented at a cheque auction.

December 31 – the Russian joint–stock company for energy and electrification (RAO 'EAS of Russia') is registered. All of the assets of the Ministry of fuel energy of Russia that relate to electric energy are transferred to the ownership of the RAO: the unified energy system (UES), which has existed since 1961; 70 regional energy systems, 100 Gas Energy Systems and over 600 power stations, and 2.5 million km of power lines. Viktor Chernomyrdin gave his blessing to Anatoly Dyakov taking over the leadership of the company.

In December the first two production lines were launched at the St Petersburg firm RJRPetro, which was set up at the Uritsky tobacco factory owned by the transnational corporation R.J. Reynolds. Initially it only produces Russian brands. A few years later, however, it begins producing Camel and Winston cigarettes.

In December, as a result of the privatization of the Ulyanovsk car plant, the company's workforce received 25% of shares in Joint–Stock Company UAZ for free, whilst 60% had to be sold at auction. At the end of the year, the first 10% of shares in UAZ were issued, and they were picked up by JSC Kapital. The company had been set up just a few days before the auction by 11 sub–departmental directors at UAZ, including the company's CEO Pavel Lezhankin. The regional property fund only confirmed the results of the first auction of shares in UAZ six months later – after receiving special instructions from the Federal property fund.

In December, shares in the Sayansk and Bratsk aluminium plants were presented at a private cheque auction.

December 22 – the Supreme Soviet of the RF approves the law on entering and leaving the country. Henceforward it was sufficient to obtain an entry visa at the relevant embassy in order to travel to a foreign country. From this day forth, traders in markets in Istanbul start learning Russian, whilst Chinese entrepreneurs learn to sew big striped bags for Russian stall owners.

In December Charabank was established. The bank accepted deposits from its customers at high rates of interest.

At the end of the year food assistance began to come into the country from the countries of the EU (the first swathe was worth $774 million) and the USA ($1 billion). The country learns all about 'Bush's knives' and boneless slabs of meat.

In 1992, the Ministry of finances and the State property committee prescribe that by the end of the year all shipping organizations must prepare the documents required for privatization. Shipping in Murmansk, Baltic (St Petersburg), Northern fleet (Arkhangelsk), Sakhalin, Kamchatka, Novorossiysk and the Far Eastern Region are privatized. Major share packages in all these shipping organizations remain held by the state. And only Primorskoye maritime shipping becomes a fully private company.

In the middle of 1992 it was announced that a draft decree by the president of Russia regarding share flotations of companies in the oil industry had been devised. The order was accepted in November. Under this order, the first oil companies, in which up to 49% of shares might be owned by private investors, were LUKOIL, Yukos and Surgutneftegaz.

In 1992, the corporatization of Gazprom, which had been under the stewardship of Viktor Chernomyrdin, was approved, in accordance with the plan of the gas company's directors. The initial distribution of shares was as follows: 40% reverted to the property of the state until 1999, with a transfer to Gazprom of voting rights for 35% of these shares; 28.7% were designated for sale in exchange of privatization cheques; 15% reverted to Gazprom's workforce; 10% were set aside for subsequent sale by Gazprom on foreign stock exchanges; 5.2% reverted to the population of the Yamalo–Nenetsk autonomous district; 1.1% were transferred to Rosgazifikatsiya.

In 1992 the privatization of the black metals industry began with the sale of 34.3% shares in the Saldinsk metallurgy plant (Sverdlovsk Region) – the oldest company in the sector.

In 1992, a graduate of the Academy of national management, Vladimir Lisin, became vice–president of the off–shore company TransCIS Commodities Ltd. Thus began the process of building the metals empire Trans World Group (TWG), in which Lisin was to be the director of Russian affairs until 1997.

In 1992, the Nizhegorodsk company Akron, which produced mineral fertilizers, was one of the first in Russia's chemicals industry to be privatized. A few years later, under the guidance of Vyacheslav Kantor, it began to play a leading role in the European fertilizer market. The crisis in the European chemicals industry coincided with a complete rupture in the technological inter–industry networks in Russia. The first project for the consolidation of the Russian chemicals industry emerges – the head of Menatep, Mikhail Khodorkovsky, sets the bar high with a proposal to invest 1.8 billion roubles in the industry in exchange for control of the property of a host of companies. Menatep's proposal was not accepted. Privatization was launched in the sector, too. Analysts from the RFFI assessed the move as an unsuccessful one at the time: people were reluctant to invest their vouchers in chemicals firms. Only later did it transpire that the chemicals was precisely the industry in which they ought to have been invested: a person holding a voucher and investing it in a company in this sector received seven times as many shares as someone investing in oil. For some reason it was only residents of Mordovia that cottoned on to this: statistically, they were more active than anyone else when it came to investing their "share of the nation's wealth" in the chemicals industry.

In 1992, the Joint–Stock Company Roslegprom is founded. Its president was Alexander Biryukov. Its shareholders were over 400 companies in light industry, retail and wholesale trade companies, academic and teaching institutions and also car manufacturing plants. The state concern Rostekstil was reformed as an open–type joint–stock company, which over time became the biggest operator in the textiles market: it was to own a controlling majority of shares in 15–20 companies in the sector. The factory 'Trekhgornaya manufaktura' was transformed into a joint–stock company. Staff at the factory owned a controlling majority of the shares.

In 1992 the Joint–Stock Company MMM is set up (it was never registered anywhere, incidentally).

In 1992 the closed JSC Russky Dom Selenga is set up.

In 1992 Valentina Solovieva sets up the company Vlastilina.

In 1992 the Moscow tobacco factory Dukat and the American company Brook Overseas (an affiliate of the Liggett Group) set up the company LiggettDukat.

In 1992 the joint vodka production enterprise Pernod Ricard – Altai is set up at the Zmeinogorsk distillery. The initiator of the deal was Europe's biggest manufacturer of alcohol, Pernod Ricard, which was to be bought seven years later by the Yerevan cognac plant.

In 1992 the Dutchman Dirk Sauer began publishing the first independent English–language newspaper in Russia – The Moscow Times, thereby laying the foundations for the future publishing house Independent Media.

In 1992 local entrepreneur Vladimir Melnikov founds the company Gloria Jeans in Rostov–on–Don, which makes denim clothing for children.

In late 1992 it is announced that a large number of major players in the forestry industry, including VEC Eksportles and the concern 'Russian forestry industrialists', were going to be turned into joint–stock companies.

1993

January 3 – the START–II agreement between the USA and the Russian Federation is signed.

January 5 – JSC 'AvVAZ' is founded.

In January, six different agencies had a share of the market for TV advertising. Premier CV, 'Video International', 'Lot', 'Contact', 'Blik communications' and and 'Avrora' signed an agreement with RSTRC Ostankino, under which they were given significant exemptions on the cost of advertising in exchange for being required to buy up fixed amounts of air–time on Ostankino's channel one and channel four.

February 17 – RJSC Gazprom is founded.

February 19 – the Russian parliament adopts a directive 'On the issuing of state short–term coupon–free obligations'.

In February the first issue of the newspaper *Sevodnya* is published.

In February the first privatization scandal in the metallurgy industry breaks out. The workforce of the Chelyabinsk metals combine (Mechel) accuse their managers of an illegal attempt to seize a controlling share in the company via JSC Tomet. The CEO of Mechel, Rafshat Maksutov, is forced to resign.

In February, mass privatization of the aluminium sector begins. In the course of 1993 all the aluminium plants get new owners: the Volgograd and Kandalaksh aluminium plants are put in the hands of the company RIAL (RaznoimportAluminii); Alinvest, an affiliate of JSC Aluminprodukt, buys up shares in SaAZ; and Mikhail Zhivilo's MIKOM appears at NkAZ. The Russo–American Joint Enterprise Renova, which was then under the control of Vladimir Balaeskul, goes to IrkAZ.

In April, by a government decree, open joint–stock companies such as LUKOIL, Yukos and Surgutneftegaz are formed. The state receives 45% of their main capital. The companies are headed by the heads of the concerns at which they were founded – Vagit Alekperov, Sergei Muravlenko and Vladimir Bogdanov. The remaining oil production companies are united within the state company Rosneft. Its president is Alexander Putilov. By the end of the year, however, 30 oil production associations, whose shares were transferred to Rosneft, began to insist on being divided up into individual companies. The main stimulus for this was the example of the 'independent' corporations Yukos, LUKOIL and Surgutneftegaz, who were able to export oil without the help of state middlemen.

In April the first companies in the forestry complex began to be privatized – the forestry production companies in the Far Eastern region, the biggest of which was JSC Nakhodkales. The privatization process moves at a slow rate, without drawing much attention to itself, and forms a layer of small–scale private owners in the forestry sector who will go on to determine the market situation over the course of the coming years.

May 18 – the first auction of State Short–term Debt Obligations.

July 6 – Boris Yeltsin signs the decree 'On aspects of the corporatization and privatization of the Russian state concern for the production of non–ferrous and valuable metals 'Norilsk nickel'. 51% of the vote–carrying shares are reverted to federal ownership. July 26 – August 7: monetary reforms in Russia.

September – October – the height of the constitutional crisis in Russia: armed clashes in Moscow and the break–up of the Supreme Soviet of Russia.

October 3 – armed raid on the TV company Ostankino.

October 4 – the storming of the White House in Moscow.

October 5 – Boris Yeltsin bans opposition parties and newspapers in Russia.

October 10 – NTV begins broadcasting.

October 19 – individuals are given the right to buy State Short–term Debt Obligations. Thus the pyramid of SSOs began to be constructed; five years later it was to collapse.

In October, CJSC Mobile telesystems (MTS) is registered. 'Mobile telesystems' was founded by the Moscow State Telephone Network (MGTS), Deutsche Telekom, Siemens and several other shareholders.

In October, the independent commercial TV company NTV makes its debut on channel five (the St Petersburg channel), by broadcasting the programme *Itogi*. The TV company is financed by a consortium consisting of the group *Most* and the banks Stolichny and National credit.

In October, JSC Automobile all–Russian Alliance (AVVA) is founded – a joint project by Boris Berezovsky, the director of an affiliate of LogoVAZ, and Alexander Voloshin, the head of the firm Esta Corp. 'Alliance' was founded at AvtoVAZ, which receives 25% of its share capital, amounting to 10 billion roubles. JSC Logo VAZ, the Swiss firm Forus and the Federal property fund receive 15% of the shares each. JSC Kubyshevneft and the Unified bank receive 10% each, whilst the administrations of Samara and AvtoVAZbank receive 5% each. Boris Berezovsky is approved as CEO of AVVA.

November 12 – an investment tender is held for shares in the knitted goods factory Bolshevichka (the CEO of which is Vladimir Gurov). The corporation Illingworth Morris Ltd. from the UK (the owner and managing director of which is Alan Lewis) acquires 49% of the shares in the factory.

November 22 – JSC Alkur is registered in Ekaterinburg. It incorporates JSC Sevuralboksitrud and JSC Urals Aluminium Plant, among others.

In December, applications are opened for the auction of shares in the Gorkovsk car manufacturing plant. The auction was initially due to be started on November 12, and applications were only accepted in the Nizhny Novgorod Region and in Saransk. As it turned out, GAZ attempted to sell its shares to middlemen loyal to the company's directors. But the State property committee managed to insist on the sale of shares in GAZ at a Russia–wide auction. But the percentage of shares put up for sale was not 30%, as the plant's administration had suggested, but 50% of its main capital. However, due to an over–valuation of GAZ's property (mainly items of social or cultural value or for everyday use), the package of shares rose to 50.7%. The auction was consequently declared invalid. A state commission, set up after a letter was sent by governor Boris Nemtsov to the government, outlining violations of the law during the course of the auction, transferred material to the prosecutor's office in Russia. It was established that GAZ's administration had used state resources to buy up its own shares. All the bids were recalled with the exception of the one from the company GAZinvset, which made no attempt to hide the fact that it had once again acted on behalf of GAZ. This led people to believe that all the fuss surrounding the auction was instigated by the directors of the car manufacturing giant, in order to prevent other shareholders from getting to the plant by creating the pretence of conflict.

December 12 – a new Constitution of the Russian Federation is adopted by a national vote.

In December 1993 the acceptance house RJSC UES of Russia was set up – a structure which, over the next three years, was to take control of 40% of the monetary resources in the country's electric energy sector by monitoring the circulation of its promissory notes.

In December, Mikhail Khodorkovsky becomes chairman of the board of directors of JSC Avisma, which manufactures rolled metal titanium. He did not sell the plant until 1997, to the corporate blackmailer Kenneth Dart, via the Investment Company Kreditanshtalt grant.

At the end of the year, the radio station Echo of Moscow received credit from MostBank in exchange for 51% of its shares.

The radio station achieved fame in 1991 following reports about events in Vilnius (the storming of the TV tower) and the August putsch in Moscow.

In 1993, the Scandinavian group Baltic Beverages Holdings (BBH) buys up 43.5% of shares in the Baltika brewery, situated in St Petersburg. BBH installed new equipment at the plant, and Baltika becomes the first Russian producer of a barley–based drink, begins to release high–quality, long–life beer in industrial quantities. As a result, the plant quickly becomes the leading player in Russia's beer market.

In 1993, the St Petersburg factory Nevotabak and the tobacco company Rothmans International Tobacco sign an agreement to set up the Joint Enterprise RothmansNevo. At practically the same time, construction of a factory with the same name commences in the Northern capital, with a capacity of 12 billion cigarettes a year.

In 1993, two more McDonald's outlets appear, in addition to the famous one on Pushkin Square: one on Orageva Street (now known as Gazetny pereulok) and one on Old Arbat. The company announces that by 1995 it will have built approximately five more restaurants in Russia. They will all be opened by the company itself. None of the franchising schemes which McDonald's operates in other parts of the world will be used in Russia.

In 1993, the Nestle group opens an office in Moscow, whose activity in Russia is limited for the time being to the supply of products from abroad.

In 1993, North–Western river shipping is transformed into a holding company and begins to be known by the abbreviated form of its name – North–Western shipping.

In 1993, the planning stage begins for a distribution of shares in the Moscow tobacco factory Java. During the document collection stage rumours begin to circulate to the effect that the most likely buyer of shares in Russia's most famous tobacco complex is British American Tobacco (BAT). One year on, the rumours are to be confirmed: BAT is to take full control of the company. At the same time, the company Philip Morris buys up a package of shares in JSC Krasnodartabakprom (in Krasnodar) from a local property fund. R.J. Reynolds also put in a claim for shares in the company, but the factory's directors decided in favour of Philip Morris, whose representatives had put forward a better development programme for the company. The high level of investment activity by the tobacco companies led to some very interesting results – advertising tobacco was banned on the TV.

In 1993, the final stage of the privatization of the company 'Trekhgornaya Manufaktura' is brought to an end. According to the preliminary results of the cheque auction, 56% of the shares in Trekhgorki remain in the possession of the workforce, whilst 29% are owned by the State property commission. A further 15% are bought up by three Russian companies, whilst 5% are transferred to the shareholder fund for the company's employees.

In 1993, privatization of the chemicals industry is in full swing. Ilya Vaisman, who was completely unknown at the time, was one of its architects, at the St Petersburg production company Plastpolymer. The concern ORIMI was to emerge at the company Plastpolymer, where Sergei Krizhan and Dmitry Varvarin were in charge of business. They were shot in 1999. Ilya Vaisman was killed too...

In 1993, full–scale privatization of the metallurgy sector began. In May, 35% of the shares in the WestSiberian Metallurgical Combine (Zapsib) and 27% of the shares in Nizhnetagilsk Metkombinat (NTMK) were put up for auction, whilst in November 35% of shares in the Kuznetsk Metkombinat (KMK) were put up for auction.

1994

January 11 – the RF State Duma begins to operate.

In January, President Boris Yeltsin signs an order allowing the TV company NTV to broadcast on channel four. The president's adviser on sport, Shamil Tarpischev, had lobbied on behalf of this order at the request of his friend, the banker Alexander Smolensky, who became one of the sponsors for the project.

In February, the all–Russia coordination centre announces the privatization of AOOT Rostelekom, the monopoly holder in TV broadcasting and international telephone calls. The firm's staff are given 24.086% of preferred shares and 10% of ordinary shares, whilst the administration's staff receive 5%. A further 10% are transfered to the auction fund, whilst 38% revert to federal ownership, and 22.014% are presented at a Russia–wide cheque auction.

In March, shares in the Cherepovets metallurgical combine (in Severstal) are put up for sale at a Russia–wide cheque auction. Severstal's financial director Aleksei Mordashov sets up the firm Severstalinvest at the request of its general director Yury Lipukhin, in order to buy up shares in the combine.

April 7 – the top–level national domain .ru is registered for Russia.

April 29 – the first assembly of shareholders in AMO ZIL. 180,000 shareholders are added to the register. The majority shareholder turns out to be the firm Mikrodin; its president and chairman of the board of directors is Alexander Yefanov, and the chairman of its steering committee is Dmitry Zelenin.

In April, the government directive 'On the approval of the charter of the joint–stock company Aeroflot – Russian international airlines'. The document entitled Aeroflot to represent the country's interests in the global aviation industry.

In May and June, shares in the Nizhny Novgorod ship–building plant Krasnoye Sormovo are sold at cheque and cash auctions. The firm's biggest private shareholder is Kakhi Bendukidze's firm AlmazMarketing (over 10%).

On May 27, Alexander Solzhenitsyn returns to Russia. After flying from the USA to Vladivostok, he travelled right across the country by train, finishing his journey in Moscow, where he gave a speech to deputies in the State Duma.

In May, the government announced its plans to set up new holding companies using shares in Rosneft: the Siberian and Far Eastern oil company (SIDANKO), the Eastern Oil Company (VNK) and the Russian and Belarussian state company Slavneft.

In June, a cheque auction for the sale of shares in the Mil Moscow Helicopter Plant (MHP) – which manufactured Mi helicopters – was held. 29% of the shares were bought up by JSC MMMInvest and SadkoArkada. It was maintained that under cover of these firms shares were purchased by the American aviation construction companies Boeing and Sikorsky, in order to take on their main Russian rival.

In June, shares in Nornickel are presented at a cheque auction. Anatoly Chubais describes these shares as the 'pearl of the privatization process'.

In June, the Russia–wide coordination centre announces that a cheque auction for shares in Vnukovskiye Airlines is going to be held. 29% of the main capital is put forward at the auction, whilst the remaining 41.4% of the shares, which have not been allocated, are put forward for an investment tender.

In June, an attempt is made on the life of Boris Berezovsky. A remote–controlled bomb is detonated in a car parked outside a reception building owned by the company Logo VAZ. Berezovsky, who is sitting nearby in his Mercedes, escapes with minor injuries, whilst his driver is killed. Four years later, Berezovsky would write an open letter to the director of the FSB, Vladimir Putin, in which he informed him that another attempt on his life was being prepared by the previous director of one of the FSB's sub–divisions.

In July, Leonid Fridland and Leonid Strunin founded the company Mercury – Russia's biggest exporter of luxury goods. The company became an exclusive supplier to world–famous labels such as Prada, Armani and Gucci, and sold items at incredible discounts. By the end of the 1990s the company's sales had reached $100 million a year.

In July, the mobile networks MTS and Vympelkom begin operating almost simultaneously, selling their services under the label Bee Line. The operators announced that they would begin selling services after a one–day interval.

In the middle of 1994, the holding company UstIlimsky LPK is set up.

August 4 – Sergei Mavrodi is arrested.

In August, unknown organizations obtained 17% of the shares in the Novolipetsk metkombinat (NLMK) via the bank CSFB. The investors paid $1 million for the shares. The local authorities, and TWG, which managed the combine, demanded that the deal be annulled. The mysterious investor (one year later it would emerge that these organizations represented Vladimir Potanin's group Interros and Boris Iordan's foundation Sputnik) gave no clues as to his identity. The war on the NLMK has to be waged for a further two years.

In August, the company Sovintorg begins buying up shares in Sakhalinsk Maritime Shipping (SakhMP) from its workforce and from cheque funds in the far–east of Russia.

In September 1994, ONEKSIMbank and the bank MFK set up FPG Interros, which incorporates several chemicals companies.

In November, Charabank stops paying dividends to its investors.

In November, the holding company Telekominvest is set up in St Petersburg. Initially, its shareholders were the Petersburg telephone network (95%) and the Dutch company Waza Invest Consulting (5%).

In November, 'Community Russian television' (ORT) was set up. A controlling package of shares (51%) is owned by the state, in the shape of the State property committee. The remainder of the shares, in accordance with the order, are divided up between the banks Menatep, Stolichny, Russian credit, Inkmobank and JSC Aeroflot – Russian international airlines and JSC AvtoVAZ.

In December, Khopyorinvest stops paying dividends to its investors.

December 11 – troops are sent into Chechnya. The start of full–scale military operations in the Chechen Republic.

December 31 – the storming of Grozny by federal troops.

In 1994, JSC Kondopog – Karelia's second biggest PPM – is privatized. It is the most peaceful privatization in the entire sector – 80% of shares are handed over to the workforce.

In 1994, law enforcement agencies start talking seriously, for the first time, about the regular shootings of oil men perpetrated by criminal organizations. The murder of Anatoly Kuzmin was the first. Two months later, the vice–president of Yukos, Vladimir Zenkin, was shot outside his apartment building. In May, unidentified individuals stabbed the director of JSC Neftebur, Oleg Litvinov. In September the commercial director of the company Neft Samara, Yury Shebanov, was murdered. Viktor Tarkhov, who replaced Vladimir Zenkin as vice–president of Yukos, was somewhat luckier: when his company jeep was blown up in Novokuibyshev (in the Samara region), the entrepreneur was not in it.

In 1994, thanks to an active advertising campaign, Khopyorinvest set up affiliates in dozens of regions throughout Russia.

In 1994, conflicts break out over the payment of dividends at Vlastilina.

In 1994, the government signs an order on the setting up of the Orenburg oil company (ONAKO). Prime Minister Viktor Chernomyrdin personally oversees the creation of ONAKO. By a special decree, the company is exempted from most federal taxes (rumour has it that this amounts to a 'reserve airbase' for Chernomyrdin, in case he is forced to resign).

In 1994, the CocaCola Refreshments Moscow plant opened its doors in Solntsevo, outside Moscow.

In 1994, BAT buys up 75% of the shares in the Saratov tobacco plant. The plant is soon renamed BATSTF, and it begins selling Pall Mall cigarettes instead of Prima cigarettes.

In 1994, at the St Petersburg yarn spinning mill combine 'Soviet star' and the 'Red thread' factory, OJSC Concern 'Kvarton' is founded.

In 1994, at Stupino, outside Moscow, construction of two Mars factories begins – one that produces confectionary (Snickers bars, Mars bars etc.) and one that manufactures foodstuffs (Uncle Ben's sauces), as well as a pet–food production plant (Wiskas).

1995

In mid–January, the new head of the State Property Commission, Vladimir Polevanov, announced that he intended to nationalize the aluminium industry. Anatoly Chubais would successfully push for his retirement in the spring.

In January it is announced that Aeroflot is going to be re–constituted as a joint–stock company: 51.15% of the shares would be held by the state, and the rest would be owned by the workforce. During the course of the year, rumours circulate to the effect that the owner of LogoVAZ, Boris Berezovsky, has a commercial interest in Aeroflot. In October, Aeroflot acquires a new CEO, Yevgeny Shaposhnikov, and managers from LogoVAZ begin to take charge of the airline's affairs. In November, the former CEO of LovoVAZ, Samat Zhaboyev, is appointed first deputy CEO of Aeroflot for commerce; the former deputy CEO of LogoVAZ Alexander Krasnenker takes up the role of deputy to Shaposhnikov for commerce and advertising, and the development director at LogoVAZ, Mikhail Denisov, is given the post of deputy CEO of Aeroflot for automation and commercial development. On November 16, Boris Berezovsky told the newspaper *Kommersant*: Aeroflot is the biggest airline in Russia, and it is only natural that the business world should take an interest in it as a source of considerable profits. Our interest here – I'll say it again – is abundantly clear… If I can put it like this, privatization in Russia goes through three phases: in the first phase, profits are privatized; in the second phase, property is privatized, and in the third phase debts are privatized. Aeroflot is going through an intermediary phase between the privatization of profits and of ownership. We want to take part in both forms of privatization."

In January, the government changed the rules in relation to the privatization of the Mil MVZ, securing, by means of a directive, 25% of its shares in federal ownership for a period of three years.

At the start of the year word got out that one of the biggest confectionery companies in the country – the Rossiya factory in Samara – had come under the control of the Swiss group Nestle.

March 1 – Vladislav Listev, a TV presenter and journalist, is killed.

March 6 – a unit of insurgents led by the Chechen field commander Shamil Basayev retreats from Chernorechya – the last district of Grozny under the control of the separatists, and the city comes under the control of Russian troops once and for all.

March 15–23 – Argun is taken by Russian forces.

March 30 and 31 – the cities of Shal and Gudermes are taken without a fight.

In March, the businessman Oleg Boiko (the owner of the OLBI concern and the bank National credit), who had described himself in an interview with *KommersantDaily* as a representative of a so–called 'big group of eight' (Alphabank, Imperial, Menatep, National credit, SBS, JSC Mikrodin, JSC LogoVAZ and RAO Gazprom), proposed that channel one be privatized in favour of the 'group of eight'. The goal of 'countering Gusinsky's anti–government propaganda' on NTV was put forward as the reason for doing so. Soon, the organizations listed (with the exception of Imperial) were given 46% of shares in Channel One.

In March, Interros Kapital, part of the Interros group, wins an investment tender for the sale of 20% of shares in Leningrad optical and mechanical association (LOMO).

In March, IFK Dinamika, part of the Mikrodin group, gets involved in the privatization of the chemicals industry. Along with Khimtrastkonsalting it promised to cancel the debts of Korund and Orgstyokol and invest $60 million in them, thereby acquiring major packages of shares in the companies. The chairman of Mikrodin's governing board, Dmitry Zelinin, thus gets involved in the chemicals industry for a short time.

At the end of March, the president of ONEKSIMbank, Vladimir Potanin proposes a deal to the government on behalf of a consortium of banks (Imperial, Stolichny savings bank, Menatep, Alfabank and others): the country's biggest banks are prepared to lend money to the government in exchange for the right to manage state–controlled sets of shares. Industry was going through the worst period in the non–payment crisis, and the state was suffering from a desperate shortage of money. The oil companies alone owed 7.536 trillion roubles to the state budget – that would have been enough to deal with the debts in relation to the payment of pensions, soldiers' salaries, employees of the MIA and the FSB, miners etc. The proposal was upheld. The authorities thought up a unique format in which state–controlled packages of shares could be held on trust – deposit auctions (the real–terms value of the share packages presented with them are now at least ten times greater than the level of debt).

April 7–8 – an operation takes place in the village of Samashka Achkhoi, in the Martanovsk district of the Chechen Republic, during which, according to a host of witnesses, federal forces commit mass murder of innocent civilians.

April 18 – an attempt on the life of the CEO of the finance company Grant, Andrei Orekhov, is made in Moscow. Grant's biggest and most controversial project is the organization of auction trading of shares in RAO EAS Rossii, during privatization.

April 28 – the Russian side calls a halt to military intervention in Chechnya from its side until May 11.

May 24 – the city of Bamut and the Lysaya mountain, which dominates it, are taken by soldiers fighting under General–major Vladimir Shamanov. A unit led by Ruslan Khaikhoroev, which was protecting Bamut, broke through the line of troops encircling the area under cover of dusk and the descending fog.

In May, the Moscow investment corporation Nipek obtained control over one of Russia's biggest and most modern companies in the oil and chemicals industry – JSC 'Tomsk oil and chemicals combine' (TNKhK). The main director of the Nipek corporation is Kakha Bendukidze; he is to leave the chemicals business two years later.

June 2 – the banks in the 'big group of eight' send to the government a list of companies whose shares interest them at deposit auctions. The companies in the black metallurgy sector on the list include Magnitogorsk combine, Mechel, Severstal, NLMK, Zapsib, NTMK and the Oskolsk Electro–metallurgical combine (OEMC). The directors of most of these companies demand, via the minister for metallurgy, Oleg Soskovets, to be removed from the list.

June 3 – Russian troops take the Chechen mountain village of Vedeno.

June 8 – Vyacheslav Ivankov, 'the little Japanese', is arrested, accused of extortion.

June 12 – Russian forces take the regional centres of Shata and NozhaiYurt, in Chechnya.

June 14–19 – the terrorist attack in Budyonnovsk. 195 Chechen insurgents, led by commander Shamil Basayev, take the city hospital, where they take innocent civilians hostage. It transpires that the terrorists have approximately 2000 hostages under their command. Basayev demands an end to military operations, the withdrawal of Russian troops from Chechnya and negotiations with Dudayev, overseen by UN representatives. The command is given for the hospital to be stormed. The storming of the hospital lasts four hours; a special ops team takes control of all the wings of the hospital (except the main building), freeing 61 hostages. Three members of the special ops team were killed. On the same day, an unsuccessful second attempt to storm the building was made. Prime Minister Viktor Chernomyrdin ordered the special ops team to stand down. After this, negotiations began between Viktor Chernomyrdin and Shamil Basayev. The terrorists were provided with buses, in which they travelled with the 120 hostages to the Chechen village of Zandak, where the hostages were released. According to official data, the death toll on the Russian side was 143 (of whom 46 were members of the security agencies), with 415 people wounded, whilst on the terrorists' side 19 people were killed and 20 were wounded.

June 18 – in the programme 'Head to head' on Channel One, presented by Alexander Lyubimov, Vladimir Zhirinovsky pours orange juice over Boris Nemtsov during a debate. This incident goes down in the history of Russian television, and is still frequently recreated to this day.

July 5 – the only successful attempt to escape from the Matrosskaya Tishina (Sailor's Rest) penitentiary – the escaped prisoner is a murderer named Alexander Solonik.

In July, the owner of Vlastilina, Valentina Solovieva, is arrested.

August 31 – the president meets a representative delegation of bankers from Moscow and the provinces (V. Gusinsky (MostBank), Y. Dubenetsky (Promstroibank), N. Raevskaya (Avtobank), S. Rodionov (Imperial bank), G. Tosunyan (Technobank), M. Khodorkovsky (Menatep), V. Khokhlov (Tokobank), S. Yegorov (the Association of Russian banks), A. Kozyreva (Tveruniversalbank), E. Koluga (Sibtorgbank), V. Popkov (Uralvneshtorgbank)) and, on the same day, signs an order on the auctioning of bank credit to the government, based on contracts. As a result, significant state–owned shares in major industrial firms are deposited with the banks; in 1997, after the failure by the state to return the loans, these are bought up at repeat auctions by the banks, from themselves.

September 1 – the managing company of the Menatep group is registered – Rosprom. Mikhail Khodorkovsky becomes the chairman of the board of directors at Rosprom. By this time, Menatep already has a controlling proporation of shares in 29 Russian companies. In addition, the bank also owns 'near–controlling' shares (20%–30% of main capital) in approximately 50 companies. Most of these are in the metallurgy, mining, chemicals, oil production, pulp and paper, construction, textiles and food industries. Companies in light industry, in which Menatep bank owns a controlling share, include Rostekstil, the factories Silk, Sobinteks and Paris Commune, JSC Moscow cotton fabrics factory, JSC Artistic paintings.

September 18 – AOOT Svyazinvest is officially registered.

September 25 – a list of companies presented at deposit auctions is published. The list includes NLMK, OEMK, Zapsib, NOSTA and Mechel. On the same day, Oleg Soskovets flies to Sochi to meet Boris Yeltsin and returns to Moscow in the evening with a directive creating JSC Russian Metallurgy. It is to incorporate Magnitka, Severstal and NLMK. This directive represents an open challenge to Chubais. But the State Cooperative Institute wins this war, whilst 'Russian metallurgy' remains in existence on paper only.

In September, FPG Interros merges with the Mikrodin group. The companies in the chemicals industry include members of the Interros – Mikrodin alliance: Azot from Cherepovets, JSC Phosphorite (Kingisepp), JSC Khimvolokno (Saratov). After a few months, Dmitry Zelenin, the head of Interros, leaves the chemicals industry.

In September there is a major privatization scandal in the forestry market: the governor of Komi, Yury Spiridonov, cancels an auction of 15% of shares in Syktyvkarsky LPK. Menatep and Ilim Pulp are the favourites for the tender (the governor refers to them as 'investor–speculators') and the management company LPK – a joint enterprise involving the governments of the Komi Republic and Moscow, Kommos – feared losing control of the combine. Spiridonov postpones the tender by three years.

October 6 – by order of the president of the RF, Boris Nemtsov, RGTRK Ostankino is liquidated.

In October, the Arkhangelsk PPM files a lawsuit against the State property committee, which, instead of putting forward share packages in the PPM for an investment tender, put them forward for a shares–for–loans auction on December 7. The court prohibits the shares–for–loans auction. Later, the Solombalsk and Bratsk LPK follow suit, and in December, not without support from Roslesprom, three more companies in the forestry sector manage to avoid sales at shares–for–loans auctions. Not a single one of the other 26 companies put on sale in the auction manage to repeat this success.

In October, the State Control Institute puts a 15% state–owned share package in Severstal up for sale and gives the remaining 5% of the state–owned property to the workforce. The company Severstalinvest (owned by Aleksei Mordashov) trades in Severstal's metal. This company has a controlling package of shares in Severstal, although nobody knows this yet.

At the start of November the non–payment crisis in the sector brings a host of companies in the metallurgy sector to a complete standstill. The Korshunovsk and Mikhailovsk Mining and Concenetrating Combines are brought to a standstill; the defence resources of Zapsib and Magnitok are not operating due to the deficit in defence resources, and due to a lack of coal, coke batteries were installed at Mechel and NOSTA. To all intents and purposes, all of the country's ferrous metals companies are bankrupt.

November 17 – the first shares–for–loans auction is held in Moscow. The winner of the auction of Nornikel is ONEKSIMbank. It obtains 51% of Norilsk nickel for $170.1 million. The other candidate was Rossisky kredit, but this bank was thwarted in its efforts to take part in the Nornikel auction.

In November, a shares–for–loans auction for 40.16% of the oil company Surgutneftegaz was won by the Surgutneftegaz pension fund, at a cost of 1.4 trillion roubles (the company, which owed 1 trillion roubles to the state coffers, immediately stumped up the money).

On November 28, the Sukhoi OKB, at the insistence of Goskomoboronprom and the company's directors, is excluded from the programme of shares–for–loans auctions. It was proposed that 51% of the company's shares, which belonged to the state, be sold for $12 million. By that time, ONEKSIMbank controlled 14% of the shares in OKB, and Inkombank controlled 25%.

December 10–12 – the city of Gudermes, which Russian troops had taken without meeting any resistance, is seized by units led by Salman Raduev, KhunkarPashi Israpilov and Sultan Geliskhanov. Fighting continued in the city from December 14 to December 20, and Russian troops needed approximately one more week of 'clean–up' operations in order to take decisive control of Gudermes.

In December dozens of shares–for–loans auctions are held. The bank MFK (in effect a consortium of MFK and Alphagroup) obtained 51% of SIDANKO for $130 million; CJSC 'Oil financing company' (guaranteed by the Capital savings bank) obtained 41% of Sibneft for $100 million (the men behind this deal were Boris Berezovsky and a little–known oil trader based in Moscow, Roman Abramovich); the oil production firm Surgutneftegaz (guaranteed by ONEKSIMbank) obtained 40.12% of Surgutneftegaz for $88.9 million; and the bank MFK (effectively Renessans Kapital) obtained 14.87% of NLMK for $31 million. LUKOIL avoided the shares–for–loans auctions – only 5% of shares in the company were sold at them.

In December, Inkombank was given control of JSC SAMECO, the biggest aluminium production plant in Europe. The head of SaAZ, Oleg Deripaska, conducts negotiations on the purchase of SAMECO, but the price is too high.

In December a shares–for–loans auction is held for shares in Novorossiysk maritime shipping. After offering a maximum credit reserve of $22.65 million, the shipping company easily beats off competition from its rivals.

In December 1995, the Russian Fund for Fundamental Research puts up for sale state shares in the NOSTA metals combine (12.7% of the shares), and completes the first privatization of a metals company in the country.

In 1995 ONEKSIMbank starts buying up shares in the Sukhoi OKB from the company's workforce. In response, the CEO of OBK, Mikhail Simonov, joins forces with Inkombank, which also starts to buy up shares in the company.

In 1995, as the process of privatization of the shipbuilding plant 'Severnaya Verf' nears completion, a struggle for control of the company begins: at the time, preparations were already being made for the signing of a $1 billion contract for the supply to China of two 'contemporary' class destroyers which had been held by 'Severnaya Verf' since Soviet days. By 1995, 32.9% of the shares were under the control of Soyuzkontrakt.

In 1995, following a series of cheque and money auctions for the sale of shares in the Baltic plant, the company's biggest shareholders were IST and Promstroibank.

In 1995, the Japanese sect Aum Shinrikyo is banned in Russia.

In 1995, the Siberian and Urals Region oil, gas and chemicals company (SIBUR) is established.

In 1995, the Baskin Robbins ice cream factory opens in Moscow.

In 1995, construction of a Heinz factory begins in Stavropol. The factory produces foodstuffs for children.

In 1995, supplies of the most famous luxury alcoholic drinks brands to Russia are effectively monopolized by the company Roust, which was set up at the beginning of 1992 by Rustam Tariko. At first, the company obtained exclusive rights to sell Martini, and then in 1995 Roust signed a distribution agreement with United Distillers (the makers of Johnny Walker whisky) and began supplying Bacardi rum.

In 1995, a consortium of companies led by Inkombank obtains a $13 million controlling share in the Babaev combine, Moscow's second–largest confectionery factory.

1996

On January 9 a unit of 256 insurgents under the command of Salman Raduev, TurpalAli Atgeriev and KhunkarPashi Israpilova raid the city of Kizlyar. The terrorists seized the hospital and birth centre, taking approximately 3000 people hostage inside. During the negotiations, agreement was reached on the provision of buses for the insurgents that would take them to the Chechen border, in exchange for the release of the hostages, who were to be let down at the border itself. On January 10, a convoy consisting of the insurgents and the hostages made its way towards the border. When it became clear that the terrorists were going to go back to Chechnya, warning shots were fired to stop the convoy of buses. Taking advantage of the intervention by the Russian leaders, the insurgents seized the village of Pervomaiskoye, blowing up the police checkpoint situated there. Negotiations were conducted from January 11 to January 14, and an unsuccessful attempt to storm the village was made on January 15 and January 18. During the storming of Pervomaiskoye, on January 16, a group of terrorists seized the passenger craft Avraziya in the Turkish port of Trabzon and threatened to shoot all the Russian hostages unless the storming of the village was brought to a halt. After two weeks of negotiations the terrorists surrendered to the Turkish authorities.

On January 18, under cover of darkness, the insurgents broke through the lines of soldiers and departed for Chechnya.

On January 16 Anatoly Chubais retired from his post as Russia's first ever deputy prime minister.

In January, Nikolai Glushkov, a member of the board of directors at LogoVAZ, was named first deputy to the CEO of Aeroflot for commerce. By now there were more than 30 people at Aeroflot who had come from LogoVAZ, or were simply close to Boris Berezovsky. Under Shaposhnikov's precedecessor, Vladimir Tikhonov, Aeroflot's accounts had been transferred to AvtoVAZbank (LogoVAZwas one of this bank's four main shareholders). Under Evgeny Shaposhnikov they found themselves at Associated bank, which was controlled by Berezovsky.

On February 8, the Stolichny savings bank declares its interests. Alexander Smolensky's bank managed to secure a loan from the German bank Commerzbank of $1 billion for 'technical refurbishment of its metallurgical companies in the Chelyabinsk region' (i.e. Mechel and Magnitka). The deputy head of the administration of the Chelyabinsk Region, Viktor Khristenko, actively lobbies on behalf of the project. Neither Mechel nor Magnitka ever see Commerzbank's money, incidentally.

On February 28 Russia joins the Council of Europe.

In February the State property committee attempts to initiate a new wave of privatization in the forestry sector on behalf of sub–divisions of Roslesprom, which manages but does not own the country's biggest forestry companies. OJSC Severoleseksport was put up for sale.

On March 6, several units of insurgents attacked Grozny, which was under the control of Russian troops, from various sides. The insurgents seized the Staropromyslovsk district of the city, and blocked off and started shooting at the Russian checkpoints and cabins. Although Grozny remained under the control of the Russian armed forces, the separatists, as they departed, took with them supplies of food, medicines and ammunition. According to official reports, 70 people died on the Russian side and 259 people were wounded.

In March the CB revokes Charabank's license.

In March the trial of the owner of Vlastilina, Valentina Solovieva, gets under way.

In early April Roslesprom blocks the sale of the company Severolesexport, which it manages, proposing that instead of being privatized it should be the base for the finance and industrial group (FIG) Severoles, which had to include the holding company Northern cellulose, owned by the Arkhangelsk PPM, the state companies Konoshales and Severoles, Onezhsk lesdrevkombinat, a host of forestry combines, Lesobank from Arkhangelsk and the leasing company Lesnoi leasing. The sector is gripped by a trend for building Finance and Industrial Groups, although not a single successful FIG was to be built.

April 16 – the 245th Motor Rifle Regiment of the Russian army is ambushed at the small town of Yaryshmarda in

Chechnya. According to official data, 73 soldiers are killed and 52 are wounded.

April 21 – following an operation by Russian special forces, Dzhokar Dudayev, the first president of the self–styled Chechen Republic of Ichkeria, is killed.

April 27 – a letter signed by 13 oligarchs entitled 'Turn back out of this dead–end!' is published. It is an open letter from Russia's biggest entrepreneurs to the general public, politicians and each other, calling on them not to allow the communists to win the election.

In spring, the financial and industrial group 'Consortium 'Russian textiles' is formed, at seven industrial companies; controlling shares in the companies are owned by the company Rosprom, owned by Mikhail Khodorkovsky's Menatep.

June 16 – the first round of the presidential elections in the Russian Federation. G.A. Zyuganov and B.N. Yeltsin go through to the second round. The other candidates include A.I. Lebed, G.A. Yavlinsky, V.V. Zhirinovsky, S.N. Fyodorov, M. S. Gorbachev.

June 18 – the organizer of the election campaign 'Vote or lose', Sergei Lisovsky, and Chubais's assistant Arkady Evstafiev are arrested as they leave the government building with a cardboard box for photocopy paper. The box contains over half a million dollars in cash. After being questioned, Lisovsky and Evstafiev are released, and the men behind their arrest are fired.

July 3 – Boris Yeltsin is elected for a second term as president.

August 6 – 14 – Chechen insurgents storm Grozny.

August 30 – peace agreements are signed between the federal powers and Chechnya in Khasavyurt.

In August, the city government in Moscow secures agreements with the directors of the Interros group to buy shares in ZIL, which had belonged to the Mikrodin group, for $6 million. The relevant agreement is signed by the mayor of Moscow, Yury Luzhkov, and the president of ONEKSIMbank, Vladimir Potanin.

In September there is a cash auction for the sale of 34% of shares in SIDANKO. ONEKSIMbank, represented by Interrosoil and AlphaEko, bids for the shares. The winner is Interrosoil, which proposed a package worth 326.1 billion roubles for the shares (AlphaEko offered 325.5 billion roubles). SIDANKO's vice–president for commercial affairs, Ziya Bazhaev, is appointed the company's first vice–president.

In September Michael Jackson visits Moscow.

On September 6 a condemned man is executed – the last occasion on which the death sentence is implemented in Russia.

In October the biggest chemicals FIG in the country's history, Interkhimprom, is set up. It includes the Cherepovetsk and Novomoskovsky Combines for Fertilizers, JSC Ventamonyaks (Latvia), the bank 'Strategiya', CJSC 'Port Kavkaz' and JSC 'InterkhimpromOKSOsyntez'. Also part of the FIG was the Sovalub group (whose head office was in London) and the Russian investment company Analaize. The president of FIG Interkhimprom, Boris Titov, the chairman of the board of directors.

December 1 – the channel STS begins broadcasting.

In 1996, an investment competition for the sale of 19% of the shares in Sibneft was won by Sins, a company owned by Boris Berezovsky. In October, Roman Abramovich's firm Refineoil won a tender for the sale of 15% of shares in Sibneft, promising to invest $35.31 million in the company.

In 1996, the term 'Seven Bankers' Cabal' is coined, perhaps thanks to Boris Berezovsky: Alexander Smolensky ('Stolichny' bank), Vladimir Potanin (ONEKSIMbank), Mikhail Khodorkovsky (Menatep), Vladimir Gusinsky (MostBank), Mikhail Fridman (Alphagroup), Pyotr Aven (Alphabank) and Boris Berezovsky (LogoVAZ and Associated bank).

In 1996 Nestle creates a joint enterprise with the Zhukov khladokombinat and starts selling ice cream in Russia.

1997

January 1 – RENTV begins broadcasting.

February 19 – the State Duma passes an order on the nationalization of RAO Norilsk nickel. ONEKSIMbank is required to return the federally owned shares of RAO, which it had held as a deposit.

February 26 – the arbitration court in Moscow declares the bank Natsionalny kredit bankrupt.

In March, VAO 'Intourist' and the airline 'Vnukovskiye Airlines' signs a general memorandum of understanding in the field of passenger airline journeys on both international and domestic lines. This is the first long–term exclusive agreement between tour operators and airlines in Russia.

In April, the businessman Evgeny Chichvarkin founds Evroset along with his partner. Two years later the company becomes the biggest company in the mobile telephone market, thanks in no small part to its risque advertising slogan.

In April, Ziya Bazhaev was appointed president of SIDANKO – the holders of 99% of the shares voted for him.

In April, the Arkhangelsk PPM led negotiations on the conclusion of privatization and the restructuring of the business. As a result, a large package of shares is concentrated in the Vladimir Krupchak's 'Titan' group, and significant portions of shares are owned by western investors, most of them German.

In May, the Oil financing company (the chairman of the board of directors is Badri Patarkatsishvili) puts 51% of the shares in Sibneft on sale at a starting price of $101 million. The winner of the auction is Financial oil company, which offered $110 million. It was founded by affiliates and affiliated companies of the SBSAgro bank.

In June, controlling shares in four companies – OJSC Rostelekom, OJSC Central telegraf, OJSC Ekaterinburg telefon and OJSC Hyprosvyaz are transferred to Svyazinvest by a presidential decree.

In July, the investment group Neftekhimprom is set up, based at the Maksim group – the latest attempt at consolidation within the industry, this time on the Volga. Neftekhimprom, to which Viktor Pelevin wrote his novel *Chapaev and Emptiness* as a hymn, got off to a fairly good start. It is said that the group's owner, Maksim Vasiliev, began collecting BMWs after just a few months. Just eighteen months later the group was to be torn apart by a group of more successful 'consolidators'.

In July there was an auction of shares in OJSC Svyazinvest (25% plus one share). The winner was the Cypriot consortium Mustcom Ltd., which included ONEKSIMbank, the investment bank Deutsche Morgan Grenfell, the investment bank Morgan Stanley and George Soros's fund Quantum.

In July there was an auction of 40% of the shares in TNK. The winner was the company 'Novy kholding', which represented the interests of Alphagroup and the company Renova; it offered the gigantic sum, in those days, of $810 million.

In July AOZT Russky Dom Selenga was declared bankrupt. In February 2000 a court sentenced its owners to 9 years behind bars.

August 4 – the decision to de–value the rouble and alter the scale of prices by a thousand times is approved. Banknotes and coins from the Bank of Russia, in the 1997 issue, were put into circulation. The CB decided not to effect a direct exchange of money for older versions: the old money was removed from circulation throughout the whole of the year 1988 and accepted by all organizations in Russia as being worth the same as the new money. Starting on January 1, 1999, the old versions of the banknotes lost their status as RF currency, but could still be exchanged at Bank of Russia branches for a further three years.

In August, the co–owner of the firm Khopyorinvest was arrested. In 2001 she was sentenced to 8 years behind bars.

In August the fate of Purneftegaz was decided once and for all – a three–year battle between SIDANKO and Rosneft for a controlling share of the business ended in Rosneft's favour. With the signing of a worldwide agreement on Purneftegaz, the last impediment to the privatization of Rosneft disappeared. The sale of the company was scheduled for the first half of 1998.

On September 17 Russia acceded to the Paris lenders' club. The first deputy prime minister of the RF government, Anatoly Chubais, as Russia's representative, signed a memorandum 'On mutual understanding...', setting out the terms of Russia's entry to the Paris club as a member with full rights (a lender country). Russia received tangible support in its negotiations with its debtors in the form of this assembly of creditors. Under the club's terms, if a debtor country which accepted a decision of the Paris club failed to fulfil its obligations, the international programmes of the International Currency Fund would be used against it. $52 billion of Soviet–era debts was transferred to the members of the Paris club, of which Russia, after joining the organization, forgave $40 billion.

September 22 – AOOT MMM is declared bankrupt. On January 31, 2003, Sergei Mavrodi was arrested at a rented apartment in Moscow. On April 28, 2007, Sergei Mavrodi was found guilty of fraud and sentenced to 4 years and 6 months' imprisonment (of which he had already served 4 years and five months when he was sentenced). Sergei Mavrodi was released on May 22, 2007.

September 23 – the search engine yandex.ru was opened.

In September, in Moscow and Nizhnevartovsk, the first ever mutually exclusive shareholder meetings in the sector, for shareholders of JSC Nizhnevartovskneftegaz, took place. (This practice was to become commonplace in later years. Under this practice, both meetings were able to declare themselves completely legitimate and elected quorums, elect their own CEOs and boards of directors, and litigate in respect of each other's decisions. A meeting of shareholders supporting TNK, as well as Alphagroup and Renova, which were behind it, took place in Moscow. Supporters of Viktor Paly attended a meeting of shareholders in Nizhnevartovsk.

In September, the court of arbitration in Moscow decided to

return 41% of shares in 'Azota', from Cherepovets, to ownership by the state. A month later, the head of OONEKSIMbank, Vladimir Potanin, was called to the MIA's investigative committee. It was probably the first time an oligarch was interrogated in Russia.

October 6 – the RTS index reaches 571.66 points before falling sharply. The so–called Asian crisis has begun, the effects of which are to be felt by a large number of countries. Not until six years later was RTS able to return to this level.

October 6 – Russia signs an agreement with the London creditor bank club.

October 27 – the Dow Jones index falls by more than 550 points. As a result the Russian securities market collapses, and for the first time in Russia's history trades halted.

In October 1997 CocaCola opens four new factories, in Vladivostok, Nizhny Novgorod, Rostov–on–Don and Krasnoyarsk. CocaCola's total level of investment in Russia reaches $600 million.

From November 1 onwards, payments in foreign currency are prohibited in Russia. Henceforth a new monetary unit appears in Russia – the *uchetnaya edinitsa* ('conventional unit').

In November, ONEKSIMbank, the British company BP and SIDANKO sign an agreement on strategic partnership. BP obtains 10% of the main capital of SIDANKO for $571 million.

In December Yukos acquired 44% of the shares in VNK from an auction of 50% of the oil company's shares. Taken together with the 9% of shares in VNK that it already had, the newly acquired stake amounted to a controlling share – and Yukos thereby rose to second place in Russia in terms of the volume of oil produced. Mikhail Khodorkovsky announced that Yukos intended, in conjunction with Sibneft, to take part in the privatization of Rosneft.

December 21–22 – an attack by 40–60 members of the

Khattaba group on the barracks town in the 136th Motor Rifle Brigade in Buinaksk.

In 1997 the corporation Dovgan – Zaschischonnoye kachestvo (DZK) ceases to exist. DZK was created by Vladimir Dovganem and the owner of the Aktiv bank, German Lillevyali. In the first instance, the corporation, which organized the release of over 200 lines of Dovgan food and drink products, was quite successful. Later, however, its costs began to exceed its profits, and the partners panicked.

1998

In January the Law on bankruptcy was adopted. Over the next four years this law was to become the main tool for the raids that had become common throughout the country. Major companies were subjected to fictitious bankruptcy, and as a result their rivals retake control of them. Raiders in the oil, metals and coal industries are particularly active.

In early March, global prices for Russian 'Urals' oil fall to a nine–year low of $11 a barrel.

March 23 – Viktor Chernomyrdin retires.

April 23 – Sergei Kirienko is appointed chairman of the government.

April 30 – Anatoly Chubais is appointed chairman of the board of directors of RJSC 'UES of Russia'. The first act of Chubais's team is to set about accelerating bartering processes and increasing the frequency with which payment for electricity is collected; approvals procedures with the state bodies for the future division and privatization of the company's shares went hand in hand with this.

May 5 – Russia ratifies the European convention on human rights and principle freedoms and acknowledges the jurisdiction of the European Court of Human Rights. Residents of Russia were given the ability to turn to this international body if they were unable to find a way to protect their rights inside the country.

May 8 – Centrobank introduced a temporary administration at Tokobank. This was the first sign of the forthcoming banking crisis.

By May, as a result of the mass purchase of shares in Krasny Sormov, the share of Kakhi Bendukidze's organizations owned by the workers at the factory reaches 30%. The firm's management, which had also bought up shares from the workers, controlled about 13% of the shares. A battle broke out between Bendukidze and the plant's directors for representation on the board of directors.

During the sale of shares in the Rostov helicopter plant Rostvertol, the plant began to be 55% owned by major Moscow banks and foreign companies. The shareholders included the bank Russian credit, ONEKSIMbank, the bank Olympisky, the company Belukha, Rostpromstroibank, CSFirst Boston and the VertoServis group. The joint–stock company itself controlled about 25.7% of its shares.

On June 19, at the AGM for shareholders in RJSC 'UES of Russia', Anatoly Chubais was once again elected a member of the board of directors of the RAO.

June 29 – the board of directors of RAO 'EAS of Russia' elects a new team to govern the company, headed by Anatoly Chubais.

July 6 – the profits of state obligations in the market exceeds the rate of refinancing. The profits of long State Short–term Debt Obligations shoots up to 93%, and Federal Loan Obligations – to 80%. Despite the fact that by the end of July, emergency external loans are paid to Russia by the IMF ($14 billion) and the International Bank for Reconstruction and Development ($1.5 billion), by the start of August the Bank of Russia acknowledges a complete loss of trust among investors.

July 17 – the remains of the family of Nikolai II, the last Russian emperor, are buried at the Peter and Paul cathedral in St Petersburg.

August 14 – the banks Imperial and SBSAgro stop making payments, three days before the general crisis sets in.

August 14 – Boris Yeltsin declares that there is not going to be a default.

August 17 – a joint declaration by the Bank of Russia and the government is issued. The government of the Russian Federation announces that there has been a default, i.e. it unilaterally decides not to cancel, on contractual conditions, state rouble obligations (SSO Simultaneously, the government and the CB introduce a 90–day moratorium on the performance by the banks of their obligations to foreigners. On the same day, the principle of setting an official exchange rate for the dollar is changed: Centrobank begins to take into account the exchange rate of the inter–banking market, which is significantly higher than the rate set by the Bank of Russia and the MMVB. A currency corridor of 6.0–9.5 roubles per dollar was established, but on September 2 the Bank of Russia rejected it and moved to a floating rate. It thereby paved the way for the collapse of the rouble.

August 24 – the government of Sergei Kirienko, after confirming the crisis of the previous day, is dismissed.

August 25 – Imperial bank has its license revoked. It is the first bank to suffer this fate following the crisis of August 17. The bank was only able to have its license returned two years later, and achieved a sensational court verdict against the Bank of Russia: a ban on revoking the license of Imperial bank.

August 28 – the bank SBSAgro brings in a temporary administration and announces that the bank is taking a two–week holiday. A year later, another order is signed on the introduction of a temporary administration at SBSAgro. After this, the bank was transferred to the Agency for the restructuring of credit organizations (ARCO).

September 3 – the Bank of Russia, for the first time since August 26, sets an official exchange rate – 13.46 roubles to the dollar. It was at this exact rate that the only transaction ever carried out by the electronic lot trade system (ELTS) was effected.

September 3 – private savings accounts at the banks SBSAgro, Menatep, Inkombank, Promstroibank, MostBank and Mosbiznesbank are frozen. Savers from these banks were able to exchange their money at a rate of 9.33 roubles a dollar at Sberbank. The promotion lasted a month.

September 7 – the head of the Bank of Russia, Sergei Dubinin, tenders his resignation to the president of the RF.

September 9 – Evgeny Primakov becomes prime minister.

September 12 – Viktor Geraschenko once again becomes the head of the Bank of Russia, replacing Sergei Dubinin. His old team, including the bank's first deputy chairman, Tatiana Paramonova, returns to the CB with him.

In September, AvtoVAZ begins working on a round–the–clock basis. In the middle of the summer the plant faced the threat of bankruptcy: its annual plan was twice adjusted downwards, and its staff went unpaid for several months. However, the default meant that demand for *Zhiguli* cars went through the roof – they were now three to four times cheaper than the cheapest foreign–made car, and in order to save themselves from inflation people were rushing to invest money in cars.

In September, according to data from the Federal Aviation Service, the volume of passenger journeys fell by 20% in comparison with the same period in 1997. Airlines had great difficulty securing money from the agencies for tickets that had been sold, since the banks were not making payments. Ticket prices rose slightly, however.

October 27 – Vladimir Vinogradov left his post as president of Inkombank.

October 29 – the Bank of Russia revoked Inkombank's license. Inkombank was declared bankrupt just a year later.

Right after the default, oil companies declared the launch of cost–cutting programmes.

Right after the default, all supplies of imported food into our country were brought to a complete stop. A whole host of importers were forced out of the market – most of the products imported after the crisis were now four times more expensive due to the exchange rate for the dollar, and demand for them had fallen dramatically. Foreign foodstuffs had disappeared from the shops. A shortage of food was avoided, however. Russian manufacturers increased production in record time and closed the gaps in the market.

In 1998, the pride of Russia's meat–reprocessing industry – the Moscow meat combine Mikoms (formerly known as the Mikoyan meat combine) went bankrupt. The majority of its staff were sacked. The combine's property was divided up between its creditors – several major banks, as well as importers of meat who had supplied products to the meat combine.

1999

February 4 – the General prosecutor's office publicizes the results of an inspection by the Bank of Russia. Thus began the scandal surrounding FIMACO, which was registered on the island of Jersey (in the Channel Islands). Under the agreement between the company and the Bank of Russia, CB systematically entrusted it with the management of the country's foreign currency reserve, IVF credits and securities from the Ministry of Finance.

March 22 – the Agency for the restructuring of credit organizations (ARKO) begins operating.

May 29 – Imperial bank regains its revoked license.

In May, Menatep has its license revoked. Most of its liquid assets revert to the accounts of the bank Menatep St Petersburg, which was also part of the Menatep Group (this bank's shares were bought up by its managers in 2004). Later Menatep was declared bankrupt, and this decision suited all parties involved, except the creditors.

June 12 – 'The race for Pristina': a battalion of Russian paratroopers race from a peacekeeping base in Bosnia and Herzegovina to Kosovo, covering more than 600 km in 7.5 hours, and seize Slatina airport before NATO troops arrive.

June 18 – the restructuring plan for Promstroibank RF is approved. Under the plan, the bank was supposed to be dealt with by the Agency for the restructuring of credit organizations. The ARCO decided not to impose a sanitation order on Promstroibank, however, and in November the Arbitration Court of Moscow declared Promstroibank bankrupt.

June 30 – the board of directors of CB decided to revoke the licence of Mezhkombank, Mosbusinessbank and others. This mass revocation of licences was an unexpected turn of events, in spite of the difficulties that the banks experienced after the crisis in 1998.

In June, Baltic maritime shipping ceased to exist. An assembly of creditors decided that the company was completely bankrupt.

In July, the licences of ONEKSIMbank and Promstroibank were revoked. Before the crisis, ONEKSIM was the fifth biggest bank in Russia. Soon after the licenses were revoked, bankruptcy proceedings were initiated. Nevertheless, in February 2000 two creditors managed to reach an agreement on the restructuring of debt, and the bankruptcy proceedings were brought to an end. At the end of the year 2000, ONEKSIMbank merged with Rosbank. The prospects of the sanitation at Promstroibank were described as hopeless by the CB, and after bankruptcy proceedings were completed it was wound up.

August 2 – a temporary administration took charge at SBSAgro.

August 7 – units under Shamil Basayev and Khattab invade Dagestan. After a month of battles with federal troops, the insurgents were forced into Chechnya.

August 9 – Vladimir Putin is appointed acting Prime Minister of the Russian Federation. On the same day, the current president Boris Yeltsin named him his successor. The 'Putin era' in modern Russian history began on August 16 – on this day Vladimir Putin became Prime Minister of the Russian Federation.

September 4–16 – a wave of terror attacks hits Russia: residential buildings are blown up in Buinaksk, Moscow and Volgodonsk. Approximately 300 people die.

In September, in order to restrict 'shuttle' business, the government of the Russian Federation passes a decree under which products made in light industry and imported into Russia for commercial purposes will be exempted from customs tariffs. The exemptions remained in effect for items that were imported 'for personal consumption'. For imported products with a value up to $1000 and weighing up to 50kg, no customs dues were charged at all; for imported products with a value up to $10,000 or weighing up to 250 kg, the customs dues amounted to 4 euros per kg (customs dues for an imported mink coat, for example, were just 9–14 euros under decree No. 783). The new rules only affected the business of legal entities, and did not have any effect on 'shuttle' trade, the market share of which, for products from the light industries, amounted to 60–70%.

September 30 – Russian troops are sent into Chechnya. The second Chechen war breaks out.

September 30 – the academic Dmitry Sergeevich Likhachev dies.

October 9 – a mistake by Alexander Filimonov in the 88th minute of a match between Russia and Ukraine leads to Russia failing to qualify for football's European Championships for the first time in the modern era.

October 18 – the bank Russian credit stops paying out on its debts. A moratorium on payments is introduced by the ARCO, which has taken charge of the bank.

December 16 – a young man named Maksim Alekseev, using a power of attorney from the notary officer Vladimir Belyaev, to whose account the remainder of the bankruptcy assets of Tokobank (252 million roubles) was transferred, transfers the entire sum to the new, specially opened account of a notary officer at Tandembank. Between December 23 and 28, Maksim Alekseev withdrew 252 million roubles in cash and disappeared. Tokobank was thus bankrupted.

In 1999 Britain's biggest juice manufacturer, Del Monte, pulled out of the Russian market. The reason for its departure was the losses it had suffered during the crisis. Del Monte was just about the only company which, in the long run, could have competed with WimmBillDann (WBD). But WBD had luck on its side.

December 31 – Boris Yeltsin, the first president of the Russian Federation, steps down. Vladimir Putin becomes acting president.

2000

February 1 – Inkombank is declared bankrupt.

February 20 – Anatoly Sobchak, the first mayor of St Petersburg, dies.

March 26 – the presidential elections in Russia. V.V. Putin wins an overall majority in the first round of voting

May 7 – the inauguration of the Russian president Vladimir Vladimirovich Putin.

May 17 – Centrobank takes temporary administrative charge of MostBank. As a result, MostBank is put in the care of Vneshtorgbank, for sanitation. A year later, however, CB recalls its licence and MostBank's bankruptcy proceedings begin.

August 8 – a bomb explodes in Moscow, in the underground crossing at Pushkinskaya metro station.

August 12 – the nuclear submarine the Kursk is hit by disaster in the Barents Sea

August 27 – a fire breaks out at the Ostankino TV tower in Moscow. It takes several months for TV broadcasts to be fully restored to normality in Moscow.

September 14 – ONEKSIM bank and Rosbank begin to merge.

September 25 – MDM bank begins its take–over of Konversbank.

September 26 – the battle to succeed Inkombank. All–out war between Gutabank, on the one hand, and Rosbank and MFK, on the other, for control of the concern 'Babayevsky' and the 'Rot Front' factory.

October 2 – Vneshtorgbank officially announces that it has purchased 100% of the shares in MostBank.

12. CAST

Abalkin, Leonid
Abramovich, Roman
Aven, Pyotr
Averin, Viktor
Adamovich, Ales
Aisenshpis, Yury
Akchurin, Renat
Alekperov, Vagit
Aleksashenko, Sergei
Alekseev, Maksim
Aleksei II
Aleshin, Vladimir
Aliev, Geidar
Angelevich, Arkady
Andrievsky, Protogen
Andropov, Yury
Anpilov, Viktor
Apina, Alena
Arutyunova, Irina
Astafeyev, Viktor
Asuev, Sharip
Afanasiev, Yury
Akhmadulina, Bella
Achalov, Vladislav

Babichev, Ivan
Bazhaev, Ziya
Bakatin, Vladimir

Balkanov, Oleg
Balabanov, Aleksei
Balaeskul, Vladimir
Baranchuk, Leonid
Barsukov, Mikhail
Basayev, Shamil
Baskov, Nikolai
Belousov, Yevgeny
Belyaev, Sergei
Belyaev, Vladimir
Belyaev, Sergei
Bendukidze, Kakha
Berg, David
Berezovsky, Boris
Bekh, Nikolai
Biryukov, Alexander
Bogdanov, Vladimir
Bodrov Jr., Sergei
Bodrov Sr., Sergei
Boiko, Maksim
Boiko, Oleg
Boldin, Valery
Bondarev, Yury
Borzyuk, Vladimir
Borin, Alexander
Borovoi, Konstantin
Borschev, Valery
Brezhnev, Leonid
Bryntsalov, Vladimir
Bulgak, Vladimir
Buldakov, Aleksei
Burbulis, Gennady
Bykov, Anatoly
Bykov, Vasil

Bykov, Dmitry

Chelnokov, Mikhail
Chernov, Sergei
Chernomyrdin, Viktor
Chernye brothers
Cherny, Mikhail
Chesnokov, Aleksei
Chechulin, Anatoly
Chichvarkin, Yevgeny
Chubais, Anatoly
Chubais, Igor
Chumak, Alan
Clinton, Bill

Danilov–Danilyan, Viktor
Dart, Kenneth
DeBakey, Michael
Denisov, Mikhail
Deripaska, Oleg
Dobronravov, Nikolai
Dovgan, Vladimir
Dolgov, Anton
Dondukov, Alexander
Dorenko, Sergei
Dubenetsky, Yakov
Dubinin, Sergei
Dudayev, Djokhar
Dykhovichny, Ivan
Dyakov, Anatoly
Dyachenko, Tatiana

Ernst, Konstantin

Fadin, Andrei
Fyodorov, Andrei
Fyodorov, Boris
Fyodorov, Svyatoslav
Filippov, Pyotr
Filkinshtein, Andrei
Fomenko, Nikolai
Freedland, Leonid
Freedland, Mikhail

Gagauz, Dmitry
Gazmanov, Oleg
Gaidar, Yegor
Gaidar, Timur
Galkin, Maksim
Galtsova, Olga
Gamsakhurdina, Zviad
Gandelman, Leon
Gdlyan, Telman
Gelman, Marat
Geraschenko, Viktor
Glaziev, Sergei
Globa, Tamara
Globa, Pavel
Glushkov, Nikolai
Govorukhin, Stanislav
Golovnev, Leonid
Golubets, Pavel
Golutva, Alexander
Gor, Albert
Gorbachev, Mikhail
Gorbacheva, Raisa
Gorodilov, Viktor
Grachev, Pavel
Gribov, Yakov

Greenberg, Ruslan
Gromov, Boris
Gromyko, Andrei
Gryzlov, Boris
Gubenko, Nikolai
Gurevich, Alexander
Gurov, Vladimir
Gusev, Pavel
Gusinsky, Vladimir

Hubbard, Ron
Hussein, Saddam

Ivanenko, Alexander
Ivanov, Nikolai
Izmailov, Ivan
Illarionov, Andrei
Ilyumzhinov, Kirsan
Ilyukhin, Viktor
Ilyushin, Viktor
Ioselliani, Dzhaba
Iordan, Boris

John Paul II

Kabaev, Sergei
Kazakova, Rimma
Kazantsev, Viktor
Kalmanovich, Shabtai
Kalugin, Oleg
Kamensky, Mikhail
Kantor, Oleg
Kantor, Vyacheslav
Kapitsa, Sergei
Karaganov, Sergei

Karelin, Alexander
Kashin, Vladimir
Kashin, Oleg
Kashpirovsky, Anatoly
Kvantrishvili, Amiran
Kvantrishvili, Otari
Kvashnin, Anatoly
Kerestedzhiyants, Leonid
Kivelidi, Ivan
Kiknadze, Vasily
Kireienko, Sergei
Kirkorov, Philip
Kislinskaya, Larissa
Klimin, Anatoly
Kobets, Konstantin
Kobzon, Josef
Kovalev, Valentin
Kovalev, Sergei
Kozyrev, Andrei
Kokoshin, Andrei
Kolesnikov, Andrei
Kolesnikov, Mikhail
Komar, Dmitry
Konstantinov, Ilya
Korzhakov, Alexander
Korkunov, Andrei
Koroleva, Natalia
Kostikov, Vyacheslav
Kostov, Ivan
Kokh, Alfred
Kochnevsky, Igor
Kravchuk, Leonid
Krasnenker, Alexander
Krasnyansky, Eduard
Krizhan, Sergei

Krichevsky, Ilya
Krichevsky, Mikhail
Krupchak, Vladimir
Krutoi, Igor
Krylova, Galina
Kryuchkov, Vladimir
Kudrin, Aleksei
Kuznetsov, Yevgeny
Kuzmin, Anatoly
Kulikov, Anatoly
Kuraev, Andrei
Kurginyan, Sergei
Kurkova, Bella
Kutsyllo, Veronika

Lebed, Alexander
Lezhankin, Pavel
Lekareva, Vera
Lenin, Vladimir
Leontev, Mikhail
Lepeshinskaya, Olga
Lesin, Mikhail
Lesnevskaya, Irena
Leshchenko, Lev
Ligshmaa, Endel
Lillevyali, Herman
Linkov, Ruslan
Lipukhin, Yury
Lisin, Vladimir
Lisovsky, Sergei
Listev, Vladislav
Litvinov, Oleg
Likhachev, Dmitry
Lobov, Oleg
Lopukhin, Vladimir

Lotorev, Alexander
Lubenchenko, Konstantin
Luzhkov, Yury
Lukin, Vladimir
Lukianov, Anatoly
Lysenko, Vladimir
Lewis, Alan
Lyubimov, Yury

Mavrodi, Sergei
Mavrodi, Vyacheslav
Maganov, Ravil
Makashov, Albert
Makustov, Rafshat
Malinin, Alexander
Mamalashvili, Shota
Mandela, Winnie
Maslachenko, Vladimir
Maskhadov, Aslan
Matvienko, Igor
Matetsky, Vladimir
Matyukhin, Georgy
Medvedev, Dmitry
Melamed, Leonid
Melnikov, Vladimir
Menshikov, Oleg
Menshov, Yevgeny
Milashevich, Anatoly
Milyukov, Yury
Minkin, Alexander
Mitkova, Tatiana
Mitrofanov, Aleksei
Mikhailov, Sergei
Mikhailov, Viktor
Mikhalkov, Nikita

Mogilevich, Semyon
Moiseev, Mikhail
Mordashov, Aleksei
Morozov, Oleg
Moskovchenko, Nikolai
Mostovoi, Pyotr
Moon, Sun Myung
Muravlenko, Sergei
Muromov, Mikhail

Nagibin, Yury
Nazarbaev, Nursultan
Naitshul, Viktor
Nevzlin, Leonid
Nevzorov, Alexander
Nekipelov, Alexander
Nemtsov, Boris
Nenakhov, Anton
Nechaev, Andrei
Nikolaev, Aleksei
Nikolaev, Andrei
Nikolaev, Igor
Nikonov, Vyacheslav
Novodvorskaya, Valeriya
Nudel, Mark

Okudzhava, Bulat
Orekhov, Andrei
Orlov, Dmitry

Pavlov, Valentin
Pavlovsky, Gleb
Palm, Viktor
Pamfilova, Ella
Panikin, Alexander

Panichev, Valentin
Panyushkin, Valery
Paramonova, Tatiana
Parfyonov, Leonid
Pekshev, Valery
Pelevin, Viktor
Perepelkin, Vladimir
Petrov, Boris
Petrov, Yury
Petrosyan, Yevgeny
Platonov, Vladimir
Plakhov, Andrei
Polevanov, Vladimir
Politkovsky, Alexander
Poltoranin, Mikhail
Popov, Gavriil
Potanin, Vladimir
Pochinok, Alexander
Primakov, Yevgeny
Prokhanov, Alexander
Pugacheva, Alla
Pugo, Boris
Pulikovsky, Konstantin
Putilov, Alexander
Putin, Vladimir

Raduev, Salman
Razgon, Lev
Rappoport, Andrei
Rasputin, Valentin
Rastorguev, Nikolai
Rakhimov, Murtaza
Renard, Andrei
Rich, Mark
Rogozhkin, Alexander

Rodionov, Igor
Rodionov, Sergei
Rozenbaum, Alexander
Rokhlin, Lev
Rokhlina, Tamara
Rudakov, Aleksei
Rutskoi, Alexander
Ryzhkov, Nikolai
Ryklina, Marina
Ryazanov, Eldar

Sabonis, Arvidas
Svostyanov, Yevgeny
Sauer, Dirk
Safaryan, Igor
Sakharov, Andrei
Seleznev, Gennady
Semago, Vladimir
Semenov, Vladimir
Sergeev, Igor
Shaimiev, Mintimer
Shakkum, Martin
Shadybin, Vasily
Shantsev, Valery
Shaposhnikov, Yevgeny
Sharapov, Alexander
Shafranik, Yury
Shakhrai, Sergei
Shebanov, Yury
Shevardnadze, Eduard
Shevchenko, Vladimir
Shelov–Kovedyaev, Fyodor
Shenderovich, Viktor
Sheremet, Vyacheslav
Shlyafshtein, Yury

Shmonov, Alexander
Shoigu, Sergei
Shokhin, Alexander
Shumeiko, Vladimir
Shchelkanov, Alexander
Shcherbakov, V.P.
Sianuk, Narodom
Silaev, Ivan
Simonov, Mikhail
Sitdikov, Ravil
Skokov, Yury
Skuratov, Yury
Smirnov, Boris
Smolensky, Alexander
Smolkin, Igor
Sobolev, Oganes
Sobchak, Anatoly
Sokolov, Maxim
Solzhenitsyn, Alexander
Solovieva, Valentina
Sorokin, Vladimir
Soros, George
Soskovets, Oleg
Spiridonov, Yury
Staller, Ilona
Stankevich, Sergei
Starovoitova, Galina
Staroselsky, Alexander
Stashevsky, Vlad
Stepashin, Sergei
Sterligov, German
Steele, Doug
Stolyarov, Nikolai
Streletsky, Valery
Strunin, Leonid

Surkov, Vladislav
Sysuev, Oleg

Tarantino, Quentin
Tarasov, Artyom
Tariko, Rustam
Tarpischev, Shamil
Tarkhov, Viktor
Tatum, Paul
Tilipman, Yakov
Timofeyev, Sergei (Silvester)
Titov, Boris
Titov, Konstantin
Titov, Yury
Titomir, Bogdan
Tikhonenko, Valery
Tikhonov, Alexander
Tikhonov, Vladimir
Tishkovskaya, Yevgenia
Tosunyan, Garegin
Travkin, Nikolai
Trubin, Nikolai
Tsaregradskaya, Maryana
Tsoi, Viktor
Tsvigun–Mamonova, Marina
Tuleev, Amangeldy

Umalatova, Sazhi
Usov, Vladimir
Utkin, Vladimir

Vavilov, Andrei
Veissman, Ilya
Varvarin, Dmitry
Vardanyan, Ruben

Varennikov, Valentin
Vasiliev, Valery
Vasiliev, Georgy
Vasiliev, Dmitry
Vasiliev, Maksim
Vasiliev, Sergei
Venediktov, Aleksei
Viktyuk, Roman
Vinogradov, Vladimir
Vinokur, Vladimir
Vovk, Angelina
Voloshin, Alexander
Vyakhirev, Rem

Yavlinsky, Grigory
Yazov, Dmitry
Yakovlev, Vladimir
Yakunin, Gleb
Yakushev, Alexander
Yanayev, Gennady
Yastrzhembsky, Sergei
Yevstafiev, Arkady
Yevtushenkov, Vladimir
Yegorov, Sergei
Yegorov, Mikhail
Yegorov, Nikolai
Yeltsin, Boris
Yeltsina, Naina
Yerin, Viktor
Yefanov, Alexander
Yefimov, Vitaly
Yugin, Viktor
Yumashev, Valentin
Yursky, Sergei
Yushenkov, Sergei

Zhaboev, Samat
Zhechkov, Vladimir
Zhivilo, Mikhail
Zhirinovsky, Vladimir
Zavarzin, Viktor
Zadornov, Mikhail
Zamiralov, Dmitry
Zapol, Yury
Zelenin, Dmitry
Zenkin, Vladimir
Zimin, Dmitry
Zorkin, Valery
Zrelov, Pyotr
Zykina, Lyudmila
Zyuganov, Gennady

SOURCES

http://ria.ru / trend / russia_referendum /

Mikhail Gorbachev. On My Country and the World (О моей стране и мире). Columbia University Press. 2000. P. 96.

* * *

E. Aleeva, P. Rushailo Children of the decade // Money. 2001. No. 32 (336). 15.08.

Alexander Rutskoi: I'm not the kind to lie down underneath someone // *Kommersant.* 1998. No. 184 (1587). October 3.

Alexander Smolensky: Yeltsin did not sink so low as to imprison everyone who was not on his side. An interview with M. Builov // *Kommersant Money.* 2011. No. 41 (848). October 17,

V. Alexandrov, M. Stepenin How Starovoitova was killed // *Kommersant Power.* 1998. No. 46 (298). December 1.

Andrei Illarionov: I replied to Medvedev that this was nonsense. An interview with E. Sigalu // *Kommersant Money.* 2011. No. 40 (847). October 10.

Artyom Tarasov: "The options open to me were to become an oligarch or a dead man." An interview with A. Nikolaeva // Echo of Moscow. 7.02.2009 // http://www.echo.msk.ru / programs / features / 570656–echo /

Artyom Tarasov: we killed the USSR's management system. An interview with E. Drankina // *Kommersant Money.* 2011. No. 36 (843). September 12.

'Aum sinrikyo' in Russia // *Kommersant.* 1999. No. 178 (1822). September 30.

Bagrov A. Ydar // *Kommersant.* 1999. No. 48 (1692). March 25.

Baku. Timeline // *Kommersant Power.* 1990. No. 4 (4). January 29.

Belchenko V., Beider V., Belyaninov K. The shooting at Novodevichy // *Ogoniok*. 2009. No. 26 (5104). November 9.

Berres L. Kobets brings an end to the matter // *Kommersant* 2000. No. 113 (1998). June 24.

Berres L., Korobov P., Tregubova E., Tueva E. The failed *coup d'etat* // *Kommersant Power*. 2001. No. 33 (435). August 21.

The biography of Galina Starovoitova // *Kommersant*. 1998. No. 219 (1622). November 24.

Bovt G. A purely European drama // *Kommersant* (the newspaper). 1996. No. 75 (1033). May 7.

Borin A. 'Politics tests a person to breaking point' // *Ogoniok*. 2009. No. 32 (5110). December 21.

Brodsky L. It's Chubais's birthday // *Kommersant*. 1995. No. 111 (829). June 17.

Builov M. Banks // *Kommersant Power*. 2001. No. 49 (451). December 11.

Bulavinov I. The trough of the Russian Federation. The Family // *Kommersant Power*. 2003. No. 44 (547). November 10.

Bulavinov I. Commanders in the parliament building // *Kommersant Power*. 1998. No. 26 (278). July 14.

Bulavinov I. The military–industrial complex // *Kommersant Power*. 2001. No. 48 (450). December 4.

Bunin, I. Union Republics: the putsch as an indication of chemical make–up // *Kommersant Power*. 1991. No. 34 (78). August 26.

D. Butrin History 1991–2000 // *Kommersant Power*. 2001. No. 36 (438). September 11; No. 37 (439). September 18.

D. Butrin How Comrade Cheque became Mr. Voucher // *Kommersant Money*. 2002. No. 27 (382). July 17.

D. Butrin The forestry industry // *Kommersant Power*. 2002. No. 3 (456). January 29.

D. Butrin The undersigned // Power. 2006. No. 16 (670). April 24.

D. Butrin The non–ferrous metals industry // *Kommersant Power*. 2001. No. 40 (442). October 9.

D. Butrin The energy industry // *Kommersant Power*. 2001. No. 45 (447). November 13.

D. Butrin, S. Kozitsyn. Who is in charge of Russia's finances // *Kommersant Money*. 2001. No. 16 (320). April 25.

D. Bykov, I. Izmailov The tale of Olegovich the prophet // *Moskovskaya Komsomolka*. 2001. No. 15 March 26 // http://www. newlookmedia.ru / ? p=7529

An attempted coup has taken place in Estonia // *Kommersant Power*. 1990. No. 19 (19). May 21.

N. Vardul, K. Smirnov The trough of the Russian Federation // *Kommersant Power*. 2003. No. 46 (549). November 24.

The century suited him down to the ground // *Kommersant Money*. 1999. No. 39 (243). November 6.

Viktor Gerashchenko: everyone here wanted to have someone under their thumb – all that began with Putin. An interview with M. Builov // *Kommersant Money*. 2011. No. 39 (846). October 3.

Could you have become the country's leader? // *Kommersant Power*. 2000. No. 7 (358). February 22.

The gas industry // *Kommersant Power*. 2001. No. 47 (449). November 27.

N. Gevorkyan. Operation 'Face–down in the snow' // *Kommersant Power*. 1997. No. 5 (211). February 11.

N. Gevorkyan, N. Timakova. Ilich's Outpost // *Kommersant Power*. 1999. No. 11 (312). March 23.

N. Gevorkyan, N. Timakova Berezovsky is heading to the bottom // *Kommersant Power*. 1999. No. 9 (310). March 9.

V. Gendlin 1991: brave new world // *Kommersant Money*. 2011. No. 33 (840). August 22

V. Gendlin 1992: shock therapy // *Kommersant Money*. 2011. No. 34 (841). August 29.

V. Gendlin 1994: fun and fearsome // *Kommersant Money*. 2011. No. 36 (843). September 12.

V. Gendlin 1995: the criminal branch // *Kommersant Money*. 2011. No. 37 (844). September 19.

V. Gendlin 1996: everyone has a price // *Kommersant Money*. 2011. No. 38 (845). September 26.

V. Gendlin 1997: the illusion of developed capitalism // *Kommersant Money*. 2011. No. 39 (846). November 3.

V. Gendlin 1998: ruin and relief // *Kommersant Money*. 2011. No. 40 (847). October 10.

V. Gendlin 1999: our everything and all that is ours // *Kommersant Money*. 2011. No. 41 (848). October 17.

V. Gendlin 1993: the age of adventurers // *Kommersant Money*. 2011. No. 35 (842). September 5.

V. Gendlin The ducat has been edged out // *Kommersant*. 1997. No. 17 (1199). February 22.

German Sterligov: "I'm not even sure myself how rich I was." An interview with D. Tikhomirov // Money. 2007. No. 5 (611). February 12.

A. Grigoriev, '600 seconds' was not broadcast // *Kommersant* 1993. No. 54 (277). March 25.

'Even if all the profits coming into the budget were put towards paying off the debt, that still wouldn't be enough' // *Kommersant Money*. 2011. No. 40 (847). October 10.

E. Degot Solzhenitsyn didn't accept awards // *Kommersant*. 1998. No. 233 (1636). December 15.

Batallions of deputies // *Kommersant*. 2005. No. 56 (3140). March 31.

Kommersant is ten years old // *Kommersant Power*. 1999. No. 49 (350). December 14.

Dmitry Likhachev: the testament of current affairs // *Kommersant*. 1999. No. 179 (1823). October 1.

D. Dobrov The food industry // *Kommersant Power*. 2001. No. 38 (440). September 25.

V. Dorofeyev, One Boris more, one Boris less... // *Kommersant Power*.
1997. No. 40 (246). November 4.

V. Dorofeyev, The one–reporter show // *Kommersant Power*. 1997. No. 46 (252). December 23.

V. Esipov, E. Gridneva Farewell // *Kommersant*. 1998. No. 220 (1623). November 25.

R. Zhuk The automobile industry // *Kommersant Power*. 2001. No. 39 (441). October 2.

M. Zhukov, N. Timakova, D. Lukaitis Korzhakov on the FSB // *Kommersant*.

1998. No. 222 (1625). November 27.

L. Zavarsky. Passenger air journeys // *Kommersant Power*. 2001. No. 43 (445). October 30.

G. Zaichenko Checheno–Ingushetia: Yeltsin's Caucasian friends have taken power // *Kommersant Power*. 1991. No. 36 (80). September 9.

The USSR law dated March 14 No. 1360I 'On the establishment of the post of president of the USSR and the introduction of amendments and addenda to the Constitution (Primary Law) of the USSR'.

E. Zapodinskaya The naked truth about the Justice Minister // *Kommersant*. 1997. No. 94 (1276). June 21.

E. Zapodinskaya. The Justice Minister is not ashamed // *Kommersant*. 1997. No. 95 (1277). June 24.

N. Zubov. The procession of sects in Russia // *Kommersant Power*. 1996. No. 11 (170). April 2.

E. Ivanova The gas industry // *Kommersant Power*. 2001. No. 47 (449). November 27.

E. Ivanova The media // *Kommersant Power*. 2001. No. 50 (452). December 18.

'Inflation went from 40–70% to 120%» // *Kommersant Money*. 2011. No. 37 (844). September 19.

Irina Khakamada: we need to switch on our emotions // *Kommersant*. 1999. No. 156 (1800). August 31.

A. Kabakov, A. Grishkovets. The history of the CPRF. Short course // *Kommersant Power*. 1999. No. 28 (329). July 20.

O. Kabanova Cultural words, the people's music // *Kommersant*. 1997. No. 1 (1183). January 31.

E. Kaverneva. Dark forces are oppressing us malevolently // *Kommersant Money*. 1994. No. 3 (4). November 9.

R. Kadyrova. The iron lady of perestroika // http://spb.mironov.ru / round–leader / section_1768 /

S. Kanunnikov, M. Kochetova Light industry // *Kommersant Power.* 2001. No. 44 (446). November 6.

O. Kashin The children of homo Sovieticus // *Kommersant Money.* 2011. No. 33 (840). August 22.

O. Kashin Yegor Gaidar's last meeting // *Kommersant.* 2009. No. 238 / (4293). December 21.

N. Klimontovich. The people are ready for Solzhenitsyn's idea of Russia // *Kommersant.* 1993. No. 240 (463). December 14.

I. Klochkov, A. Bagrov. The cost of a power vacuum // *Kommersant.* 1998. No. 219 (1622). November 24.

A. Knyazev The mass media // *Kommersant Power.* 2001. No. 50 (452). December 18.

A. Kolesnikov. Shoigu over the city // *Kommersant Power.* 1999. No. 48 (349). December 7.

A. Kolesnikov, The cabin // *Kommersant.* 1999. No. 119 (1763). July 9.

A. Kolesnikov. Soon the Serbs will hate us more than the Albanians do! // *Kommersant.* 1999. No. 121 (1765). July 13.

Kommersant Power. 2001. No. 43 (445). October 30.

Kommersant Power. 2001. No. 50 (452). December 18.

Kommersant Money. 2011. No. 33 (840). August 22.

Kommersant Money. 2011. No. 34 (841). August 29.

Kommersant Money. 2011 No. 35 (842). September 5.

Kommersant Money. 2011. No. 36 (843). September 12.

Kommersant Money. 2011. No. 37 (844). September 19.

Kommersant Money. 2011. No. 38 (845). September 26.

Kommersant Money. 2011. No. 39 (846). October 3.

Kommersant Money. 2011. No. 40 (847). October 10.

Kommersant Money. 2011. No. 41 (848). October 17.

Who does Russia belong to? // *Kommersant Power.* 2001. No. 38 (440). September 25; No. 41 (443). October 16; No. 44 (446). November 6; No. 46 (448). November 20; No. 47 (449). November 27.

P. Korobov, Y. Taratuta, A. Kozenko. The patriarch gave God a soul // *Kommersant*. 2008. No. 223 (4040). December 6.

V. Kostikov. Without Solzhenitsyn // *Arguments and facts*. 2008. August 6.

"Whatever you were sitting on, that was what you got." Interview with P. Rushailo by Pyotr Naishulya // *Kommersant Money*. 2002. No. 27 (382). July 17.

V. Kutsyllo, Borya from wit // *Kommersant Power*. 2000. No. 29 (380). July 25.

V. Kutsyllo // *Kommersant*. 1993. No. 190 (413). October 5.

V. Kutsyllo. The civil war has already happened // *Kommersant*. 1998. No. 184 (1587). October 3.

V. Kutsyllo. A career that might never have happened // *Kommersant*. 2009. No. 224 (4279). December 1.

M. Lepina. The sect that you can never leave // *Kommersant*. 1998. No. 89 (1492). May 21.

M. Kamensky. A tunnel in blood // *Kommersant Power*. 1991. No. 34 (78). August 26.

M. Poletayev. A defeat with fatal consequences // *Kommersant*. 2000. No. 29 (1914). February 22.

M. Mamedov, Y. Chubchenko Baku marks the anniversary of "black January" // *Kommersant*. 2000. No. 7 (1892). January 21.

K. Makhnenko. Our little boy has grown up // *Kommersant*. 1992. No. 60 (213). December 14.

"We are doing all we can to make sure there isn't enough money" // *Kommersant Money*. 2011. No. 34 (841). August 29.

"We didn't bring about privatization in Russia, we created private property in Russia // *Kommersant Money*. 2011. No. 39 (846). October 3.

I. Nagibin. Y.: The man who sets fire to 'stars' // *Kommersant Money*. 1995. No. 10 (20). March 12.

L. Novikov. You steer well clear of complicated ideas, like Ramob – day by day // *Kommersant*. 2003. No. 157 (2760). September 2.

F. Nordhausen. There's a problem with Scientology in Luzhkov's house (Ein Problem mit Scientology im Hause Luschkow) // *Kommersant*. 1999. No. 209 (1853). November 12.

"This country's image in the West is so awful that there's no demand for Russian honesty" // *Kommersant Money*. 2011. No. 41 (848). November 17.

The October madness // *Kommersant*. 1998. No. 184 (1587). October 3.

Oligarch. That has a nice ring to it // *Kommersant Power*. 2001. No. 41 (443). October 16.

The Osh Uprising in 1990 // *Kommersant*. 2005. No. 48 / P (3132). March 21.

V. Panyushkin. The female choice in Russia // *Kommersant*. 1996. No. 168 (1126). October 5.

Y. Papilova, V. Pakin. 'Aum Shinrikyo' accuses Oleg Lobov of trading in sarin // *Kommersant*. 1997. No. 60 (1242). April 25.

The black sheep // *Kommersant Power*. 2001. No. 5 (407). February 6.

Pyotr Mostovoi: the problem in our country is that we don't have a ruling class. An interview with E. Drankina // *Kommersant Money*. 2011. No. 37 (844). September 19.

Writers are calling for decisive action by the government // *Izvestiya*. 1993. No. 189 (24044). October 5.

A. Plakhov. A hero in age without heroes // *Kommersant*. 2002. No. 175 (2544). September 27.

A. Plakhov. A river with two banks // *Kommersant*. 2001. No. 195 (2325). October 24.

A. Plakhov. The outcome of the cinema forum in St Petersburg // *Kommersant*. 1995. No. 121 (839). July 1.

"By our estimates, $6–8 billion has been taken out of the country" // *Kommersant Money*. 2011. No. 38 (845). September 26.

Entrepreneurs // *Kommersant*. 1997. No. 17 (1199). February 22.

The investigation into the murder of Otari Kvantrishvili // Kommersant. 1994. No. 64 (532). April 9.

The referendum has passed us by. And so has the plebiscite // *Kommersant Power*. 1991. No. 12 (62). March 18.

The birth of a president: *plus ça change?* // *Kommersant Power*. 1990. No. 11 (11). March 19.

A novel that looks like a 'P' // *Kommersant Power*. 1999. No. 9 (310). March 9.

P. Sapozhnikov The oil industry // *Kommersant Power*. 2001. No. 42 (444). October 23.

A. Sborov. Yegor Gaidar has died // *Kommersant Power*. 2009. No. 50 (854). December 21.

E. Sigal. Andrei Illarionov: I replied to Medvedev that it was nonsense // *Kommersant Money*. 2011. No. 40 (847). October 10.

A word to the people // *Soviet Russia*. 1991. July 23.

The death of a general // *Kommersant*. 1998. No. 119 (1522). July 4.

A. Snpov. Nevzorov established the popular liberating movement 'Ours' // *Kommersant Power*. 1991. No. 46 (90). December 2.

A. Sokovnin. The 'Aum Shinrikyo' sect has been banned in Russia // *Kommersant*. 1995. No. 71 (789). April 19.

M. Sokolov. March 28: has a great centre died? // *Kommersant Power*. 1991. No. 13 (63). March 25.

M. Sokolov. Alexander Solzhenitsyn: the second 'Letter to the leaders' // *Kommersant Power*. 1990. No. 38 (38). September 24.

M. Sokolov The rise and fall of enlightened authoritarianism // *Kommersant Power*. 1995. No. 1 (112). January 17.

M. Sokolov. Gorbachev 90: "For six years now I've ruled the country calmly..." // *Kommersant Power*. 1990. No. 50 (50). December 24.

M. Sokolov. What is the best way to usurp power? // *Kommersant*. 1992. No. 60 (213). December 14.

M. Sokolov. The morphology of the puppet // *Kommersant*. 1995. No. 131 (849). July 15.

M. Sokolov. A new parliamentary chapter in the creative output of a great writer // *Kommersant*. 1994. No. 206 (674). October 29.

M. Sokolov. Perestroika is over, thank God // *Kommersant Power*. 1991. No. 34 (78). August 26.

M. Sokolov. The congress has burst the president // *Kommersant*. 1992. No. 60 (213). December 14.

M. Sokolov. Fomino represents the rebirth of executive power // *Kommersant Power*. 1993. No. 16 (16). April 26.

M. Sokolov. The Union collapsed into free republics… // *Kommersant Power*. 1991. No. 36 (80). September 9.

M. Sokolov, L. Skoptsov. August 1991: how not to carry out a *coup d'etat* // *Kommersant Power*. 1991. No. 34 (78). August 26.

G. Starovoitova. Interview // *Arguments and facts*. 1995. No. 16

M. Stravinskaya. The master of re–clothing // *Kommersant Power*. 2004. No. 33 (586). August 23.

A. Timofeyevsky, M. Sokolov. Solzhenitsyn has come to Russia // *Kommersant*. 1994. No. 97 (565). May 28.

M.L. Tirmaste. Anatoly Chubais applied over Yury Luzhkov's head // *Kommersant*. 2010. No. 12 (4312). October 26.

S. Topol, D. Pavlov. A leader in the law // *Kommersant Power*. 1997. No. 18 (224). May 20.

Triumphs and awards for Russian peacekeepers // *Kommersant*. 1999. No. 162 (1806). September 8.

M. Trofimenkov. Shoot and score // *Kommersant Power*. 2008. No. 20 (774). May 26.

Russia no longer has a conscience // *Kommersant*. 1999. No. 179 (1823). October 1.

Going away in order to stay longer // *Kommersant Power*. 1990. No. 11 (11). March 19.

Yegor Gaidar has died // KommersantOnline. 2009. December 16. 10:39.

Fedorov spent his whole life cooking cutlets and stealing. Andrei Fedorov interviewed by V. Gendlin // *Kommersant*. 1997. No. 17 (1199). February 22.

A. Fedorov. 16 years on a stool // *Kommersant Power*. 2007. No. 34 (738). September 3.

V. Khamraev. Viktor Ilyhin has died // *Kommersant*. 2011. No. 47 / P (4588). March 21.

V. Khamraev. The State Duma refuses to honour the memory of Yegor Gaidar // *Kommersant*. 2009. No. 238 (4293). December 19.

I. Cheberko. Telecommunications // *Kommersant Power*. 2001. No. 51 (453). December 24.

S. Chereshnev. Water transport // *Kommersant Power*. 2001. No. 46 (448). November 20.

G. Cherkasov. Forever on the right // *Kommersant*. 2009. No. 236 (4291). December 17.

What's going to happen in 1991? // *Kommersant Power*. 1990. No. 50 (50). December 24.

What would you have written in your exercise book about Yegor Gaidar? // *Kommersant Power*. 2009. No. 50 (854). December 21.

What happened in the week // *Kommersant Power*. 1990. No. 50 (50). December 24.

What did Yegor Gaidar do? // *Kommersant*. 2009. No. 236 (4291). December 17.

So as not to hear all this // *Kommersant Power*. 2009. No. 33 (837). August 24.

A. Chugunov. Zhirinovsky vs. Nemtsov: the battle of Ostankino // *Kommersant*. 1995. No. 113 (831). June 21.

S. Shelin. The story has not yet begun // Gazeta.ru 2009. August 19 // http://gazeta.ru / column / shelin / 3237971.shtml

O. Shkurenko What will we remember Yegor Gaidar for // *Kommersant*. 2009. No. 236 (4291). December 17.

'It's not a market, it's worse than a bazar' // *Kommersant Money*. 2011. No. 35 (842). September 5.

* * *

V. Dorofeyev, V. Bashkirova, A. Solovieva. The 13 retirements of Luzhkov. – M.: Kommersant; Eksmo, 2011.

V. Dorofeyev, V. Bashkirova, A. Soloviev. How Chernomyrdin rescued Russia. – M.: Kommersant; Eksmo, 2011.

V. Bashkirova, A. Soloviev. The outcasts of Russian business. – M.: Kommersant; Eksmo, 2011.

E. Tregubova. The old wives' tales of the Kremlin's diggers. – M.: Ad Marginem, 2003.

The new Russian fraud. – M: Kommersant; Eksmo, 2010.

Glagoslav Publications Catalogue

www.ingramcontent.com/pod-product-compliance
Lightning Source LLC
Chambersburg PA
CBHW022130020426
42334CB00015B/831